Questions & Answers

Evidence

Questions & Answers Series

Series Editors: Rosalind Malcolm and Margaret Wilkie

The ideal revision aid to keep you afloat through your exams

Q&A Company Law
Stephen Judge

Q&A Criminal Law
Mike Molan and Geoff Douglas

Q&A Employment Law
Richard Benny, Malcolm Sargeant, and Michael Jefferson

Q&A English Legal System
S.Kunalen and Susan McKenzie

Q&A Equity and Trusts
Margaret Wilkie, Rosalind Malcolm, and Peter Luxton

Q&A EU Law
Nigel Foster

Q&A Evidence
Maureen Spencer and John Spencer

Q&A Family Law
Penny Booth with Chris Barton and Mary Hibbs

Q&A Human Rights and Civil Liberties
Steve Foster

Q&A International Law
Susan Breau

Q&A Land Law
Margaret Wilkie, Peter Luxton, and Rosalind Malcolm

Q&A Landlord and Tenant
Mark Pawlowski and James Brown

Q&A Law of Contract
Adrian Chandler and Ian Brown

Q&A Law of Torts
David Oughton, Barbara Harvey, and John Marston

Q&A Public Law
Richard Clements and Philip Jones

- advice on exam technique
- summary of each topic
- bullet-pointed answer plans
- model answers
- diagrams and flowcharts
- further reading

Questions & Answers

Evidence

SIXTH EDITION

Maureen Spencer
MA (Oxon), MA (Open) LLM, PhD, PGCertHE

John Spencer
MA (Oxon), LLM, MMath, Barrister

2009 and 2010

OXFORD
UNIVERSITY PRESS

OXFORD

UNIVERSITY PRESS

Great Clarendon Street, Oxford OX2 6DP

Oxford University Press is a department of the University of Oxford.
It furthers the University's objective of excellence in research, scholarship,
and education by publishing worldwide in

Oxford New York

Auckland Cape Town Dar es Salaam Hong Kong Karachi
Kuala Lumpur Madrid Melbourne Mexico City Nairobi
New Delhi Shanghai Taipei Toronto

With offices in

Argentina Austria Brazil Chile Czech Republic France Greece
Guatemala Hungary Italy Japan Poland Portugal Singapore
South Korea Switzerland Thailand Turkey Ukraine Vietnam

Oxford is a registered trade mark of Oxford University Press
in the UK and in certain other countries

Published in the United States
by Oxford University Press Inc., New York

© Maureen Spencer and John Spencer 2009

The moral rights of the author have been asserted

Crown copyright material is reproduced under Class Licence
Number C01P0000148 with the permission of OPSI
and the Queen's Printer for Scotland

Database right Oxford University Press (maker)

First published 1996
Second edition 2001
Third edition 2003
Fourth edition 2005
Fifth edition 2007
Sixth edition 2009

British Library Cataloguing in Publication Data

Data available

Library of Congress Cataloging-in-Publication Data

Data available

Typeset by Laserwords Private Ltd, Chennai, India
Printed in Great Britain
on acid-free paper by
Ashford Colour Press Limited, Gosport, Hampshire

ISBN 978–0–19–955957–2

10 9 8 7 6 5 4 3 2 1

Contents

The Q&A Series

Key features

The Q&A series provides full coverage of key subjects in a clear and logical way.

This book contains the following features:

- Questions
- Commentary
- Bullet-pointed answer plans
- Suggested answers
- Flowcharts
- Further reading
- Bibliography

 online resource centre

www.oxfordtextbooks.co.uk/orc/qanda/

Every book in the Q&A series is accompanied by an Online Resource Centre, hosted at the URL above, which is open-access and free to use.

The Online Resource Centre for this book contains revision and exam advice, a glossary of evidence law terms, and links to websites useful for the study of evidence law.

Preface

'So what's the answer?' said Laura, a rather literal-minded girl who wrote down everything Robyn said in tutorials. 'Is it a train or a tram?'

'Both or either,' said Robyn. 'It doesn't really matter. Go on Marion.'

'Hang about,' said Vic. 'You can't have it both ways.'

Nice Work by David Lodge (Secker & Warburg, London 1988)

Like David Lodge's fictional English Literature tutor, Evidence teachers are fonder of setting questions than giving answers. But in these days of modularisation and semesterisation, not to mention larger classes, students do sometimes need ready access to the answers outside the lecture theatre or the seminar room. The authors believe there is a place for modest study aids like this book. It does not pretend to replace the standard Evidence textbooks or the great practitioners' manuals as a source of authoritative information yet will be more portable and perhaps more accessible to the student in a hurry.

This sixth edition takes full account of changes in evidence law over the last two years. It reflects the developing case-law under the Criminal Justice Act 2003, particularly in relation to character and evidence. It also includes much case-law, including that on anonymous witnesses and inferences to be drawn from the defendant's silence. It reflects the law as it is in August 2008. We thank the ever-patient editors at OUP, particularly Helen Swann.

Maureen Spencer
John Spencer
August 2008

Table of Cases

Table of Statutes

Table of Statutory Instruments

1

Introduction

Evidence is often regarded as one of the trickier subjects studied in undergraduate law courses. It is a mixture of arcane old rules and opaque new statutes and sometimes seems to offend common sense. Technical precepts are intermingled with judicial discretion and matters of high constitutional principle. The subject covers such matters as the defendant's right to silence, the treatment of witnesses, the role of the presumed victim in the trial process, whether or not intercept evidence should be used in court, the extent of judicial discretion in admitting evidence, for example of the complainant's sexual history in rape trials. Since we started producing this book 12 years ago, there has been a great deal of legislative activity in the field of evidence, much of it dealing with issues which are politically controversial. The courts have struggled to digest complex new law while upholding the human rights of the various parties to litigation, both criminal and civil. As well as absorbing his or her course material, the alert student will follow these changes both in the general media and in legal journals.

Question and answer books are not a substitute for learning the law. They are at best a supplementary aid to coursework preparation and particularly to revision for examinations and coursework. But we hope this book will help the many students who find it difficult to visualise what satisfactory coursework looks like, as well as those for whom answering examination questions poses particular challenges. We hope it will also reassure superior students that their answers are on the right lines. These are not model answers to be slavishly copied (of course, this would constitute plagiarism), but rather examples to help the student understand the topic and see how it might be approached. Assessment in law courses can take many different forms and it is important that students respond to it in their own voice, rather than merely parroting rote responses.

One of the skills which law students have to acquire is the art of doing well in examinations. This is not merely a matter of knowing the subject, but requires self-organisation and a disciplined approach to the task of writing the examination itself. Obviously, students should reach the examination hall with an adequate knowledge of their subject. The problem so often is putting that knowledge to proper use once they get there.

Put crudely, the examinee's objective in any examination is to accumulate in the time allowed as many marks as possible. To be manageable this task needs to be broken down into three stages: planning, execution and review.

First, planning. Make sure you arrive at the examination hall in time, with adequate equipment, including statute books if these are allowed in the hall. When you are given the examination paper, read it, read the rubric (the instructions at the top of the paper) carefully, then take five minutes to read the paper itself right through. Turn it over to make sure there's nothing on the back you have missed. You will usually be required to answer a set number of questions (say four out of ten). You must answer the number of questions required. A surprising number of candidates fail because they answer fewer questions than required. There is very little the examiner can do even for a good candidate in this position. Most papers are marked between 40 and 70 per cent, so if four questions are required and you have only produced three answers you will have a mediocre grade even if they are brilliant answers. If your answers are average you will have failed. You may also be required to choose one or more questions from a particular section of the paper. At this point you should begin to pick out the questions you will answer. If, for example, you have always found presumptions a source of confusion, this is no time to try and clarify your mind by answering a question about them. Try and pick the questions to display what you know, even if that is not a great deal.

Having chosen the required number of questions try and sketch out in telegraphic note form your answer to each. In problem questions in law examinations this is very often a matter of spotting the issues, as several different areas of the subject are mixed together. If at this point you can recall the names of the cases which are authority for particular propositions in the area concerned, all the better. If you can't, pass onto the next of your chosen questions. By the end of this process, which should not take more than perhaps 20 minutes, you will have sketched out in rough form your answer to each of your chosen questions. Many of your fellow examinees will already be scribbling frantically. Don't panic. Before you go to the stage of execution make a simple calculation. Take the length of the examination in minutes (180 minutes for the classic three-hour examination). Subtract the time you have spent on the planning stage (perhaps 25 minutes) and allow five minutes review time for the end of the examination. Then divide the remainder equally between the questions you have chosen. So if the examination started at 9.00 and you were asked to answer four questions you would have 150/4 = 37 minutes to answer each question. If you start your first answer at 9.30, you should begin your next at 10.07, your third at 10.44, and your fourth at 11.21. Write those times down.

Now you can start writing your first answer. If you think your handwriting may be difficult to read, remember that the examiner will have dozens if not hundreds of scripts to deal with and is unlikely to look kindly on any candidate whose script needs to be decyphered. So come armed with a good pen, and write clearly. Break your answer into paragraphs, underline the names of cases and don't write in the margins.

It is very important to remember that the examiner is interested in what you do know, not what you don't know. So if you are uncertain about a particular point, it is generally better to put down what you think is the answer, provided it is relevant to answering the question. If you are right, you will gain marks, if you are wrong you will usually not have marks taken away. Don't be tempted to exceed your time limit. You are more likely to pick up marks at the beginning of your answer than at the end. Once your self-imposed time limit is up, stop writing and go on to the next question. It is poor time management to chase one or two extra marks on question three and leave yourself short of time to accumulate the marks you need on question four. If necessary start the next question in a different answer book so that you have space to come back to the previous question during your review period at the end of the examination.

When the time gets to 10.45 your concentration may start to sag. It is at this point that you will appreciate having made your sketch answer to your third question at the beginning of the examination period. Your fellow examinees who rushed to get pen to paper at the start of the examination will be flagging too, but they won't have tried to think through the issues in the question when they were fresh. Your aim will be to get as many marks for your last answer as for your first.

The approach required to answering questions will vary with the type of question. There are broadly two types you will encounter in Evidence examinations: problems and essays. Briefly, in answering problem questions, the student must first identify the areas of law in which the problem falls. Almost invariably, there will be more than one issue and it is important that you identify them at the start. Having done so, you should be able to outline the legal principles which are relevant to the issues in the problem, citing the relevant cases and statutes. Ideally, citations should include the principle on which the case was decided, the significant facts which explain the principle and the name of the case. But examiners do recognise that case names can be forgotten under the stress of examination and will probably be reasonably satisfied if the examinee can give the relevant principle and facts. The next stage is to apply these authorities to the facts. This involves discussion of the facts in the light of the relevant principles, analysis of the facts to select which are significant, and, where appropriate, a comparison of the problems' facts with those of the authorities, in such a way as to support your argument. Finally, come to a practical conclusion, which need not be a definitive answer, may suggest more than one alternative and should where necessary indicate what additional factual material would be required to give a definitive response.

A different approach is required when answering essay questions. These are likely to figure largely in your coursework and to be related to current controversies in the field. The good student will have spent time during the year dipping into such publications as the *International Journal of Evidence and Proof*, *Criminal Law Review*, *New Law Journal*, *Law Quarterly Review* and *Solicitors' Journal*. Even if you are not of their number, it is well worth spending a few hours of revision time before the examination in the library looking through recent issues and making a note of evidence topics which have drawn academic comment. In many cases this is where the examiner will have looked when drafting the exam paper. Another authoritative source of material is *Criminal Evidence* by Roberts and Zuckerman (Oxford 2004), which analyses many of the issues thrown up by the Criminal Justice Act 2003. Background reading will help you to see what the question-setter is looking for in answer to essay questions. You should analyse the question to establish whether you are asked to discuss, explain or criticise a particular area of the law. You should not attempt an essay question unless you are clear what it is asking for.

We hope this book will give some idea of what your answers in Evidence ought to look like. The authors aim to give some practical guidance on handling specific issues which should be fairly typical of those likely to come up on an undergraduate examination paper. It is not a substitute for a textbook and though efforts have been made to cover the typical syllabus it cannot claim to be exhaustive. To some extent the format is rather artificial because each topic in evidence has been treated for the most part discretely except for the mixed questions at the end. In some questions material from earlier chapters has been included. Thus, for example, the questions on character here require you to draw also on your knowledge of competence and compellability. In practice, examination questions usually contain several issues taken from different parts of the syllabus and part of the examiners' aim is to test the students' skill in spotting what the issues are. That skill can be acquired only by a student who has already covered the various issues in some depth. For the same reason the answers vary somewhat in length, our aim being to give the issue the attention it merits. The answers on character, which often occur as a free-standing question in examination papers, are longer than those for example on competence, which rarely occur as single issue questions. We have included a mixture of problem and essay questions, as do most university examinations.

These days law examinations can take different forms, including seen questions, open book exams and so on. To take account of this, we have included among the essay answers in this book some which are closer to more fully researched pieces rather than to off-the-cuff answers in a traditional exam. Many courses now require coursework as well as exams and we have tried to supply material which might help students faced with assessments other than by three-hour unseen examination. You therefore will notice, particularly in the essay questions, much lengthier quotations are given than you could possibly remember in an examination. We have included them because it is artificial for us not to check the exact wording. We would recommend that at least you try to recall comments from academic writers in your answers to essay questions, although clearly you will mostly paraphrase (of course acknowledging the source) rather than quote verbatim. Perhaps perversely examiners often award more marks for a student's recall of how an academic deals with a problem of legal analysis rather than the student's intuitive response.

We have tried in the introductory sections of each chapter to give some guidance as to the appropriate way of dealing with the types of questions likely to arise in that area. Examination technique is an important part of preparation for examinations in law and attention to it will not be wasted. But technique is ultimately only a means of demonstrating effectively the student's knowledge of the relevant law. We hope this book will help students to learn how to communicate better what they know. The sixth edition has been extensively revised and rewritten to reflect the state of the law of evidence in summer 2008. We cannot stress too strongly the benefits of reading widely as the most effective way of preparing for both coursework and examination.

Recommended additional reading is given at the end of each chapter. The more general texts are listed in the Selected Bibliography on page 307.

2

Burden and standard of proof; presumptions

Introduction

These two subjects are closely related and sometimes but not always taught together. Both are a terminological minefield and you should make sure you are thoroughly familiar with the definitions and their meanings. Behind the allocation of the burden of proof operating in both civil and criminal trials is the decision as to who should bear the risk of losing the case. That allocation is decided by common law and by statute. In criminal trials the 'presumption of innocence' means that the burden of proof will be on the prosecution, unless this is reversed by some express or implied statutory provision. Here the law of evidence safeguards what in some other jurisdictions is a matter of individual civil rights backed up by a tenet of the constitution. The **Human Rights Act 1998** has had a significant impact in this area.

You must understand the difference between the legal and the evidential burden and the occasions where they are separately allocated. Students often have difficulty in differentiating the two in criminal trials. It is helpful to see the evidential burden primarily as an aspect of the sensible proposition that there must be a degree of evidence on asserted issues before they can be a matter for the trial. It is for the judge then to decide whether the assertion can go before the jury. Thus the prosecution has to adduce enough evidence of the guilt of the accused for the judge to be satisfied that there is a case to answer. In other words, it has the evidential burden. Here, the prosecution also has the legal burden on the same matter and this is the normal state of affairs directed at convincing the jury of the defendant's guilt beyond reasonable doubt (the criminal standard). The tricky areas are those where there is a divorce of the legal and evidential burden. These arise primarily in situations where the prosecution cannot be expected to put up evidence to anticipate every specific defence the accused may present. Thus in order to plead self-defence the accused will have to provide some evidence to enable the court to consider the matter. The legal burden stays with the prosecution. You must be clear that these instances differ from the occasion when statute has expressly or impliedly shifted the burden on a fact in issue. Here, both the legal and the evidential burden are shifted. The allocation of the burden of proof in civil cases is evident from the pre-trial pleadings.

In a sense it is somewhat misleading to refer to the burden of proof in a trial. The burden may relate to several different specific facts in issue. Burdens may be allocated between the parties in relation to these different facts in issue. This is particularly so in civil cases but may also occur in criminal cases. In civil cases the principle 'He who asserts must prove' means that the burden may shift according to who is trying to establish a relevant fact in issue. In criminal cases the presumption of innocence means that as a general principle the burden of proving actus reus and mens rea lies on the prosecution. Statutes may impliedly or expressly shift that burden, however. It has been said that there is a clear case for rationalising the terminology in this area. For example, the legal burden is sometimes called the 'persuasive burden', and the evidential burden, the 'burden of passing the judge'. A third expression is sometimes employed, namely the 'tactical burden'. This is not, however, a precise legal concept unlike the evidential and legal burdens, but rather an exposition of how during a trial the parties are well advised to respond to the production of evidence if they are to claim or maintain an advantage.

The enactment of the **Human Rights Act 1998** has affected the allocation of the burden of proof in criminal cases. It is arguable that to place the burden on the accused violates the presumption of innocence in art. 6(2) of the European Convention on Human Rights. The Strasbourg case-law suggests, however, that placing the burden on the prosecution is not an absolute rule. For example, in *Salabiaku v France* (1988) **13 EHRR 379** the ECtHR found that there was no principled objection to the imposition of strict liability in criminal cases. However, it stressed that this should be applied 'within reasonable limits'. In other words the test of proportionality will apply. One consideration would be the seriousness of the offence in question. The House of Lords has considered the impact of the **Human Rights Act** on the allocation of the burden of proof in several important cases. In *R v DPP, ex parte Kebilene* [2000] 2 AC 326 the House of Lords considered whether the reverse burden provisions in the **Prevention of Terrorism (Temporary Provisions) Act 1989** violated art. 6(2). In the Divisional Court Lord Bingham had stated that these sections 'in a blatant and obvious way' undermined the presumption of innocence. In the event the House of Lords did not have to pronounce on this point since it was held that the issue in the trial was not reviewable, but it did take the opportunity to demonstrate a pragmatic approach to the shifting of the burden of proof. Lord Hope stated that 'As a matter of general principles. . .a fair balance must be struck between the demands of the general interest of the community and the protection of the fundamental rights of the individual.' It was important to consider in particular whether the defendant was being required to prove an essential element of the offence or establish a special defence or exception. In the latter instance it would be less objectionable to reverse the burden.

The next leading case was *R v Lambert, Ali and Jordan* [2002] 2 AC 545. There the House of Lords held in a majority decision that it was not justifiable to use s. 28 of the **Misuse of Drugs Act 1971** so as to transfer the legal burden onto the accused and require him to prove that he did not know that the bag he was carrying contained a controlled drug. The majority found it possible to construe the section as imposing an evidential rather than a legal burden and such an interpretation was not a violation of the Convention. Lord Hutton dissented on this point, stating that 'it is not unprincipled to have regard to practical realities where the issue related to knowledge in a drugs case'. Lord Steyn on the other hand argued for outlawing reverse burdens where the defence bears directly on the moral blameworthiness of the defendant. This decision is of great importance in reassessing the crucial nature of the presumption of innocence and you should be familiar with the judgment. It is likely to form the topic of essay questions for some years to come. As Roberts and Zuckerman put it, 'the practical implication of *Lambert* appears to be that the post-**Human Rights Act 1998** effect of every single reverse onus clause in English criminal law must be determined on an individual, case-by-case, basis' (2004, at p. 383). The result is that sometimes a reverse onus clause is construed as imposing merely an evidential burden and in other cases a full probative burden on the defence. In other cases the burden may remain on the prosecution. Table 1 overleaf lists the leading judgments; Tables 2 and 3 set out practical examples.

The standard of proof is a less complex topic. In this area, as in all areas of evidence, you must be careful to apply the appropriate rules according to whether the case is a civil or a criminal one. You will be unlikely to have questions which mix the two. In problem questions you may be asked to comment on the possible flaws in a judge's summing-up. You will then have to see if the legal burden has been allocated according to law and if the appropriate standard has been applied. Other questions may ask you to advise on burden and standard and here it is probably helpful to dissect the facts in issue into their various components and decide how the legal and evidential burdens should be distributed.

Presumptions can obviate the need for proof, or make the process easier; on occasions they are irrebuttable. The word presumption has been used in various ways. Evidence courses nowadays usually concentrate on what are known as 'rebuttable presumptions of law', i.e., those of death, legitimacy, marriage and here we deal only with them. Other presumptions, including 'irrebuttable presumptions of law', such as the age of criminal liability, belong more properly to the substantive law. Finally 'presumptions of fact' are really aspects of logical reasoning.

Example of Allocation of Burden of Proof in a Criminal Case

Joan is accused of growing an illegal drug in a window box at her flat, contrary to ss. 5 and 28 of the **Misuse of Drugs Act 1971**. She pleads not guilty, arguing that she thought the plants she was growing were tomato plants since they looked similar to a picture she had in a book 'Growing Tomatoes in Small Places'. See Table 2, page 9.

Example of Allocation of Burden of Proof in a Civil Case

Cowboys Ltd are engaged to transport a racehorse, Diana, belonging to Sam Sloane. The contract specifies that Cowboys will not be liable for damage caused to Diana in transit if Sloane has not organised to have her given a clean bill of health by a veterinary surgeon before the journey. Diana dies of a heart attack during the journey. Sloane is suing Cowboys Ltd for breach of contract. Cowboys rely on the exclusion clause. See Table 3 below.

Table 1 The **Human Rights Act** and the burden of proof

Case	Court	Statute	Outcome
R v DPP ex parte Kebilene [2000]	HL	Prevention of Terrorism (Temporary Provisions) Act 1989 ss. 16A and 16B	No conclusion possible since **HRA** not in force but reverse legal burden might have to be interpreted as only an evidential burden[1]
R v Lambert, Ali and Jordan [2004]	HL	(a) **Misuse of Drugs Act 1971** s. 28 (3) (b) **Homicide Act 1957** s. 2	(a) Evidential burden only on accused (b) Legal burden on accused[2]
R v Davies [2002] EWCA Crim 2949	CA	**Health and Safety at Work Act 1974** s. 40	Legal burden on defendant to prove 'it was not reasonably practicable to do more than was in fact done'[3]
R v Johnstone [2003] 1 WLR 1736	HL	**Trade Marks 1994** s. 92 (1)(b) and s. 92(5)	Legal burden on accused
Att.-Gen. Ref. (No. 1 of 2004) [2004] 1 WLR 2111	CA	(a) **Insolvency Act 1986** ss. 353, 357 (b) **Protection from Eviction Act 1997** s. 1(2) (c) **Homicide Act 1957** s. 4 (d) **Criminal Justice and Public Order Act 1994** s. 51(1)	(a) Legal burden on accused in s. 353 but evidential burden in s. 357 (b) Legal burden on accused (c) Legal burden on accused (d) Legal burden on accused[4]
L v DPP [2003] QB 13	Divisional Ct	**Criminal Justice Act 1988** s. 139 (4)	Legal burden on accused[5]

(contiinued overleaf)

Table 1 *continued*

Case	Court	Statute	Outcome
Sheldrake v *DPP*; **Attorney General's Reference (No. 4 of 2002) [2004] 3 WLR 976**	HL	(a) **Road Traffic Act 1988** s. 5(2) (b) **Terrorism Act 2000** ss. 11(1) and (2)	(a) Legal burden on accused (b) Evidential burden on accused[6]

[1] In the **Terrorism Act 2000**, replacing the 1989 Act, Parliament included s. 118 converting some, but not all, reverse legal burdens in the Act to evidential burdens

[2] Relevant factors in deciding that proof of diminished responsibility lay with the defence were that there was no power to examine a defendant and that the prosecution was required to prove all the elements of the defence.

[3] This is just one example of offences which are not regarded as truly criminal and so reverse burdens are acceptable. See also, however, *R* v *S* [2003] 1 Cr App R 602, where a conviction under the **Trade Marks Act 1994** could result in imprisonment.

[4] The Court, noting the different approaches in *Lambert* and *Johnstone,* stated that if in doubt courts should follow that of Lord Nicholls in *Johnstone*. Lord Woolf CJ set out 10 general principles as guidance but see now *Sheldrake* v *DPP*; **Attorney General's Reference (No. 4 of 2002)**.

[5] *Lambert* was distinguished in this case involving a defence to possession of a flick-knife in a public place. The defendant had to prove he had good reason or lawful authority.

[6] This section was not covered by s. 118 (see above n. 1). Six reasons were given for the decision. The House acknowledged that there could be no doubt that Parliament intended to impose a legal burden on the accused. The House held that both *Lambert* and *Johnstone* were the primary domestic authorities on reverse burdens and that *Johnstone* did not depart from *Lambert*. Lord Woolf's guidance notes (see n. 4 above) were not endorsed, Lord Bingham questioning the assumption that Parliament would not have made an exception without good reason. See also *R* v *Keogh* [2007] EWCA Crim 528.

Table 2 Burden of proof—criminal cases

Facts in issue	Who has evidential burden?	Who has legal burden?	What is the standard of proof of the legal burden?
Possession of window-box	Prosecution	Prosecution	Beyond reasonable doubt
Defendant's knowledge of possession of window-box	Prosecution	Prosecution	Beyond reasonable doubt
Identity of plant as cannabis	Prosecution	Prosecution	Beyond reasonable doubt
Defendant's knowledge of identity of plants	Defence*	Prosecution*	Beyond reasonable doubt

*Following *R* v *Lambert*.

Table 3 Burden of proof—civil cases

Fact in issue	Who has legal burden?	Who has evidential burden?	What is the standard of proof on legal burden?
Existence of contract	Sloane	Sloane	Balance of probabilities
Death of Diana	Sloane	Sloane	Balance of probabilities
Absence of veterinary surgeon's examination	Cowboys	Cowboys	Balance of probabilities

Question 1

'In order to merit its reputation as a fundamental constitutional guarantee, the presumption [of innocence] must be reasonably extensive and not too easily defeated.' (Roberts and Zuckerman, *Criminal Evidence* (Oxford, 2004, p. 328).) Discuss the development of the presumption of innocence.

Commentary

The **Human Rights Act 1998** has played a part in generating an increasingly jurisprudential approach to the law of Evidence and this question requires you to demonstrate your appreciation of the principles enshrined in the technically somewhat complex law relating to the presumption of innocence. This presumption is also fully acknowledged by the common law. Your answer will therefore have to examine the law before and after the 1998 Act and the extent to which inroads into the presumption were and are currently allowed.

There have been a number of House of Lords decisions in this area including *Woolmington* v *DPP* [1935] AC 462, *R* v *Hunt* [1987] AC 352, *R* v *Lambert, Ali and Jordan* [2002] 2 AC 545 and *Sheldrake* v *DPP*; *Attorney General's Reference (No. 4 of 2002)* [2004] 3 WLR 976. (See Table 1, page 8.) But you must avoid giving a bare narrative of the decisions, since the question is clearly centred on analysing an abstract constitutional principle.

Answer plan

- Outline the constitutional basis of the presumption of innocence and its importance in ensuring a fair trial
- The common law protection of this principle; *Woolmington* and its aftermath—pragmatism versus principle

- Article 6(2) guarantee of presumption of innocence but not an absolute principle—*Salabiaku*
- Competing principles—individual rights and protection of the public; *Lambert*, *Johnstone* and other post-*Lambert* cases
- Risks of confusing substantive and procedural right in application of Article 6(2)

Suggested answer

A criminal conviction and subsequent state-imposed punishment subjects individuals to moral denunciation and physical hardship. The constraints imposed by the law of evidence on the trial process exist in large part to try to ensure that only the guilty are convicted and that the trial process is fair. In other words trials should have factual and moral legitimacy. The presumption of innocence is recognised in many jurisdictions as one of the most important foundations of this legitimacy. Its constitutional significance is that it recognises the vulnerability of the defendant faced with state prosecution and concomitant 'inequality of arms'. The individual liberty of the subject is safeguarded by placing the task of proving the case firmly on the prosecution. The prosecution, in other words, has the burden of proof, must carry out the task of amassing and presenting the evidence and in order to succeed has to do this to an exacting standard. The defendant is entitled to receive the benefit of reasonable doubt. The prosecution bears the risk of losing. Reference to the presumption of innocence is to be found in all major international human rights treaties but until the enactment of the **Human Rights Act 1998** its acknowledgement by UK law is to be found in judicial observations. Viscount Sankey's 'golden thread' speech in *Woolmington* v *DPP* **[1935]** is one of the most celebrated passages in English criminal law: 'No matter what the charge or where the trial, the principle that the prosecution must prove the guilt of the prisoner is part of the common law of England and no attempt to whittle it down can be entertained.'

However, closer examination reveals that the *Woolmington* principle itself has never been absolute. Indeed, if it is so much part of the common law of England, it does seem strange that a trial judge and the Court of Criminal Appeal as late as the twentieth century could have made so fundamental an error as to place the burden of proving lack of mens rea on the defendant. In fact, the concept that the prosecution bears the legal burden on mens rea and actus reus was still somewhat undecided until the last century. For example, the common law recognised the principle that if the defendant has possession of facts known only to him, it is for the defendant to produce the relevant evidence. McEwan (1998, p. 76) cites *R* v *Turner* **(1816) 5 M & S 206**, where there were ten possible justifications in the relevant statute for the defendant's possession of pheasants or hares. Only Turner could know which if any were applicable and the burden was on him to prove them. Furthermore, *Woolmington* itself cited exceptions to the principle, notably the common law defence of insanity and statutory exceptions. It is important to stress the rationale behind the *Woolmington* principle which McEwan points out (at p. 74), 'derives not only from paternalistic concern as to the fate of accused persons, but is an application of the basic theory of the trial, that parties who wish the machinery of the law to assist them should have the obligation of proving their case'. The state should bear the legal burden if it seeks to convict someone of a crime.

Yet the defendant's right to the presumption of innocence was not absolute. The constitutional principle of parliamentary sovereignty meant that parliament could expressly shift the burden of an element of the offence to the defendant. Research by Ashworth and Blake (1996) revealed that the 40% of offences triable in the Crown court appeared to violate the presumption of innocence by placing a legal burden of proof on the defendant or imposing a form of strict liability. Doubtless the number has increased in the subsequent ten years. The justification for this is the consequentialist argument that on occasion the social good of crime reduction achieved by reducing the burden on the prosecution takes precedence over the defendant's rights. Considerable controversy arose, however, over the clearer acknowledgement, post-*Woolmington,* of a third exception to the 'golden thread', namely implied statutory exceptions. Historically the starting point was what is now s. 101 of the **Magistrates' Court Act 1980,** which covers situations where a defendant relies for his defence on an 'exception, exemption, proviso, excuse or qualification' whereby specified conduct is allowed in permitted circumstances. In such situations it was for the defendant to prove that he falls within the exception, etc.

The objective of such legislation was to make it easier for the authorities to prosecute certain regulatory offences, such as driving without a licence. The approach of the courts, however, was to extend the possibility of shifting the burden to the defendant in a wider range of circumstances. This was illustrated in the landmark cases *R* v *Edwards* and *R* v *Hunt*. In both cases it is arguable that the constitutional principle of the presumption of innocence was secondary to policy considerations. Thus in *Edwards* the Court of Appeal adopted what Stein (1991, p. 1) called a 'syntactical approach' and classified defences on their syntactical status or sectional location in the statute. It held statutes could be interpreted to have impliedly shifted the burden for trials on indictment as well as summary offences, and that where the burden shifted it would be the legal not simply the evidential burden. One safeguard was that the standard imposed on the defendant was only the balance of probabilities. In the subsequent case of *Hunt* the House of Lords set out more fully the circumstances in which the courts would interpret legislation as permitting placing the legal burden on the defendant. Stein points out that the House of Lords in *Hunt,* while upholding *Edwards,* saw the issue as more complex. Attention should be paid not only to the linguistic structure of the Act but also to the mischief at which it was aimed and various practical matters which affect the burden of proof.

As regards general guidelines these were as follows. Firstly, the courts should recognise that Parliament can never lightly be taken to have intended to shift the burden of proof onto the defendant. Secondly, a factor of great importance was the ease or difficulty that parties met in discharging the probative burden. Here the courts drew on the House of Lords decision in *Nimmo* v *Alexander Cowan & Sons Ltd* [1968] AC 107, where the plaintiff employer was allocated the burden of proof on the issue of whether it was 'reasonably practicable' to observe health and safety standards. Finally, the gravity of the offence should be borne in mind.

In *Hunt* itself the House of Lords reversed the Court of Appeal and held that on the proper construction of the statute, the composition of the alleged prohibited drug was an element of the offence which the prosecution should prove. However, a number of critics, while applauding the actual decision, pointed out its dangerous implications. By abdicating on the matter of principle the House opened the door to serious inroads on the presumption of innocence. Mirfield (1988, p. 19) drew a distinction between the judgments of Lord Templeman on the one hand and Lords Griffiths, Ackner, Keith and Mackay on the other. All but Lord Templeman expressly supported the notion that Parliament may impliedly place the burden of proof on the accused. In cases of ambiguity in the statute, instead of relying unequivocally on the presumption of innocence, their Lordships were prepared only to see the necessity of avoiding the imposition of 'onerous burdens' on the defendant.

Bennion (1988, p. 34) took a less critical stance and argued that the exception in Hunt could only be taken to apply to offences of strict liability for 'Where the ingredients of the offence require mens rea, the onus must always remain on the prosecution to prove the evidence of this.' He suggested that this is illustrated by the House of Lords decision in *Westminster City Council* v *Croyalgrange Ltd* (1986) 83 Cr App R 155, where the House agreed that the prosecution should prove the landlord company knew a necessary licence had not been obtained by their tenants. On the other hand, Mirfield (1988) examined the **Public Order Act 1986** to show how on the basis of the *Hunt* guidelines the statute could be interpreted to shift the burden of disproving the mental element of riot. He suggested (at p. 234) that Lord Templeman distinguished *Woolmington* in that it dealt with mens rea not actus reus but that Lords Griffiths and Ackner would accept 'judicial sovereignty over the burden of proof at common law, but not, for constitutional reasons, over statute'. In theory after *Hunt*, Parliament could be taken to have shifted, impliedly, the burden on the mens rea. Mirfield argued that this is unlikely in the case of riot, but possible in less 'obvious' cases, because the policy considerations set out in *Hunt* did not stress the most important one, namely that of maintaining the *Woolmington* principle.

Stein (1991) took this approach further in analysing *R* v *Alath Construction Ltd* [1990] 1 WLR 1255, the first reported case decided under the *Hunt* guidelines. In this case the defence that the tree was dying or dead and therefore not subject to a preservation order was for the defendant to prove. This case shows how sectional separation between offences and defences could not be relied upon to obviate a shift in the burden of proof. Stein claimed the Court of Appeal, relying on *Hunt,* was confusing justification where there should be no legal burden on the accused and an 'actor-related "excuse" ' where s. 101 would apply. Traditional common law defences such as duress or necessity only require an evidential burden from the accused, but, in sanctioning reversal of the burden of proof in some cases under statute, *Hunt* confirmed that both the evidential and the legal burden should shift.

If *Hunt* and *Edwards* marked a retreat from constitutional principle then the **Human Rights Act 1998** clearly signalled a return. It required the courts to take account of the Strasbourg jurisprudence in interpreting legislation. The outcome has been to a large extent a return to the *Woolmington* principled approach. This has been examined by the House of Lords in several landmark cases. Firstly in **R v DPP, *ex parte Kebilene* [2000] 2 AC 326** the House of Lords was asked to consider, inter alia, whether s. 16A of the **Prevention of Terrorism (Temporary Provisions) Act 1989** violated the principle of the presumption of innocence guaranteed by art. 6(2) of the European Convention on Human Rights. It held that it was open to the accused on a prosecution under that section to argue that no more than an evidential presumption had been raised which could be displaced by the raising of a reasonable doubt as to guilt rather than a reverse onus of persuading the jury as to guilt or innocence. Lords Cooke, Hope and Hobhouse held that it was open to argument that art. 6(2), although expressed in absolute terms, was not to be regarded as imposing an absolute prohibition on reverse onus provisions. The House considered some of the Strasbourg cases which indicated that reverse onus of proof provisions are not necessarily a violation of the Convention. In *Salabiaku* v *France* (1988) 13 EHRR 379, for example, the Strasbourg Court accepted that there was no objection in principle to the operation of strict liability in criminal law. However, it clearly indicated that a powerful consideration will be the question of proportionality since presumptions of fact or law were not to be regarded with indifference in criminal cases. States should confine them within reasonable limits which take into account the importance of what is at stake and maintain the rights of the defence. In *Kebilene* Lord Bingham in the Divisional Court had held that s. 16A of the 1989 Act undermined in a blatant and obvious way the presumption of innocence. He observed: 'Under section 16A a defendant could be convicted even if the jury entertained a reasonable doubt whether he knew the items were in his premises and whether he knew he had the items for a terrorist purpose.' Although the House of Lords did not pronounce on the matter in *Kebilene,* it is clear that courts will have now to weigh a number of considerations in applying statutes which appear to place the onus of proof on the defendant. Following *Hunt* they were not restricted to the form or wording of the statutory provision but must consider also policy matters. *Pepper* v *Hart* [1993] 1 All ER 42, of course, allows recourse to Hansard as a means of statutory interpretation. The **Human Rights Act** has now, however, reasserted the *Woolmington* principle.

This is even clearer in the second of this series of House of Lords cases namely, *R* v *Lambert, R* v *Ali, R* v *Jordan* [2001] 3 WLR 206. By a majority of four to one the House decided that in the context of reverse burdens of proof, 'prove' in a statute could be interpreted as imposing an 'evidential burden'. Lord Steyn, in giving the majority judgment, stated that 'legislative interference with the presumption of innocence requires justification and must not be freer than necessary. The principle of proportionality must be observed.' A transfer of the legal burden would amount to a disproportionate interference with the presumption of innocence. Ashworth (2001, p. 865) contrasted *Lambert* with that of the Strasbourg Court in *Salabiaku* v *France* (1988) 13 EHRR 379. In the latter case the Court accepted that legislatures may reverse the burden of proof 'within reasonable limits which take into account the importance of what is at stake and maintain the rights of the defence'. Ashworth comments that it 'must be said that the Strasbourg jurisprudence on art. 6(2) is underdeveloped, not to say flaccid, and it is British judges, taking their cue from Commonwealth constitutional courts, who have sought to give greater sharpness to the right and any exceptions'.

In *R* v *Johnstone* [2003] UKHL 28 the House of Lords gave fuller guidance on reverse burden provisions. They were permitted so long as they were confined within reasonable limits that took account of the importance of what was at stake and maintained the rights of the defence. The case involved an offence under s. 92 (6) of the **Trade Marks Act 1994** and the section concerned with the burden of proof read, 'it is a defence for a person charged with an offence under this section to show that he believed on reasonable grounds that the use of the sign in the manner in which it was used, or was to be used, was not an infringement of the registered trademark'. Lord Nichols gave the majority judgment, cited a number of policy reasons why there should be a legal burden on the case and also identified s. 92 as imposing an offence of almost strict liability. Subsequent case-law has demonstrated that the courts place much importance on the nature of the offence and are more ready to allow a shift of the burden in the case of regulatory offences. Reverse legal burdens were probably justified if the overall burden remained on the prosecution but Parliament had for significant reasons concluded that it was fair and reasonable to make an exception in respect of a particular aspect of the offence (*Attorney General's Reference (No. 1 of 2004)* [2004] **EWCA 1125**). However, Parliament's intentions may be disregarded if the fairness of the trial is threatened (**Attorney General's Reference (No. 4 of 2002)** [2004] **UKHL 43**). In the latter case there was no doubt that Parliament in the **Terrorism Act** intended to shift the legal burden but 'it was not the intention of Parliament in the 1998 Act' (para. 51) and the House imposed only an evidential burden on the accused. It held that both *Lambert* and *Johnstone* were both leading cases on reverse burdens and that, despite the statement of Lord Woolf in *Attorney General's Reference No. 1 of 2004, Johnstone* did not depart from *Lambert*.

Lambert itself left a number of unanswered questions. First, Lord Hutton argued in a powerful dissenting speech that the effect of upholding the defendant's right was to endanger society. Defendants would now easily be able to raise defences under the statute. He stated that 'the threat of drugs to the well-being of the community and the peculiar difficulty of proving knowledge in such cases justifies an exception to the general principles. . .In my opinion, it is not unprincipled to have regard to practical realities where the issue relates to knowledge in a drugs case.'

Secondly, the law is left in a state of some uncertainty. As Munday argues (2007, p. 106) 'one ought not to run away with the idea that *Lambert* has led to wholesale abandonment of the idea that Parliament can legitimately cast a legal burden of proof on a defendant'. He pointed out that in *L* v *DPP* [2003] QB 137 the Divisional Court interpreted s. 139(4) of the **Criminal Justice Act 1988** as amended as placing a legal burden on the accused 'to prove that he had good reason or lawful authority for having [an offensive weapon] with him in a public place'. This interpretation struck the correct balance between protecting society on the one hand and the rights of the defendant on the other. Here, by contrast to *Lambert*, derogation from the principle of the presumption of innocence was acceptable. As Munday (2007, p. 110) commented; 'whenever construing a statutory provision that purports to impose a legal burden of proof upon a defendant, the court will find itself wandering in Tennyson's "wilderness of single instances (see *Aylmer's Field*)"'.

A further criticism of the *Lambert* approach is elegantly argued by Roberts and Zuckerman. They point out (2004, p. 388) that: 'Article 6(2) was extended to the proof of facts that were not elements of the offence that the prosecution had to prove to secure a conviction.' By treating an affirmative defence as if it were an element of the offence, thereby applying Article 6(2), they argue, the court imbues the presumption of innocence 'with a measure of substantive content in English law'. English courts are not equipped for this degree of statutory judicial review and the risk is that Parliament might withdraw affirmative defences altogether. This, they suggest, has happened in the US. Roberts was very critical of the reasoning in *Lambert*. He wrote (2002(a), p. 36), 'The result achieved in *Lambert* was arrived at with scant regard for established evidentiary concepts and taxonomies. Once the presumption of innocence is given substantive content, there are no obvious conceptual limits on the scope for judicial reworking of the elements of criminal law offences. This would be questionable enough in an exclusively domestic context, without the prospect of the Strasbourg Court acquiring the notion that it can use Article 6(2) to rewrite States Parties' substantive criminal codes, for example by striking down what it deems to be objectionable strict liability offences.' Roberts argued that the legislative precursors of the 1971 Act created absolute liabilities for possessing drugs and that this was 'wholly dispositive' of art. 6(2) issues.

These observations illustrate the difficulty of deciding the parameters of a 'fundamental constitutional guarantee' and that the courts have not taken an absolutist stance. They have been prepared, however, on occasion to depart from the intention of Parliament, which does suggest that the presumption of innocence may override the popular will.

Thus in English law, as in the Strasbourg jurisprudence, the presumption of innocence is not quite an absolute. In *Lambert* however the Court moved closer to the *Woolmington* principle by requiring close examination of all statutory reverse onus provisions. But reverse onus provisions will still exist either by virtue of unambiguous wording of the statute or judicial interpretation of ambiguous statutes. As the above analysis has shown, the current position has left some uncertainty and theoretical incoherence. One way forward suggested by Roberts and Zuckerman is a 'planned programme of de-criminalisation' of the regulatory offences which are most often at issue in this area of statutory interpretation. Such criticisms are endorsed by Padfield (2005). She writes (p. 19): 'The time has come for a category of administrative regulations which would carry little stigma and no possibility of imprisonment. Only for such "non-crimes" should strict liability or reverse burdens be acceptable.'

Finally, the constitutional importance of the presumption of innocence has been highlighted in an even more controversial way by the case of *R (Mullen) v Secretary of State for the Home Department* [2005] 1 AC 1. The judgment raised also international constitutional obligations under the International Covenant on Civil and Political Rights and the European Convention on Human Rights, both of which enshrine the presumption of innocence. The House of Lords, overturning the Court of Appeal on this issue, upheld the executive's decision to deny compensation to a man whose conviction for conspiracy to cause explosions had been overturned on the grounds of pre-trial unlawful action by the executive. The accuracy of the original conviction was not questioned. The issue then becomes whether the presumption of innocence is restored when a conviction is overturned on what is often referred to as a 'technicality'. Schiemann LJ's view in the Court of Appeal ([2003] QB 993, 1007) had been that 'in a case where this court has quashed a conviction the presumption of innocence requires that Acts of Parliament are to be interpreted on the basis that it is not intended that the state should proceed on the basis that a wrongly convicted man is guilty'. In a wide-ranging review of the judgments in this 'exceptional' case Nobles and Schiff (2006, p. 90) explain that, '*Mullen* exposes a tautology at the heart of criminal justice, which is that guilt established by the legal system is always legal guilt—guilt according to law. And as such innocence is simply the condition which exists when the legal system has not established guilt. This tautology does not disappear when successful appeals are routinely treated as sufficient conditions for the award of compensation. Those appeals have not established innocence. They have merely restored the condition of guilt not having been legally established.'

The presumption of innocence, together with the high standard of proof required, is generally regarded as a necessary right, safeguarding the citizen against an all-powerful state. The above account has illustrated, however, that it is also accepted that there may be compromises to this principle. Some parts of the burden may be shifted to the defendant in some cases. This has been imposed by both Parliament and the judges. In *Lambert* the House of Lords, stretching the linguistic interpretation somewhat, signalled a return to the principled approach of *Woolmington* away from the pragmatism of *Hunt*. The principles should, the majority held, not be easily defeated. Public interest arguments for the opposite stance did not prevail, a stance that showed more respect for the presumption of innocence than Strasbourg showed in *Salabiaku*. However, principle and pragmatism currently go hand in hand, creating what Roberts and Zuckerman have called (2004, p. 383) a 'blizzard of simple instances'.

There has been to some extent a difference of approach between the Court of Appeal and the House of Lords. In *Attorney-General's Reference (No. 1 of 2004)* the Court of Appeal in reviewing *Lambert* preferred the approach of Lord Nicholls to that of Lord Steyn. It stated: 'In practice a legal burden is, much more likely to have to be reduced to an evidential burden on Lord Steyn's approach than it is on Lord Nicholls of Birkenhead's approach. . . . We suggest that until the position is clarified by a further decision of the House of Lords lower courts should follow the approach of Lord Nicholls of Birkenhead rather than that of Lord Steyn if they are in doubt as to what should be the outcome of a challenge to a reverse burden.' The House of Lords subsequently did clarify the law in *Sheldrake* v *DPP* and *Attorney-General's Reference* (No. 4 of 2002). Lord Bingham stated that 'Both *R* v *Lambert* and *R* v *Johnstone* are recent decisions of the House, binding on lower courts for what they decide. In *R* v *Keogh* [2007] 1 WLR 1500, the Court of Appeal, applying *Lambert, Johnstone* and *Sheldrake* held that ss 2(3) and 2(4) of the **Official Secrets Act 1989** imposed only an evidential burden on the accused. These sections related to mens rea. Referring to *Sheldrake* the court stated that the 'essential effect of the authorities is summarised by Lord Bingham at paragraph 31: "The task of the court is never to decide whether a reverse burden should be placed on a defendant, but always to assess whether a burden erected by Parliament unjustifiably infringes the presumption of innocence."'

Question 2

Answer all parts:

(a) Harry is refused entrance to a nightclub by a bouncer called George. A scuffle breaks out and George suffers a broken nose. Harry is prosecuted for assault and claims that George struck the first blow. In her summing up the judge says, 'Ladies and gentlemen of the jury you have heard the defendant claim that he acted in self-defence. It is for the prosecution to prove however that he did not act in self-defence.'

Comment on the judge's summing-up.

(b) 'Are we to infer that *M'Naghten* (and *Woolmington*) have been overruled, to the extent that the accused no longer has to prove insanity (on the balance of probabilities) but only to raise enough evidence to pass the judge?' P. Roberts (2002) 'Criminal Procedure, Drug Dealing and the Presumption of Innocence: The Human Rights Act (Almost) Bites', **International Journal of Evidence and Proof** 6(2), p. 37.

Comment.

(c) Under the imaginary Bicycle Tuition Act (1996) it is an offence for a person to give lessons in cycling for payment to pupils without a licence from the Highway Authority unless the pupils are aged 16 years or more. Gloria has been charged with an offence under this Act. Advise her on the burden and standard of proof.

Commentary

These three questions require you to be familiar with situations where the burden of proof may shift in criminal trials. You will need some knowledge of the evolution of the law in this area and the impact of recent case-law under the **Human Rights Act 1998**. You must be careful to use the correct terminology and in particular to understand the difference between the legal and the evidential burdens. The legal burden is the obligation placed on a party to prove a fact in issue, whereas the evidential burden (the 'burden of passing the judge') is that placed on a party to adduce sufficient evidence on a fact which is asserted for it to become an issue in the trial. There is a significant amount of academic literature in this area and your answers would be improved by familiarity with it.

(a) This part requires an outline of the evidential rules concerning a plea of self-defence.

(b) In this article Paul Roberts is critical of the logic behind the majority ruling of the House of Lords in **Lambert**. He outlines the uncertainties it has created in the law over reverse onus clauses, including the defence of insanity.

(c) Your answer to this question would have been different before the implementation of the **Human Rights Act**. It requires knowledge of the nature of implied statutory exceptions in relation to the burden of proof. The law in this area has been dominated by the cases of *R* v *Hunt* and *R* v *Edwards*. Doak and McGourlay point out (at p. 76) that these cases 'should be seen as being of historical interest only'. In your answer however you should demonstrate an academic knowledge of the historical development of the law but concentrate on giving practical advice in the light of the more recent cases since 2000. It is important to show you understand that there may be several elements to an offence and the allocation of the legal and evidential burdens of proof will not be the same for all of them.

Answer plan

(a)

- Trace the common law position through the case-law
- Distinguish the evidential and legal burdens and the standard of proof in both

(b)

- State the **Woolmington** position on insanity
- Discuss the potential impact of the **Human Rights Act** in this area
- Law Commission reform proposals

(c)

- Identify the elements of the actus reus
- Refer to s. 101 **Magistrates Court Act**, **Hunt** and **Edwards**
- Assess the impact of the **Human Rights Act** and the possibility of construing a statutory provision to place an evidential burden on the defendant
- Show some familiarity with relevant recent case-law, **Sheldrake** v DPP **[2004] 3 WLR 976**, and **L** v **DPP [2003] QB 13.**

Suggested answer

(a) The judge in her summing-up has directed the jury's attention to Harry's use of self-defence based on the common law. It is a well-established principle that the prosecution does not have to anticipate every claim the defendant makes. If the defendant wishes to plead self-defence then he must adduce sufficient evidence to convince the judge that this can be a live issue at the trial. In other words the defendant has what is popularly known as the evidential burden. As Roberts (2002(a), p. 34) points out the 'evidential burden is not a burden of proof at all, but only a burden of adducing evidence'. The judge therefore does not have to refer to the evidential burden in her summing-up because it is not a matter for the jury at all. Here the judge is correct to point out that the legal burden remains with the prosecution on this issue (*Lobell* [1957] 1 QB 547). A failure to do this could lead to an appeal (*R* v *Moon* [1969] 1 WLR 1705). More recently in *R* v *O'Brien* [2004] EWCA Crim 2900 the Court of Appeal held that a failure by the judge to direct the jury that it was the task of the prosecution to prove the defendant was not acting in self-defence was 'an important misdirection in relation to a very significant aspect of the law of self-defence'. In the question set there is no reference to the standard of proof in the summing-up. There is considerable case-law on the words judges should use in directing juries on the standard of proof. Where the prosecution bears the legal burden the standard of proof required for conviction is beyond reasonable doubt. The Judicial Studies Board has drafted a model direction as follows:

> How does the prosecution succeed in proving the defendant's guilt? The answer is—by making you sure of it. Nothing less than that will do. If after considering all the evidence you are sure that the defendant is guilty you must return a verdict of 'Guilty'. If you are not sure your verdict must be 'Not Guilty'. (www.jsboard. co.uk/specdir)

The judge would therefore be expected to include in her summing-up a direction along those lines. The Court of Appeal has over the years pronounced on unacceptable judicial directions in this area. In *R* v *Yap Chuan Ching* (1976) 63 **Cr App R 7**, 11 Lawton LJ observed that 'if judges stopped trying to define that which is almost impossible to define there would be fewer appeals'. In this case, however, the Appeal Court stated that judges should avoid defining 'reasonable doubt'. Lord Denning in *Miller* v *Minister of Pensions* [1947] 2 **All ER 372, 373** gave a celebrated definition:

> Proof beyond reasonable doubt does not mean proof beyond a shadow of a doubt. The law would fail to protect the community if it admitted to fanciful possibilities to deflect the course of justice. If the evidence is so strong against a man as to leave one a remote possibility in his favour which can be dismissed with the sentence, 'of course it is possible, but not in the least probable,' the case is proved beyond reasonable doubt but nothing short of that will suffice.

Thus the judge's summing-up in this instance is correct on the burden of proof but incomplete on the question of the standard of proof.

(b)   The classic common law summary of the burden of proof in criminal cases is given in *Woolmington*. Lord Sankey identified two exceptions to the placing of the burden of proof on the prosecution, namely statutory exceptions and that created in *M'Naghten's Case* (1843) **10 Cl & Fin 200**. The latter specifies that where the defendant in a murder trial makes a plea of insanity the burden of proving insanity is on him.

The quotation in this question acknowledges the importance of this exception to the 'golden rule' while at the same time acknowledging its status may be under threat from current judicial attitudes. To take the first point it is salutary to realise that, as Roberts and Zuckerman point out, the insanity exception is 'of limited practical significance' (2004, p. 373). They point out that a finding of 'not guilty by reason of insanity' meant 'mandatory detention in a secure hospital', and although other sentencing options are now available, 'a plea of insanity remains an unattractive option for most accused, and the defence is seldom raised'.

In the article cited in the question, however, Roberts goes further by outlining the shaky intellectual basis for the exception. The House of Lords in *Lambert*, argues Roberts, is close to saying that the only burdens on the defence should be evidential ones. He finds the reasoning in this case doctrinally incoherent, 'with scant regard for established evidentiary concepts and taxonomies'. In particular he criticises the judgment because the analysis fails to acknowledge the conclusive nature of the specific statutory section, namely that it creates an offence of strict liability and therefore the discussion on burden of proof in relation to guilty knowledge is theoretically incoherent.

This approach leads Roberts to speculate about the possible implications for other seemingly entrenched doctrines, including the burden of proof on an insanity defence. He mentions that the Canadian courts have re-examined the approach to this in the light of fair trial right considerations, although this is not specifically included in the House of Lords' *Lambert* ruling. Roberts points out, however, that the Canadian courts have acknowledged that the traditional reverse onus clause in relation to insanity was upheld as a justifiable derogation from the presumption of innocence under the general saving cause, s. 1 **Canadian Charter of Rights of Freedoms**. He adds that there is no comparable provision in art. 6, **ECHR**.

In short, Roberts is arguing that the implications of the *Lambert* judgment are far-reaching. Although putting an evidential burden rather than a legal burden on the defence might be welcome from a human rights standpoint, the uncertainty and intellectual confusion the judgment has prompted is troubling.

In fact, since Roberts penned this observation the courts have retreated somewhat from an overly robust readiness to refuse to interpret reverse onus clauses so that the legal burden is not placed on the defence and have adopted a case-by-case approach. This, however, succeeds only in perpetuating the uncertainty, as a number of commentators have pointed out (see Choo (2006, p. 344), Ashworth (2005, p. 219)). Choo (p. 344) for example, comments in relation to the leading case *Sheldrake* v *DPP*; *Attorney General's Reference (No. 4 of 2002)* [2004] 3 **WLR 976** that it has 'served to bring the problem of uncertainty and unpredictability into even sharper focus'.

With regard to the principled question in relation to insanity, namely should the burden of proof be on the defendant, it is certainly arguable that the *M'Naghten* decision itself is a historical anomaly and is arguably difficult to justify in the light of art. 6 provisions. The European Court of Human Rights has held, however, that the rule does not violate the presumption of innocence, *H* v *UK* (1990) **App No 15023/89**. T. H. Jones (1995, p. 475) however cites arguments that the burden on the defence should be evidential only. Jones acknowledges that the courts are just as concerned with social protection as they are with issues of individual fairness or responsibility and that 'there is a constant tension between these two competing values, which goes some way to explaining (but not justifying) the complexities and paradoxes which pervade this area of law'. The Law Commission has produced a draft report on the issue, the Draft Criminal Code: Criminal Liability and Mental Disorder (2002). It proposed that the general law relating to mental illness should be rationalised and a new term 'mental disorder' should replace 'insanity'. The burden of proving the defence would remain on the accused on the balance of probabilities.

(c) The elements of the offence with which Gloria is charged are first in relation to the actus reus:

- Giving bicycle riding tuition for payment
- to a person under 16 years
- without a licence.

The section does not specify the necessary mens rea but it will be assumed that this is not an offence of strict liability since there is a presumption of mens rea

(*Sweet* v *Parsley* [1970] AC 132). There should therefore be little doubt that the task of proving mens rea lies on the prosecution because there is nothing in the statute quoted to suggest that Parliament has implicitly affected this burden. This approach was affirmed in *B (A Minor)* v *DPP* (2000) 2 AC 428 and *R* v *K* [2001] 3 All ER 897.

It is necessary therefore to examine where the burden of proof lies on each of the elements of the actus reus. The general rule in criminal cases is that it is for the prosecution to prove all the elements of an offence beyond reasonable doubt (*Woolmington* v *DPP* [1935] AC 462). This principle is upheld also by the presumption of innocence provision in art. 6(2) of the **European Convention on Human Rights**. However, the principle is also subject to statutory exceptions either expressed or implied. The questions to be addressed here are whether the statute reverses the legal burden of proof on any aspect of the offence, whether the evidential burden may be placed on the defendant on any aspect or whether the legal and evidential burden should remain exclusively with the prosecution. An additional question is whether the position differs depending on whether the matter is tried summarily or on indictment. It is important to recognise that the burden of proof regarding each aspect of the offence may be placed on the defendant while the prosecution may retain others. Similarly the courts may split the evidential and legal burdens between defence and prosecution on a specific issue.

The (imaginary) statute in this question must be analysed in the light of the application of the **Human Rights Act 1998** (HRA) with some acknowledgement also of the earlier case-law. It would seem that the first of the elements, teaching cycling for payment, requires proof for the prosecution to the standard of beyond reasonable doubt. There is nothing in the wording of the statute to suggest otherwise. More complex is the question of where the burden of proof should lie in relation to the two other elements, namely the existence of a licence for the local authority and the age of the pupils taught by Gloria. There is considerable case-law on implied statutory exceptions. At issue is the effect of s. 101 of the **Magistrates Court Act 1980,** which provides that where 'a defendant relies for his defence on any exception, exemption, provision, excuse or qualification' he bears the burden of proving the exception, etc. The House of Lords held that this enacted a principle of common law that the statute could implicitly shift the burden of proof from prosecution to defence. This approach must now be examined in the light of the application of the HRA.

The first preliminary issue is whether it is significant that the statute precedes the HRA. The current judicial stance is that what is decisive is the date of the original trial, not the statute. The same approach to allocating the burden of proof will apply whether the trial is held in a Crown Court or a magistrates Court (see *R* v *Hunt*).

In the leading case of *Sheldrake* v *DPP* (UKHL) 43 the House of Lords examined the status of the burden of proof in a case involving the application of the

Road Traffic Act 1988. At issue was whether where the defendant was on trial for being in charge of a car while intoxicated, contrary to the **Road Traffic Act**, the defence under s. 5(2) placed the burden on him or on the prosecution. The defence was available on proof that there was no likelihood of the defendant driving his car. In giving the lead judgment Lord Bingham referred to Lord Griffiths' statement in *R* v *Hunt* that if the statute was unclear, 'the court should look to other considerations to determine the intention of Parliament such as the mischief at which the Act was aimed and practical considerations affecting the burden of proof and, in particular, the ease or difficulty that the respective parties would encounter in discharging the burden'. It is possible, on the wording of the statute the court would draw the conclusion that the age of the pupils, like the composition of the morphine in *Hunt*, was an element of the offence and the burden of proof lay on the prosecution. If, alternatively, the court considers that the statute creates a defence, the burden of which is placed on the accused, following *Lambert*, it will be required to consider whether placing the burden on Gloria was proportionate and therefore compatible with Article 6(2). In particular the court must consider whether placing the evidential burden only on Gloria could achieve the intention of Parliament.

Lord Griffiths' statement cited in *Sheldrake* may, however, be a useful guide to the question of who has the burden of proof on the existence of a licence. The post-**HRA** cases, *Lambert, Johnstone* and *Sheldrake,* indicate that the courts in the cases of ambiguous statutory provisions will go beyond s. 101 of the **Magistrates' Court Act**. In *Sheldrake* the House placed the burden of proof on the defendant on the issue in question. Lord Bingham acknowledged that the Strasbourg jurisprudence did not mean that the burden of proof being on the prosecutor was an absolute. It was important to strike a reasonable balance between the public interest and the interest of the individual. Here it is arguable that the protection of minors in an age which is increasingly conscious of their vulnerability to abuse could mean that the burden of proof should be on the defendant to prove she had the licence. *In L v DPP* [2002] QB 13 the Divisional Court interpreted s. 139(4) of the Criminal Justice Act 1988 so as to place the legal burden on the accused to prove that he had a good reason or lawful authority as a defence to a charge under s. 139(1). The actus reus was having a bladed article in his possession in a public place. The prosecution had to prove possession, and that the accused knew he had the relevant article. There was strong public interest in suppressing this crime. The accused was being asked to prove something within his knowledge. Placing the burden on him was a proportionate response which maintained the balance between the public interest and individual rights. It may be that the defence may counter this argument by referring to the seriousness of a penalty and the likelihood that the defendant would lose her livelihood.

If the legal burden is placed on the defence, the standard of proof will be the balance of probabilities.

Question 3

Loamshire District Council is suing Amy for money they allege was paid her in error while she was working under contract as a temporary gardener. They claim she has fraudulently retained the money. She claims she has no idea she was overpaid since her pay was paid directly into her bank account and she did not receive pay slips. She has no records relating to the period and simply denies the liability. Amy claims further that if there were payments beyond her wages it was for a bonus the council promised to pay her. Loamshire are also claiming for a rake which they say she broke. She relies on a clause in the contract which exempts her from liability for damage to any tools providing she was not negligent.

   Advise the parties on burden and standard of proof.

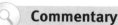 ## Commentary

Questions on the burden and standard of proof in civil cases do not raise as many controversies as those in criminal cases. The simplest approach is to realise that the burden generally lies on the party who pleads an issue. Two possibly problematic issues arise here. One is whether the standard of proof is affected because the council are alleging fraudulent retention by Amy of money not owing to her; secondly the burden in the exemption clause and its proviso will arguably shift from one to the other as assertion meets counter-assertion.

 ## Answer plan

- General principle in civil cases, he who asserts must prove. Council has burden on issue of overpayment, Amy has burden of proving her defence; both burdens are legal and evidential
- Case may be decided on burden of proof—***Rhesa Shipping*** v *Edmunds* [1985] 1 WLR 948
- General rule that civil standard of proof is balance of probabilities
- Examine cases where quasi-criminal accusation is made in a civil case; despite some deviation from balance of probabilities House of Lords has decided there is no third standard—***Re H and Others (Minors)*** [1996] AC 563
- Concerning rake, council to prove breach of contract, Amy that she falls within the exemption clause—***Munro Brice and Co*** v *War Risks Association* [1918] 2 KB 78

Suggested answer

The general principle in civil litigation is that the burden of proof lies on the asserter of a claim. It is thus for the council to prove the excessive payment under the contract. The incidence of the burden is thus here a matter of substantive law and the House of Lords held that it is usually clear from the pleadings: *Wilsher* v *Essex Area Health Authority* [1988] AC 1074. The council therefore have the legal burden of proof on the issue of the overpayment. They also have the evidential burden in the sense that they must put in some evidence to convince the court there is a case to answer.

Amy may simply deny liability but she runs the risk tactically of losing. She is, however, putting up a specific defence, namely that the overpayment was money due from a bonus. She has the legal and evidential burden of mounting this defence. The incidence of the legal burden of proof will decide the outcome of the case if the tribunal is not able to come to a decision on which to prefer. In *Rhesa Shipping Co. SA* v *Edmunds* [1985] 1 WLR 948 the House of Lords, overturning the Court of Appeal, held that the judge had not been obliged to choose between two versions merely because the defendants had chosen to put forward their explanation of events.

Thus, the plaintiff, Loamshire District Council, has the task of proving its case more probable than not, not more probable than Amy's version of events.

The standard of proof is on the balance of probabilities. There is a possible further consideration in that the council are alleging that Amy held the money fraudulently.

The Bar's Code of Conduct provides that counsel may not draft an allegation of fraud without specific instructions and unless he or she has reasonably credible material which, as it stands, establishes a prima facie case of fraud.

There have been some examples in civil cases where courts have held that certain matters must be proved to the criminal standard of proof, in *Re a Solicitor* [1992] QB 69 for example. The issue was the standard of proof in a case before a solicitors' disciplinary tribunal, where allegations of professional misconduct were made. The Divisional Court held that since what was alleged was tantamount to a criminal offence the criminal standard should apply. However, this has not been generally followed. In *Hornal* v *Neuberger Products Ltd* [1957] 1 QB 247, a case involving an allegation of fraudulent misrepresentation, the Court of Appeal rejected the view that there was a higher standard necessary than balance of probability but rather puzzlingly commented per Denning LJ at p. 258 'the more serious the allegation the higher the degree of probability that is required' and per Morris LJ at p. 266 'the very elements of gravity become a part of the whole range of circumstances which have to be weighed in the scale when deciding as to the balance of probabilities'. In *Re H and Others (Minors) (Sexual Abuse: Standard of Proof)* [1996] AC 563 the House of Lords in a majority decision rejected the concept of a third standard in civil cases of this sort.

In some previous Court of Appeal decisions there had been some doubt expressed on this. Some had argued for a standard higher than the balance of probabilities but lower than the criminal standard. In *R* v *B (A Child)* [2004] EWCA Civ 567 the Court of Appeal reaffirmed that in care proceedings the standard of proof remained the balance of probabilities test set out in *Re H* and that the more improbable the event the stronger must be the evidence that it had occurred.

Lord Nicholls in *Re H* suggested that if there were a third standard in some civil cases it would be necessary to identify what that standard was and when it applied. Since any such formulation would risk causing confusion it would be better to leave things as they were. Dennis (2002, p. 398) comments: 'This is not a wholly persuasive argument. The existence of a third standard of proof is well recognised in the United States in the form of the "clear and convincing standard".' He suggests (p. 486) that 'the rejection in *Re H (Minors)* of a third standard of proof was perhaps over-hasty. It is not apparent that leaving the matter of serious allegations as one affecting the weight of the evidence needed to tip the balance of probability is significantly more certain and less confusing.' Dennis points out that in fact there are two identifiable strands from the case law in this area. The first view is that the degree of probability varies with the seriousness of the issue and will occasionally approach the criminal standard (see *Khawaja* v *Secretary of State* [1984] AC 74.) In *R* v *Chief Constable of Avon and Somerset* [2001] 1 All ER 562 Lord Bingham stated (at p. 573) that proof of the conditions for making a sex offender order under s. 2 of the **Crime and Disorder Act 1998** should be to 'a civil standard of proof which will for all practical purposes be indistinguishable from the criminal standard'. The second view, according to Dennis (p. 486), is that evidenced in *Re H (Minors)*, where 'the matter is not one of the degree of probability required, but is a matter of weight of evidence needed to tip the balance of probabilities'. In *R (N)* v *Mental Health Review Tribunal (Northern Region)* [2006] 2 WLR 850, the Court of Appeal confirmed that "the civil standard is one single standard, namely proof on the balance of probabilities." On the facts as they are given here it is likely that the position stated in *Re H* should be applied and that the standard of proof required will be on the balance of probabilities but that cogent evidence of Amy's alleged fraud will be required.

As regards the rake, again the council have the burden of proving that it was broken and that this constituted breach of contract. It is for Amy to prove it is a tool which falls within the exemption clause, although this is a matter of construction for the court: *Munro Brice and Co.* v *War Risks Association* [1918] 2 KB 78. However, it is arguable that if a plaintiff relies upon a proviso to an exemption clause the burden of proving that the facts fall within the proviso may be on the plaintiff: *The Glendarroch* [1894] P 226. Amy may argue by analogy with this reasoning that the plaintiff council will have to prove she was negligent.

Question 4

Jane and Harry are legally married in 1960 in Birmingham. In 1961 Harry leaves to join a revolutionary group in Bolivia, but tells Jane he will return in a year. In fact Jane does not hear from him again and in 1963 gets a letter from the group leader saying Harry has been missing for six months following an expedition against counter-revolutionaries. Jane hears no more and in 1972 marries Oliver, an older man, in Paris. In 1973 Jane gives birth to twins Barry and John and in 1975 to Margaret. In 1995 Jane and Oliver are both killed instantly in a car crash. Shortly before he was killed Oliver told John that Margaret could not be his child because he had not had intercourse with Jane for a year before her birth. At the funeral, Alan, an old college friend of Jane and Harry's, who has been out of touch for years, tells John that he saw Harry in a cafe in La Paz in 1971 but says Harry disappeared before he could speak to him. Jane's will said that if she died after Oliver her estate should be divided between her children and a charity for distressed Bolivian revolutionaries. Oliver's will left all his property to his 'legitimate children'. When John and Margaret, after the car crash, look through old photographs in the attic they come across one showing Oliver and an unknown woman. On the back is noted 'Wedding day, 29 March 1969'.

Advise whether Margaret can claim under Oliver's will and whether all children can succeed under Jane's will.

Commentary

Presumptions do not figure in all evidence courses, so you should check your syllabus. This is conceptually quite a tricky area and you need to keep in mind the difference between presumptions in civil cases and criminal cases and the traditional classification of irrebuttable presumptions of law, rebuttable presumptions of law and presumptions of fact. It is mainly the second with which you need to be concerned in this question. In addition, you will need to distinguish persuasive presumptions, that is those where the effect of the presumption is to put the legal burden of disproof on the party who wishes to challenge it, and evidential presumptions where the evidential burden only is placed on the party against whom it operates. As regards criminal cases it is generally accepted that presumptions can place an evidential burden on the accused only. Thus, for example, the Privy Council held that the prosecution could not rely on the presumption of regularity in *Dillon* v *R* [1982] AC 484. In this question, the examiner is looking for a clear application of the law on presumptions to the facts, rather than discussion on the rationale of presumptions more appropriate to an essay question. You should begin by listing the events in chronological order and stating the relevant presumptions. In your approach to presumptions, you must first acknowledge that the primary facts must first be proved; if they are, the specific presumption must be drawn from them, although it may be rebutted by other conflicting facts. Thus you must first see if the presumptions apply and then see if they can be rebutted.

Answer plan

- 1960 Jane and Harry marry—presumption of validity of marriage
- 1972 Jane and Oliver marry—does presumption of Harry's death operate?
- What is the effect of the 1971 sighting of Harry? Is validity of marriage challenged by 1969 'wedding photograph' of Oliver and unknown woman?
- Does it matter marriage takes place in Paris?
- 1973 John and Barry born
- 1975 Margaret born—presumption of legitimacy but does what Oliver told John rebut presumption of Margaret's legitimacy? Does the 'wedding photograph' affect all children's legitimacy?
- 1995 Jane and Oliver killed—presumption of order of death and effect on inheritance.

Suggested answer

The order of death of Jane and Oliver is determined by their seniority (**Law of Property Act 1925**, s. 184, but see **Administration of Estates Act 1925**, s. 46(3), **Intestates' Estates Act 1952** and **Law Reform (Succession) Act 1995**). As Jane is the younger of the two, Oliver will be presumed to have died first, thus in accordance with the terms of her will her estate is divided between John, Barry and Margaret and the Bolivian charity.

Oliver's estate raises more complicated issues. John, Barry and Margaret can inherit only if they are legitimate. The validity of the marriage between Jane and Oliver could affect the legitimacy of all three. The validity of the marriage is threatened by two pieces of evidence. One is the evidence of Alan that Harry may have been alive after he was presumed to have died. The other is the photograph which suggests that Oliver was not free to marry Jane. The presumption of the validity of a marriage is a very strong one. There are two presumptions which may be operative here. On proof of the celebration of a marriage ceremony, that is one which is capable of producing a valid marriage, the law will presume the formal validity of the marriage, that is to say that the formalities have been complied with. The primary facts thus are the evidence of the ceremony that is valid according to local law. In *Mahadervan* v *Mahadervan* **[1964] P 233** it was argued that the presumption did not apply in favour of a foreign marriage but Sir Jocelyn Simon P said (at p. 247):

> To accept it would give expression to a legal chauvinism that has no place in any rational system of private international law. Our courts in my view apply exactly the same weight of presumption in favour of a foreign marriage as of an English one, and the nationality of any later marriage brought into question is quite immaterial.

It is not significant therefore that the marriage took place in Paris.

This presumption is a persuasive one and there is a legal burden on the party seeking to rebut formal validity. The standard of proof to be met by that party is high. In *Mahadervan* Sir Jocelyn Simon P held that the presumption can only be rebutted by evidence which establishes beyond reasonable doubt that there was no marriage.

On proof of the celebration of a marriage ceremony, relying on the same primary facts, the 'essential validity' of the marriage will be assumed. This is that the parties had the necessary capacity of marrying and that their respective consents were genuine. There appears to be little doubt about the formal validity of the marriage of Jane and Oliver: the issue is its essential validity, in other words, were the parties free to marry? Again in civil proceedings the presumption is persuasive rather than an evidential presumption, but the standard of proof is lower than that in the case of the presumption of formal validity. In *Re Peete, Peete* v *Crompton* [1952] 2 All ER 599 the issue arose as to the essential validity of a formally valid marriage in 1919. There was some evidence of the existence of an earlier marriage and the presumption of validity of the 1919 marriage failed. Even so, the photograph in itself is unlikely to be sufficient evidence to undermine the presumption that Oliver was free to marry Jane.

The issue whether Jane was free to marry is more complicated. Evidently, she relied on the presumption that Harry was dead when she went through the ceremony with Oliver. The rules relating to presumption of death were set out in *Chard* v *Chard* [1956] P 259. Harry is presumed dead when four circumstances apply: there is no acceptable evidence that he has been alive for at least seven continuous years; there are persons likely to have heard of him, had he been alive; who during that period have not so heard; all due enquiries have failed to locate him. We aren't told whether Jane made inquiries about Harry after his disappearance, but assuming she did she was entitled to presume his death by 1970. Had she been properly advised she would have followed the special procedure laid down by s. 19 of the **Matrimonial Causes Act 1973**, petitioning for a decree dissolving the marriage and presuming the death of the spouse. This does not require that enquiries be made, takes no account of the likelihood that the petitioner would have heard of the person had they been alive and restricts the issue whether the petitioner had no reason to believe in the spouse's continued existence to events taking place in the last seven years.

If she had married Oliver without petitioning for a s. 19 decree, the marriage would not necessarily have been an act of bigamy since she could still rely on the common law presumption. Those wishing to challenge the presumption will have the evidential burden. In *Prudential Assurance Co.* v *Edmonds* (1877) 2 App Cas 487, a niece standing in a crowded street in Australia had briefly caught sight of a man she recognised as her uncle. The judge had first to decide whether or not she was mistaken. If she was, it made no difference to the presumption. If she was not, the onus was on the side claiming that he was dead to establish that he was. The House of Lords held that it was for the tribunal of fact to decide whether or not to accept the niece's evidence and that if the jury had been satisfied that she was mistaken the basic facts giving rise to the presumption were established. Here Alan is available for cross-examination and the preliminary issue is ultimately one of fact.

The next issue concerns Margaret. Does what Oliver told John affect her legitimacy and claim under Oliver's will? There is a presumption that a child born to the wife in lawful wedlock and conceived while the husband was alive is legitimate. This persuasive presumption can be rebutted by evidence which shows that it is more probable than not that the person is illegitimate and it is not necessary to prove that fact beyond reasonable doubt: Family **Law Reform Act 1969**, s. 26 and *S v S* **[1972] AC 24**. Oliver's remark to John (admissible under the **Civil Evidence Act 1995**; see Chapter 5) is evidence which might be capable of rebutting the presumption that Margaret is legitimate. The presumption is a persuasive one, so the legal burden of disproof falls on John and Barry, assuming it is they who are challenging Margaret's claim. However, against the remark should be set the provisional presumption (or presumption of fact) that sexual intercourse between husband and wife is likely to follow where opportunities for it occur. This is a weaker presumption: *Piggott* v *Piggott* **(1938) 61 CLR 378**, probably destroyed here by the remark itself. John and Barry have only the tactical burden of disproving it. The issue might be resolved by DNA testing.

Question 5

Arnold's widow is suing Harnet Transport Company over his death. The claimant alleges that a coach in which Arnold was travelling crossed the central reservation on the motorway, crashing into a car coming in the opposite direction. At the trial the claimant put forward no evidence about the circumstances of the accident. The defendants, however, gave evidence that a motorcycle had swerved in front of the coach causing the driver to lose control. The judge held that the burden of disproving negligence fell on the defendants and that they had not discharged the burden. He found for the claimant. Comment on the judge's decision and critically evaluate the law of evidence in this area.

Commentary

The main problem with a question of this sort is in recognizing the issue. It turns on rather a narrow point, namely whether the doctrine of res ipsa loquitur (literally, the thing speaks for itself) operates to reverse the burden of proof. There is not a great deal of case-law on this issue but it has aroused sharp differences of opinion. You need to explain the differing views of this doctrine, namely whether it is an evidential presumption, a persuasive presumption or a presumption of fact.

Answer plan

- Res ipsa loquitur, a controversial maxim
- Debate over whether it is an evidential assumption, a persuasive presumption or a presumption of fact
- Examine **Ng Chun Pui** v **Lee Chuen Tat [1988] RTR 298**, approving **Lloyd** v **West Midland Gas Board [1971] 1 WLR 749**—emphasis on common sense approach
- **Fryer** v **Pearson, The Times, 4 April 2000,** where scepticism was expressed by the Court of Appeal about 'unhelpful Latin phrases'; practice in other jurisdictions

Suggested answer

The judge here has interpreted the doctrine of res ipsa loquitur to mean that the burden of proof had shifted to the defendant. This is by no means generally accepted in law. The doctrine itself turns on the presumption of negligence. Its *raison d'être* was set out by the Court of Exchequer Chamber in *Scott* v *London and St Katherine Docks Co.* (1865) 3 H & C 596, 601 per Erle CJ:

> There must be reasonable evidence of negligence. But where the thing is shewn to be under the management of the defendant or his servants, and the accident is such as in the ordinary course of things does not happen if those who have the management use proper care, it affords reasonable evidence, in the absence of explanation by the defendants, that the accident arose from want of care.

However, the effect of the presumption remains open to debate. There are conflicting views on whether it is an evidential presumption, a persuasive presumption or a presumption of fact. In *Lloyd* v *West Midland Gas Board* [1971] WLR 749 the court described the principle as 'no more than an exotic, although convenient, phrase' which enshrined a common-sense approach. This judgment refuted the viewpoint that the burden of proof shifted the defendant in a case where res ipsa loquitur applied. This stance was approved by the Privy Council in 1988. In *Ng Chun Pui* v *Lee Chuen Tat* [1988] **RTR 298,** the Privy Council upheld the decision of the Court of Appeal of Hong Kong that the trial judge had misunderstood the doctrine of res ipsa loquitur which was no more than a legal maxim to describe a state of the evidence from which it was proper to draw an inference of negligence. The court said that it was misleading to talk of the burden of proof shifting to the defendant in a res ipsa loquitur situation because the burden of proving negligence rested throughout on the plaintiff. The case involved a road accident in which a coach driven by the second defendant and owned by the first defendant had crossed the central reservation and collided with a bus driven in the opposite direction. At the trial the plaintiffs called no oral evidence and relied on the fact of the accident or, as the judge referred to it, the doctrine of res ipsa loquitur. They relied on the inference that the coach was self-evidently not being driven with the appropriate standard of care. The defendants, however, called evidence to explain the loss of control. Because the plaintiffs had relied on res ipsa loquitur the judge wrongly held that the burden of disproving negligence lay on the defendants and they had failed to discharge it. If the defendant adduced no evidence there was nothing to rebut the inference of negligence, but if he did that evidence had to be evaluated to see if it was still reasonable to draw the inference of negligence from the mere fact of the accident. Lord Griffiths said (at p. 301) that:

> resort to the burden of proof is a poor way to decide a case . . . In so far as resort is had to the burden of proof, the burden remains at the end, as it was at the beginning upon the plaintiff to prove that his injury was caused by the negligence of the defendants.

If the doctrine is an evidential presumption the party against whom it operates will lose unless he adduces some evidence. But if the probability of negligence is equal to that of its not being present the defendant will succeed since the plaintiff has failed in his legal burden of proving negligence on the balance of probabilities. In *The Kite* [1933] P 154, involving a dispute over the cause of a collision of a barge with a bridge where the probabilities of the explanations were equal, the court found for the defendants.

If the doctrine, however, is a persuasive presumption negligence must be presumed if there is no evidence to the contrary. Thus the party against whom the presumption operates will lose if the probabilities are equal. This is how the Court of Appeal interpreted the presumption in *Barkway* v *South Wales Transport Co. Ltd* [1948] 2 All ER 460. The case concerned a bus which had fallen down an embankment. The Court held that it was insufficient for the defendants to show the bus had left the road because of a burst tyre. This was an event which was as consistent with negligence as not. The House of Lords in *Henderson* v *Henry E Jenkins & Sons Ltd* [1970] AC 282 also held that res ipsa loquitur was a persuasive presumption. It held that the plaintiff had proved negligence. On this issue PS Atiyah (1972, p. 340) thought the question of negligence was simply not proved either way. He argued that English judges, without acknowledging it, were shifting the burden of proof.

As Atiyah shows some authorities, particularly Australian, hold that res ipsa loquitur is no more than a presumption of fact whereby the party against whom it operates has only the tactical burden of disproving negligence. He is not bound to lose. If the defendant adduces no evidence he runs the risk of losing but is not bound to lose. A finding by the tribunal of fact in his favour could be reversed on appeal. Atiyah concludes:

> . . .the distinction between a legal and an evidential burden is much less significant in a trial by a judge than in a trial by jury for in the latter case the significance of an evidential burden means that a jury finding that the burden has not been discharged cannot be upset on appeal. However where trial is by judge alone an appellate court

may today be willing to review findings of negligence or non-negligence claims as freely as though it were trying the case itself. Where this is done the distinction between a legal and an evidential burden seems to be reduced to vanishing point.

Thus, the difficulty in this case is deciding which authority to follow. Is res ipsa loquitur a rebuttable presumption of law? Does it do no more than permit but not require a finding of negligence? It seems, however, that in *Ng Chun Pui* it is only a presumption of fact, placing a tactical burden on the opponent. This approach has been taken even further by the Court of Appeal in *Fryer* v *Pearson*, **The Times, 4 April 2000**. There house owners were not liable for an accident caused by a visitor kneeling on a needle in the carpet when, on the evidence, it was not established that they knew that it was there and that they permitted it to remain there. It was not possible to infer from the evidence that the respondents had caused or permitted the needle to remain in the carpet. The Court also held (obiter) that 'one should take care not to use unhelpful Latin phrases whose meaning does not express a defined principle'. In the consequent case of *Widdowson* v *Newgate Meat Corporation* **[1998] PIQR 138** the Court of Appeal held that the maxim applied. The case involved a claim for personal injuries suffered when the claimant was knocked down by a van driven by Mr A. Scullion whose employer was the defendant. Scullion did not give any evidence. Brooke LJ stated, 'Since Mr Scullion had elected to call no evidence, the judge's task was to determine whether on the evidence before him the plaintiff had established a prime facie case that Mr Scullion had been negligent. Although it is now common for liability to be established in a road traffic accident on the application of the maxim, res ipsa loquitur, it is also rare for a judge to be invited to determine liability for such an accident without hearing from either of the parties who were involved in the accident.' Referring to *Scott* v *London & St Katherine Docks Co, Barkway* v *South Wales Transport Co.* and *Lloyd* v *West Midlands Gas Board*, he stated, 'These cases show that a plaintiff in Mr Widdowson's position is taken as establishing a prime facie case that a defendant was negligent if it is not possible for him to prove precisely what was the relevant act or omission which set in train the events leading to the accident but if on the evidence before the judge it is more likely than not that the effective cause of the accident was some act or omission of the defendant which constituted a failure to take proper care for the plaintiff's safety.' However, as Choo (2006, p. 375) points out, 'The question remains, however, whether the presumption is a persuasive or evidential one. Does the defendant in providing an explanation for the accident, need to *prove* the absence of negligence? Or is the defendant required merely to adduce sufficient evidence of absence of negligence to make it a "live issue" with the burden of proving negligence resting ultimately with the claimant? Support for the presumption being an evidential one is found in the House of Lords' decision, *Royal Bank of Scotland* v *Etridge (no.2)* **[2001] 3 WLR 1021**.

McInnes reports that the doctrine has been laid to rest by the Supreme Court of Canada in *Fontaine* v *Loewen Estate* **[1998] 156 DLR (4th) 181** (1998, p. 547). He points out:

The reality of the litigation process also explains why it is often misleading, suggesting that res ipsa loquitur invariably raises an inference of negligence. For while it is necessary in a jury trial to distinguish between the roles played by the trier of law (in determining whether or not some non-perverse inference of negligence could be drawn from the circumstantial evidence) and the trier of fact (in actually quantifying the permissible interference) most cases are resolved by a judge alone. And in that situation it can hardly be expected that a judge will assiduously separate his duties; because he will exercise both functions simultaneously he will not have recourse to the maxim as a possible basis of proof unless he believes that a probable case of negligence has actually been established. . . . Recognition of the fact that res ipsa loquitur is capable of supporting a range of inferences from unpersuasive to virtually conclusive, is significant in so far as it reveals the maxim's true nature.

McInnes advises the abolition of the doctrine in England and Wales and Witting (2001, p. 397) in his comment on *Fryer* concludes, 'Even if *Fryer* proves not to have dealt it a fatal blow, this is, perhaps, a taste of what is to come when the concept is next discussed in the House of Lords. Is it dead now? It may be hoped so.' Thus the current position is that in an appropriate case a claimant in a negligence suit may establish a prima facie case by relying on the fact of the accident. It may be that if no evidence is produced in rebuttal of the inference of negligence that the claimant has discharged the burden of proof. If, however, the defendant has adduced evidence it must be examined to see its effect on the inference of negligence. Here the defendant had adduced evidence. Thus, the judge's summing-up is possibly a ground of appeal in that he appears to place the legal burden of proof on the defendants.

Additional Reading

Ashworth, A., 'Criminal Proceedings After the Human Rights Act: the First year' (2001) Crim LR 855.

Ashworth, A, 'Four threats to the Presumption of Innocence' (2006) 10 E & P 241.

Ashworth, A. and Blake, M., 'The Presumption of Innocence in English Criminal Law' [1996] Crim LR 306.

Ashworth, A. and Rees, T., 'Burden of Proof: Reverse Burden of Proof' [2004] Crim LR 832–836.

Atiyah, P.S., 'Res Ipse Loquitur in England and Australia' [1972] MLR 337.

Bennion, F., 'Statutory Exceptions: A Third Knot in the Golden Thread' [1988] Crim LR 31.

Birch, D.J., 'Hunting the Snark: The Elusive Statutory Exception' [1988] Crim LR 221.

Cooper, S., 'Human Rights and Legal Burdens of Proof' [2003] 3 Web JCLI.

Dennis, I, 'Reverse Onuses and the Presumption of Innocence' [2005] Crim LR 901.

Dingwall, G., 'Statutory Exceptions, Burden of Proof and the Human Rights Act 1998' (2002) MLR 450.

Hamer, 'The Presumption of Innocence and Reverse Burdens: A balancing act' (2007) CLJ 142.

Healy, P., 'Proof and Policy: No Golden Threads' [1987] Crim LR 355.

Jones, T.H., 'Insanity, Automatism and the Burden of Proof on the Accused' (1995) 111 LQR 475.

Lewis, P., 'The Human Rights Act 1998: Shifting the Burden' [2000] Crim LR 667.

McInnes, M., 'The Death of *Res Ipsa Loquitur* in Canada' (1998) LQR 114, 527.

Mirfield, P., 'The Legacy of Hunt' [1988] Crim LR 19.

Mirfield, P., 'An Ungrateful Reply' [1988] Crim LR 233.

Nobles, R. and Schiff, D., 'Guilt and Innocence in the Criminal Justice System: A Comment on *R (Mullen) v Secretary of State for the Home Department*' [2006] MLR 80.

Padfield, N., 'The Burden of Proof Unresolved' (2005) CLJ 17.

Pattenden, R., 'Silence. Lord Taylor's Legacy' [1998] 2 E&P 141.

Roberts, P., 'Taking the Burden of Proof Seriously' [1995] Crim LR 783.

Roberts, P., 'Criminal Procedure, Drug Dealing and the Presumption of Innocence: the Human Rights Act (at last) Bites' (2002(a)) 6 E & P 17.

Roberts, P., 'The Presumption of Innocence Brought Home? *Kebilene* Deconstructed' (2002(b)) 117 LQR 40, Part VIII.

Smith, J.C., 'The Presumption of Innocence' (1987) 38 NILQ 223.

Stein, A., 'After *Hunt*: The Burden of Proof, Risk of Non-persuasion and Judicial Pragamatism' (1991) 54 MLR 570.

Stein, A., 'An Essay on Uncertainty and Fact-Finding in Civil Litigation, with Special Reference to Contract Cases' [1998] U of Toronto LJ 299.

Tadros, V. and Tierney, S. 'The Presumption of Innocence and the Human Rights Act' (2004) 67 MLR 402.

Williams, G., 'Evidential Burdens on the Defence' (1977) 127 NLJ 182.

Williams, G., 'The Logic of Exceptions' (1988) CLJ 261.

Witting, C., '*Res lpsa Loquitur*: Some Last Words?' (2001) 117 LQR 392.

Zuckerman, A.A.S., 'The Third Exception to the Woolmington Rule' (1976) 92 LQR 402.

3

Witnesses: competence and compellability; special measures

Introduction

Witnesses are a principal source of evidence in a trial and the rules relating to their attendance indicate their importance. The starting point is that all witnesses with relevant information are assumed to be competent to give evidence. This is now reinforced by s. 53(1) of the **Youth Justice and Criminal Evidence Act 1999,** which states that at every stage in criminal proceedings all persons are (whatever their age) competent to give evidence. Such witnesses are also usually compellable to give evidence, in that the court may summon them to attend. Other interests of the witness are secondary to the need for the court to have all the necessary information. The exceptions to compellability are predominantly to be found in criminal law.

The competence of witnesses in criminal proceedings was historically a particularly controversial area, certain groups of people being excluded on moral or religious grounds. In addition, parties to the proceedings were held to be incompetent because they had an interest in the outcome. There are now no such legal objections to such groups of witnesses. The difficulties previously faced by the court in respect of children's testimony have to some extent been clarified by the **Youth Justice and Criminal Evidence Act 1999**. This Act specifies that there is a presumption of competence for all witnesses: 'At every stage in criminal proceedings all persons are (whatever their age) competent to give evidence' (s. 53(1)). This is subject to a general test: 'A person is not competent to give evidence in criminal proceedings if it appears to the court that he is not a person who is able (a) to understand questions put to him as a witness, and (b) to give answers to them that can be understood.'

Guidance on the application of the test in s. 53(3) is given in *R* v *Sed* [2004] **1 WLR 3218**. The witness, a rape victim, was 81 years old and suffering from Alzheimer's disease. Auld LJ stated that it was 'for the judge to determine the question of competence almost as a matter of feel, taking into account the effect of the potential witness's performance as a whole, whether there is a common and comprehensive threat in his or her responses to the questions, however patchy—bearing always in mind that, if on critical matters, the witness can be seen and heard to be intelligible, it is for the jury and no one else to determine matters of reliability and general cogency.' Thus s. 53 does not expressly require 100% comprehension by either the witness or the jury.

Some witnesses who are competent may, however, claim a privilege not to give evidence; thus they are not in contempt of court if they refuse to appear or if they do appear but refuse to answer certain questions. These witnesses include defendants on their own behalf, although the evidential consequences of their failure to testify under s. 35 of the **Criminal Justice and Public Order Act 1994** should be borne in mind.

The other main group of witnesses that has to be considered is spouses or civil partners testifying for the prosecution, a rule based on the rather quaint idea that any compulsion may lead to marital discord. However, this lack of compellability is subject to a number of important exceptions set out in **PACE** s. 80(3).

Questions on competence and compellability are easy to spot in that they will usually include a reference to a reluctant witness. You are unlikely to be asked about the position of spouses in civil cases since the rules there are quite straightforward, e.g. spouses of the parties are both competent and compellable. The position of children's testimony is complex. In criminal cases, the earlier statutory provisions contained in the **Criminal Justice Act 1988** as amended by the **Criminal Justice and Public Order Act 1994** have now been replaced by ss. 53 to 57 of the **Youth Justice and Criminal Evidence Act 1999**. This Act has the effect of treating child witnesses in general in the same way as adult witnesses. There are two situations where the child's age and maturity is of relevance. The first is that in the case of a child under the age of 14 or that of a person who is over the age of 14 but fails to appreciate the solemnity of the occasion and the responsibility for telling the truth under oath, the witness must give unsworn evidence: ss. 55(2) and 56. The second is where an issue arises under ss. 53 and 54 of the 1999 Act, i.e. whether the child is able to understand the questions being put to him and to give intelligible answers. In civil cases, the common law principles set out in *R* v *Hayes* [1977] **1 WLR 234** have been incorporated in the **Children Act 1989**, s. 96(1) and (2). Under these provisions, if any child, in the court's opinion, does not understand the nature of the oath, his evidence may still be heard unsworn. As far as criminal procedure is concerned ss. 16–30 **YJCEA** enable courts to give 'Special Measures Directions' (SMDs) to protect children and other vulnerable witnesses. For example, evidence may be given in a video-taped pre-trial hearing. Further measures were introduced in the **Criminal Justice Act 2003**. Like children, adults suffering from mental disorder or mental illness are presumed now to be competent.

The same test of competency under s. 53(3) **YJCEA** applies to all potential witnesses. Section 55 deals with the question of whether witnesses should be sworn. All witnesses over 13 years of age may testify on oath if they have 'sufficient appreciation of the solemnity of the occasion and of the particular responsibility to tell the truth which is involved in taking an oath' (s. 55(2)(b)). Under s. 55(3) 'the witness shall, if he is able to give intelligible testimony, be presumed to have a sufficient appreciation of those matters if no evidence tending to show the contrary is adduced (by any party)'. If a party fails to prove on the balance of probabilities that the witness qualifies to give sworn testimony the witness may give unsworn testimony if he satisfies the general test of competence set out in s. 53(3).

If a question is raised by the court or the opposing party about the competence of a witness, s. 54 specifies that is for the party calling the witness to satisfy the court that on the balance of probabilities the witness is competent to give evidence in the proceedings. The general expectation is that all witnesses aged 14 years and over will give sworn evidence, and witnesses under 14 cannot give sworn evidence. Section 55(2)(b) provides that a witness who has reached the age of 14 can give sworn evidence if 'he has sufficient appreciation of the solemnity of the occasion and of the particular responsibility to tell the truth which is involved in taking the oath'.

Tables 4 and 5 may help you remember the various permutations of the status of witnesses with regard to competence and compellability in criminal trials. Note under the **Criminal Justice Act 2003** the defendant who elects not to testify will face the same risk of having previous convictions admitted as one who testifies (see Chapter 4). Table 6 gives an outline of the Special Measures Directions for vulnerable witnesses introduced in the **YJCEA 1999** and the **Criminal Justice Act 2003**. Note that these only apply to non-defendant witnesses. However, some limited changes were introduced for vulnerable defendants in the **Police and Justice Act 2006**, amending the **Youth Justice and Criminal Evidence Act 1999** to create s. 33A. This came into force in January 2007. Under this provision the accused may give oral evidence through a live link if the court is satisfied that it is in the interests of justice and one of the following conditions apply. If the accused is under 18 years a live link may be allowed if:

(a) his ability to participate effectively in the proceedings as a witness giving oral evidence in court is compromised by his level of intellectual ability or social functioning, and

(b) use of a live link would enable him to participate more effectively in the proceedings as a witness (whether by improving the qualify of his evidence or otherwise).

Where the accused has attained the age of 18 the conditions are that:

(a) he suffers from a mental disorder (within the meaning of the **Mental Health Act 1983**) or otherwise has a significant impairment of intelligence and social function, and

(b) he is for that reason unable to participate effectively in the proceedings as a witness giving oral evidence in court, and the terms set out in (b) for under-18s apply.

Table 4 Competence and compellability: single defendant and co-defendant situations

Witness	For prosecution		For own defence		For co-defendant	
	Comp't	Comp'able	Comp't	Comp'able	Comp't	Comp'able
Defendant where no co-defendant	No. **YJCEA,** s. 53(4)	No	Yes. **YJCEA,** s. 53(1)	No. **CEA 1898,** s. 1(1)	n/a	n/a
Co-defendant pleading not guilty	No. **YJCEA,** s. 53(4)	No	Yes. **YJCEA,** s. 53(1)	No. **CEA 1898,** s. (1)	Yes. **CEA 1898,** s. 1(1)	No. **CEA 1898,** s. 1(1) **PACE** s. 80(4)
'Ex-co-def', i.e., pleading guilty, acquitted, or *nolle prosequi* entered	Yes. **R v Boal [1965] 1 QB 402**	Yes	n/a	n/a	Yes. **R v Boal**	Yes
Accomplice where proceedings are pending	Yes	As a matter of practice (not law) only if undertaking made that proceedings will be discontinued. **R v Pipe (1966) 51 Cr App R 17**	n/a	n/a	Yes	Yes. **R v Richardson (1967) 51 Cr App R 381**

Notes: **CEA 1898**—Criminal Evidence Act 1898
PACE—Police and Criminal Evidence Act 1984
YJCEA—Youth Justice and Criminal Evidence Act 1999

Table 5 Competence and compellability—spouse and civil partner of defendant

	For prosecution		For spouse's defence		For co-defendant	
Witness	Comp't	Comp'able	Comp't	Comp'able	Comp't	Comp'able
Spouse of defendant jointly charged with him or her (whether or not the same offence(s)) and pleading not guilty	No. **YJCEA,** s. 53(4)	No. **PACE,** s. 80(4)	Yes. **YJCEA,** s. 53(1)	No. **PACE,** s. 80(4)	Yes. **YJCEA,** s. 53(1)	No. **CEA 1898,** s. 1(1) **PACE,** s. 80(4)
Spouse of defendant not jointly charged	Yes. **YJCEA,** s. 53(1)	Only for offences in **PACE,** s. 80(3)	Yes. **YJCEA,** s. 53(1)	Yes. **PACE,** s. 80(2)	Yes. **YJCEA,** s. 53(1)	Only for offences in **PACE,** s. 80(3)

Notes: 1: *CEA 1898—Criminal Evidence Act 1898*
PACE—Police and Criminal Evidence Act 1984
YJCEA—Youth Justice and Criminal Evidence Act 1999
Notes: 2: former spouses to be treated as other witnesses (**PACE,** s. 80(5)).
Notes: 3: The failure of the wife or husband of a person charged in any proceedings to give evidence shall not be made the subject of any comment by the prosecution (**PACE,** s. 80A).
Notes: 4: In ***R*** v ***Pearce* [2002] 1 WLR 1553** the Court of Appeal held that the word 'spouse' in the statute does not cover cohabiting partners, even interpreted in the light of Art. 8 ECHR.

Question 1

John is charged with assaulting Fred after an argument about football in a bus queue. John claims self-defence in that he says Fred was wearing knuckleduster rings and he was afraid he would be hurt. Fred denies he threatened John. The only other witness to the brawl was John's wife, Hilda. Discuss whether she is competent and compellable as a witness for John or the prosecution and critically evaluate the law of evidence in this area.

Commentary

Have in your mind a clear picture of the position of spouses under s. 80 of the **Police and Criminal Evidence Act 1984** as amended by the **Youth Justice and Criminal Evidence Act 1999**. You are expected to outline the law and then comment on its rationale. It is an area which previously has raised a number of controversial issues, but arguably the 1999 Act has resolved some of these issues. Be careful not to be too expansive on the historical background of the law but it is quite appropriate to set the development of the law in context.

Table 6 Special measures in criminal cases[1]

Statute	Protection	Circumstances
CJA 2003, s. 51	Live link	Court must consider if it is in the interests of the efficient or effective administration of justice; relevant factors include availability of witness and need for witness to attend in person
CJA 2003, ss. 137, 138	Video recordings	Need Crown Court trial; need for events to be fresh in witness's memory
YJCEA 1999, ss. 19–30	• Screens • Live links • Evidence given in private • No wigs or gowns • Video recorded evidence • Use of intermediaries • Aids to communication	Apply to four categories of witness: • Under 17 years • Quality of evidence likely to be impaired by physical or mental disorder • Witness in fear of distress (automatically includes complainants in sexual cases)
YJCEA, s. 35	Any video-recordings must be admitted	Three categories of child witness covered: cases concerning sexual offences, other specified offences, and other offences
YJCEA, s. 32	Judicial warning so that direction does not prejudice the accused	May be given during the trial or in the summing up

1 These do not apply to defendants.

Answer plan

- Presumption of competence and compellability
- **YJCEA**, s. 53(1), **PACE**, s. 80 and competence of spouses
- Compellability of spouses for defence—Hilda
- Compellability of defence only specified offences—Hilda compellable if Fred under 16, **PACE**, s. 80(2A)(a) and s. 80(3)(b)
- Comment by prosecution on failure of spouse to give evidence (archaic)
- Competing social interests involved and arguably archaic nature of the current law

Suggested answer

The general rule is that any person is competent and compellable as a witness provided he or she is able to communicate coherently. Thus he or she may lawfully give evidence. It is for the court to decide issues as to the competence and compellability of witnesses, as the Court of Appeal held in *R* v *Yacoob* (1981) 72 Cr App R 313. A competent witness is generally compellable. The main exceptions apply in differing degrees to spouses, children and those of unsound mind.

By virtue of s. 53(1) of the **Youth Justice and Criminal Evidence Act 1999**, all persons are competent to give evidence. There is no longer any necessity to consider the issue of competence in terms of the spouse being called as a witness for the prosecution or for the defence. Hence, Hilda is a competent witness for the prosecution. She is also compellable for the defence: s. 80(2) of the **Police and Criminal Evidence Act 1984**. But by s. 80(2A)(b) and (3) of the 1984 Act, she is compellable for the prosecution only if Fred was under 16 at the time of the alleged assault. If she does choose to give evidence for the prosecution, provided the right of refusal has been clearly explained to her, she can be treated like any other witness, as the Court of Appeal held in *R* v *Pitt* [1983] QB 25. The prosecution has the burden of establishing the competence of a prosecution witness and the standard of proof is on a balance of probabilities: s. 54(2) of the **Youth Justice and Criminal Evidence Act 1999** (reversing *R* v *Yacoob* (1981) 72 Cr App R 313).

Section 80A of the 1984 Act as amended forbids comment by the prosecution on the failure of a defendant to call his or her spouse to give evidence. This provision originally appeared in s. 1 of the **Criminal Evidence Act 1898** and in s. 80(8) of the 1984 Act. Thus, in *R* v *Naudeer* (1984) 80 Cr App R 9, the Court of Appeal quashed a conviction because the prosecuting counsel had told the jury it had been deliberately deprived of material evidence as the defendant had not called his wife as a witness. The case was one of shoplifting and the wife had been in the shop at the relevant time. The court may, however, correct the damage by making a relevant comment. It should be stressed that the prohibition in s. 80A is with regards to comment by the prosecution only. It does not prevent the judge from commenting on the defendant's failure to call his or her spouse, as the Court of Appeal held in *R* v *Gallagher* [1974] 1 WLR 1204, just as he may comment on the failure to call any witnesses.

In relation to spouses, their exemption from a general duty to testify for the prosecution has been a matter of some controversy. At present, spouses are only compellable for the prosecution if the offence in question is a crime of violence or a threat to one of the spouses or a person under 16, if it is a sexual offence committed against a person under the age of 16, or it consists of an attempt or a conspiracy to commit or of aiding or abetting the commission of one of the offences stated above (s. 80(3) of the 1984 Act). Until the 1984 Act came into force, spouses were at common law not competent nor compellable for the prosecution. If there was a co-accused, he or she was treated as being in the same position as the prosecution and similar changes in relation to the co-accused as to the prosecution were enacted in **PACE**, which has since been amended by the **Youth Justice and Criminal Evidence Act 1999**. A spouse could, under the **Criminal Evidence Act 1898**, give evidence on behalf of the accused. The reasoning for this was based on the legal fiction of the single personality of the husband and wife and the policy of attempting to preserve the institution of marriage.

It should be noted that by s. 80(9) of the 1984 Act, a spouse who testifies cannot refuse to disclose the content of marital communications even if they are confidential, nor refuse to answer relevant questions on when sexual intercourse took place.

The changes enacted (in the 1984 Act and subsequently as amended by the 1999 Act) go in some ways further than had been recommended by the Criminal Law Revision Committee in its 11th report (1972, Cm 4991). A spouse is thus compellable even in cases involving violent or sexual offences against persons under 16 who are not members of the same household. Once the marriage is over spousal privilege ceases (s. 80(5)).

Generally, even with the changes introduced by the 1999 Act, the present law can still be criticised as being too restrictive and inconsistent.

The historic reason for spousal privilege was stated by Lord Salmon in *R v Hoskyn* [1979] AC 474, at p. 495: 'This rule seems to me to underline the supreme importance attached by the common law to the special status of marriage and to the unity supposed to exist between husband and wife. It also no doubt recognised the natural repugnance of the public at the prospect of the wife giving evidence against her husband in such circumstances.' This case has been overruled by **PACE** on the facts. Spouses may now be compelled to testify if they are alleged victims of domestic assault. In cases other than those specified in s. 80(4) a spouse may claim exemption from testifying against the husband or wife. Roberts and Zuckerman have expressed a number of criticisms of the current law. They write (2004, at p. 232): 'Marital harmony is not, to be sure, a trivial consideration. Whether it should be allowed to take priority over doing justice in contemporary society is however, another matter entirely.' They make the following points to illustrate the illogicality of the present position. First, marriages are more easily dissoluble today so a married couple are no longer so constrained to remain together. Second, non-compellable spouses have to make a morally repugnant choice between their civic duty to testify and upholding marital harmony. Third, although the exceptions to non-compellability in **PACE** s. 80(3) are welcome, they are also illogical. There are other vulnerable groups than battered partners and children: these include older people, racial minorities, etc. Roberts and Zuckerman (2004, p. 233) cite Cross and Tapper **on Evidence** (1999, at p. 222): 'The accused's wife is compellable against him if he kissed a 15-year-old. . . but not if he raped and murdered a 16-year-old.' Fourth, the position in relation to co-defendants is confused; Roberts and Zuckerman point out (at p. 234) that 'It is difficult to comprehend why a wife should be compellable for her husband's co-accused when both men are jointly charged with child abuse but not in other cases. If the co-accused requires the wife's assistance to prove his innocence, the law should compel her testimony regardless of the impact on the wife's marital harmony; or at least, in the alternative, should sanction separate trials.' These arguments are indeed persuasive. Munday (2007, p. 127) also points out that the scope of s. 80(3) 'is not necessarily as straightforward as at first might appear'. There might be some controversy over whether an alleged offence falls within its ambit. As he suggests, 'the word "involves" is not the most precise of terms'.

In *McAndrew-Bingham* [1991] 1 WLR 1897 the Court of Appeal took a broad interpretation in holding that every child abduction under the **Child Abduction Act 1984** should be taken as an assault for the purposes of the **Criminal Justice Act 1988**, s. 32(2)(a), allowing video recording of a child's evidence. The section has identical wording to s. 80(3)(a). Finally, one might suggest that the very concept of a spouse is somewhat outmoded in these days of same-sex unions and more varied domestic liaisons. It is indeed difficult to see why the husband and wife relationship deserves special protection but not the equally sensitive relationship between parent and child.

It is arguably offensive that parties who are cohabiting but are not married or civil partners are outside the scope of s. 80 and are treated as ordinary witnesses. In *R v Pearce* (2002) Kennedy LJ stated, 'there may be much to be said for the view that with very limited exceptions all witnesses who are competent should also be compellable, and certainly the material before us does not enable us to conclude that because a concession has been made to husbands and wives proper respect for family life requires that a similar concession be made to those in the position of a husband or wife'.

Another anomaly in the current legislation is the question of permissible comment on the spouse's failure to testify. Section 80A of **PACE** states, 'the failure of the spouse or civil partner of a person charged in any proceedings to give evidence in the proceedings shall not be made the subject of any comment by the prosecution'. This prohibition is a wide one and thus prevents comment even if it may be based on logical inferences. It is perhaps surprising that it still exists since comment on the accused's failure to testify may be permissible (s. 35 **CJPOA 1994**); see *R v Davy* [2006] **EWCA Crim 565**.

In short, the theoretical coherence of the current law is flawed and it is suggested that the criminal law treats spouses as witnesses in an unsatisfactory way. In civil cases, by contrast, spouses are treated as any other witness, although arguably the threat to the institution of marriage exists in these cases too. There is a powerful argument that the privilege afforded to spouses as witnesses in criminal cases should be removed, subject to discretionary exception. As Dennis (2007, at p. 542) concludes '. . . it might be preferable to abandon attempts at compromise and to adopt a general rule that a spouse should be a compellable witness in all cases'.

Question 2

Dido is charged with causing criminal damage to some gnomes in the garden of 14 Churchill Road. The prosecution case is that she was hawking flowers door to door with her daughter Janet, aged 12. Mr and Mrs Baldwin refused to buy from her. As she left she allegedly kicked down the gnomes in anger. Hector, the Baldwins' 20-year-old son, who has a mental age of 10, was looking out of the window. The prosecution wish to call Janet and Hector as witnesses. Advise whether they are competent and compellable and comment critically on the law in this area.

Commentary

This is a similar question on two other groups of witnesses who are to some extent a deviation from universal competence and compellability. The law relating to children in criminal cases is now relatively simple and amended after much research in this area. However, it has only reached this state after a number of statutory measures. Children are now assumed to be as competent in criminal trials as other witnesses. Adults may be incompetent to testify through drunkenness, or some physical or mental disability. In this, as in all other cases, the question of competence in any specific case remains one for the trial judge.

Answer plan

- Jane—competence of children under **YJCEA**, s. 53
- **YJCEA**, s. 55(2) and s. 56—evidence of children under 14 is unsworn
- Pigot Committee recommendations and change in approach to children's evidence; SMDs under **YJCEA**
- Hector—mental capacity, *R* v *Bellamy* **(1985)**—**YJCEA**, s. 53, s. 54(5) and s. 55(3)
- Possibility of evidence being admitted as exception to hearsay rule—but see *R* v *Setz-Dempsey* **(1994)**
- Special Measures Directions

Suggested answer

Janet is a competent witness (**Youth Justice and Criminal Evidence Act 1999**, s. 53) and compellable for the prosecution. The fact that a witness could not be imprisoned for failure to comply is not a good reason for refusing to issue a witness summons to compel her attendance: *R* v *Greenwich Justices, ex parte Carter* **[1973] Crim LR 444**. As a child under 14 Janet must give evidence unsworn: **Youth Justice and Criminal Evidence Act 1999**, ss. 55(2) and 56. This provides that the evidence of children under 14 is to be given unsworn and that a child's evidence must be received unless it appears to the court that the child is incapable of understanding questions put to her and unable to give answers which can be understood: **Youth Justice and Criminal Evidence Act 1999**, s. 53(3). The court must decide not whether she is competent on grounds of age but whether she is capable of giving intelligible evidence. It is submitted that a normal 12-year-old would be. The importance of giving truthful evidence must be explained to her by the tribunal as part of the process of putting her at her ease. If it is decided to receive her evidence it is a matter of fact for the tribunal as to how much weight to attach to it. The position of child witnesses was the subject of much controversy and research. The Pigot Committee on Video Evidence set up by the Home Office, reporting in 1989, condemned the existing position as being founded on an archaic belief that children could not be honest and coherent witnesses. The law was subsequently changed so that there is now no preliminary examination of the child's ability to give evidence. The present practice is that the child should give evidence and only be stopped if it becomes clear she could not give an intelligible account. The result is that there is now no minimum age below which a child cannot give evidence, although in practice judicial discretion may be exercised. In *R v N* **(1992) 95 Cr App R 256**, the Court of Appeal said that the fact that a child was too young to be prosecuted for perjury was not a reason for excluding her evidence. The present state of the law arguably brings it into line with psychological research on the veracity of children. The emphasis on judicial discretion rather than strict rule is a welcome development. It should be noted that under ss. 54 and 55 of the **Youth Justice and Criminal Evidence Act 1999** the determination of the question of the competence of the witness should be done in the absence of the jury and that the court may question the child's competence of its own motion.

The changes in the law relating to children's evidence were the result particularly of the difficulty of achieving successful prosecutions in the case of child victims of sexual abusers. As Birch (1992, p. 269) argues, 'Children contrary to what was once thought, are not necessarily unreliable at all, and are certainly no less dangerous as witnesses than those who abuse them.'

As regards Hector, the court will probably take a pragmatic view and allow him to testify if it considers he understands the nature of the proceedings and can speak the truth to the best of his ability. The competence of witnesses may be raised by the parties or by the court of its own motion (s. 54(1)). It is for the party calling the witness to satisfy the court on the balance of probabilities that the witness is competent (s. 54(2)). In *R v Bellamy* **(1985) 82 Cr App R 222**, the Court of Appeal held that the cases then pertaining to the swearing of children applied in the case of an alleged victim in a rape case who was 33 years old but had a mental age of 10. It was not necessary for her to appreciate the divine sanction of the oath. This decision was welcomed as a break from earlier emphasis on the theological implications of understanding the oath. Under the **YJCEA 1999**, ss. 53–57 witnesses who suffer from mental disorder, disability or mental illness do not form a separate category but are subject to the same test of competence as any other witness. This is that they must understand questions put to them as a witness and give answers to them which can be understood: s. 53(3). If Hector is judged to have insufficient understanding to take the oath (s. 55(2)(b)), and there is a presumption that he has sufficient understanding, then he may be able to give evidence unsworn provided he passes the basic test of competence (s. 56(1) and (2)). Expert evidence may be admitted as to the witness's mental state but it was held in *R v Deakin* **[1994] 4 All ER 769** that it should not be taken with the jury present over the defendant's objection. This is now confirmed in s. 54(5).

If Hector is held incompetent as a witness it is unlikely that his evidence may be admitted under the statutory exceptions to the hearsay rule. The hearsay provisions of the **Criminal Justice Act 1988** have now been repealed and replaced by ss. 114–136 of the **Criminal Justice Act 2003**. Section 23 of the **CJA 1988** made it a pre-condition of the admission of documentary hearsay evidence that there was no other objection to the admission of the evidence than the one based on hearsay. Under s. 114 **CJA 2003**, in deciding whether a hearsay statement is to be admitted the court must have regard, inter alia, to 'how reliable the maker of the statement appears to be' (s. 114 (2)(e)).

The Court of Appeal held in *R* v *Setz-Dempsey* **[1994] Crim LR 123** that the admission of documentary statements from a mentally ill witness under s. 23(1)(a) of the **Criminal Justice Act 1988** was a material irregularity. The judge had erred in law in not exercising discretion under s. 26 and should have considered the psychiatrist's evidence about the likely quality of any evidence given by the witness and also that the statements could not fairly be admitted without the jury hearing the witness's evidence.

Another possibility to be considered is the use of Special Measures Directions under the **Youth Justice and Criminal Evidence Act 1999**. It may be considered that Hector might encounter special difficulty in testifying. Under ss. 16(1)(b) and 16(2) witnesses other than the accused who suffer from a physical or mental disorder, or have a disability or impairment of intelligence and social functioning that is likely to diminish the quality of their evidence, may give evidence by means such as live video link or pre-recording. In *R (on the application of D)* v *Camberwell Green Youth Court* **[2003] EWHC Admin 22**, the Divisional Court held that special measures provisions, here involving children, were compatible with Article 6(3)(a), which embodies the defendant's right 'to examine or have examined witnesses against him'.

Question 3

(a) Jane (an adult) and her nephew Tony who is 15 are charged with an indecent assault on Freda who is 13 years old. John, Jane's husband, told police he witnessed the assault but now refuses to testify. Freda is very frightened about giving evidence. Advise Freda, Tony and John about their likely treatment as witnesses.

(b) James and his wife Helen are being sued for negligence. They were proprietors of a riding school and one of their horses has injured Grace, aged 11 years. Advise on Grace's status as a witness.

Commentary

(a) This question requires you to be familiar with the statutory provisions on the competence and compellability of spouses as witnesses and that of children. You should also cover special measures provisions and whether they apply to child defendants.

(b) Note that this is a question on civil law. You need to consider whether children may give sworn evidence and any specific protections affecting them.

Answer plan

(a)

- Competence and compellability of spouses—**PACE**, s. 80
- Competence and compellability of children and whether they can give sworn evidence—see **YJCEA 1999**, s. 55(2)(a) and **YJCEA 1999**, s. 53(1)
- Special measures for children—**CJA 2003**, s. 51, **YJCEA 1999**, s. 19

(b)

- Section 96 **Children Act 1989**
- **Hearsay and Civil Evidence Act 1972**
- Special protective measures for children

Suggested answer

(a) The general presumption is that all witnesses are competent and compellable. However, Freda and Tony may prove exceptions to this general rule by virtue of their age, as may John by virtue of his relationship to the defendant, Jane.

In principle Freda is eligible to give evidence and also therefore compellable. If she were to testify, since she is under the age of 14 she cannot be sworn (**YJCEA 1999**, s. 55(2)). Nowadays children are no longer regarded as unreliable witnesses and there is no need for special warnings about their evidence. However, child witnesses, particularly child victims, may be reluctant to appear in court and we are told here that this is the case with Freda. Recent statutory changes have considerably eased the potential trauma of court appearances for vulnerable and frightened witnesses. The **YJCEA 1999** contains Special Measures Directions for vulnerable and intimidated witnesses. Freda qualifies for these under two categories. First she is a witness 'under the age of 17 at the time of the hearing' (s. 16(1)(a)) and second, a witness who is a complainant of a sexual offence is automatically an eligible witness under s. 17(4) unless she has informed the court of her wish not to be so eligible. Under this category the witness is one where 'the Court is satisfied that the quality of evidence given by the witness is likely to be diminished by reason of fear or distress on the part of the witness in connection with testifying in the proceedings'. A number of different special measures are included in the statute. In outline these include the use of screens, live links, giving evidence in private, dispensing with wigs or gowns, video-recorded evidence, the use of intermediaries and the use of aids to communication. In addition, there are rules which are specifically directed at child witnesses. The relevant one here is s. 35(3)(a): a witness in a case concerning one of the sexual offences specified. More information is therefore needed about the actual offence with which Jane and Tony are charged.

If the offence falls within this category the protection offered to Freda is greater. Here, in brief, there is a presumption that any relevant video-recording must be admitted as evidence in chief, unless the court is of the opinion, having regard to all the circumstances of the case, that the interests of justice require otherwise. In addition, evidence not given in a video-recording should be given by live-link.

Freda, of course, will be giving evidence for the prosecution. Defence counsel may argue that the section violates art. 6(3)(a) in that there is no need to apply a test of the quality of the specific evidence before admitting it. But in *R(D)* v *Camberwell Green Youth Court* [2005] 1 WLR 393 the House of Lords held there was no violation. It was stated that the ECHR 'does not guarantee a right to face to face confrontation'. The statute does provide, however, that the judge must 'give the jury such warning (if any) as the judge considers necessary to ensure that the fact that the direction was given in relation to the witness does not prejudice the accused' (s. 32). This can be given at the time the evidence is presented or in the summing-up (*R* v *Brown* [2004] EWCA Crim 1620).

Another protection offered Freda is that Jane or Tony will not be allowed to cross-examine her in person (s. 34). Freda is additionally protected from such cross-examination since she is a 'protected witness' (s. 35(3)(a)) by virtue of her age. Under s. 41 there are restrictions on the introduction of Freda's prior sexual behaviour, if any, with the defendants or third parties (see further **Chapter 10** below.)

Turning to Tony, who at 15 is also a child, it will be seen that there is far less protection offered to him as a witness. We are not told where this trial is taking place but if it is in the Juvenile Court Tony will be protected by anonymity. (There is no specific protection for child defendants who testify in the Crown Court.) But the limit of this protection is illustrated in *R(S)* v *Waltham Forest Youth Court* [2004] Cr App R 21 (p. 335), which held that even where a 13-year-old defendant was intending to give evidence against her co-defendants she was not entitled to the statutory Special Measures. Tony may, however, place some reliance on the Practice Direction issued in the wake of *Tvv UK* [2000] 30 EHRR 121 where art. 6 was found by the Strasbourg Court to have been breached in the trial of two boys for the murder of James Bulger (see also *SC* v *UK* [2005] 40 EHRR 10). However, these provisions must be seen in the light of the amendments made to the **YJCEA** by the **Police and Justice Act 2006**. These empower a court to direct that the accused may give evidence through a video-link. Since Tony is aged under 18 years he may benefit from the provision which specifies that:

(a) his ability to participate effectively in the proceedings as a witness giving oral evidence in court is compromised by his level of intellectual ability or social functioning, and

(b) use of a live link would enable him to participate more effectively in the proceedings as a witness (whether by improving the qualify of his evidence or otherwise). In addition the court must be satisfied that the interests of justice are satisfied by the giving of evidence this way.

Finally, if Jane is proposing to engage in a 'cut throat' defence Tony may gain some protection from s. 35 whereby a person charged with the sexual offences listed may not cross-examine in person an alleged witness who is a protected witness 'including those who are co-defendants'. A protected witness is one who is under 17.

John as Jane's spouse will be advised to refer to **PACE**, s. 80 (as recommended by the **YJCEA 1999**). He is competent to give evidence for the protection (**YJCEA**, s. 53(1)) but only compellable if the offence with which Jane is charged is included in **PACE**, s. 80(3). It does appear that this is the case here since it is a sexual offence alleged to have been committed in respect of a person who at the material time was under the age of 16. Thus if John refuses to give evidence for the prosecution or for Tony he will be in contempt.

(b) If the case goes to trial it may be that Grace will be called as a witness. Under s. 96 of the **Children Act 1989**, children are allowed to testify unsworn and the then existing common law test of competency was enacted to apply in civil proceedings. The test is that the child has sufficient understanding of the duty to tell the truth to justify the reception of her evidence. A 'child' is any person who has not reached the age of 18. The judge will question Grace before she gives any evidence to see if she shows sufficient understanding of the solemnity of the oath. Dennis (2007, p. 548) comments '. . . the first condition of s. 96 of the **Children Act** is certainly stricter than the criminal law, because it retains the requirement, now dropped by the criminal law, that the child understands the duty of truth-telling. Whether this strictness is justifiable is debatable. Its effect may be to exclude the testimony of very young children in civil cases.' The section reads:

(1) Subsection (2) applies where a child who is called as a witness in any civil proceedings does not, in the opinion of the court, understand the nature of an oath.

(2) The child's evidence may be heard by the court if, in its opinion, (a) he understands that it is his duty to speak the truth; and (b) he has sufficient understanding to justify his evidence being heard.

Keane (2008, p. 130) states 'it is submitted that the court should be guided by the common law authorities which governed in criminal as well as civil cases prior to parliamentary intervention'. He refers to *R* v *Hayes* [1977] 1 WLR 234 adding that the court adopted a "secular approach" and appeared to have accepted a concession made by counsel for the defence that 'the watershed dividing children who are normally considered old enough to take the oath and children normally considered too young to take the oath, probably falls between the ages of eight and ten'.

Grace may benefit from two further provisions. It is possible that some of her evidence may be heard as hearsay under the **Civil Evidence Act 1995**. Section 5 of the 1995 Act makes it clear that the child will be a competent witness if he or she satisfies the requirements of s. 96 **Children Act 1989**, thereby making any hearsay evidence by the child admissible. In *R* v *B, ex parte P* [1991] 2 All ER 65, 72 Butler-Sloss LJ referred to the need to treat such evidence 'anxiously and consider carefully the extent to which it can properly be relied on'. Secondly, **Civil**

Procedure Rules rule 32.3 provides that the court may permit a witness to give evidence through a video link or other means. The court has a broad discretion to allow this.

Question 4

Margaret, a partner in a hairdressing salon, is charged with conspiracy to defraud. It is alleged that at a meeting she and her partners agreed to send false VAT returns. At the trial, she refuses to testify but claims through her counsel that she left the meeting early before the matters alleged were discussed. Advise the prosecution on how they can treat these facts.

Commentary

This question deals with a defendant's failure to respond to police questioning and also failure to testify. The question does not make it clear whether Margaret gave the explanation about leaving the meeting earlier when questioned by police. If she did not then this may permit adverse comment by the prosecution under s. 34 CJPOA. Pre-trial silence is covered in **Chapter 6**.

Answer plan

- Duty of disclosure—**Criminal Procedure and Investigations Act 1996**
- Procedure on alibi notices
- ss. 34 and 35 **CJPOA**
- Permissible judicial comment on failure to testify—see **Cowan (1995)**

Suggested answer

The **Criminal Procedure and Investigations Act 1996** requires the prosecution and the defence to disclose evidence prior to the trial. It imposes a duty on the defence, which goes further than previously required. Prior to the 1996 Act, the obligation on the defendant to disclose evidence pre-trial was limited including, for example, issuing an alibi notice under s. 11 of the **Criminal Justice Act 1967**. This has been superseded by s. 5 of the 1996 Act. This requires the defendant to disclose evidence of the defence that will be raised at trial, after the prosecution has made primary disclosure and the defence has been served with relevant documents, including copies of the indictment and the prosecution's evidence. Disclosure provisions are strengthened under Part 5 of the **Criminal Justice Act 2003** amending the 1996 Act.

Under s. 11 of the 1967 Act, the defence could not adduce evidence of an alibi if they had not served an alibi notice on the prosecution without leave of the court. In practice leave was often given. However, s. 5 of the 1996 Act adopts a different approach. It is silent on whether the court can refuse to admit evidence for which particulars of the alibi had not been served on the prosecution in accordance with the section. Section 11(2) of the 1996 Act allows the court or any other party (with leave of the court) to make such comment on the defendant's failure to provide pre-trial particulars of alibi as appears appropriate. The court and jury may draw such inferences from such failure as appear proper in the circumstances of the case. Arguably, although s. 5 is silent on the court's power to refuse to allow such evidence, the court retains its discretion under s. 78 of the **Police and Criminal Evidence Act 1984** to exclude evidence which would have an adverse impact on the fairness of the trial. Thus, even though Margaret may not have served particulars of alibi with her defence statement in accordance with s. 5 of the 1996 Act, she will be permitted to adduce evidence that she was not at the meeting at the time the agreement to send false VAT returns was made. However, the court and the prosecution, with leave of the court, may comment on this and the jury can draw such adverse inferences as are proper.

By s. 35 of the **Criminal Justice and Public Order Act 1994**, adverse inferences can be drawn by the court from the refusal to give evidence at trial. It is not, however, contempt of court for Margaret to fail to testify at trial. Under s. 35(4) of the statute the common law principle is retained that the accused is not compellable to give evidence on his own behalf.

Before the **Criminal Justice and Public Order Act 1994** it was forbidden for the prosecution to comment on the accused's failure to testify, although comment was allowed by the judge. The law in this regard was restated by the Court of Appeal in *R* v *Martinez-Tobon* [1994] 1 WLR 388. The judge had to direct that the defendant was under no obligation to testify and that the jury should not assume he is guilty because he had not given evidence. The prosecution is now permitted by s. 35 of the 1994 Act to comment on Margaret's failure to testify but the section does not specify what kind of comment is appropriate and, unlike s. 11(2) of the **Criminal Procedure and Investigations Act 1996**, does not require leave of court before such comment can be made. It may be some comfort to Margaret to rely on s. 38(3) of the **Criminal Justice and Public Order Act 1994**:

> A person shall not have the proceedings against him transferred to the Crown Court for trial, have a case to answer or be convicted solely on an inference drawn from such a failure as is mentioned in section 34(2), section 35(3) . . .

The procedure which must be followed by the court in relation to a defendant's refusal to testify is set out in s. 35 and in addition a Judicial Studies Board Specimen Direction clarifies the process. In particular, before adverse comment may be considered the defendant must have pleaded not guilty, be physically and mentally fit to testify and be aware of the risks attached to silence. Margaret should be aware that the same risks apply if she did decide to testify but then refused to answer some questions put to her. Under s. 35(5) a failure to answer questions is presumed to be 'without good cause' unless the accused is either entitled under statute not to answer particular questions or has a legal privilege not to answer or 'the court in its general discretion excuses him from answering'. Guidance on judicial comment where the accused does not give evidence is to be found in the Court of Appeal's judgment in *R v Cowan* [1996] QB 373. In three separate cases, heard together on appeal, defendants who had not given evidence appealed against conviction on the grounds of non-compliance with sections 35 and 38(3) of the **Criminal Justice and Public Order Act 1994**. The court held that s. 35(4) had expressly preserved the right to silence but that while the burden of proving guilt beyond reasonable doubt lay throughout on the prosecution the court or jury might draw the inference from a defendant's failure to testify to be a further evidential factor in support of the prosecution's case. A specimen direction from the Judicial Studies Board was a sound guide and before any inferences from silence could be drawn the jury had to be satisfied that a case to answer had been established by the prosecution. In G and C's case misdirections had been made and the convictions were quashed. In C's case the judge had failed to tell the jury that they could not infer guilt solely from silence or to warn them that they could not hold his silence against him unless the only sensible explanation was that he had no answer to the case against him which could have stood up to cross-examination. In G's case there were also shortcomings in the summing-up. In R's case the judge had directed the jury correctly. The guidance given in *Cowan* is amplified in Judicial Studies Board Specimen Direction No. 39. The direction is detailed and complex and underlines that jurors should take into account any evidence which might explain why the defendant elected not to testify. It is only if jurors are satisfied that the only sensible reason for Margaret not testifying is that she has no answer to the charge, or none that would stand up in cross-examination, can they draw an inference which will support the prosecution case. The prosecution may argue that Margaret may reveal incriminating details about the meeting if she takes the stand.

A key question is the extent of the prosecution case against Margaret. In *Doldur* [2000] **Crim LR 178**, Auld LJ set out the specific requirements of a s. 35 direction which differ from those under ss. 34, 36 and 37. In the case of s. 35 the jury should be directed to restrict its consideration to the prosecution case in deciding whether to draw adverse inferences. By contrast, in relation to s. 34 the jury would have to consider both prosecution and defence cases since it was the contrast between the defendant's earlier silence and reliance on facts at trial which permitted the drawing of an adverse inference (see further **Chapter 6**). If the judge fails to give clear directions on the drawing of permissible inferences Margaret may have strong grounds of appeal under Article 6 provisions (see *Condron* v *UK*).

Additional Reading

Birch, D., 'Children's Evidence' [1992] Crim LR 262.

Birch, D., 'A Better Deal for Vulnerable Witnesses?' (2000) Crim LR 223.

Cooper, D., 'Pigot Unfulfilled: Video-recorded cross-examination under S28' [2005] Crim LR 456.

Creighton, P., 'Spouse Competence and Compellability' [1990] Crim LR 34.

Dwyer, D., 'Can a Marriage be Delayed in the Public Interest so as to Maintain the Compellability of a Prosecution Witness?' (2003) E & P 7(3), 1916.

Gillespie, A., 'Compellability of the Child Victim' (2000) 64 J Crim L 98–105.

Home Office Research Study. 'Are Special Measures Working?' (2004) www.homeoffice.gov.uk/rds/pdfs04/hors283.pdf.

Hoyano, L.C.H., 'Striking a Balance between The Rights of Defendants and Vulnerable Witnesses: Will Special Measures Directions Contravene Guarantees of a Fair Trial?' (2001) Crim LR 948.

Jackson, J., 'Inferences from Silence—from Common Law to Common Sense' (1993) 44 NILQ 103.

Spencer, J.R., 'Child Witnesses, Video Technology and the Law of Evidence' (1987) Crim LR 76.

Spencer, J.R. and Flin, R., *The Evidence of Children: The Law and the Psychology* (2nd edn, Blackstone, London 2003).

4

Character of defendant

Introduction

This chapter is concerned with one of the most complex questions in criminal evidence, namely, those situations in which the accused may adduce evidence of his good character to suggest lack of guilt and support credibility and those in which the prosecution counsel or the counsel for the co-defendant may cross-examine him on previous discreditable behaviour. Before the **Criminal Justice Act 2003** was in force, such cross-examination was for the purpose of eliciting evidence to show the defendant's lack of credibility. It was not for the purpose of suggesting he was guilty of the offence for which he was charged. Thus it was different from the purpose for which Similar Fact evidence was called, namely to suggest guilt. The exclusionary rule was fundamental to the English legal system and based on the principle that the defendant should have a fair trial based on the instant charge. As is the case with all exclusionary rules in evidence, there were exceptions to it. These occurred both at common law, which applied when the defendant did not give evidence, and in the **Criminal Evidence Act 1898**, which applied to cross-examination. The rule on exclusion of character evidence only applied to the defendant under the **CEA 1898** and different rules applied when the defendant gave evidence and thus laid himself open to cross-examination and when he elected not to testify. The law has now changed but it is important that you have some grasp of the historical background of this huge area.

This topic makes a regular appearance on examination papers on the law of Evidence, both in the form of problem questions and, since it has generated a certain amount of theoretical debate, also essay questions. Whether or not you are allowed to take a statute book into the examination, you must be very familiar with the somewhat tortuous text of the 2003 statute.

Referring to the difficulty which Evidence students and criminal practitioners have in understanding character evidence Roberts and Zuckerman (2004, p. 500), stress that it is essential to stay focused on the underlying evidentiary principles and keep the practical nature of the subject firmly in mind. They add 'One might otherwise easily miss the wood by staring too long and too hard at the individual trees, several of which were misshapen or sickly specimens. Extensive pruning of dead wood and selective renewal were long overdue in the English law of character evidence.' Renewal, or rather wholesale reform, was carried out in the **Criminal Justice Act 2003**. The law made comprehensive changes to the rules relating to the *admissibility* of evidence of bad character of both the defendant and witnesses providing that 'the common law rules governing the admissibility of evidence of bad character in criminal proceedings are abolished' (s. 99(1)). Common law rules therefore arguably may apply to:

- the meaning of character, including good character
- the admissibility of good character
- rules relating to judicial directions on the meaning of good or bad character.

In addition, although provisions of the **Criminal Evidence Act 1898** are repealed, some of the case law under this provision may still be worthy of note. In any case, in order to understand the current law it is necessary to appreciate its historical evolution. More generally the meaning of character and the extent to which previous behaviour can explain the present has been the subject of a great deal of scientific investigation. A helpful review of this research is to be found in the Law Commission Paper, 'Evidence in Criminal Proceedings: Previous Misconduct of a Defendant' (1996). Commentators have referred to the extent to which it is accepted that character evidence can be helpful in deciding guilt or innocence. Redmayne (2002, p. 690) writes, 'The main lesson to draw from the psychological literature is a negative one: that it provides no strong reason to doubt that information about past behaviour can be useful in working out whether a person committed a particular act.' Choo (2006, p. 194) outlines the prejudicial effect of bad character evidence on a jury and also the lack of 'a significant link between bad character evidence and lack of veracity as a witness'.

One further complication is that the **CJA 2003** has changed the law relating to the admissibility of bad character evidence of witnesses other than defendants: this is dealt with in **Chapter 10**.

With regard to the character of the defendant, you need to be familiar with the law on:

1. The definition of good character
2. The admissibility of good character
3. 'Putting character in issue'
4. The evidential value of good character
5. The definition of bad character
6. The admissibility of bad character
7. The evidential value of bad character.

You must appreciate that historically 'evidential value' refers to two possible impacts: that of issue, i.e. whether the defendant is more likely to be guilty or not, and that of credit, whether the defendant (or other witness) is more or less likely to be believed. In relation to the issue of credit the assumption seems to have been that those who have previous criminal records are less likely to be honest, although this is of course a dubious assertion.

The **Criminal Justice Act 2003** is a major statute which creates a new regime for the admissibility of character evidence. The Act was the result of over a decade of discussion and is based on a belief that the existing law was over-complex and on the view, expressed by the government, that it was too favourable to defendants. Note also that it will apply to testifying and non-testifying defendants.

Reports Leading to CJA 2003

1993   Runciman Royal Commission reports that rules on accused's bad character were unsatisfactory

1996   Law Commission Consultation Paper No. 144, *Previous Misconduct of Defendant*

2001   Law Commission Report No. 273, *Evidence of Bad Character in Criminal Proceedings*

2001   *Review of Criminal Courts of England and Wales Report* (Auld Report) recommends 'introducing some reality into this complex corner of the law'

2002   Government White Paper *Justice For All* recommends that '. . .where a defendant's previous convictions, or other misconduct are relevant to an issue in the case, then unless the court considers that the information will have a disproportionate effect, they should be allowed to know about it'

2003   November, **Criminal Justice Act 2003** receives Royal Assent. Introduced in stages. Sections 98–113 cover character evidence, repealing s. 1(3) of the 1898 Act (see Table 7). The key section is s. 101 (with explanatory sections 102–6):

s. 101 Defendant's Bad Character

(1) In criminal proceedings evidence of the defendant's bad character is admissible if, but only if—
(a) all parties to the proceedings agree to the evidence being admissible,
(b) the evidence is adduced by the defendant himself or is given in answer to a question asked by him in cross-examination and intended to elicit it,
(c) it is important explanatory evidence,
(d) it is relevant to an important matter in issue between the defendant and the prosecution,
(e) it has substantial probative value in relation to an important matter in issue between the defendant and a co-defendant,
(f) it is evidence to correct a false impression given by the defendant, or
(g) the defendant has made an attack on another person's character.
(2) Sections 102 to 106 contain provisions supplementing subsection (1).
(3) The court must not admit evidence under subsection (1)(d) or (g) if, on an application by the defendant to exclude it, it appears to the court that the admission of the evidence would have such an adverse effect on the fairness of the proceedings that the court ought not to admit it.

(4) On an application to exclude evidence under subsection (3) the court must have regard, in particular, to the length of time between the matters to which that evidence relates and the matters which form the subject of the offence charged.

Note that the discretion to exclude character evidence applies only to evidence admitted under s. 101(1)(d) or s. 101(1)(g). Note also that ss. 101(1)(e), (f) and (g) overlap to some extent. It is therefore crucial in determining whether statutory discretion is available to first consider which subsection is triggered by the defendant's tactics.

Key Features of Provisions on Character in CJA 2003

* Section 99 abolishes common law rules on admissibility (but not on other aspects of character, e.g., definition of good character or judicial directions to jury). It also repeals s. 1(3) **Criminal Evidence Act 1898**

* Section 98 defines a person's 'bad character' as 'evidence of, or of a disposition towards, misconduct on his part' other than evidence which has to do with the alleged facts of the offence with which the defendant is charged or is evidence of misconduct in connection with the investigation or prosecution of that offence

* Applies whether defendant is testifying or not

* Section 100 covers admissibility of bad character of persons other than defendants (see **Chapter 10**)

* Section 101(1) (d) is comparable to what was Similar Fact (see below)

* The 2003 Act as a whole enshrines government policy on what the Home Office press release described as 'end-to-end reforms to modernise and balance the system in favour of victims, witnesses and communities'.

Historical Background to Propensity Evidence

Students used to study character evidence and Similar Fact evidence as distinct areas. This is no longer appropriate in the light of the **CJA 2003**; however, you need to be aware of the historical background (see Table 8).

Strictly speaking, the term Similar Fact was a misnomer. Whilst evidence of previous offences which were strikingly similar to the one with which the accused was being tried (hence the term 'Similar Fact evidence') fell within this category, it also included evidence of extraneous acts and disposition and of incriminating articles. In the light of cases such as *DPP* v *P* **[1991] 2 AC 447** and *R* v *H* **[1995] 2 AC 596**, the stringent requirements of striking similarity prevalent in the older cases had been eroded, the effect being to lower the threshold of admissibility. The **CJA** takes this process much further.

Ultimately, the admissibility of the type of evidence under discussion depends generally on concepts of relevance, probative value and an assessment of the prejudicial effect of such evidence.

Table 7 Definition evidential value of good and bad character, common law, and **CJA 2003**

Question	Source/leading cases	Comment
Definition of good character	**Rowton (1865)** **Redgrave (1982)**	Evidence of general reputation only to be admitted*
Admissibility of good character	**Rowton** Section 118 **CJA 2003** preserves common law rule on reputation and good (and bad) character	Good character may be admitted by testimony of defendant on other witnesses, or by cross-examining prosecution witnesses
Ways of putting good character in issue	See below for examples Section 105 **CJA 2003**—giving 'false impression'	Assertions of innocence alone do not put good character in issue; **R** v **Lee [1976] WLR 71**
Evidential value of good character	**R** v **Vye [1993] 1 WLR 471** **R** v **Aziz [1996] 1 AC 41** **R** v **Gray [2004] 2 Cr App R 498**	Relevant to credit and propensity. Judicial direction must be given
Definition of bad character	Section 98 **CJA 2003**	Includes previous acquittals, may include sexual interest in children or being a racist. Does not include matters relating to current charge, such as attempts to intimidate witnesses
Admissibility of bad character	See Table 8 below	
Evidential value of bad character	**R** v **Hanson [2005] EWCA Crim 824**	'The focus upon the abolition of rules of admissibility seems to leave the common law on guidance to juries and directions relating to the weight to be attached to evidence of bad character unscathed.' (Tapper 2004, p. 540)

*Examples of under **CEA 1898** putting good character in issue (and therefore triggering admission of bad character, see below):
- **R** v **Ferguson [1909] 2 Cr App R 250**—attending mass for 36 years
- **R** v **Samuel [1956] 40 Cr App R 8**—had previously found lost property and handed it back.

Examples of not putting good character in issue:
- **R** v **Stronach [1988] Crim LR 48**—in regular work with London Transport (contrast **Coulman [1927] 20 Cr App R 106**)
- **R** v **Hamilton [1969] Crim LR 486**—wearing a regimental blazer (but see now s. 105 **CJA 2003**, making a misleading impression by conduct includes appearance or dress).

Table 8 Admissibility of D's bad character etc (see Note 1): history and current law

Summary of differences between common law (CL), CEA 1898 and CJA 2003			
Gateways for evidence from defendant with bad character	Under the common law, i.e. not testifying (presumption of non-admissibility of D's bad character (*Makin*))	Under the now repeated sections of CEA 1898, i.e. D testifying (presumption of non-admissibility of D's bad character but set out triggers for loss of 'shield')	Under CJA 2003, i.e. whether D testifies or not (presumption of admissibility of D's bad character if any of s. 101 conditions apply)
D gives evidence of own good character (**CEA**)/gives evidence which 'creates a false impression' (**CJA 2003**)	N/A	D's bad character admissible Discretion to exclude	D's bad character admissible, s. 101(1)(f) (see also s. 105)
D calls good character witness (CL, **CEA**)/'creates a false impression' (**CJA 2003**)	Prosecution could call bad character evidence in rebuttal	D's bad character admissible Discretion to exclude	D's bad character admissible, s. 101(1)(f) (see also s. 105)
D cross-examines prosecution witness to establish own good character (CL, **CEA**)/'creates a false impression' (**CJA 2003**)	Prosecution could call bad character evidence in rebuttal	D's bad character admissible Discretion to exclude	D's bad character admissible, s. 101(1)(f) (see also s. 105)
D casts 'imputations on prosecution witness, or dead victim, by cross-examination' (**CEA**)/'has made an attack on another person's character'(**CJA 2003**)	Prosecution could not call evidence in rebuttal (*Butterwasser*)	D's bad character admissible Discretion to exclude	D's bad character admissible, s. 101(1)(g) (see also s. 106), i.e. *Butterwasser* reversed. Discretion to exclude, s. 101(3)

Table 8 *(continued)*

D casts imputation on prosecution witness during own evidence in chief (**CEA**)/'has made an attack on another person's character' (**CJA 2003**)	N/A	D's bad character admissible Discretion to exclude	D's bad character admissible, s. 101(1)(g) (see also s. 106). Discretion to exclude, s. 101(3)
D1 gives evidence against co-accused (D2) (**CEA**)/D1's 'bad character' has substantial probative value in relation to an important matter in issue between the defendant and a co-defendant (**CJA 2003**)	N/A	D's bad character admissible No discretion to exclude	D1's bad Character admissible by D2, s. 101(1)(e). Not covered by discretion in s. 101(3)

Notes: (1) **Criminal Evidence Act 1898** (**CEA**) applied only to defendants who chose to testify. The non-testifying defendant was covered by the common law. The **Criminal Justice Act 2003** covers the defendants who do not testify as well as those who do. (2) The wording of s. 101(1)(f) 'correcting a false impression' includes also the concept of undermining other witnesses, so overlaps with s. 101(1)(g).

The **Criminal Justice Act 2003** abolishes the common law rules on admissibility of evidence of bad character (s. 99). The relevant sections of the **CJA 2003** in relation to what was known previously as Similar Fact evidence are summarised below:

(1) Admissibility

Under s. 101(1)(d) the defendant's bad character is admissible if 'it is relevant to an important matter in issue between the defendant and the prosecution'.

Sections 103(1) and (3) define 'matter in issue between the defendant and the prosecution' as including: '(a) the question whether the defendant has a propensity to commit offences of the kind with which he is charged, except where his having such a propensity makes it no more likely that he is guilty of the offence; and (b) the question whether the defendant has a propensity to be untruthful except where it is not suggested that the defendant's case is untruthful in any respect.'

The section specifies that where this applies, a defendant's propensity to commit offences of the kind with which he is charged may be established by evidence that he had been convicted of an offence of the same description as the one with which he is charged or an offence of the same category as the one with which he is charged. The section also specifies that the Secretary of State may make orders for prescribing particular offences as offences of the same category. The **Criminal Justice Act 2003** (**Categories of**

Offences) Order 2004 (SI 2004 No. 3346) lists offences in the two categories of theft and sexual offences against persons under the age of 16.

(2) Discretion to Exclude

Sections 101(3) and 103(4) set out two provisions for exclusion of otherwise relevant evidence under this heading. Under s. 101(3) the court must not admit evidence under subsections (1)(d) or (g) if on application by the defendant to exclude it, it appears to the court that the admission of the evidence would have such an adverse effect on the fairness of the proceedings that the court ought not to admit. Particular regard should be had to the length of time between the matters to which that evidence relates and the matters which form the subject of the offence charged. In addition, s. 103(3) specifies that evidence of propensity to commit offences of the kind with which the defendant is charged should not be admitted if the court is satisfied, by reason of the length of time since the conviction or for any other reason, that it would be unjust. Note that s. 101(3) includes the words 'must not admit', which is stronger than the provision s. 78 **PACE** 'may refuse to allow'.

(3) Danger of Collusion

Sections 107 and 109 deal with situations of cross admissibility where two or more witnesses give supporting evidence of the defendant's alleged misconduct on other occasions and there is a danger of potential collusion or concoction. Under s. 107 where evidence of the defendant's bad character has been admitted into the trial without his agreement (under s. 101(1) paragraphs (c)–(g)) and the judge is satisfied at any time after the close of the case for the prosecution that the evidence is contaminated such that a conviction would be unsafe, he should either direct the jury to acquit or prepare for a retrial. Contamination may arise through deliberate or unwitting confabulation (s. 107(5)).

(4) Court's Duty to Give Reasons

Section 110 requires the court, in the absence of the jury, to give reasons for relevant rulings.

(5) Background Evidence

Under the common law there had sometimes been a lack of clarity between evidence of extraneous misconduct in relation to other offences (Similar Fact evidence) and extraneous misconduct which is part of the events forming part of the current charge. This had on occasion been admissible and was known as 'background evidence'; in *R* v *M* [2000] 1 All ER 148 the Court of Appeal said: 'Where it is necessary to place before the jury evidence of a continued background of history relevant to the offence charged in the indictment and without the totality of which the account placed before the jury would be incomplete or incomprehensible, then the fact that the whole account involves including evidence establishing the commission of an offence with which the accused is not charged is not of itself a ground for excluding the evidence.' Roberts and Zuckerman give as an example (at p. 529) the information given to the jury that *Straffen* had recently absconded from Broadmoor, which was not challenged by the defence, as opposed to information about his previous offences, which was. They suggest that given the laxity of the pre-existing common law the **Criminal Justice Act 2003** has increased the threshold of admissibility of such evidence. It is identified in s. 101(1)(c) as 'important explanatory evidence' and defined in s. 102 as evidence either without which the court or jury would find it impossible or difficult properly to understand other evidence in the case or evidence whose value for understanding the case as a whole is substantial.

Table 9 compares in simplified form the common law and **CJA 2003** provisions.

Table 9 Admissibilty of evidence of propensity/previously known as 'Similar Fact' evidence

Issue	Common law	CJA 2003
Description	Similar Fact evidence	Need for bad character evidence to be relevant to an important matter at issue (s. 101(1)(d))
Admissibility	Leading case **DPP** v **P**. Admissible if probative value exceeds prejudicial effect	s. 101(1)(d) and s. 103 admissibility of bad character evidence (for definition see s. 98);
Fairness/discretion to exclude	s. 78 common law discretion	s. 101(3) & (4) and s. 103(3)
Possibility of collusion	**R** v **H** [1995] 2 AC 596	ss. 107, 109
Need for judge to give reasons		s. 110
'Background' evidence	Generally admissible; **R** v **M**	Test for admissibility s. 101(1)(c) (see also s. 102)

Comment on Character Evidence

One problem with the pre-existing law was that by stressing the non-admissibility of bad character evidence it served to make such evidence, when it was admitted, assume too much importance. A number of commentators argued that it might be simpler and more intellectually acceptable to admit criminal record as a matter of routine. For example, Zuckerman (1989, p. 245) wrote 'A more effective way of combating prejudice would be to bring into the open the scope of prejudice created by evidence of poor criminal record and strive to persuade juries that the principles of criminal justice, which require resistive prejudice, reflect their own perceptions of justice. If members of the jury are made to understand this, they would be better able to resist the temptation of convicting because of the accused's bad character.'

The subsequent case-law now suggests that the **Criminal Justice Act** has led to an increase in prosecution submission of the defendant's previous convictions. The Court of Appeal stated in *R v Edwards (Stewart Dean)* [2006] 1 WLR 1524 that it 'was apparent that Parliament intended that evidence of bad character would be put before juries more frequently than had previously been the case'. But it should also be noted that in *R v Campbell* [2007] EWCA Crim 1472 (see further discussion below) the court stated that it was highly desirable to warn the jury not to attach too much weight to bad character evidence.

Detailed guidance on the provisions has also been provided in *R v Hanson* [2005] 1 WLR 3169 and *R v Highton* [2005] 1 WLR 3472. Some of the main points from the judgments are:

- Three questions are to be considered where propensity to commit the offence is relied upon: (1) Does the history of convictions establish a propensity to commit offences of the kind charged? (2) Does that propensity make it more likely that the defendant committed the offence charged? (3) Is it unjust to rely on the convictions of the same description or category; and, in any event, will the proceedings be unfair if they are admitted?

- Decisions under ss. 101(3) and 103(3) should take into account the degree of similarity between the previous conviction and the offence charged, the respective gravity of the past and previous offences and the strength of the prosecution case. If there is no or very little other evidence against a defendant, it is unlikely to be just to admit his previous convictions.

- Old convictions with no special features shared with the offence charged are likely seriously to affect the fairness of proceedings adversely unless they show a continuing propensity.

- Propensity to untruthfulness is raised only if truthfulness is an issue in the present case.

- Pre-2003 Act authorities may apply to s. 101(1)(g). However, in *Campbell* (2007) the court stated previous decisions on judicial directions on the evidential worth of bad character evidence are unhelpful and should not be cited.

- Court of Appeal will be slow to interfere with the judge's ruling. It will not interfere unless the judge's judgment as to the capacity of prior events to establish propensity is plainly wrong, or discretion has been exercised unreasonably in the *Wednesbury* sense.

- Where the Crown begins the process of applying to adduce evidence of bad character it must specify the relevant gateway. This may include the facts of the conviction or, additionally, the surrounding circumstances.

- Judge should warn jury against placing undue reliance on previous convictions. Evidence of bad character cannot be used simply to bolster a weak case or to prejudice the minds of a jury against a defendant.

- Once evidence was admitted through one of the s. 101(1) gateways, the use to which it could be put by the jury depended on the matters to which it was admitted, not the gateway through which it had been admitted; *Highton* (2005), followed in *Campbell* (2007).

The Court of Appeal further summarised the application of the new provisions in *R v Edwards (Stewart Dean)* [2006] 1 WLR 1524.

- It does not follow that merely because evidence fails to come within s. 101 gateways it will be inadmissible. Where exclusions in s. 98 are applicable, evidence is admissible without more ado.

- Parties should reflect at time of application on likely use of the evidence. There can be difficulties for the judge in summing-up when bad character evidence that has been admitted turns out to have only marginal relevance.

- Parliament intended more bad character evidence to be put than under **CEA 1898**; judge determines admissibility; weight is for the jury, subject to judge's summing-up on relevance; see *Hanson* para. 28 and *Highton* para. 11.

- During trial ground may have shifted since bad character evidence admitted and judge may need to direct it has little weight.

- Difference between s. 101(1)(d) and (e)–in determining an application under s. 101(1)(e) analysis with a fine toothcomb is unlikely to be helpful. Context of the case as a whole matters.

- Co-defendants cannot use s. 101(1)(d), (f) and (g), which are open only to prosecution.

- Section 104(1) not exhaustive of scope of s. 101(1)(e)–it limits evidence relevant to a defendant's propensity to be untruthful.

- Whether defendant's stance amounts to no more than a denial of participation (*R v Varley* [1982] 75 Cr App R 24) or gives rise to an important matter in issue between a defendant and a co-defendant turns on facts of the individual case.

- *Bovell* [2005] 2 Cr App R 27, p. 21 distinguished–mere making of an allegation is capable of being evidence within s. 101(1).

- 'Feel' of trial judge is very important and appeal court will only interfere where conviction is unsafe.

Two areas of particular controversy have been subject to critical academic comment. The first is the meaning of 'reprehensible behaviour', which in s. 112(1) defines 'misconduct', referred to in s 98 as 'the commission of an offence or other reprehensible behaviour'. Leading cases are *R v Weir* [2006] 1 WLR 1885, *R v He* [2006] 1 WLR 1885, *R v V* [2006] EWCA Crim 1901, *R v Renda* [2006] 1 WLR 2948 and *R v Hanson (P)* [2005] 1 WLR 3169. Goudkamp (2008, p. 139) sees little guidance on general principle in these cases. He writes, 'the closest thing to a general principle that has emerged from the authorities is that conduct is not "reprehensible" unless it reveals culpability. Needless to say, this hardly advances matters very far.' He points out that the term 'reprehensible behaviour' has not featured before in an English statute and it is not a term of art with an accepted meaning at common law. The courts are consequently required to feel their way in the dark, with precious little illumination to guide them.

Another area of controversy is judicial directions on the evidential value of bad character evidence, namely whether it is evidence of lack of credibility as well as propensity. In *R* v *Campbell* (2008) CLR 303 the defendant was charged with false imprisonment and assault against a woman with whom he had a sexual relationship. The prosecution was allowed to adduce evidence of recent crimes of violence against girlfriends on that they showed the relevant propensity under s 101(1)(d) CJA 2003. He had pleaded guilty to those offences. On conviction, the defendant argued on appeal that the judge should not have directed the jury that the previous convictions might be relevant to credibility as well as propensity. The following principles are derived from the report of the case.

- The CJA 2003 had introduced a change in simplifying directions to juries and earlier decisions should not be cited.

- Where evidence of bad character was introduced the jury should be given assistance as to its relevance that was tailored to the individual. Relevance could normally be deduced by the application of common sense.

- Once evidence was admitted through one of the s. 101(1) gateways, the use to which it could be put depended on the matter to which it was admitted, not the gateway through which it had been admitted. *Highton* (2005) applied.

- The courts had in the past drawn a distinction between propensity to offend and credibility. This distinction was usually unrealistic.

- It could be comparatively rare for the case of a defendant who has pleaded not guilty not to involve some element that the prosecution suggested was untruthful. However, the question of whether a defendant had a propensity for being untruthful would normally not be capable of being described as an *important* matter in issue between the defendant and the prosecution; cf. s. 101(1)(d).

- Whether or not a defendant was telling the truth was likely to depend simply on whether or not he committed the offence. The jury should focus on that question.

- Failure to follow specimen directions in this area should not automatically be grounds for appeal.

The above account, drawn from the Criminal Law Review report of the case (2008, 303–6) indicates that the Court of Appeal found difficulties with a strict application of the legislative scheme. The Criminal Law Review comment notes, 'Having been meticulously drafted it cannot be right for the courts to render significant aspects of the legislative scheme superfluous . . . under the general approach advocated by the court in the present case the jury are to focus on whether or not the defendant committed the offence and his previous convictions for similar offences, rather than the issue of truthfulness.' Murphy (2008, 4–5) comments on this case, 'So now it seems that even previous convictions, such as those for perjury that demonstrate a very specific propensity to lie at trial, fail to pass muster. Paying attention to such a past record serves only to divert the jury from the key question of guilt or innocence in the case in hand. . . . One gets to the credibility of the witness via the evidence that is relevant to the issue, not the other way round.'

Question 1

Andy, Ben and Catherine are charged with theft of video machines brought to their shop for repairs by David. They all plead not guilty. Andy testifies in his own defence. He claims that Ben had asked him to help steal the machines but he had refused. Andy has several convictions for criminal damage. At the trial counsel for the prosecution and for Ben cross-examine Andy on these convictions. Ben gives evidence and claims he had nothing to do with the theft and that Andy had stolen the machines. He calls several witnesses to give evidence that he has done extensive charitable work for a local pensioners' club for many years. Catherine does not testify at trial but claims at interview that David was falsely implicating her out of resentment because she refused to have an affair with him. She also said at interview that Doris, David's girlfriend, had a grudge against her. David is a prosecution witness, Doris is not. Catherine's conviction is referred to by prosecution counsel. Catherine has a conviction for theft. All the defendants' previous convictions are admitted. In her summing-up, the judge tells the jury that they may take Ben's good character evidence as relevant to credibility and his propensity to commit offences and that Andy was more likely than Ben to have committed the offence. Ben is acquitted. Andy and Catherine are convicted.

Advise them whether they have any grounds of appeal on the grounds that evidence is wrongly treated.

Commentary

This question requires you to be familiar with the complex provisions in ss. 98–113 **Criminal Evidence Act 2003** and the recent case-law, particularly the cases of **Hanson** and **Highton**. The issues to address are the specific gateways of the admissibility of previous convictions, whether the court exercised discretion reasonably and the use to which the evidence is put and how the judge directed on this.

Answer plan

- Definition of 'bad character' in s. 98
- Andy—gives evidence against a co-defendant; application of s. 101(1)(e); prosecution not allowed to adduce bad character evidence under this section
- Catherine—gives evidence against a prosecution witness; application of s. 101(1)(g) and s. 101(3) and (4)
- Ben—direction on good character; impact of this on Andy and Catherine

Suggested answer

Andy has previous convictions for criminal damage. These convictions fall within the 'bad character' definition of s. 98 **CJA 2003** as 'evidence of, or of a disposition towards, misconduct on his part, other than evidence which (a) has to do with the alleged facts of the offence with which the defendant is charged, or (b) is evidence of misconduct in connection with the investigation or prosecution of that offence'. The term 'misconduct' is further defined in s. 112 as the commission of an offence or other reprehensible behaviour.

These convictions are admissible if, but only if, they are covered by one of the provisions in s. 101. Andy has given evidence against his co-defendant Ben in stating that Ben had asked him to help steal the machines. Ben denies this. Section 101(1)(e) permits bad character evidence to be admissible if 'it has substantial probative value in relation to an important matter in issue between the defendant and a co-defendant'. The Explanatory Note accompanying the Act states that evidence is admissible on issues between the defendant and co-defendant if it has substantial probative value in relation to an important issue in the case. In other words, evidence that has any marginal or trivial value would not be admissible in the case as a whole. One issue in the trial is who is telling the truth, Andy or Ben. The question then arises whether the convictions for criminal damage do not have substantial protective value in helping the jury decide whether Andy is untruthful. Section 104 specifies that 'Evidence which is relevant to the question whether the defendant has a propensity to be untruthful is admissible on that basis under Section 101(1)(e) only if the nature or conduct of his defence is such as to undermine the co-defendant's defence.'

The convictions may therefore be admissible if they are relevant to Andy's lack of credibility. In *R* v *Edwards (Stewart Dean)* [2006] **1 WLR 1524** the Court of Appeal stated that 'Section 104(1) is not exhaustive of the scope of Section 101(1)(e). It limits evidence relevant to a defendant's propensity to be untruthful.' It also stated 'Simply because an application to admit evidence of bad character is made by a co-defendant, the judge is not bound to admit it. The gateway in Section 101(1)(e) must be gone through. Sections 101(1)(d) and (e) give rise to different considerations. In determining an application under 101(1)(e) analysis with a fine tooth comb is unlikely to be helpful; it is the context of the case as a whole that matters. Section 112 makes this clear by its definition of what amounts to an important matter in issue.'

In *Edwards* the appellant claimed that a conviction for handling could not properly be regarded as evidence relevant to his propensity for truth. The court acknowledged that a 13-year-old handling offence had marginal relevance to the question of whether the co-defendant was telling the truth. Relevant issues here will be how old the convictions are and whether Andy pleaded not guilty to them, thus suggesting lack of truthfulness.

The earlier cases give some limited guidance on the application of the new provision. The meaning of 'evidence against another person' was examined by the House of Lords in *Murdoch* v *Taylor* [1965] AC 574. The case established that it means evidence which supports the prosecution case in a material respect or which undermines the defence of the co-defendant in a material respect. The intention with which the evidence is given is irrelevant.

Andy claims that Ben asked him to help steal the machines but that he refused. Is this 'evidence against'? In *R* v *Crawford* (1998) 1 Cr App R 338, Lord Bingham CJ (at p. 343) said:

> If the defendant's evidence supports the Crown on a significant matter in issue between the Crown and the co-defendant and relative to proof of the commission by the co-defendant of the offence alleged against him, then that is evidence potentially damaging to the defence of the co-defendant and is to be regarded. . .as evidence by the defendant against the co-defendant.

Lord Morris in *Murdoch* v *Taylor* suggested that one test is: would the evidence be included in a summary of the evidence in the case which, if accepted, would lead to the conviction of the co-defendant? Andy's motive in giving evidence is irrelevant; the evidence need not be given with hostile intent. It appears to be the case that Andy is going beyond mere denial of participation in the offence. In *R* v *Varley* (1982) 75 Cr App R 241 the principles of law in this area were set out. There the defendant V and his co-accused D were jointly charged with robbery. D's defence was that he was acting under duress from V, who denied both that he had taken part and that he forced D to commit it. The Court of Appeal upheld the judge's ruling to allow D's counsel to cross-examine V on his previous conviction. Here V's evidence was 'evidence against' D because the effect of his denial of involvement was to suggest that D committed the offence. May (1999 at p. 153), however, points out that Lord Bingham CJ in *Crawford* said that *Varley* was not a statutory provision and there was a danger of over-complicating an easily applicable test. The application of *Varley* was also examined in *R* v *Hatton* (1976) 64 Crim App R 88. If Andy's denial of complicity does not damage Ben's defence then he would not be protected (see *R* v *Kirkpatrick* [1998] Crim LR 63), but this does not appear likely on the facts of this case.

Here, from the facts we are given, it is very likely that Andy's evidence contradicts Ben's denial of involvement. There is no statutory discretion to prevent Ben's counsel questioning Andy on his previous offences. The statutory discretion in s. 103 CJA does not cover s. 101(1)(e). Furthermore, the right to cross-examine is arguably only limited on grounds of relevance. It is likely that Andy's bad character will be held to have been rightly admitted. The Court of Appeal is reluctant to interfere with the judge's discretion (see *R* v *Lawson* [2007] 1 WLR 1191).

Has Andy a ground of appeal in that the judge may not have properly directed the jury on the evidential value of the cross-examination on previous convictions, particularly since he is being tried alongside a person of good character? The defendant has long been entitled to adduce evidence of his good character with the aim of inducing the jury to conclude that a person with that character would not commit the alleged offence. The general common law rule is that evidence of character is confined to evidence of general reputation (*R v Rowton* (1865) *Le & Ca* 520; *R v Redgrave* (1982) 74 Cr App R 10), though as an indulgence, such evidence is often admitted for the defendant. After 1898, when the defendant became capable of giving evidence at his trial, his good character was said to go primarily to his credibility: *R v Bellis* [1966] 1 WLR 234. Where a defendant of good character has given evidence, the judge is required to direct the jury about the relevance of good character to the defendant's credibility, but also to refer to the likelihood that a person of good character would act as charged. Problems arise where, as here, a person without a blot on his record (Ben) is tried alongside a defendant of bad character (Andy). By drawing the jury's attention to the fact that a person of Ben's good character is less likely than a person of bad character to have committed the offence, the judge inevitably suggests that Andy is more likely to have committed it. This is a connection between character and propensity, the very chain of reasoning the jury is not supposed to make. However, there is authority that the judge should refer to the issue of whether a person of good character would commit the alleged offence, even where the co-defendant is of bad character: *R v Vye* [1993] 1 WLR 471. The defendant who possesses the bad character is entitled to a direction as to the limited relevance of his previous convictions. Without such a direction, the jury might assume that the previous convictions are relevant to the same issues as good character, and particularly to propensity to commit crime and, by extension, guilt. In *R v Cain* [1994] 1 WLR 1449, a case involving three defendants, one defendant had previous convictions, including an offence of dishonesty. The judge directed the jury as to the significance of one co-defendant's good character and said of another defendant only that he had 'had a spot of trouble with the police before'. However, the Court of Appeal dismissed the appeal of the latter on conviction. It accepted that the judge should have warned the jury to disregard the convictions as irrelevant to guilt but came to the conclusion that his dismissive language had reduced any adverse inferences which the jury might otherwise have drawn. Since a full direction would have reminded the jury that the convictions were relevant to credibility, the overall effect was not less favourable to the defendant than it would have been if a full direction had been given.

Again, the fact that Andy's convictions are for criminal damage, not an offence involving dishonesty, is unlikely to change the position, though it will probably rule out, as irrelevant, examination on the details of the offences for which he was convicted. It is therefore submitted that Andy may not have any good ground of appeal on this issue of direction on the evidential worth of his bad character.

Catherine has a previous conviction for theft and her attack on David is arguably covered by s. 101(1)(g); 'The defendant has made an attack on another person's character.' The prosecution may therefore adduce evidence of her previous convictions although the court has a discretion to exclude under s. 101(3) and (4). The section was applied in *R v Nelson (Ashley George)* [2006] EWCA Crim 3412; [2007] Crim LR 709–711. The defendant was charged with affray and assault occasioning actual bodily harm. The prosecution case was that the defendant had swung a machete to the alleged victim. The defence argued that the victim and neighbour had conspired to fabricate the allegations. The defendant, in interview, had claimed that the neighbour was a liar who used illegal drugs. The neighbour was not a witness at trial. The judge ruled that there had been an attack on another person's character. Nelson was convicted and appealed on the ground that the comments in interview should not have been admitted. The Court of Appeal dismissed the appeal, holding that 'an attack on another person's character' did not confine that gateway to the situation where a defendant, personally or through his advocate, attacked the character of a prosecution witness. It had to be taken as Parliament's intention deliberately to widen the gateway in that fashion. The trial judge had a discretion, however, to exclude evidence of a defendant's bad character when he had merely made imputations about the character of a non-witness. That discretion could be exercised under s. 78 **PACE** or s. 101(3) of the 2003 Act. The court stated that it would be a matter for the judge how he exercised that discretion but that it would be unusual for evidence of a defendant's bad character to be admitted when the only basis for so doing was an attack on the character of a non-witness who is also a non-victim. In the instant case, however, the attack by the defendant could provide the basis for the admission of the defendant's previous convictions.

The prosecution therefore will try to argue that Carol's comments at the interview have opened the gateway to admission of her previous convictions. It will, however, on the authority of *Nelson*, have to convince the judge that a proper basis has been laid for putting Catherine's comments at interview in front of the jury. In *Nelson* the court considered that it would have been improper for the prosecution to seek to get such comments before a jury simply to provide a basis for satisfying gateway (g). However, in the event the requirements of gateway (g) were met by referring to the attack on the victim in cross-examination. David is being called as a witness and if the defence refers to Catherine's claims in cross-examination that would provide a stronger ground for admitting Catherine's conviction.

One further issue arises as to whether bad character evidence is admissible when the imputations made by the defendant are an integral part of the defence case. The comment on the case in the Criminal Law Review (2007, p. 711) states, 'the old law was criticised on the grounds that it made no exception to adduction of evidence of the defendant's bad character in cases in which the imputations that were cast were integral to the defence that was being run, e.g. that a confession had been fabricated. In this respect no change has been effected by the 2003 Act. Consequently, those who are interviewed under caution by the police are now required to navigate a perilous path on one side of which is the risk of providing a detailed account of matters which might trigger the expectation of gateway (g) at trial, and on the other the danger that any circumspection in the interview might lead to adverse inferences being drawn under the provisions of the **Criminal Justice and Public Order Act 1994**.' (This, of course, assumes a defendant with previous form.) The comment on *Nelson* adds: 'In the light of this, the view expressed by the court in the present case, that it would be improper for the prosecution to seek to adduce parts of an interview which were not relevant to the matters in issue merely to trigger the operation of gateway (g) is to be welcomed.'

Thus the attack on David, if not that on Doris, may trigger the admissibility of Catherine's previous convictions.

The fact that Catherine does not testify does not in itself prevent her conviction being admitted. Section 106(1)(c) is a departure from the position under the **Criminal Evidence Act 1898.** It was applied in **R** v **Renda** [2005] **EWCA Crim 2826.** Section 100 and subsection 106 set out guidelines for attacks on non-defendants' bad character. The court has a discretion to exclude under s 101(3) and (4). If the conviction is admitted it may in principle be used as evidence of propensity or lack of credibility (**Highton, Campbell**). However, in **R** v **Meyer** [2006] **EWCA Crim 1126,** the Court of Appeal held that the part of the direction that referred to a person of bad character as being less likely to tell the truth rendered the conviction unsafe. Section 103(1)(b) did not apply. On the other hand, in **Campbell** (2007) the court did not consider that the jury had been led astray by a similar direction. Catherine should be warned that the court in **Campbell** stressed that it was not helpful to rely on previous decisions, which were confined to their particular facts.

Both Catherine and Andy should be warned that the Court of Appeal has indicated it will not readily interfere with the judge's discretion in this area (**Hanson**).

Question 2

Thelma and Louise are jointly charged with murdering Harry. Both plead not guilty to the charge. Their explanation is that Harry had tried to rape Thelma and in the course of protecting her they both were obliged to push him and he fell down some stairs. Both had fled the scene but later gave themselves up to the police. Louise chooses not to give evidence but her counsel calls her local vicar to state that Louise had been a Bible School teacher and sang in the church choir. Her counsel also suggests, in cross-examining a prosecution eye witness, Gary, that he had been high on heroin on the night of the alleged murder and that his account of events was not therefore reliable. Louise has two previous convictions for theft. Thelma elects to testify and in the course of giving evidence explains her flight from the scene of the incident by saying she was afraid of the police because she had cannabis in her pocket. Thelma has several drug-related convictions and is awaiting trial on a charge of violent disorder. The police claim that Thelma had confessed to attempting to kill Harry but Thelma denies making such an admission. They are tried on indictment.

Discuss the evidential issues involved.

Commentary

The provisions of the **Criminal Justice Act 2003** on character created, as Lord Phillips of Worth Matravers put it in *O'Brien* v *Chief Constable of South Wales* **(2005) UKHL 26**, 'rules of some complexity'. The developing case-law often raises more questions than answers. Reviewing the first seven cases to be heard on appeal, Waterman and Dempster said (2006, p. 628), 'some of the new provisions are very difficult. Practitioners and judges are in a better position because of these rulings than they were without them. It is not, however, the case that these principles are now clear: far from it! It is to be hoped that the Court of Appeal will continue to wrestle with them so that through the normal process of development of a body of case law further principle and practical guidance will emerge.' You will need to familiarise yourself with the developing case-law and academic commentary.

Answer plan

- Thelma and Louise appeared to attack Harry by claiming he tried to rape Thelma—consider s. 101(1)(g) and whether the case-law under the 1898 Act applies
- Louise does not testify. Does the **Criminal Justice Act 2003** apply to testifying and non-testifying defendants?
- Bad character—meaning of, s. 98 **CJA 2003**
- Louise called good character evidence—consider s. 101(1)(f)
- Louise's counsel makes an imputation on Gary as prosecution witness—consider s. 101(1)(g)
- Thelma—explanation of flight may include admission of misconduct; denies police version of events

Suggested answer

The main issues in this case involve questions as to whether Thelma and Louise's character can be brought into the trial under the **Criminal Justice Act 2003**, which repealed both the common-law provisions and those in the **Criminal Evidence Act 1898**. The 2003 Act applies to both testifying and non-testifying defendants and so both Thelma and Louise are covered by its provisions.

With regard to Louise's failure to testify, the scope of permissible comment by the judge and counsel for the prosecution is covered by s. 35(3) of the **Criminal Justice and Public Order Act 1994**, whereby the court or jury in determining whether the accused is guilty of the offence charged may draw such inferences as appear proper from the failure of the accused to give evidence. The prosecution can therefore now comment on her failure to testify but under s. 35(3) no conviction can be made solely on the inferences drawn under s. 35. Moreover, Louise's position may be aided by the common-law case of *R* v *Martinez-Tobon* [1994] 1 WLR 388, which underlines the principle that silence in itself is neutral; it simply leaves the prosecution case unchallenged. The Court of Appeal in *R* v *Cowan* [1996] QB 373 laid down guidelines. Provided an inference under this section is not the only evidence against the defendant, the section will usually operate. The judge in summing-up should refer to the points covered in the Judicial Studies Board specimen direction:

> The defendant has not given evidence. That it is his right. He is entitled to remain silent and to require the prosecution to make you sure of his guilt. You must not assume he is guilty because he has not given evidence. But two matters arise from his silence:
>
> In the first place you must try this case according to the evidence, and you will appreciate that the defendant has not given evidence at this trial to undermine, contradict or explain the evidence put before you by the prosecution.
>
> In the second place silence at this trial may count against him. This is because you may draw the conclusion that he has not given evidence because he has no answer to the prosecution's case, or none that would dare examination. If you do draw a like conclusion you must not convict him wholly or mainly on the strength of it, but you may treat it as some additional support for the prosecution's case.
>
> However you may draw such a conclusion against him only if you think it is a fair and proper conclusion, and you are satisfied about two things: first that the prosecution's case is so strong that it clearly calls for an answer by him, and second that the only sensible explanation for his silence is that he has no answer, or none that would bear examination.

The prosecution may rely on *Murray* v *UK* **[1996] 22 EHRR 29**, where the European Court of Human Rights held that there was no breach of art. 6(1) of the Convention arising from the drawing of adverse inferences due to the defendant's failure to answer questions during interrogation or his failure to give evidence during his trial. In this case the judge may draw attention to strengths in the prosecution case, such as Louise's flight from the scene, which she does not explain.

Under the common law the accused is entitled to adduce evidence of her own good character with the aim of persuading the jury that a person with that character is unlikely to have committed the alleged offence. The rule at common law, unaffected by the **Criminal Justice Act 2003**, is that evidence of character is confined to evidence of general reputation and not of specific creditable acts. The leading case on this is *R* v *Rowton* **(1865) Le & Ca 520**, which was followed in *R* v *Redgrave* **(1981) 74 Cr App R 10**. In the latter case the accused, who was charged with offences relating to homosexuality, was not allowed to prove his heterosexuality by evidence of past liaison with members of the opposite sex. The question that arises is whether the evidence of Louise's vicar is evidence of her general reputation, which is relevant to the case. It is likely that the court will accept that this evidence is admissible since the common-law rule that it is, despite *Redgrave*, is not often strictly applied. The application of s. 101(1)(f) of the **Criminal Justice Act** must then be considered. The prosecution may be permitted to adduce evidence of bad character to correct any false impression that may have been created. The provision reads: 'In criminal proceedings evidence of the defendant's bad character is admissible if, but only if. . . it is evidence to correct a false impression given by the defendant.'

The preceding case-law under s. 1 of the **Criminal Evidence Act 1898** may be helpful in determining what is meant by 'creating a false impression'. The previous case-law under the 1898 Act centres on the meaning of claiming to be of good character such as the shield would be lost and bad character evidence put. Each case turns on its own facts but, for example, in *R* v *Baker* [1912] 7 Cr App R 252 the defendant lost his shield by giving 'evidence that for four years he had been earning an honest living'. In *R* v *Reade* (2006) 2 All ER 553 the defendant was held to be seeking to convey a misleading impression about his life and history by claiming that he had been a serving soldier in the Armed Forces, who had, while still employed, sustained serious head injuries, which had resulted in long-term brain damage. He said that at the date of his arrest he was in regular employment as a security guard. The court commented:

> Our attention was drawn to earlier authorities which considered the impact of section 1(3)(ii) of the Criminal Evidence Act 1898. However it is unnecessary to refer to them in this judgment. It is most unlikely to be useful to refer to authorities which were no more than factual examples of occasions when it was decided that an individual defendant had put his character in issue. For the purposes of section 101(1)(f) the question whether the defendant has given a false impression about himself and whether there is evidence which may properly serve to correct such a false impression under section 105(1)(a) and (b) is fact-specific.

Louise's claim to be a Bible School teacher and sing in the church choir is likely to fall under s. 101(1)(f). The question then arises what is permissible evidence to correct this impression. Section 98 and s. 112 of the **Criminal Justice Act 2003** indicate what is meant by 'bad character'. The Explanatory Note to the Act (at para. 353) reads, 'the definition covers evidence of or a disposition towards misconduct. The term "misconduct" is further defined in section 112 as the commission of an offence or other reprehensible behaviour. This is intended to be a broad definition and recover evidence that shows that the person has committed an offence, or has acted in a reprehensible way (or is disposed to do so) as well as evidence from which this might be inferred.' Do Louise's two previous convictions for theft qualify for admission under s. 101(1)(f)? Although this section is largely a reflection of s. 1(3) of the **Criminal Evidence Act 1898** the wording of the new section makes it clear that evidence is only now admissible if it goes no further than is necessary to correct the false impression, in contrast to the draconian common law position in *R* v *Winfield* [1939] 4 All ER 164 that character was indivisible. Louise may take advantage of s. 105(3) in withdrawing or dissociating herself from the false or misleading impression. There is no statutory discretion to exclude evidence under s. 101(1)(f) except the general discretion under s. 78 of the **Police and Criminal Evidence Act**.

Louise and Thelma claim that Harry tried to rape them. Their argument possibly is self-defence. In *R* v *Selvey* [1970] AC 304 the House of Lords stated 'cross-examination of the accused as to character [is permissible] both when imputations on the character of the prosecutor and his witness are cast to show their own reliability as witnesses independently of the evidence given by them and also when the casting of such imputations is necessary to enable the accused to establish his defence'. This is likely to apply under s. 101(1)(g). In *Hanson* the Court of Appeal stated that 'pre-2003 authorities will continue to apply when assessing whether an attack has been made on another person's character, to the extent that they are compatible with the [new legislation]'.

Thus Louise's convictions may be admissible by the prosecution under this head also although under s. 101(3) such evidence is not likely to be admissible 'if on application by the defendant to exclude it, it appears to the court that the admission of the evidence would have such an adverse effect on the fairness of the proceedings that the court ought not to admit it'. One factor is 'the length of time between matters to which that evidence relates and the matters which form the subject of the offence charged'. In *R* v *Bovell* the Court of Appeal made it clear that the trial judge was not expected to conduct an investigation into why the defendant made the attack: 'the impact on the fairness of proceedings had to be assessed by reference to matters and other than what the defendant's particular intention may or may not have been'.

Thelma's explanation of her flight from the scene of the alleged crime has arguably introduced evidence of reprehensible behaviour, namely that she had cannabis in her pocket, which is unlawful. This is analogous to the position under the 1898 Act of *DPP* v *Jones*, who had himself revealed his bad character to explain his change of alibis. Doak and McGourley (2008, p. 179) comment: 'The *Jones* case is likely to fall under s. 101(1)(b) in that "the evidence is adduced by the defendant himself or is given in answer to a question asked by him in cross-examination and intended to elicit it".'

It follows therefore that the prosecution may cross-examine Thelma on her previous conviction. Thelma has also arguably 'made an attack on another person's character' under s. 101(1)(g) by claiming Harold had attempted rape and by denying the police version of her alleged confession. In relation to the latter in *Hanson* the Court stated that 'as to section 101(1)(g) pre-2003 authorities will continue to apply when assessing whether an attack has been made on another person's character, to the extent that they are compatible with section 106'. It is not clear under the new law how the pending charge will be treated. Misconduct is defined in s. 112 as 'the commission of an offence or other reprehensible behaviour', a broader definition than before. Support for the argument that the evidence of a pending charge may be admitted is that s. 99(1) specifies that 'the common law rules governing the admissibility of evidence of bad character in criminal proceedings are abolished'. Thelma is advised that the Court will most likely protect this privilege and not allow reference to the charge. In relation to the admissibility of her previous bad character, in *R* v *Smith* [1989] Crim LR 900 the Court of Appeal decided that the accused cannot be asked in cross-examination about pending charges since they may tend to undermine her privilege against self-incrimination.

One question which arises is may the prosecution cross-examine on the details of previous offences where they are admitted? In *R* v *McLeod* **[1994] 1 WLR 1500** the Court of Appeal had set out guidelines on this. In *Hanson* (para. 17) the Court stated, 'in a conviction case the Crown needs to decide at the time of giving notice of the application whether it proposes to rely simply upon the fact of conviction or upon the circumstances of it. The former may be enough when the circumstances of the conviction are apparent from its description, to justify a finding that it can establish propensity, either to commit an offence of the kind charged or to be untruthful and that the requirement of section 103(3) and 101(3) can, subject to any particular matter raised on behalf of the defendant, be satisfied.' It added 'We would expect the relevant circumstances of previous convictions generally to be capable of agreement, and that, subject to the trial judge's ruling as to admissibility, they will be put before the jury by way of admission. Even where the circumstances are genuinely in dispute we would expect the minimum indisputable facts to be thus admitted. It will be very rare indeed for it to be necessary for the judge to hear evidence before ruling on admissibility under this Act.' Finally the judge should direct on the evidential value of the bad character. In *Highton* the Court of Appeal held that evidence which was admitted through one gateway, for example gateway (g), is nonetheless capable of being used according to the definition of another section. It stated (para. 10):

> We therefore conclude that a distinction must be drawn between the admissibility of evidence of bad character, which depends upon it getting through one of the gateways, and the use to which it may be put once admitted. The use to which it may be put depends upon the matters to which it is relevant rather than upon the gateway through which it was admitted. It is true that the reasoning that leads to the admission of evidence under gateway (d) may also determine the matters to which the evidence is relevant or primarily relevant once admitted. This is not true, however, of all the gateways. In the case of gateway (g) for example admissibility depends on the defendant having made an attack on another person's character, but once the evidence is admitted, it may, depending on the particular facts, be relevant not only to credibility but also the propensity to commit offences of the kind with which the defendant is charged.

This approach also underlines the importance of the guidance that was given in the case of *Hanson* and others as to the care that the judge must exercise to give the jury appropriate warnings when summing-up. In *Edwards* (para. 18) Lord Justice Rose said:

> What the summing up must contain is a clear warning to the jury against placing undue reliance on previous convictions, which cannot by themselves prove guilt. It should be explained why the jury has heard the evidence and the way in which it is relevant to and may help their decision. Bearing in mind that relevance will depend primarily, though not always exclusively, on the gateway in section 101(1) of the **Criminal Justice Act 2003** through which the evidence has been admitted. For example some evidence admitted through Gateway (g) because of an attack on another

person's character, may be relevant or irrelevant to propensity, so as to require a direction on this aspect.

In *Hanson* (para. 15) the court stated 'if a judge has directed himself or herself correctly this court will be very slow to interfere with the ruling either as to admissibility or as to the consequences of non-compliance with the regulations for giving notice of intention to rely on bad character evidence. It will not interfere unless the judge's judgment as to the capacity of prior events to establish propensity is plainly wrong, or a discretion has been exercised unreasonably in the *Wednesbury* sense.'

Question 3

Critically evaluate the approach of the courts in relation to the evidential value of bad character and assess the extent of the change brought about in this area by the **Criminal Justice Act 2003**.

Commentary

You are asked here to comment on the approach taken by the courts to the evidential value of bad character, namely whether it goes only to credibility. This question requires a brief historical outline of the compromise achieved by the **Criminal Evidence Act 1898**, which allowed the accused to appear as a witness for the first time. Unlike other witnesses, however, he was allowed a shield in that he was protected from cross-examination on his past record unless he put his own good character in or impugned a prosecution witness. You should deal with the first aspect of the proviso, putting in good character, and discuss *R* v *Winfield* [1939] 4 All ER 164. Deal then with the circumstances of loss of shield by impugning a prosecution witness, the 'tit for tat' principle (*Selvey* v *DPP* [1970] AC 304; *R* v *Watts* [1983] 3 All ER 101; *R* v *Powell* [1985] 1 WLR 1364). The question requires you to discuss judicial directions on credibility and propensity and the difficulties faced where one defendant is of good character and the other has a criminal record. This raises the question of whether it is possible to differentiate credibility and propensity (the House of Lords in *R* v *Aziz* [1996] 1 AC 41, differentiated between the two on the basis that no direction as to credibility need be given when the defendant had not given evidence, and dealt with the circumstances in which a judge could refuse a direction to a defendant with no convictions; see also *R* v *Cain* [1994] 1 WLR 1449). You should then discuss the changes in law to include imputations against a deceased victim, and deal finally with any academic discussion on the statutory provision. You should demonstrate knowledge of the report of the Law Commission in this area and the relevant provisions of the **Criminal Justice Act 2003**. Your answer will be improved if you can show familiarity with the work of academics such as McEwan (1992), Zuckerman (1989) and Munday (1985). Roberts and Zuckerman (2004) have written a very clear account of the new law. Note also the recent articles by Waterman and Dempster (2006) and Munday (2006).

Answer plan

- Account of compromise reached now repealed s. 1(3) **Criminal Evidence Act 1898**—defendant allowed to testify but given a shield
- Review of effect of defendant who testifies and claims to be of good character
- 'Tit for tat' principle—impugning a prosecution witness
- Difficulty of differentiating credibility and propensity—**R** v **Aziz**
- Review of provisions of **CJA 2003**, academic comment and recent case-law

Suggested answer

English law has traditionally only allowed the jury to hear about discreditable events in the accused's past (apart, of course, from evidence about the instant charge or charges) in exceptional circumstances. The **Criminal Evidence Act 1898**, which for the first time allowed the accused to testify in his own defence, provided five of these in relation to cross-examination of the accused. These were Similar Fact evidence; those occasions where the accused undermines the evidence of the co-accused; and the three referred to in this question, namely where the accused puts himself forward as a person of good character; where he impugns a prosecution witness; and since the implementation of s. 31 of the **Criminal Justice and Public Order Act 1994**, where the accused impugned a deceased victim. The rationale behind the three last exceptions are examined and the background to the provisions of the **Criminal Justice Act 2003**, which repeals s. 1(3) of the 1898 Act outlined below. However, the Act covers admissibility and so in principle the law on judicial directions on the evidential worth of the bad character evidence is not affected.

Munday (1985, p. 79) referred to the 'commonsensical' principle behind the first limb of s. 1(3) of the **CEA 1898** in that there is a clear logic in the proposition that a man who claims to be of good character and therefore not the sort of person to commit the offence with which he is charged, should be cross-examined if there is evidence from his past that he is in fact the sort of man to commit that kind of offence. The cross-examination may indicate past criminal acts and suggest whether the defendant is the sort of person who is likely to tell the truth on oath. There is a paradox here in that, as Viscount Sankey pointed out in the House of Lords in *Maxwell* v *DPP* [1935] AC 309, evidence of good character is likely to be taken by the jury as evidence that the accused is a person who is unlikely to have committed the offence with which he is charged. Here the common law established before 1898 the principle that such evidence went to the issue of guilt, clearly credibility being not an issue since the defendant did not testify. The case of *R* v *Vye* [1993] 1 WLR 471 makes it clear that a direction as to the relevance of good character to the likelihood of the defendant having committed the offence charged, was to be given whether or not he had testified. This was to be accompanied by a direction as to the relevance of the good character to credibility as well where the defendant testifies, or alternatively, relies on pre-trial 'mixed' statements. The *Vye* direction need not be given when a defendant without previous convictions is shown beyond doubt to have been guilty of serious criminal behaviour similar to the offence charged. In these circumstances, the House of Lords held in *R* v *Aziz* [1996] 1 AC 41 that it would be an insult to common sense for the judge to give the *Vye* direction. The difficulties suggested in the question of differentiating credibility and guilt are illustrated in *R* v *Cain* [1994] 1 WLR 1449. Here the issue arose of what direction was appropriate if an accused of good character is jointly tried with an accused of bad character whose previous convictions have been placed before the jury. Here the former is entitled to the *Vye* direction and the jury should be directed that the previous convictions of the other are not relevant to guilt, but are relevant to credibility. Thus, one difficulty of the application of the principle that bad character is relevant to credibility arises when good character of a co-defendant is also presented at the trial.

Related to this was the further difficulty of appreciating the rationale of the first limb of s. 1(3). It was made clear in *R* v *Winfield* [1939] 4 All ER 164 that the purpose of the question was to match the favourable impression created by the good character evidence. Humphreys J pointed out (at p. 165) that 'there is no such thing known to our procedure as putting half your character in issue and leaving out the other half'. This led to the somewhat anomalous position that the trial judge would allow cross-examination on previous offences even if they bore no relation to the good character evidence. McEwan (1998, p. 195) argued that *Winfield* was 'indefensible' in that it allowed exclusion of offences close in nature to the current offence because the defendant chose not to lose his shield, but admited offences that were totally irrelevant because he had lost it. She pointed out that the tribunal of fact was directed to assess the defendant's overall creditworthiness in the light of his bad character rather than judge if the prosecution has refuted the specific claims made. Thus, the jury was told to consider that convictions for theft was a relevant response to a claim made by a witness that the defendant was not the sort of person to assault women. The House of Lords cited *Winfield* in *Stirland* v *DPP* [1944] AC 315.

Furthermore, it is indeed questionable whether it is conceptually possible to draw a distinction between evidence going to propensity and evidence going to credibility, let alone whether the judge could convey this to the jury. Munday (1985 p. 65) quoting Cross refers to this as 'one of those distinctions without a difference'. Partly he draws on psychology to show the fallacy of the belief that there exists some unitary entity which can be called credibility and that dishonesty in one situation suggests dishonesty in all. In any case the jury is being asked to accept that there is a recognisable distinction between the statement that the accused is of bad character and is not telling the truth and that the accused is of bad character and the sort of person who commits the instant offence. The difficulties of trying to maintain the distinction were illustrated in the case of *Jones* v *DPP* [1962] AC 635. In holding that cross-examination about Jones' earlier offence was permissible under what became s. 1(3) of the 1898 Act, not s. 1(2).

Zuckerman (1989, p. 253) complained that the House of Lords had added to the 'notorious distinction between relevance to the issue and relevance to credibility'. The terminology used in the case referred also to 'direct' as opposed to 'indirect' relevance and the objective was the arguably laudable one to protect the defendant. The House held that if s. 1(2) was used to justify questions about Similar Fact evidence then the prosecution should have brought it out in examination-in-chief. The somewhat tortuous nature of the reasoning here is due in no small measure to the attempt to uphold a distinction between relevance to credibility and relevance to guilt. However, as the discussion below shows the **CJA 2003** is still wrestling with this problem.

This questionable conceptual device was even more marked in relation to the second limb of s. 1(3)(b). Here the accused lost his shield if he impugned the character of a witness for the prosecution and, since November 1994, a dead victim. The problem of what amounts to an imputation was a difficult one but is not the subject of this question. Here, the protection against revelation of past record referred to by Munday (1985 at p. 63 quoting Wigmore) as the 'inborn sporting instinct of Anglo Normandom' can give way to what he calls the 'crude retaliatory notion of tit for tat'. The rationale seemed to be that, if the accused attacked the character of a prosecution witness, and there was no such tit for tat response, the jury would not be able to judge who was telling the truth. There are, as Munday shows, several weaknesses in this argument. First, it is not clear why it should not apply when the accused is not impugning the prosecution witness. The usual explanation is that the character evidence is too prejudicial in that it might make the jury lower the standard of proof and convict for emotional not rational reactions to the evidence. These same concerns arguably apply whatever evidence has been given against the prosecution witness.

Second, an analysis of *R* v *Britzman* **[1983] 1 WLR 350**, the leading case under the **CEA 1898** on the guidelines to be applied in cases where the defendant impugned a police officer, contains a particularly odd formulation. The prosecution are told not to rely on the proviso if other evidence against the defendant is overwhelming. But why should legally admissible evidence be excluded on this strange ground? It suggests the courts are worried about this form of prejudicial evidence, reflecting as Munday (1985 at p. 76) says 'the fragility of the conceptual framework' of the section. This approach is continued under the **CJA 2003**, where the courts will not admit bad character evidence if the prosecution case is strong (*Hanson*).

Third, the courts have shown a readiness to admit criminal convictions even where the imputation made was a necessary part of the defence, illustrating that the section is not only based on compensating for an intended discrediting of a prosecution witness and severely hampering the defence tactics of a defendant with a record. Thus, despite this inconsistency, the House of Lords in *Selvey* v *DPP* **[1970] AC 304** held that the words of the statute should be given their ordinary and natural meaning. 'Nature and conduct of the defence' was taken to mean that which was inherent in the defence and the actual handling of the case by the defendant or his advocate. This approach does not appear to have been changed by the CJA 2003.

Fourth, the exercise of the discretion to exclude evidence under this head shows the courts had moved away from only admitting cases which reflected dishonesty, again blurring the distinction between credit and propensity. Thus in *Selvey* cross-examination was actually limited to offences of a similar type to that charged, i.e., indecency, although the effect must have been to suggest an inference of guilt since the defendant had previous convictions for similar offences. In what was described at the time by Munday (2003, p. 261) as an 'ugly decision' the Court of Appeal extended the scope of cross-examination. Relying on *Selvey* the court held in *Chinn* (1996) 160 JP 765 that while it was normal practice for prosecuting counsel to apply to cross-examine, the judge was also entitled to take the initiative and cross-examine. This extended the danger of prejudice to the defendant. In *R* v *Powell* [1985] 1 WLR 1364, the court felt that it had interfered too lightly with the discretion in the earlier case of *R* v *Watts* [1983] 3 All ER 101 and the fact that the defendant's convictions are not for offences of dishonesty, or are for offences bearing a close resemblance to the offence charged, are factors to be taken into consideration when the court is exercising its discretion but does not oblige the court to disallow the proposed cross-examination. Munday (2006) demonstrates how under the CJA propensity evidence may be admissible under s. 101(1)(g) even though the Explanatory Note to the statute says this section 'will primarily go to the credit of the defendant'.

Finally, the changes made in the **Criminal Justice and Public Order Act 1994** and retained in the CJA made the argument that the purpose of the section was to assess relative credibilities increasingly threadbare. The credibility of a dead victim could hardly have been at issue.

The Law Commission produced a consultation paper on 'Evidence in Criminal Proceedings: Previous Misconduct of a Defendant' (Consultation Paper No. 141) in 1996. It noted the difficulty of maintaining the distinction between relevance for guilt and credibility. It pointed out (at para. 12.34, pp. 215–216):

> . . . when the shield is lost the jury will be directed that the evidence of previous misconduct goes only to the defendant's credibility and not directly to the issue of his or her guilt. Such a direction may be impossible to follow and there is a serious danger of prejudice to the accused. Moreover the cases suggest that the courts do not always adhere to the theory that bad character evidence admitted under this provision goes only to the defendant's credibility.

The Commission issued a note of warning that, although past behaviour can be probative on the question of propensity, 'the probative value of a single previous instance can be easily over-estimated; the psychological research supports the emphasis currently placed on the importance of close and unusual similarities between past conduct and that now alleged' (p. 257). The report was cautious about the sort of offences which are relevant to credibility and suggest that behaviour not involving dishonesty is unlikely to be relevant. However, the Commission did 'not think it appropriate to prescribe in a statute which kinds of conviction are and are not probative'.

In 2001 the Law Commission produced its Report No. 273 (Cm 5257), 'Evidence of Bad Character in Criminal Proceedings'. Among its recommendations were the proposal that misconduct of the defendant surrounding the offence, for example, witness intimidation, should be admissible, with discretion under s. 78 of **PACE** to exclude. It also recommended that with leave of the court there should be three areas of admissibility of character evidence as exceptions to the exclusionary rule. These were first where misconduct is evidence of guilt; second where the defendant makes bad character relevant through the nature of the defence by suggesting another person, whether or not a witness, has a propensity for untruthfulness; third where the defendant creates a false impression about himself misconduct evidence may be admissible if relevant to credibility or propensity. McEwan (2002) stressed that such measures would require clear directions by the judge to the jury in order to minimise the risk of prejudice.

The Report rejected the option of routinely disclosing the defendant's record at the beginning of every trial. This would involve 'the admission of prejudicial and irrelevant evidence for no very clear purpose, with potentially damaging consequences for the administration of justice and public confidence in it'. Many of the Law Commission proposals are contained in the **Criminal Justice Act 2003**, which repeals s. 1(3) **Criminal Evidence Act 1898** and makes radical changes to the law on character evidence. However, there is great similarity between the **CEA** and the **CJA** in that neither give clear guidance on the evidential worth of bad character evidence and to date the case-law does not shed much light.

The 2003 Act represents a reaction to what were perceived as failures of the 1898 statute. As Tapper (2004, p. 535) put it, 'the situation was seen as one of incoherence complexity and uncertainty'. However, he sees also 'disturbing' differences between the 'good intentions' of the Law Commission proposals and the final version of the 2003 Act, the latter starting with an inclusionary stance on bad character, the former an exclusionary stance. Thus as Munday (2006 p300) argues 'Although Pt II of the 2003 Act swept aside virtually every rule that previously had governed the admission of bad character evidence, structurally the statute retains features that will seem dimly familiar to those conversant with the old law.'

The intellectual difficulties revealed in the **Criminal Evidence Act 1898** and its application has prompted several writers however to propose more radical reforms. Thus Zuckerman (1989, p. 245) suggested that:

[a] more effective way of combating prejudice would be to bring into the open the scope of prejudice created by evidence of past criminal record and strive to persuade juries that the principles of criminal justice, which require resisting prejudice, reflect their own perception of justice.

There was thus an argument for saying that criminal record should be routinely admitted as in continental jurisdictions. This would avoid highlighting the criminal record and also the almost accidental way a defendant can lose his protection.

Zuckerman (1989, p. 246) concluded that if his proposals were accepted, 'the question of admissibility [would be] less important because the tools will be in place for counteracting prejudice'. But this position arguably underestimates the amount of prejudice juries frequently draw from convictions and also presupposes that the judiciary are able to convey such complex ethical messages to a jury of differing experiences and moral standpoints. Some commentators appear sympathetic towards the position that all character evidence concerning the defendant should be excluded, while others, such as Seabrooke, put forward the argument that only experiences in the defendant's past that are similar to the allegations he makes against the prosecution witness should be allowed. This would ensure a real balance of retaliatory evidence. The weight of academic evidence criticising the 1898 Act does suggest that this question implies how complex and intellectually muddled was the long-standing attempt to differentiate credit and propensity. As Munday (1986) pointed out, strictly speaking, if the distinction was to be maintained as purely a logical proposition, the only previous convictions that should be admitted under s. 1(3)(b) were those for perjury, an approach the courts were unlikely to adopt.

How far does the **Criminal Justice Act 2003** address the intellectual incoherence of the 1898 provision cited in the question? It does overcome the problem of the 'difficult feats of intellectual acrobatics' under attack in *Watts*, but permitted in *Powell*, since it applies to both testifying and non-testifying defendants. Since it applies the same regime whether the defendant testifies or not, the distinction between credibility and guilt is marginalized. The Law Commission in its 2001 Report had noted: 'giving juries directions which they will find bizarre or incomprehensible or which require them to engage in mental gymnastics, does no credit to the law. In our view the way forward is to seek to ensure that the evidence which is adduced is limited to that which is substantially relevant to the issues of importance . . . and not marginal to the issues in the trial.' The result of the new provisions is, as Roberts and Zuckerman point out, that 'the technical evidentiary constraint on the logic of inference perpetuated in cases such as *Powell* and *McLeod* in relation to proviso (f) [later renumbered as s.1(3)(ii)] of the **Criminal Evidence Act 1898** is no longer applicable' (at p. 571). The test of admissibility is relevance to an issue and the judiciary will no longer need to draw technical distinctions between credibility and guilt. The apparently illogical differences between implications of bad character and good character are to some extent overcome. In particular the new law overcomes some of the incoherence generated by several heavily criticised cases. First, the strictures of the *Winfield* doctrine that 'character is indivisible' are tempered. In contrast to this case s. 105 of the **Criminal Justice Act 2003** sets out a more logical framework for allowing retaliatory evidence of an accused's bad character by referring to the need to 'correct a false impression'. Section 105(6) provides that 'Evidence is admissible under section 101(1)(f) only if it goes no further than is necessary to correct the false impression.'

However, in other respects although the **Criminal Justice Act 2003** may now make the law more logical it is arguably more unfair to the defendant in admitting more bad character evidence. In his commentary on *Highton* Munday (2006) demonstrates how evidence admitted under s. 101(1)(g), the successor to the **CEA**, may go to issue, not only to credibility and argues that the court took a stance 'clearly adverse to the interests of the defendant'. Another anti-defendant move is that the *Butterwasser* principle will go, largely because it was seen as unfair to victims that the defendant could impugn a prosecution witness without losing his 'shield', provided he did not go into the witness box himself. Similarly, *Selvey* still survives in that even where an attack on a prosecution witness is necessary for the defence, this may trigger revelation of the defendant's bad character. The tit-for-tat principle remains since the bad character of the defendant may be revealed if he 'makes an attack on another person's character' (s. 101(1)(g)), which might not necessarily be that the other person is of 'bad character' within the definition of the Act. There is, however, a discretion not to admit bad character under s. 101(3).

The Court of Appeal in *Hanson* stated (para. 53): 'We have not heard full argument as to whether it is right or indeed necessary to give a credibility direction where evidence of bad character has been admitted under this Act, nor as to whether the nature of the direction should be dependent on the gateway through which the evidence has been admitted.' They added that in *Hanson* 'The defendant's credibility was so inextricably bound up with whether he had committed the offences that no sustainable criticism can be made of this aspect of the summing up.'

Arguably, however, *Hanson* and the later case of *Highton* have blurred the boundaries between propensity and credibility. The intellectually more coherent position now advocated by the Court of Appeal (para. 10) in *Highton* is that the use to which the evidence could be put depended upon the matters to which it was relevant rather than upon the gateway through which it was admitted. The Court of Appeal continued to say that although it was true that the reasoning that might lead to the admission of evidence under s. 101(1)(d) may also determine the matters to which the evidence was relevant or primarily relevant once admitted, that was not true of all the gateways. For example, in the case of gateway s. 101(g) admissibility depended on the defendant having made an attack on another person's character, but once the evidence was admitted, it was, depending on the particular facts, relevant not only to credibility but also to propensity to commit offences of the kind with which the defendant was charged. Thus the distinction between credibility and propensity is maintained by the Court of Appeal in *Highton* and there are two stages at which relevance is considered with regard to admissibility and then in the summing-up. Sections 101(1)(e), (f) and (g) operate on the 'tit for tat' principle in that the evidence of bad character is admitted in response to a specific stance by the defendant. Once admitted, however, the evidence may be used not only to redress the imbalance the defendant has created but as evidence either of more general propensity or lack or credibility. The Court in (*Stewart*) *Edwards* pointed out that 'admissibility' and 'use' give rise to different questions.

References to 'untruthfulness' occur in s. 103(1)(b), amplifying s. 101(1)(d) and s. 104(1) on s. 101(1)(e). Section 103(1)(b) is broader, stating that matters in issue between the defendant and the prosecution can include 'the question whether the defendant has a propensity to be untruthful'. Section 104(1) reads 'Evidence which is relevant to the question whether the defendant has a propensity to be untruthful is admissible only if the nature or conduct of his defence is such as to undermine the co-defendant's defence. It is possible that the nature of the relevance will change during the trial.' Lord Justice Scott Baker stated in *R* v (*Stewart Dean*) *Edwards* [2006] (para 1(iv)), 'Where evidence of bad character is admitted, the judge's direction is likely to be of the first importance. It will need to cover the matters canvassed in *Hanson* and *Highton*. It may also need to pull threads together on an issue where the ground may have shifted considerably since the evidence was admitted. In an appropriate case, the judge's direction may need to underline that given the course taken by the trial, the evidence of bad character is by then of very little weight indeed.'

The Explanatory Notes on the Act state (para. 382): 'Evidence admissible under Section 101(1)(g)—as under Section 101(1)(f)—will primarily go to the credit of the defendant. Currently a jury would be directed that evidence admitted in similar circumstances, under the 1898 Act, goes only to credibility and is not relevant to the issue of guilt. Such directions have been criticised and the new statutory scheme does not specify that this evidence is to be treated in such a way. However, it is expected that judges will explain the purpose for which the evidence is being put forward and direct the jury about the sort of weight that can be placed on it.'

Thus it is difficult to argue that that the new statute has simplified the law, since added to the distinction implied in this question between credibility and guilt is that also between dishonesty and untruthfulness. The Court of Appeal in *Hanson* (para. 13) pointed out the distinction between untruthfulness and propensity to dishonesty remarking that 'Parliament deliberately chose the word "untruthful" to convey a different meaning, reflecting a defendant's account of his behaviour, or lies told when committing the offence. Previous convictions, whether for offences of dishonesty or otherwise, are therefore only likely to be capable of showing a propensity to be untruthful where, in the present case, truthfulness is an issue and, in the earlier case, either there was a plea of not guilty, and the defendant gave an account, on arrest, in interview, or in evidence, which the jury must have disbelieved, or the way in which the offence was committed shows a propensity for untruthfulness, for example by making false representations.' Emson (2008, p. 83) comments'. . .so the question is not whether the previous conviction is for an offence of dishonesty but whether the *facts* of the previous extraneous misconduct demonstrate a propensity for untruthfulness'. He also points out that 'the judgment of the Court of Appeal in *R* v *Highton* [2005] 1 WLR 3472 suggests that . . . 'any evidence of the accused's "bad character" admitted under s101(1)(d) with reference to s103(1)(a) which, logically, has a bearing on his truthfulness may be taken into consideration by the tribunal of fact when considering the accused's credibility (or the credibility of the defence) even though the evidence could not have been admitted under s101(1)(d) with reference to s103(1)(b)'. This approach was confirmed in *R* v *Campbell* [2007] 1 WLR 2798, in which

Highton was applied. Evidence of previous convictions was admitted to show that the defendant had a propensity for violence against women. The judge in the summing-up followed the Judicial Studies Board's specimen directions. The jury were also directed that the evidence of the previous convictions was relevant to his lack of credibility as well as propensity to commit crimes of the sort with which he was charged. On appeal the Court of Appeal did not accept that the judge had erred in directing that his previous convictions were relevant to credibility. The court stated: 'The summing up that assists the jury with the relevance of bad character will accord with commonsense and assist them to avoid prejudice that is at odds with this . . . It is open to the jury to attach significance to it in any respect in which it is relevant. To direct them only to have regard to it for some purposes and to disregard its relevance in other respects would be to revert to the unsatisfactory practices that prevailed under the old law. . .'

The summary and case note in the Criminal Law Review (*R* v *Campbell* (2008) **Crim LR 303**) puts the situation as follows: 'the change in the law relating to character evidence introduced by the 2003 Act should be the occasion for simplifying the directions to juries. Earlier decisions were unhelpful and should not be cited. Where evidence of bad character was introduced the jury should be given assistance as to its relevance that was tailored to the individual case . . . once evidence was admitted through one of the s. 101(1) gateways, the use to which it could be put by the jury depended on the matters to which it was admitted, not the gateway through which it had been admitted.'

The Criminal Law Review comment (by AJR, p. 306) notes that this approach does not fit will with the statutory framework since '. . .if evidence of previous convictions adduced under s. 101(1)(d) and s. 103(1)(a) in order to show propensity to commit offences of the type charged are also treated as tending to show that a defendant is generally less likely to tell the truth, as the court suggests, there would be little work left for s. 103(1)(b)'. Lord Phillips CJ in this case stated that '. . . the only circumstances in which there is likely to be an important issue as to whether a defendant has a propensity to tell lies is where telling lies is an element of the offence charged. Even then, the propensity to tell lies is only likely to be significant if the lying is in the context of committing criminal offences, in which case the evidence is likely to be admissible under s. 103(1)(a)'.

Highton and *Campbell* suggest the new law has brought prosecutorial advantages, although by contrast directions on other cases such as *R* v *Meyer* [2006] **EWCA Crim 1126** do indicate a more restrictive approach to lack of credibility particularly s.101(1)(d). Thus while the new Act may have moved away from over-technical distinctions of evidential worth, it has aroused criticism as sacrificing fairness for intellectual coherence and the early case-law suggests that the courts are, as in *Highton,* continuing to blur propensity and credibility, leaving Munday (2006, p. 318) to ask 'Does the old common law "credibility" concept then survive the 2003 Act?'.

Mirfield (2008, p. 1) suggests that the court is taking 'a more coherent view of what items of bad character really do go to incredibility of the accused's evidence'.

He pointed out that that would rule out offences other than those of dishonesty but might rule out even such offences if the charge in question did not involve an element of deception. He considered such a broad approach could also be applied to s. 101(1)(g).

The current position therefore seems to be a move away from technically complex distinctions between credibility and propensity to one where the starting point is the relevance of the evidence to the issue. This is a welcome move away from the earlier often frustrated attempts to distinguish propensity and truthfulness.

Question 4

'There can be no doubt that it was the intention of parliament to relax the strictness of the common law by dropping any requirement for enhanced relevance for similar fact evidence!' (I. Dennis *The Law of Evidence* (2007) at page 803).

Comment on this observation in the light of the provisions of s.101(1)(d) of **Criminal Justice Act 2003**.

Commentary

You are being asked here to make a critical review and evaluation of the various tests for admissibility of evidence of extraneous misconduct by the defendant. In order to answer this question well, students need to be aware of the history of the law and why it was changed in **CJA 2003**.

Answer plan

- Common law background: weaknesses in Lord Hershell's proposition in *Makin*
- Move towards probative force test—*Boardman*
- *DPP* v *P* and *R* v *H* illustrate further erosion of *Boardman*
- Reform of the law in this area—**CJA 2003** and recent case-law *Highton, Hanson, Weir*
- Academic comment, Munday (2006), Waterman and Dempster (2006).

Suggested answer

Roberts and Zuckerman (2004, p. 515) point out in relation to 'similar fact evidence (SFE)' that 'Even after sections 99 and 101–103 of the **CJA 2003** have abolished the common law SFE rule and replaced it with a new statutory framework of admissibility it would not be surprising if lawyers and judges continued to make reference to "similar facts" in certain types of cases.' However, as Munday (2006) and Waterman and Dempster (2006) show, deriving a coherent set of principles from the new law is complex. Munday (2006, p. 318) says that trying to extract meaning is 'not wholly unlike shovelling smoke'.

This is an area where the terminology keeps shifting, as Murphy points out. To some extent the terminology has survived after the legal rationale for the concept has been disapproved. Thus although the expression 'Similar Fact' evidence was criticised in *DPP* v *P* it was still employed by academic commentators. The Law Commission in its report confirmed that the key concept is relevance. The Commission pointed out that the evidence of previous misconduct or of discreditable propensity on the part of the defendant ran the risk of misleading a jury. First, it may be thought to be more relevant than it is and the jury exhibits a 'reasoning prejudice'. Second, the actual relevance of the evidence to the facts in issue may be discounted and 'moral prejudice' may lead the jury to condemn the defendant as a disreputable person. The history of this area of law, however, shows the difficulty of defining tests to assess the weight of the contested evidence. The trend has been towards lowering the threshold of admissibility most recently in s. 101(1)(d) of the **Criminal Justice Act 2003**. A review of the pre-2003 cases does help illuminate how the law has developed. As Dennis (2007, p. 844) points out, the earlier cases are not binding, '. . . all the common law rules governing the admissibility of evidence of bad character have been abolished by s. 99 of the 2003 Act . . . But the principles canvassed in the cases may prove helpful if and when the same problems arise under the [Criminal Justice] Act [2003].'

Lord Herschell in the leading, case *Makin* set out a presumption of exclusion of evidence tending to show that the accused has been guilty of criminal acts other than that with which he is being tried, and then provided various examples where this presumption could be displaced. In this case the evidence of previous instances where the Makins had fostered children for money and then buried them in the garden when the money was exhausted rebutted the defence that they were involved in a series of accidents. The evidence went beyond that of showing a disposition to act in a certain way. The 'forbidden chain of reasoning' did not allow an argument from disposition to guilt but evidence of disposition may become admissible if it sufficiently lowered the likelihood of an issue in the case.

Lord Herschell in this early case recognised the importance of the concept of relevance. He stated (at p. 65):

> It is undoubtedly not competent for the prosecution to adduce evidence tending to show that the accused has been guilt of criminal acts other than those covered by the indictment, for the purpose of leading to the conclusion that the accused is a person likely from his criminal conduct or character to have committed the offence for which he is being tried. On the other hand, the mere fact that the evidence adduced tends to show the commission of other crimes does not render it inadmissible if it be relevant to an issue before the jury, and it may be so relevant if it bears upon the question of whether the acts alleged to constitute the crime charged in the

indictment were designed or accidental, or to rebut a defence which would otherwise be open to the accused.

However, the development of the law showed the difficulty of putting flesh on the concept of relevance and suggests that in part the approach of the courts was one that was naturally a consequence of prevailing attitudes and perceptions as much as a search for a perfect legal formulation.

Lord Herschell's proposition contained several weaknesses. First, despite *Makin*, in a number of cases the reasoning was clearly from disposition to guilt. Evidence was adduced for the purpose of showing that the accused is a person likely from his past conduct to have committed the offence charged. *R v Straffen* [1952] 2 QB 911, *R v Ball* [1911] AC 47 and *Thompson v R* [1918] AC 221 are instances of this. In *Ball*, the evidence of earlier incestuous acts between a brother and sister charged with incest was held admissible to show a propensity to commit incest. However, the evidence was admissible only because it went to an issue in the case, namely the defence of innocent association. Again, in *Straffen* the evidence of previous murders was admissible not to show that the accused was a persistent strangler but to show that it defied coincidence that the same person who had committed the earlier murders had not also strangled Linda Bowyer. It is arguable therefore that a recitation of Lord Herschell's propositions as an explanation of how such evidence is admissible is misleading because in extreme cases reasoning from disposition is allowed.

A further objection to the formulation in *Makin* was the emphasis on categories of admissibility. This led in subsequent cases to much effort being expended into fitting the cases under somewhat artificial headings such as proof of identity, system or design. Thus the move away from the *Makin* emphasis on the purpose for which the evidence was admitted did not achieve a great deal more clarity.

As a result of the criticisms, as well as what Colin Tapper ([*Cross and Tapper on Evidence*, 9th edn] 1995, p. 1223) described as the 'distaste for the difficulty of operating a rule cast in such terms', the House of Lords reformulated the rule in *DPP v Boardman* [1975] AC 421. Lord Wilberforce stated that:

[t]he basic principle must be that the admission of Similar Fact evidence . . . is exceptional and requires a strong degree of probative force. This probative force is derived, if at all, from the circumstance that the facts testified by the several witnesses bear to each other . . . a striking similarity . . .

With this decision it was made clear that the basis of the admissibility of Similar Fact evidence was not dependent on whether it fell within the fixed categories but on whether there was a strong degree of probative force in the evidence. The test of admissibility, therefore, was whether the evidence of previous offence or disposition sought to be admitted is strikingly similar to the offence with which the accused is being tried and whether the probative value of this evidence outweighs its prejudicial effect. On the facts of the case, Lord Wilberforce found the case to be on the borderline of the striking similarity test.

Although the test of admissibility as set out in *Boardman* appeared straightforward, the application of it by the courts was erratic in some instances. An illustration of this can be seen in *R* v *Novac* (1976) 65 Cr App R 107 and *R* v *Johanssen* (1977) 65 Cr App R 101, where on very similar facts, the courts reached different conclusions. This apparent conflict was recognised by the Court of Appeal in *R* v *Scarrott* [1978] QB 1016, where the court made it clear that each case had to be looked at on its own facts. Scarman LJ in *Scarrott* found it difficult to explain how the inconsistency arose.

Hoffmann in *Boardman* considered that there was a need for at least one more House of Lords case 'before the law can be said to be established on a simple and rational basis'. Mirfield considered that there was 'both the need finally to lay to rest the ghost of *Makin* and the need for an authoritative statement of a more simplified, helpful and logical structure for the admission of such evidence'. The shift from *Makin* had been evidenced in two subsequent House of Lords' decisions.

In *DPP* v *P* [1991] 2 AC 447, the accused was presented with four charges of rape and four charges of incest against each of his two daughters. The Court of Appeal allowed the accused's appeal against conviction on the charge of one rape and all the counts of incest in respect of his two daughters. The Court of Appeal allowed the appeal on the basis that there was a lack of striking similarity between the offences committed against each daughter. The prosecution appealed against this decision and the House of Lords allowed the appeal. There was no need for the evidence to be strikingly similar in order for evidence of Similar Fact to be admitted. The test was one of whether the evidence has sufficient probative value to outweigh the prejudicial effect which is a question of degree in each case. In the instant case, the issue was whether there had been an offence, not who committed it. Following the implementation of the CJA there is arguably some confusion about the status of this case. It was cited in *Hanson*, but in *R* v *Weir* (2006) 1 WLR 1885 Kennedy LJ said the test in *P* was obsolete.

In *R* v *H* [1995] 2 AC 596, the accused was convicted of indecent assault and of committing gross indecency against his adopted daughter and having sexual intercourse with her when she was aged 13. He was also convicted of indecent assault on his stepdaughter. There was no suggestion that the offences were strikingly similar. The only issue was whether the evidence which was adduced in relation to one daughter could be used in relation to the other daughter.

The House of Lords decided that where there was an application to exclude alleged Similar Fact evidence and there is a risk of collusion between the victims, the court had to approach the question of admissibility on the basis that the Similar Fact evidence was true and the test in *DPP* v *P* was applicable. It would be up to the jury to decide whether the evidence was contaminated by the risk of collusion.

The change in the law, incorporated in the **Criminal Justice Act 2003**, ss. 107, 109, made the possibility of collusion a question of weight for the jury to decide in its verdict rather than relevance for the judge to decide when deciding whether or not to admit the evidence. In effect this upholds the approach to relevance generally where fact-finding is a mater for the jury. However, it is surely arguable that this is not just the outcome of more conscientious legal analysis of relevance but in part due to the need for society to prosecute serious offences more successfully, without putting alleged victims through the trauma of a voir dire as well as a trial. As Munday (2006) points out, in *Highton* the Court of Appeal was 'won over' to the view that propensity evidence was admissible under s. 101(1)(g) as well as (d), thus increasing admissibility. Thus in the recent case of *Weir* a caution received five years previously for taking an indecent photograph was admissible under s. 101(1)(a), as 'important explanatory evidence', on a charge of indecent assault on a child.

The Law Commission in its Report (No. 273) argued that the rules on Similar Fact were difficult to apply and proposed a codification of the law. It proposed that evidence which goes to a matter in issue may be admissible, applying the 'substantial value' and the 'interest of justice' test. Dennis (2007, p. 803) points out that the government rejected the Law Commission Report on this as too conservative. 'None of the proposed requirements for leave, substantial probative value or admission of the evidence in the interests of justice despite the risk of prejudice were incorporated in gateway (d).' The test is simple relevance. It is noticeable that the **Criminal Justice Act 2003** in reforming the law in this area gives much prominence to the concept of relevance rather than fine-tuning complicated phrases. Under section 101(1)(d) the defendant's bad character is admissible if 'it is relevant to an important matter in issue between the defendant and the prosecution'. Thus the word 'substantial' has been left out. Section 103(1) and (3) defines 'matter in issue between the defendant and the prosecution' as including, '(a) the question whether the defendant has a propensity to commit offences of the kind with which he is charged, except where his having such a propensity makes it no more likely that he is guilty of the offence; (b) the question whether the defendant has a propensity to be untruthful except where it is not suggested that defendant's case is untruthful in any respect'. The subsection specifies that where s. (1)(a) applies a defendant's propensity to commit offences of the kind with which he is charged should be established by evidence that he had been convicted of an offence of the same description as the one with which he is charged or an offence of the same category as the one with which he is charged. The section also specifies that the Secretary of State may make orders for prescribing particular offences as offences of the same category—a proposal which has alarmed some commentators. Under s. 101(3) there is a test of fairness for admissibility and the court must not admit such evidence if on application by the defendant to exclude it, it appears to the court that the admission of the evidence would have such an adverse effect on the fairness of the proceedings that the court ought not to admit it. The court must consider this even if the defendant has not made an application.

The Court of Appeal in *Hanson* set out the way in which propensity may now be demonstrated.

There is no minimum number of events necessary to demonstrate such a propensity. The fewer the number of conditions the weaker is likely to be the evidence of propensity. A simple previous conviction for an offence of the same description or category will often not show propensity. But it may do so where, for example, it shows a tendency to unusual behaviour or where its circumstances demonstrate probative force in relation to the offence charged (Compare *DPP* v *P* [1991] 2 AC 447 at 460E to 461A). Child sexual abuse or fire setting are comparatively clear examples of such unusual behaviour but we attempt no exhaustive list. Circumstances demonstrating probative force are not confined to those sharing striking similarity. So, a single conviction for shoplifting will not, without more, be admissible to show propensity to steal. But if the modus operandi has significant features shared by the offence charged it may show propensity.

Durston (2008, p. 200) comments on the effect of this decision. 'The approach adopted in *Hanson* is certainly at variance to that originally anticipated (in October 2004) by David Blunkett, the then Home Secretary, who suggested that there would be a "strong presumption" (albeit rebuttable) that previous convictions that were in the same category as that subsequently being tried should be admitted.' On the other hand, he notes that this restrictive approach to admissibility was not adopted in *R* v *Awaritefe* [2007] **EWCA Crim 706** where the court was more ready to admit previous offences as showing propensity although they were less serious than the current charge and took place some time ago. This case, comments Durston (p. 200) is 'indicative of the range of the trial judge's discretion'.

The Act now includes a specific reference to propensity to untruthfulness, section 103(1)(b). Tapper points out (2004, p. 548):

> In this case there is a stark, and quite explicit contradiction between the Law Commission's draft Bill and the Act. Whereas s. 8(5) provided: 'For the purposes of this section, whether the defendant has a propensity to be untruthful is not to be regarded as an issue in the proceedings.' Section 103(1) provides that matters in issue between the defendant and the prosecutor include '(b) the question whether the defendant has a propensity to be untruthful, except where it is not suggested that the defendant's case is untruthful in any respect.' It is this provision which so expands the ambit of this gateway. Under cl19 of the Law Commission's Bill not only was credibility limited to the situation in which an attack was made on the truthfulness of another, but care was devoted to detailing the factors needed to be taken into consideration. Section 103 by contrast is quite open-ended in its application and fails to include any of the relevant factors.

However, the decision in *Hanson* suggests that the courts may approach this issue cautiously. The court stated:

> As to propensity to untruthfulness, this, it seems to us, is not the same as propensity to dishonesty. It is to be assumed, bearing in mind the frequency with which the words honest and dishonest appear in the criminal law, that Parliament deliberately chose the word 'untruthful' to convey a different meaning, reflecting a defendant's

account of his behaviour or lies told when committing an offence. Previous convictions, whether for offences of dishonesty or otherwise are therefore only likely to be capable of showing a propensity to be untruthful where, in the present case, truthfulness is an issue and, in the earlier case, either there was a plea of not guilty and the defendant gave an account on arrest, in interview or in evidence which the jury disbelieved, or the way in which the offence was committed shows a propensity for untruthfulness, for example by the making of false representations.

Before assessing the impact of the new law Cross and Tapper (2008, p. 423) reviewed criticisms of the earlier provisions. Noting that, 'the test eventually adopted for the admission of evidence of the accused's bad character in chief was roughly that it should be more probative then prejudicial', Tapper continued, 'It could indeed be argued that the test, as formulated in terms of weighing probative force against prejudicial effect, was incoherent.' It was clear that 'prejudicial effect' must mean more than that the admission of the evidence would lead to an increased chance of conviction, and it was usually accepted that it meant that the trier of fact would attach more weight to the evidence than it deserved.

It is questionable whether the new law has succeeded in removing this unfairness. There are some indications that the courts have adopted a more cautious approach to admitting evidence of propensity. Thus in *Hanson* the court stated that even when offences were categorised as being of the same description, this was neither necessary, nor sufficient, to justify admission. The issue was still whether the convictions established propensity and if that propensity was relevant to the accused's guilt. But relevance again is a matter of degree. In *Edwards* the trial judge regarded convictions of over 20 years ago as not admissible, however relevant the convictions were.

The Comment by Dennis illustrates the continuing difficulty of establishing clear guidelines for the admissibility of disposition evidence. There is an inevitable conflict between fairness to the defendant, endorsed in art. 6 of the European Convention on Human Rights, and the public need to prosecute offenders successfully. As McEwan (1998, p. 52) points out, 'concepts of relevance or probative value are highly subjective'. The development of the case-law shows the intractable problem of assessing the weight of the evidence. Waterman and Dempster see the current approach as a 'half way position between the old principles and the new' (2006, p. 627). They decry the absence of a 'logical analytical basis' in recent judgments. This is not, however, a matter of semantics. In part the development of the law has reflected different social values which have of course been reflected by the judiciary. Just as the notorious case of *Thompson* [1918] AC 221 reflects prejudice and ignorance, so the lowering of the threshold in P and then even further in the **Criminal Justice Act 2003** reflects a growing awareness of the needs of victims and of the potential value of children's evidence. Perhaps too much attention has been directed to relevance as an aspect of admissibility. Just as important perhaps are clear judicial directions on matters of prejudice as well as logic on how the jury should view such evidence.

Finally it should be noted that the transparency of the reasoning in these cases is enabled by the requirement that reasons for decisions should be given in open court when making a ruling under s. 101.

Question 5

Nicholas, a taxi driver, is charged with criminally damaging a small plantation of palm trees in a country park. His fingerprints are found on a note which was pinned to the gate of the plantation which called for 'British trees only to be planted in British parks'. Nicholas denies the offence and claims that he had picked up a passenger who asked to be dropped at the park. He claims that the customer asked him to put the note in the glove compartment of the car and that he did not know what was written in it. Nicholas denies having entered the park and claims he drove away after dropping the customer off. Advise the prosecution on the following matters:

(a) Whether they can adduce evidence of three previous acquittals of Nicholas on charges of criminal damage of foreign trees in country parks. On each occasion his defence had been that he had dropped a customer at the park.

(b) Whether evidence is admissible that Nicholas is a member of a group called 'Keep our Flora British' (KFB).

Commentary

(a) The prosecution is likely to rely on s. 101(1)(d) **Criminal Justice Act 2003**. Bad character evidence is admissible if 'it is relevant to an important matter in issue between the defendant and the prosecution'. Section 103 defines this as including (i) the question whether the defendant has a propensity to commit offences of the kind with which he is charged, except where his having such a propensity makes it no more likely that he is guilty of the offence; (ii) the question whether the defendant has a propensity to be untruthful, except where it is not suggested that the defendant's case is untruthful in any respect.

(b) The prosecution will try to argue that Nicholas's membership of this organisation increases the likelihood of his guilt and that s. 101(1)(d) applies.

Answer plan

(a)

- Are previous acquittals admissible under s. 101(1)(d) **CJA 2003**?—see also *R v Z*
- What is the relevance of the number of acquittals?
- Does the categories of offences order apply?

(b)

- Does bad character evidence under **CJA 2003** include non-criminal behaviour?
- Applicability of common law cases, e.g. *R* v *Lewis* (1982) 76 Cr App R 33, *R* v *Barrington* [1981] 1 WLR 419
- Post-**CJA 2003** cases *R* v *Edwards* [2005] EWCA Crim 3244, *R* v *Hanson* [2005] EWCA Crim 824

Suggested answer

Here the prosecution will be helped by the Explanatory Notes on the statute and the decisions in *Hanson* and *Highton*. The Explanatory Note reads 'evidence might be relevant to one of a number of issues in a case. For example, it might help the prosecution to prove the defendant's guilt of the offence by establishing their involvement or state of mind or by rebutting the defendant's explanation of his conduct.' In *Hanson* Rose LJ set out a three-stage test in relation to propensity.

1. Does the history of conviction(s) establish a propensity to commit offences of the kind charged?
2. Does that propensity make it more likely that the defendant committed the offence charged?
3. Is it unjust to rely on the conviction(s) of the same description or category; and in any event will the proceedings be unfair if they are admitted?

(a) The **Criminal Justice Act 2003 (Categories of Offences) Order 2004** (SI 3346/2004) lists two categories, namely, theft and sexual offences against a person under the age of 16, on which it is not unjust to rely. The prosecution will not therefore be aided by these categorisations in this case.

The other problem is that the previous behaviour is based on a record of acquittals not convictions. In the pre-2003 Act case of *R* v *Z* [2003] 3 All ER 385 the House of Lords admitted previous acquittals on a charge of rape since they had a direct bearing on the question of consent in the current charge. The Explanatory Note to the 2003 Act makes it clear that the definition of bad character is broad. It reads:

> The definition is therefore intended to include evidence such as previous convictions as well as evidence on charges being tried concurrently, and evidence relating to offences for which a person has been charged, when the charge was not prosecuted or for which the person was subsequently acquitted. This reflects the state of the current law. On the latter point in the case of **Z** [2002] 2 AC 483, the House of Lords held that there was no special rule that required the exclusion of evidence that the person had been involved in earlier offences, even if they had been acquitted of those crimes, provided that the evidence was otherwise admissible. Thus if there were a series of attacks and the defendants were acquitted of involvement in them, evidence showing, or tending to show that he had committed those earlier attacks could be given in a later case if it were admissible to establish that he had committed the latest attack. The Act preserves the effect of this decision.

It continued: 'the scheme does not affect the admissibility of evidence of the facts of the offence. This is excluded from the definition, as is evidence of misconduct in connection with the offence.'

The approach taken in **Z** has been confirmed by **R** v **Mustapha (Mohammed Amadu)** **[2007] EWCA Crim 1702**, decided under the **CJA 2003**.

The court has discretion to exclude these acquittals under two sections. Section 101(3) reads: 'the court must not admit evidence under subsection (1)(d) if, on the application by the defendant to excluded, it appears to the court that the admission of the evidence would have such an adverse effect on the fairness of the proceedings that the court ought not to admit it'. On an application to exclude evidence under subsection (3) the court must have regard, in particular, to the length of time between the matters to which that evidence relates and the matters which form the subject of the offence charged. Section 103(2) and (3) reads:

> (2) . . .a defendant's propensity to commit offences of the kind with which he is charged may . . . be established by evidence of (a) an offence on the same description as the one with which he is charged, or (b) an offence of the same category of the one with which he is charged. (3) subsection (2) does not apply in the case of a particular defendant if the court is satisfied by reason of the length of time since the conviction or for any other reason, that it would be unjust for it to apply in his case.

Arguably more information is needed as to how long ago the acquittals were. The fact that there were three, however, makes it more likely that they will be admitted. The prosecution will need to give notice in advance that they wish to put the acquittals in evidence and since they are likely to want to adduce similarities in the defence argument about dropping off customers they will need also to specify these surrounding details. In *Hanson* (para. 17) the Court of Appeal referred to the need to specify surrounding circumstances in the context of convictions but presumably the same point applies to acquittals with even more force, since it is the similarities of the defence which are at issue. The acquittals are likely to be admitted through the gateway of s 101(1)(d). It is uncertain whether the prosecution will also be able to rely on s103(1)(b) which refers to 'the question whether the defendant has a propensity to be untruthful, except where it is not suggested that the defendant's case is untruthful in any respect'. It is clearly the prosecution case that the defendant is putting forward a lying defence and the fact that he had put forward the defence several times before increases the likelihood that his defence is not to be believed. The acquittals in themselves however do not appear to fulfil the requirement for admissibility under s101(1)(b) in that they do not in themselves demonstrate a propensity to be untruthful (see *Hanson*). The judge may have to direct that the acquittals are relevant to his guilt but not to his propensity for untruthfulness.

(b) According to the Explanatory Note bad character can include 'evidence not related to criminal proceedings . . . might include, for example, evidence that a person has a sexual interest in children or is racist'. Nicolas is claiming no involvement with the offence of destroying the trees. The likelihood of his defence that he was in the area but did not engage in the offence would be undermined by evidence that he was a member of an organisation which probably only has a small number of members. It is not of the order of membership of a gardening club for example. Someone who is a member of the KFB is more likely to be involved in direct action on this issue than someone who is not. Bear in mind that evidence does not have to reach certainty but simply increase the likelihood of guilt sufficiently to overcome the obvious prejudice of admitting it. In *R* v *Lewis* (1982) 76 Cr App R 33, membership of the Paedophilia Society was admissible to rebut the defence of innocent association. Arguably here, membership of the KFB is likely to be admitted because it is relevant to the defence of non-involvement. It surely defies coincidence that a person who belonged to such an organisation and who was in the area at the time was not involved in the offence. In *R* v *Barrington* [1981] 1 WLR 419 evidence of prior disreputable but non-criminal actions were admissible since as the court stated (at p. 430) they were 'of positive probative value in assisting to determine the truth of the charges against the appellant'. The prosecution is likely to be allowed to put this evidence to the jury.

Some guidance on what is meant by bad character under the **CJA 2003** has been given in a number of cases. Section 98(1) provides that 'References to . . . evidence of a person's "bad character" are to evidence of, or of a disposition towards, misconduct on his part . . .' Misconduct is defined in s. 112(1) as 'the commission of an offence or other reprehensible behaviour'. The Law Commission report (2002, paras 8.12–8.19) stated that, 'References in this Act to evidence of a person's bad character are references to evidence which shows or tends to show that (a) he has committed an offence, or (b) he has behaved, or is disposed to behave, in a way that, in the opinion of the court, might be viewed with disapproval by a reasonable person.'

It is arguable that Nicholas' membership of the KFB does not fall within this definition. It might therefore be admitted on grounds of relevance and not under CJA 2003. Under *R* v *Kilbourne* [1973] AC 729 evidence is 'relevant' if 'it is logically probative or disprobative of some matter which requires proof'. On the other hand, if the court considers the statute applies it could be argued that s. 101(1)(d) applies and that the membership of KFB may be considered reprehensible. Arguments in favour of admissibility can be found in *R* v *Saleem* [2007] EWCA Crim 1923, which involved possessing disturbing rap lyrics, arguments against in *R* v *Edwards* [2006] 1 WLR 1524, where lawfully possessing an antique firearm was not reprehensible behaviour. As Goudkamp (2008, p. 13) comments, reviewing these and other cases, 'it seems impossible to distil a common denominator from these authorities'.

Additional Reading

Allan, T.R.S., 'Similar Fact Evidence and Disposition: Law, Discretion and Admissibility' (1985) 48 MLR 253.

Cape, E., 'Criminal Justice Act 2003—No Debate?' (2004) *Legal Action* 6–8.

Darbyshire, P., 'Previous Misconduct and Magistrates' Courts' [1997] Crim LR 105.

Durston, G., 'Bad Character Evidence and Non-party Witnesses under the Criminal Justice Act 2003' (2004) 8 E & P 233.

Elliott, D.W., 'Cut-Throat Tactics. The Freedom of an Accused to Prejudice a Co-accused' [1991] Crim LR 5.

Goudkamp, J. 'Bad character evidence and reprehensible behaviour' (2008) E & P 116–39.

Hoffman, L.H., 'Similar Fact after *Boardman*' (1975) 91 LQR 193.

Law Commission Consultation Paper, 'Evidence in Criminal Proceedings: Previous Misconduct of a Defendant' (CP 141) London 1996.

Law Commission Report No. 273 (Cm 5257) 'Evidence of Bad Character in Criminal Proceedings' (2001).

Lloyd-Bostock, S., 'The Effects on Juries of Hearing About the Defendant's Previous Criminal Record: A Simulation Study' [2000] Crim LR 734.

McEwan, J., 'Previous Misconduct at the Crossroads: Which Way Ahead?' [2002] Crim LR 180.

Mirfield, P., 'Similar Facts—*Makin* out?' (1987) CLJ 83.

Mirfield, P., 'The Argument from Consistency for Overruling *Selvey*' (1991) CLJ 490.

Mirfield, P, 'Character, Credibility and Untruthfulness' (2008) 124 LQR 1

Munday, R., 'Reflections on the Criminal Evidence Act 1898' [1985] CLJ 62.

Munday, R. 'Stepping beyond the Bounds of Credibility. The Application of s. 1(f)(ii) of the Criminal Evidence Act 1898' [1986] Crim LR 511.

Munday, R. 'The Paradox of Cross-Examination for Credit, Too Close for Comfort' [1994] CLJ 303.

Munday, R. 'What Constitutes a Good Character?' [1997] Crim LR 247.

Munday, R., 'What Constitutes "Other Reprehensible Behaviour" under the Bad Character Provisions of the Criminal Justice Act' 2003 (2005) Crim LR 24.

Munday, R., 'The Purposes of Gateway (g): Yet Another Problematic of the Criminal Justice Act 2003' (2006) Crim LR 300.

Redmayne, M., 'The Relevance of Bad Character' (2002) 61 CLJ 684.

Roberts, P., 'Acquitted Misconduct Evidence and Double Jeopardy Principles, From *Sambasivan* to Z' [2000] Crim LR 952.

Seabrooke, S, 'The Vanishing Torch—Blurring the Line Between Credit and Issue' [1999] Crim LR 387.

Spencer, J.R., *Evidence of Bad Character* (Hart, London, 2008).

Tapper, C. *The Meaning of s. 1(f)(i) of the Criminal Evidence Act 1898' in* Crime Proof and Punishment (ed. Tapper) (London, 1981), p. 296.

Tapper, C., 'The Erosion of *Boardman v DPP*, (1995) NLJ 1223' (1987) 101 LQR.

Tapper, C. 'The Relevance of *Jones v DPP*' (1988) 51 MLR 785.

Tapper, C., 'The Probative Force of Similar Fact Evidence' (1992) 108 LQR 26.

Tapper, C. 'Criminal Justice Act 2003(3) Evidence of Bad Character' (2004) Crim LR 533.

Wasik, M., 'The Vital Importance of Certain Previous Convictions' (2001) Crim LR 363.

Waterman, A., and Dempster, T., 'Bad Character: Feeling Our Way One Year On' (2006) Crim LR 614.

Zuckerman A.A.S., 'Similar Fact Evidence—The Unobservable Rule' (1987) 101 LQR.

5

Hearsay

Introduction

The rule against hearsay is historically one of the great exclusionary rules underlying the law of evidence. Little remains of the rule, however, in civil law, after the passage of the **Civil Evidence Acts 1968, 1972 and 1995**. The **Criminal Justice Act 2003**, repealing sections of the **Criminal Justice Act 1988**, has massively eroded the rule in criminal cases. This chapter will guide you to key sections of the current law. It will give a historical overview of the development of the law in order to help you understand the current provisions.

It is important that students are familiar with the meaning of hearsay. In **R** v **Sharp** [1988] 1 WLR 7, in the House of Lords, Lord Havers adopted the definition of hearsay used by Cross (1985), namely, that it was 'an assertion other than one made by a person while giving oral evidence in the proceedings . . . as evidence of any fact asserted'. Murphy (2008, p. 206) gives what he describes as a 'longer, but perhaps more descriptive alternative definition':

> Evidence from any witness which consists of what another person stated (whether verbally, in writing, or by any other method of assertion such as a gesture) on any prior occasions, is inadmissible, if its only relevant purpose is to prove that any fact so stated by that person on that prior occasion is true. Such a statement may, however, be admitted for any relevant purpose other than proving the truth of facts stated in it.

This applies only to civil cases. The **Civil Evidence Act 1995** gave the first statutory definition of hearsay. Section 1(2) states:

> In this Act (a) hearsay means a statement otherwise than by a person while giving oral evidence in the proceedings which is tendered as evidence of the matters stated; and (b) references to hearsay include hearsay of whatever degree.

Section 13 provides that 'statement means any representation of fact or opinion, however made'.

As far as criminal cases are concerned, the definition of hearsay (although without actually using the word) is to be found in s. 114(1) **Criminal Justice Act 2003**:

In criminal proceedings a statement not made in oral evidence in the proceedings is admissible as evidence of any matter stated . . .

Section 115 states: '(2) A statement is any representation of fact or opinion made by a person by whatever means; and it includes a representation made in a sketch, photofit or other pictorial format. (3) A matter stated is one to which this chapter applies if (and only if) the purpose, or one of the purposes, of the person making the statement appears to the court to have been—(a) to cause another person to believe the matter, or (b) to cause another person to act or a machine to operate on the basis that the matter is as stated.'

The effect of this definition, which in many ways parallels that in the **Civil Evidence Act 1995**, is to settle the question that caused some considerable problems in the common law, namely, that implied assertions are not hearsay.

It must be appreciated that not all out of court statements are hearsay. It will be hearsay where it is an out of court assertion (whether orally, in writing, or by any other means) *and* it is admitted to prove the truth of the facts stated therein. An out of court statement will not be hearsay, where, for example, it is produced in court simply to assert that it was made, not that it was true. This was the case in the Privy Council decision in *Subramaniam* v *Public Prosecutor* [1956] 1 WLR 965 and *Ratten* v *R* [1972] AC 378 (see also *R* v *Nelson* (2004)). Other examples where the statement will not be regarded as hearsay include statements admissible as confirming other evidence, statements as evidence of identity (although they are included in the **CJA 2003** as exceptions to hearsay) or origin, or statements which are admitted to prove that it was made or was made in a particular way. It is also not hearsay to admit a prior statement to prove its falsity rather than the truth: *Khan* v *R* [1967] 1 AC 454. *R* v *Gilfoyle* [1996] 3 All ER 583 demonstrates the difficulties in distinguishing hearsay and original evidence.

With regard to the rule relating to implied as opposed to express assertions, until relatively recently, it was unclear whether such assertions fell under the hearsay rule. The decision of the majority of the House of Lords in *R* v *Kearley* [1992] 2 AC 228 held that such assertions were within the hearsay rule and would therefore be inadmissible unless they fell within one of the exceptions to the rule. The important question to ask is what is the task the statement is required to perform. There was no direct evidence of drug dealing, simply evidence from the police witness who reported what the callers had said in requesting drugs. This amounted to an implied assertion that the defendant was a dealer and was therefore inadmissible hearsay. The effect of s. 115 **CJA 2003** is to repeal this controversial decision. Implied assertions are not hearsay.

There were a number of common law exceptions to the non-admissibility of hearsay, the important ones included statements made as part of the *res gestae*, dying declarations, and declarations against interest. Most are preserved in **CJA 2003**. These include statements that are:

- part of the *res gestae*, i.e. related to a specific event, including the alleged crime
- related to the maker's state of mind or emotion, or physical state
- related to the maker's performance of an act
- made by persons since deceased (**not** preserved in **CJA 2003**)
- made in furtherance of common purpose

It is worth giving a brief historical overview of the gradual statutory erosion of the rule against hearsay.

Early inroads were made in the field of criminal law by the Criminal Evidence Act 1965, brought in after the House of Lords confirmed in *Myers* v *DPP* **[1965] AC 1001** that however absurd the results of its application, further exceptions to the hearsay rule could only be made by Parliament. This was a limited measure allowing documentary records of a trade or business to be admitted as evidence where direct oral evidence of the facts recorded was not available for specified reasons. It was followed in 1968 by a much more sweeping measure in the civil law field, namely the Civil Evidence Act 1968. This created a new code covering oral and written hearsay statements, as well as evidence produced by computers. The 1968 Act which applied only to hearsay statements of fact provided for a complicated notice procedure by the party seeking to adduce hearsay evidence. Another Civil Evidence Act, in 1972, extended the principles to hearsay opinion. The Civil Evidence Act 1995 abolished the rule in civil proceedings. Though such evidence is admissible, the rules of court provide for the giving of notice that it is to be adduced. Failure to give notice in accordance with the rules will affect the *weight* to be attached to the evidence and could be penalised in costs. Where a hearsay statement is adduced, the other parties can call the maker as a witness and cross-examine him. The Act spells out in section 4 the considerations which are relevant to the weighing of hearsay evidence. These are:

(a) whether it would have been reasonable and practicable for the party by whom the evidence was adduced to have produced the maker of the original statement as a witness;

(b) whether the original statement was made contemporaneously with the occurrence or existence of the matters stated;

(c) whether the evidence involves multiple hearsay;

(d) whether any person involved had any motive to conceal or misrepresent matters;

(e) whether the original statement was an edited account, or was made in collaboration with another or for a particular purpose; and

(f) whether the circumstances in which the evidence is adduced as hearsay are such as to suggest an attempt to prevent proper evaluation of its weight.

Hearsay evidence of a witness who is being called in the proceedings can only be admitted with leave of the court or to rebut a suggestion that his evidence has been fabricated. The Act also simplifies the procedure for the production of business records, providing in s. 9 that a document which is shown to form part of the records of a business or public authority may be received in evidence in civil proceedings without further proof. Its status as part of a business record must be certified by an officer of the business or public authority.

In criminal cases, major changes came in 1984 with the **Police and Criminal Evidence Act 1984 (PACE)** replacing the provisions of the 1965 Act and itself in turn substituted by provisions in the **Criminal Justice Act 1988**. Section 69 of **PACE**, covering the procedure for the admission of computer records was repealed by s. 60 of the **Youth Justice and Criminal Evidence Act 1999**.

Section 23 of the 1988 Act admitted the first-hand documentary hearsay where the maker was not available to give evidence and there was an acceptable reason for not calling him. Section 24 of the **Criminal Justice Act 1988** widened the scope of admissible multiple documentary hearsay to include documents created or received in the course of trade, business, occupation, profession or office, paid or unpaid. Section 25 and s. 26 of the 1988 Act provided for the exercise of judicial discretion over admissibility of hearsay documents.

Hearsay was thus an area where piecemeal reform was the order of the day. However, the pace of change has now accelerated. The Law Commission recommended that hearsay evidence be admitted in criminal trials if the interests of justice require it (see 'Evidence in Criminal Proceedings: Hearsay and Related Topics', Law Commission Report No. 245 (Cm 3670, 1997)); this led to a comprehensive reform in the **Criminal Justice Act 2003**. The Act in essence preserves the rule but increases the number of exceptions and safeguards. It provides a comprehensive regime for hearsay.

Table 10 gives an overview of the changes to hearsay introduced by the **Criminal Justice Act 2003**. The second column gives the earlier position under the common law and **Criminal Justice Act 1988** and the third column the position under the **Criminal Justice Act 2003**, which repeals Part 2 of the **Criminal Justice Act 1988**.

Table 10 Criminal hearsay rules: a brief history

Aspect of hearsay	Common law/CJA 1988	Criminal Justice Act 2003
Definition	'. . . an assertion other than one made by a person while giving oral evidence in the proceedings is inadmissible as evidence of any fact or opinion asserted'. (*Cross on Evidence*)	Statement not made orally in the proceedings, tendered as evidence of any matter stated (s. 114, s. 115, s. 121)
Admissibility	Inadmissible unless fell within common law or statutory exceptions	Admissible under statute, or preserved common law exceptions or after court has considered provisions in s. 114 including 'interests of justice'. See inclusionary discretion below
Implied assertions	Inadmissible hearsay (*Kearley*)	Non-hearsay (s. 115(3))
Common law exceptions	Included confessions, *res gestae*, dying declarations, common enterprise, public documents, statements against pecuniary interest by persons since deceased	Specifically preserved, s. 118, except dying declarations and statements against interest. Dying declarations arguably come under the *res gestae* exception.
Expert evidence	Experts' reports were admissible with leave if witness not attending court (s. 30), section not repealed	Experts may rely on statements prepared by other persons, at trial judge's discretion (s. 127)

(continued overleaf)

Table 10 *(continued)*

Oral hearsay statements	Only admissible under common law exceptions	May be admissible (s. 116) if witness unavailable
First-hand written hearsay	Were admissible (s. 23) if statutory reason for not calling witness with leave of court	May be admissible if statutory reason for not calling witness. Permissible reasons extended beyond those in s. 23 **CJA 1988** to include fear of death or injury to another person or financial loss (s. 116) admitted with leave of court.
Multiple hearsay non-business documents	Were not admissible s. 23	May be admissible under s. 121.
Multiple hearsay business documents	Were admissible s. 24 with leave of the court (ss. 25, 26); supplier must have personal knowledge of fact	May be admissible (s. 117). No need for leave of court (s. 121). Documents do not have to form part of a record. Supplier must have personal knowledge of fact.
Statements prepared for criminal proceedings	Were admissible under s. 23 or (s. 24) if specified reason for not calling witness and with leave of court	May be admissible if specified reason for not calling witness (s. 117(4))
Exclusionary discretion	See ss. 25, 26 **CJA 1988**, s. 78 **PACE**	See s. 126(1). Also s. 125 provides judge must direct acquittal if case rests wholly or partly on hearsay and evidence provided by statement is so unconvincing that, considering its importance to the case against the defendant, a conviction could be unsafe
Inclusionary discretion	None	Introduced; see s. 114(1)(d)
Credibility of absent witness	Evidence concerning credibility was admissible (Schedule 2)	Evidence concerning credibility is admissible s. 124(4)
Notice		Procedure under s. 132(3) (cf. Civil Hearsay); rules of Court may specify.

Safeguards under the **Criminal Justice Act 2003**

As Doak and McGourley point out (2008, p. 242), one of the greatest concerns about the use of hearsay evidence generally is that it denies the opposing party the opportunity to cross-examine the maker of the statement. The **Criminal Justice Act 2003** contains a number of safeguards aimed at protecting the integrity of this evidence. They are summarised here.

(i) Considerations on Admissibility, s. 114(1)(a)

Section 114 (1)(d) court may admit otherwise inadmissible hearsay if it is satisfied that it is in the interests of justice for it to be admissible, having regard to s. 114(2).

(a) How much probative value the statement has (assuming it to be true) in relation to a matter in issue in the proceedings, or how valuable it is for the understanding of other evidence in the case.

(b) What other evidence has been, or can be, given on the matter or evidence mentioned in paragraph (a).

(c) How important the matter or evidence mentioned in paragraph (a) is in the context of the case as a whole.

(d) The circumstances in which the statement was made.

(e) How reliable the maker of the statement appears to be.

(f) How reliable the evidence of the making of the statement appears to be.

(g) Whether oral evidence of the matter stated can be given and if not why it cannot.

(h) The amount of difficulty involved in challenging the statement.

(i) The extent to which that difficulty would be likely to prejudice the party facing it.

(ii) Fearful Witness, s. 116(2)(e)

The court may give leave if it is proposed to give a statement from a witness who is absent through fear. Leave may only be given if the court considers that the statement ought to be admitted in the interests of justice, having regard:

(a) to the statement's contents;

(b) to any risk its admission or exclusion will result in unfairness to any party to the proceedings (and in particular to have difficulty will be to challenge the statement if the relevant person does not give oral evidence);

(c) in appropriate cases, to the fact that a direction under s. 19 of the **Youth Justice and Criminal Evidence Act 1999** (special measures for the giving of evidence by fearful witnesses, etc.) could be made in relation to the relevant person; and

(d) to any other relevant circumstances.

(iii) Identity of Witnesses and Closed List of Acceptable Reasons for Witness Unavailability, s. 116(2)

This section provides that to be admissible: (a) oral evidence given in the proceedings by the person who made the statement would be admissible as evidence of that matter,

(b) the person who made the statement (the relevant person) is identified to the court's satisfaction, and (c) any of the five conditions mentioned in subsection (2) is satisfied, namely that the relevant person:

(a) is dead;

(b) is unfit to be a witness because of bodily or mental condition;

(c) is outside the UK and it is not reasonably practicable to secure his attendance;

(d) cannot be found despite such steps as is reasonably practicable to secure his attendance;

(e) through fear does not give or does not continue to give oral evidence in the proceedings (see (ii) above).

If the person in support of whose case it is sought to give the statement in evidence or a person acting on his behalf causes the reason for the non-availability of the witness the conditions for admissibility are not satisfied.

(iv) Statement Prepared for the Purposes of Pending or Contemplated Criminal Proceedings, s. 117(4)(a)

Additional requirements must be satisfied, namely:

(a) either one of the two conditions in s. 116(2) is satisfied; or

(b) the relevant person cannot reasonably be expected to have any recollection of the matters dealt with in the statement (having regard to the length of time since he supplied the information and all other circumstances).

(v) Business and other Documents, s. 117

Courts may make a declaration not to admit a statement under s. 117 if satisfied that the statement's reliability as evidence for the purpose for which it is tended is doubtful in view of its contents, the source of information contained in it, the way in which or the circumstances in which the information was supplied or received or the way in which or the circumstances in which the document concerned was created or received.

(vi) Additional Requirements for the Admissibility of Multiple Hearsay, s. 121

Multiple hearsay only admissible through ss. 117, 119, 120, or if all the parties so agree or if the court is satisfied that the value of the evidence in question, taking into account how reliable the statements appear to be, is so high that the interests of justice require the later statement to be admissible for that purpose.

(vii) Credibility, s. 124

Evidence which would have been admissible as relevant to the absent witness's credibility is admissible. The person against whom the hearsay statement is admitted may seek to use evidence to discredit the maker of the statement or to show he has contradicted himself.

(viii) Stopping the Case where the Evidence is Unconvincing, s. 125

The court must stop a case or direct an acquittal if the case against the defendant is based wholly or partly on an out of court statement so unconvincing that, considering its importance to the case against the defendant, his conviction would be unsafe. This only applies in the case of jury trials.

(ix) Court's General Discretion to Exclude Evidence, s. 126

The court may refuse to admit a statement as evidence of the matters stated if the statement was made otherwise than in oral evidence in the proceedings and the court is satisfied that the case for excluding the statement, taking account of the danger that to admit it would result in undue wasted time, substantially outweighs the case for admitting it, taking into account the value of the evidence.

(x) Rules of Court, s. 132

Rules of court may make provision about the procedure to be followed and other conditions to be fulfilled by a party proposing to tender a hearsay statement. These may include notice provisions.

(xi) Machine-Generated Records, s. 129

Where a representation of any fact is made otherwise than by a person but depends for its accuracy of information supplied (directly or indirectly) by a person, the representation is not admissible in criminal proceedings as evidence of the facts unless it is proved that the information was accurate. The common law presumption that a mechanical device has been properly set or calibrated is preserved.

Hearsay and the ECHR

Article 6(3)(d) of the ECHR provides that everyone charged with a criminal offence has the right to examine or have examined witnesses against him.

In a number of cases the court has upheld applicants' arguments that this section has been violated; see *Kostovski* v *The Netherlands* (1990) 12 EHRR 434, and *Bardin* v *France* (1994) 17 EHRR 251. In these cases the out of court statements were either the only evidence or an important part of the evidence. In some cases the defendants were unaware of the identity of the witnesses (see *Van Mechelen* v *The Netherlands* (1998) 25 EHRR 647). In other cases, however, the court has found no violation (see e.g., *Doorson* v *The Netherlands* (1996) 22 EHRR 330). In such cases the hearsay evidence was not the only or main evidence against the accused and on occasion there were other safeguards such as the possibility of cross-examination by counsel in the absence of the defendants. The hearsay provisions of the **Criminal Justice Act 1988** have not been found to be in violation of art. 6. In *R* v *Sellick* [2005] EWCA 651 the Court of Appeal has provided a helpful summary of the relevant case-law and the principles which emerge. It held that where the court had allowed a witness's statement to be read out in court under the **Criminal Justice Act 1988** ss. 3 and 26 there was no absolute rule that, where that evidence was the decisive element, its admission would automatically lead to an infringement of the defendant's rights under the ECHR, art. 6(3)(d). The

Diagram 1 Criminal hearsay—cases where a witness is unavailable, s.116 **CJA 2003**

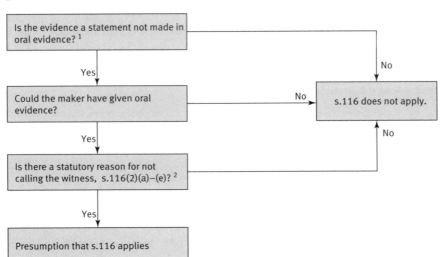

[1] The statement must be first-hand hearsay unless admissible under ss.121(1)(a) or (b).

[2] If the statutory reason is s.116(2)(e) ('that through fear &c') the statement is only admissible if the court has given leave.

court stressed the safeguards of allowing the admission of evidence relating to the credibility or inconsistency of the witness as important in considering whether a defendant's art. 6 rights had been infringed; see also *R* v *Khawaja* **[2006] 1 WLR 1078** and Diagram 1.

Birch (2004, p. 573) has little comfort for long-suffering evidence students: 'As to the Royal Commission's criticism that the hearsay rule is "exceptionally complex and difficult to interpret", it is a fair bet that law students will continue to groan whenever the word "hearsay" is mentioned.' See chapter 10 for hearsay and previous inconsistent statements and other previous statements of witnesses; also Diagram 2.

Question 1

Heather is charged with the manslaughter of Ted. The prosecution alleges that Ted and Heather, who were lovers, got into a heated argument whereupon Heather, in a fit of rage, fatally stabbed him. Consider the admissibility of the following evidence:

   (a) Evidence from Kit, a passer-by, who administered first aid to Ted when he staggered out of his house covered in blood. Ted gasped, 'It was Heather who did it, I've had it. Make sure that I have a Christian burial.'

   (b) Evidence from Ted's mother to whom Ted confided, on the morning of the stabbing, that he was going to confront Heather about her infidelity.

Diagram 2 Hearsay, business &c documents, s.117 **CJA 2003**

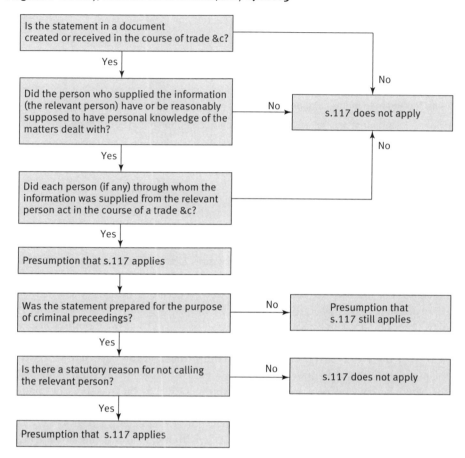

Commentary

(a) The issue here is whether the statement made to Kit is admissible under s. 166 **CJA 2003** or, in the alternative, as part of the *res gestae*, in order for it to be admissible as an exception to the hearsay rule.

(b) Again, it is clear that the statement made here infringes the rule against hearsay. What needs to be considered is whether a person's declaration of his or her intention is regarded as an exception to the hearsay rule.

Answer plan

(a)

- Purpose of adducing statement
- Arguably hearsay but may be admissible under **CJA 2003** as first-hand oral hearsay or *res gestae*

(b)

- Ted's statement to mother arguably hearsay
- If hearsay, statement may fall within 'state of mind' exception in s. 118 **CJA 2003**
- Lack of clarity in case-law whether court can infer from 'state of mind' statement that any intention was carried out

Suggested answer

(a) The statement made by Ted to Kit is a hearsay statement in that it is adduced for the purpose of establishing that what it says is true. The statutory definition of hearsay is to be found in s. 114 and s. 121 of the **Criminal Justice Act 2003**. It is a statement not made in oral evidence in the proceedings admissible as evidence of any matter stated (s. 114(1)). The statement by Ted fulfils this definition. It may, however, be given by Kit either under s. 116 or s. 118 of the **Criminal Justice Act 2003**. To take s. 116 first, this section admits first-hand oral or documentary hearsay if there is a reason for not calling the witness, in this case Ted, who was the maker of the statement or the relevant person. Section 116(2)(a) gives the reason that 'the relevant person is dead'. Under s. 116(1)(a) that person who made the statement must be identified to the court's satisfaction. If Kit is a competent and compellable witness she can give evidence of the statement. Under s. 124 the defence may call relevant evidence on Ted's credibility. If as a result of evidence admitted under this section an allegation is made against the maker of the statement the court may permit a party to lead additional evidence of such description as the court may specify for the purposes of denying or answering the allegation.

Under s. 125 if the case against the defendant is based wholly or partly on a statement not made in oral evidence and the evidence provided by the statement is so unconvincing, considering its importance to the case against the defendant, that his conviction of the offence would be unsafe, the court must either direct the jury to acquit the defendant of the offence, or if it considers that there ought to be a retrial, discharge the jury. Finally, the court may exercise its general discretion to exclude hearsay evidence under s. 126. This would apply if 'the court is satisfied that the case for excluding a statement, taking account of the danger that to admit it would result in undue waste of time, substantially outweighs the case for admitting it, taking into account the value of the evidence'.

There is little risk that art. 6 provisions would apply to exclude this evidence; see *R* v *Sellick* [2005] EWCA 651. The Court of Appeal here also accepted that in principle a conviction could be founded largely or even exclusively on hearsay evidence, in stating, that it could 'not be right for there to be some absolute rule that, where compelling evidence is the sole or decisive evidence, an admission in evidence of a statement must then automatically lead to a defendant's article 6 right being infringed'. This case was heard under the provisions of the 1988 Act.

Part 34 of the Criminal procedure Rules 2005 gave the notice requirements for introducing certain hearsay evidence. A party who receives a notice of hearsay evidence may oppose it by giving notice within 14 days to the court officer and all other parties.

Alternatively, the statement may be admissible under the common law exceptions preserved in s. 118 **Criminal Justice Act 2003**. The statement appears to be a dying declaration which is one common law exception to the rule against hearsay not preserved in the new statute. However, arguably the *res gestae* exception which is preserved is broad enough to include such a statement. The courts seemed to be moving towards accepting that the admissibility of dying declarations should be based more on the probative value of the evidence rather than the idea of impending death being equivalent to an oath. In *Mills* v *R* [1995] 1 WLR 511 the Privy Council suggested that a 're-examination of *Ratten* v *R* and *R* v *Andrews* may permit those requirements to be re-stated in a more flexible form'. It is possible therefore that Tom's statement may be admitted.

Thus it could be argued that the statement was part of the *res gestae*, as the statement was made so close to the events in question that it can be said to form part of the transaction. *Ratten* v *R* [1972] AC 378, is an example of the application of this exception. Lord Wilberforce stated (at p. 389) that:

> . . .[a]s regards statements made after the event it must be for the judge. . .to satisfy himself that the statement was so clearly made in circumstances of spontaneity or involvement in the event that the possibility of concoction can be disregarded.

Thus, the test of admissibility of such statements depends on whether the statements were made in such circumstances as to make concoction or fabrication unlikely. This test was applied in later cases such as *R* v *Turnbull* (1985) 80 Cr App R 104 and approved by the House of Lords in *R* v *Andrews* [1987] AC 281. In the latter case, the facts of which are similar to the facts of the case in hand, Lord Ackner stated that the judge had to consider all the circumstances of the case in order to satisfy himself that the event was so unusual as to dominate the thoughts of the victim, so that his utterance was an instinctive reaction to the event giving no opportunity for concoction or distortion. Where a possibility of malice on the part of the declarant is raised, the judge must be satisfied that there was no possibility of concoction or distortion. Further, the judge had to take into account the possibility of error, if only the ordinary fallibility of human recollection, but that this went to the weight of the evidence, not to its admissibility.

It could therefore be argued that Ted's statement fall within the test laid out in *Ratten* which was explained and approved in *Andrews*, in that the circumstances of the case are such that there is no possibility of concoction or distortion. In the absence of the court being satisfied that there was malice on the part of Ted, it is likely that this statement could be admitted as a *res gestae* statement under s. 118(1)4(a) **CJA 2003**.

(b) It is arguable that what Ted told his mother on the morning of the stabbing is a hearsay statement. It indicates that Ted thought that Heather was unfaithful, which is relevant to the prosecution's case on motive. Thus it would be inadmissible unless it falls within one of the common law exceptions to the hearsay rule. Statements made by a person concerning his or her contemporaneous state of mind or emotion are admissible as evidence of his or her state of mind or emotion as an exception to the hearsay rule.

This principle is preserved in s. 118(1)4(c). The importance of this exception is seen in *Neill* v *North Antrim Magistrates' Court* **[1993] 97 Cr App R 121**. The House of Lords held that the statements by police officers recounting what the two witnesses who did not give evidence through fear had told the police officers could have been given as evidence of what the witnesses had said about their fear. This was based on the law that a person's declaration of his contemporaneous state of mind was admissible. Doak and McGourlay (2006, p. 225) point out that 'It was emphasised that the evidence must not be that the witnesses were afraid (that is an inference for the Court to draw) but that the witnesses said they were afraid and that their demeanour was consistent with what they had said.' It would appear that statements as to the person's intention fall under this exception, as evidence of his or her intention at the time when the statement is made. The difficulty that arises is whether, as in the case here, the court is able to infer from the statement that the intention was carried out.

There is a lack of agreement by the courts on this issue, and the court will doubtless draw on the common law authorities. In *R* v *Buckley* **(1873) 13 Cox CC 293**, the court admitted into evidence a statement made by the victim, a police officer, to his senior officer, that he was going to watch the movements of the accused the night that he was killed. Likewise, in *R* v *Moghal* **(1977) 65 Cr App R 56**, a tape recording made six months earlier as to the intention of a third party, was admissible into evidence. However, the correctness of *Moghal* was doubted by the House of Lords in *R* v *Blastland* **[1986] AC 41**. In contrast, in *R* v *Wainwright* **(1875) 13 Cox CC 171**, the court refused to allow into evidence a statement made by the victim to a friend, on the afternoon of her murder, that she was on the way to the house of the accused. The court similarly refused to allow into evidence a statement as to where the victim was going just before her death, in *R* v *Pook* **(noted at (1875) 13 Cox CC 171)**. The reasons for the court's refusal to admit such evidence is on the basis that it was merely evidence of the victim's intention, which may or may not have been carried out. In *R* v *Callender* **(1998) Crim LR 337** a statement made by a defendant two weeks before his arrest about his intentions in relation to carrying explosive devices was not admitted. The defendant wanted to put as part of his defence that he intended to carry false explosives for publicity.

The rationale behind the admissibility of statements concerning contemporaneous state of mind was put in **R** v **Blastland**:

> It is of course elementary that statements made to a witness by a third party are not excluded by the hearsay rule when they are put in evidence solely to prove the state of mind either of the maker of the statement or of the person to whom it was made. What a person said or heard may well be the best and most direct evidence of that person's state of mind. This principle can only apply, however, when the state of mind evidenced by the statement is either itself directly in issue at the trial, or of direct and immediate relevance to an issue which arises at the trial.

Choo comments (2006, p. 237) 'What is apparently required therefore is a degree of probative value statistically above the bare minimum.' He adds in relation to the conflicting authorities on whether evidence suggesting an intent to perform a particular act is admissible to establish that the intent was in fact carried out, that is, that the act in question was performed: 'The apparent conflict remains factually unresolved but a sensible approach may be to adopt the view of Mason CJ, expressed in the decision of the High Court of Australia in **Walton** v **R** that, "out-of-court statements which tend to prove a plan or intention of the author [should be admissible in evidence] subject to remoteness in time and indications of unreliability or lack of protective value' (**1989 166 C CR 228, 290**).

There is the possibility also of admissibility under s. 114.

Question 2

David is charged with murdering his wife Heather. She had been found bound and naked hanging from the garden shed. When interviewed by the police David denies that he was at home on the day his wife died. He claims he was away on a fishing trip. A neighbour, Ron, however, states that he had overheard Heather shout on the morning of her death, 'David if you don't move those golf clubs from the lawn I will chuck them out'. David claims Heather's death must have occurred during a sado-masochistic experiment which Heather had frequently indulged in and in which he took no part. He produces a photograph of Heather bound and gagged on an earlier occasion. However, Heather's sister Jean is willing to testify that Heather had told her that David had persuaded her to pose for the photograph against her will. He had claimed, she said, that he needed it as part of his coursework for the distance learning course on erotic photography he was undertaking.

Advise whether any of the above statements may be held inadmissible because of the operation of the rule against hearsay.

Commentary

You need to consider the admissibility of the following possible 'statements'. First, whether David's denial to the police that he was in the house on the day of Heather's death can be adduced in court. The prosecution will argue that this is a lie. Here you will need to consider the status of lies and the case of **Mawaz Khan** v **R [1967] 1 AC 454**. Thus Ron's statement becomes relevant, suggesting as it does that David was in the house. The **Criminal Justice Act 2003** defined hearsay evidence as not including implied assertions.

In **R** v **Singh [2006] 1 WLR 1564**, the Court of Appeal held that when the **Criminal Justice Act**, s. 114 and s. 118, were read together they abolished the common law hearsay rules, save for those expressly preserved, and created a new rule against hearsay that did not extend to implied assertions. The majority decision in **R** v **Kearley (1992)** on hearsay was reversed. The status of the photograph as real evidence or hearsay will also need to be examined. Finally, there is the issue of Jean's evidence of what Heather had told her which requires an examination of the state of mind exception to the rule against hearsay.

Answer plan

- David's denial arguably a lie and not hearsay—see **Mawaz Khan** v **R** (see also chapter 8)
- Ron's statement possibly implied assertion and not hearsay
- Photography—real evidence or hearsay?
- Jean's statement about what Heather told her arguably *res gestae* exception—**R** v **Gilfoyle**, s. 118 CJA 2003

Suggested answer

The statement by David to the police that he was not in the house on the day of the murder is likely to be admissible because it is a statement being adduced to suggest it is a lie, not that it is true. Thus in *Mawaz Khan* v *R* [1967] 1 AC 454, false alibi statements made out of court by the defendants were admitted. The prosecution was allowed to adduce them as relevant evidence because the fact that they were made showed the defendants were in collusion and thus had a common guilt. Here the prosecution will be likely to ask the jury to infer David's guilt from his alleged lie over his whereabouts. In order to suggest that David has lied the prosecution will want to bring in Ron's account of what he heard. He claims to have heard Heather call David's name. The purpose of bringing in this statement is to infer that David was there.

As Cross and Tapper (2007, p. 605) point out, 'No question of hearsay was thought to be involved if a statement was adduced as demonstrably false.' In *Mawaz Khan* it was alleged that a false alibi had been made up by two defendants. Lord Hudson stated that these 'can without any breach of hearsay rule be used now for the purpose of establishing the truth of the assertions contained therein but for the purpose of asking the jury to hold the assertions false and to draw the inferences from their falsity'.

There is a danger that a jury may be too ready to infer guilt from a lie although the defendant may have lied for a number of reasons, not necessarily guilt. *R v Lucas* [1981] QB 720 sets out the special direction which is intended to warn juries about the dangers of relying on a lie as evidence of guilt. Further guidance is given in *R v Burge and Pegg* [1996] 1 Cr App R 163. If David is relying on an alibi which can be shown to be false a *Lucas* warning should be given (see also Chapter 8). Judicial Studies Board specimen direction No. 27 states that the following should be explained to the jury. The jury must decide whether they are convinced that David did lie and if so ask themselves why, since there may be an innocent explanation, such as panic. Only if the jury is sure that the defendant did not lie for an innocent reason may it treat the lie as supporting the prosecution case. JSB specimen direction No. 46, on alibi, should also be applied (see *R v Pemberton* (1993) 99 Cr App R 228).

The defence argument is that Heather caused her own death and so the photograph becomes relevant evidence to suggest that her death was consistent with her allegedly previous reckless behaviour. In *R v Maqsud Ali* [1966] 1 QB 688, where a tape-recording was admitted in evidence the Court of Criminal Appeal noted that the courts had long admitted photographs. The photograph here is thus a piece of real evidence and admissible. No statement is being relied on here. In s. 129 CJA 2003 the common law presumption that a mechanical device has been properly set or calibrated is maintained.

Finally the prosecution will want to undermine the defence by calling Jean to testify what Heather had told her. Statements made by a person concerning his or her contemporaneous state of mind or emotion are admissible as evidence of his or her state of mind or emotion. This common law rule is preserved in s. 118 CJA 2003. The exception was clearly acknowledged by the House of Lords in *R v Blastland* [1986] AC 41 accepting that 'statements made to a witness by a third party are not excluded by the hearsay rule when they are put in evidence solely to prove the state of mind of the maker of the statement or of the person to whom it was made'. The prosecution will argue that Heather's state of mind is of immediate relevance since it suggests that David had contrived to get her compromising photograph for his own purposes. In *R v Gilfoyle* [1996] 3 All ER 883 the accused on trial for murdering his wife produced what seemed to be a suicide note written by the wife. It appeared subsequently that the note was manufactured by the accused. The Court of Appeal held that statements by friends of the wife in which she said the accused had asked her to write the note as part of his study of suicide, should have been admitted at trial. They had been excluded as hearsay. The conversations with the friends were original evidence of the wife's state of mind in that they increased the likelihood that the 'suicide note' was not written when she was suicidal. An alternative explanation was that the statements of the wife to the friends were hearsay if tendered to show she was prompted to write the note by her husband. They were admissible, however, as a *res gestae* exception covering statements about contemporaneous states of mind or emotions. In *Gilfoyle* the *res gestae* exception extended in *R* v *Andrews* [1987] AC 281 was stretched even further to cover evidentiary facts as well as facts in issue. (Arguably now the statements would be admissible under s. 116(2) **CJA 2003**.) The Court stated (per Beldam LJ at p. 323):

> In this case the statements themselves suggested that the events which prompted them were still dominating [the wife's] mind. The statements were made in the morning after the letter had been written as soon after as would ordinarily have been expected. The possibility of invention or unreliability could be discounted and there was little room for inaccuracy in the reporting of the statements.

It is likely therefore that Helen's statement will be admitted.

Question 3

'Rather than rely on precisely defined and technically complex, and at the same time, legally inconclusive exceptions, trial judges should have the power to admit hearsay whenever it is of sufficient probative value.' (Zuckerman, 1989, at p. 216).
   Discuss in relation to criminal trials.

Commentary

This is the type of general question on the hearsay rule that occurs frequently in evidence examinations. In answering this question, students must be clear as to the rationale for the hearsay rule. They must also recognise the criticisms of the rule, the main one being that credible and reliable evidence may be excluded as a result of the rule even though in some cases this may tend to prove the innocence of the accused. The answer should also cover the academic views on the rule and how the courts have found ways of avoiding its application.

   Questions such as this, evaluating the justification for the rule against hearsay, demand you have at least an outline knowledge of the history of reform proposals in the Report of the Law Commission 'Evidence in Criminal Proceedings: Hearsay and Related Topics', No. 245 (Cm 3670, 1997), now largely enacted in the **Criminal Justice Act 2003**.

Answer plan

- Outline reasons for exclusionary rule
- Rule historically excluded apparently reliable evidence—*Myers* v *DPP*
- Devices adopted by court (hearsay fiddles) to admit hearsay
- Particular difficulty over 'state of mind' exception and implied assertions

- Law Commission proposals preserve rule but extend exceptions and allow discretion, now largely adopted in **CJA 2003**
- Dangers of Zuckerman proposal and denial of 'right to confrontation'

Suggested answer

A useful exposition of hearsay can be found in *R* v *Sharp* [1988] 1 WLR 7, where Lord Havers adopted Cross's definition of the term: '. . .[a]n assertion other than one made by a person while giving oral evidence in the proceedings is inadmissible as evidence of any fact asserted'. This exclusionary rule of evidence applies to both oral and written statements and includes what the witness said at an earlier occasion if the purpose of the admission of such evidence is to prove the truth of the facts stated therein. Murphy (2003 at p. 199) suggests, however, that this explanation of hearsay is insufficiently comprehensive. As an alternative he suggests that the following would be a more comprehensive definition of hearsay:

> Evidence from any witness which consists of what another person stated (whether verbally, in writing, or by any other method of assertion such as a gesture) on any prior occasions, is inadmissible, if its only relevant purpose is to prove that any fact so stated by that person on that prior occasion is true. Such a statement may, however, be admitted for any relevant purpose other than proving the truth of facts stated in it.

This definition is more helpful in that it makes it clear that a hearsay statement consists not only of what was said or written but includes gestures. It should be stressed that not all prior out of court statements would necessarily infringe the hearsay rule. The important criterion is that in order to be hearsay, the prior out of court statement is adduced for the purpose of proving the truth of the facts stated therein. By contrast in *Khan* v *R* [1967] 1 AC 454 the statement was admissible to prove the falsity of its contents; in *Subramaniam* v *Public Prosecutor* [1956] 1 WLR 965 an out of court statement was admitted to prove the state of mind and emotion of the witness.

There are numerous reasons for this exclusionary rule which is in principle still preserved in the **CJA 2003**. First, it has been argued that the person who made the statement may have wrongly perceived the events in question. Second, there is a risk that because of the fallibility of human nature, the memory of the person who heard the statement may be flawed. Third, there is a risk of concoction or distortion of the events in question. Finally, the statement may have been misunderstood by the person who wrote down or heard the statement. Unlike a witness who is open to cross-examination, and the accuracy of his or her testimony can be tested, this is not normally possible with a hearsay statement. Zuckerman (1989, p. 178) argued that this is the central reason for the exclusion of hearsay statements. He goes on to suggest that there is a risk that the jury may attribute too much probative force to such evidence. Lord Bridge in *R* v *Blastland* [1986] AC 41, states that '. . .The danger against which this fundamental rule provides a safeguard is that untested hearsay evidence will be treated as having a probative force which it does not deserve.' In order to answer this question it is necessary to review the development of the law.

Whilst it is clear that the risk exists that such statements are unreliable because of concoction, distortion or fallibility of human nature, the extent to which the hearsay rule applied historically was much wider than is necessary. As a result of the rule, evidence which was both credible, reliable and of probative value was excluded if it did not fall strictly within one of the exceptions. An example of this can be seen in *R* v *Blastland* [1986] AC 41, where the House of Lords suggested that a confession by a third party that he committed the crime with which the accused was being tried, would be inadmissible because of the hearsay rule. Arguably, that evidence may have been credible but the rules of evidence would have prevented it from being admitted. Likewise in *Myers* v *DPP* [1965] AC 1001, credible evidence was held to be inadmissible because of the hearsay rule. It should be noted that the evidence in question is now admissible under the statutory exceptions but the point is that at the time of the decision it was inadmissible. The other criticism of the rule is that it excluded evidence which may prove the innocence of the accused: *Blastland* and *Sparks* v *R* [1964] 1 All ER 727 is an example of this.

Bentham argued that hearsay evidence should be admissible unless there is oral evidence available on the same or similar point, on the basis that this was the best available evidence. He was of the view that to exclude such evidence may lead to mistaken factual conclusions. Other jurists, including Thayer and McCormick supported Bentham's view on this. Wigmore, on the other hand, favoured the hearsay rule, but this was on the condition that there should be reform of the rule.

In order not to exclude potentially reliable and credible evidence, the courts have over the years used numerous devices in order to avoid excluding the evidence on the basis of hearsay. An example of this is the case of *R* v *Osbourne* [1973] QB 678, where the court allowed into evidence the testimony of a police officer at an identification parade that a witness picked out the accused. The court stated that this was admissible to prove the fact of identification. The element of hearsay inherent in this was ignored. A similar approach was taken in *R* v *Okorodu* [1982] Crim LR 747. Another illustration of the courts' evasion of the hearsay rule includes cases of hearsay conduct such as *R* v *Rice* [1963] 1 QB 857 (a case which is now subject to the **Criminal Justice Act 2003** allowing documentary hearsay to be admissible). Other 'fiddles' such as the status of 'refreshing memory' documents have been largely rationalised by the **Criminal Justice Act 2003** (see **Chapter 10**).

Evasions of the rule have been described by Birch as 'hearsay fiddles' (1987). She writes at p. 35, 'it is hard to avoid the conclusion that the courts fiddle the concepts of hearsay and relevance to admit only evidence which it is considered desirable to admit'. The tortuous reasoning and somewhat desperate reliance on the concept of relevance as a justification for exclusion evidenced in *Blastland* suggest that both Birch and Zuckerman may be right. It would arguably be better to concentrate on the probative value of the evidence rather than its form. This argument gets added weight from the controversial decision in *R* v *Kearley* [1992] 2 AC 228, where a majority of the House of Lords declared that implied assertions were hearsay. The judge at first instance and the Court of Appeal had not surprisingly admitted the evidence of callers asking the defendant to supply them with drugs as evidence that Kearley was engaged in drug-dealing. But their Lordships rejected the argument that the evidence was admissible as non-hearsay because it demonstrated the state of mind of the callers. The House of Lords in *Blastland* had sanctioned the admissibility of such statements to show the state of mind of the maker. These two cases give further weight to Zuckerman's argument because as McEwan points out (1998, p. 236), 'It is sometimes difficult to disentangle that which merely indicates someone's state of mind from all manner of implied assertions which may simultaneously emerge from the statement.' An added complication is that the authorities have not agreed on whether evidence of state of mind or emotion is admissible as non-hearsay or as an exception to the rule against hearsay. There is indeed a significant lack of clarity in the current law in this area even after the implementation of the **CJA 2003**. Photofit pictures are admissible as non-hearsay, following *R* v *Cook* [1987] 1 All ER 1049, but as McEwan (at p. 239) points out the 'opportunities for error, suggestion and misunderstanding is almost endless'. Thus the courts appeared before the 2003 Act to be following somewhat contradictory paths, extending the range of exclusions on the one hand, as in *Kearley*, but increasing it on the other. Other examples of the latter approach are *Gilfoyle*, where the state of mind exception was extended to cover proof of facts which exist independently of the maker's state of mind, and *R* v *Myers* [1998] AC 124, where the exception for admissions by parties to litigation was extended to cover the use of a confession by a co-accused under certain circumstances.

In *R* v *Ward, Andrews and Broadley* [2001] Crim LR 316 the Court of Appeal extended the admission of confessions to include a statement to the police by the defendant, W, identifying himself at the scene of the crime (the police officer could not identify W later). The Court accepted that there was a circularity in the argument since it was the disputed evidence itself which was relied on to establish that there was an admission. It was persuaded by the powerful quality of the evidence. Munday (2007, 386) points out that, 'Occasionally the courts appear to have retreated from the position that the reliability of evidence, which is technically hearsay, has no bearing on its admissibility.'

Thus it is clear that the hearsay rule was to some extent disliked by both jurists and courts and the latter have been prepared in some instances to avoid its application. However, there was little consistency to this approach and the reason is simply because of the fear of letting in unreliable evidence. Zuckerman (1989, p. 216) argued that there should be the legitimisation of the inclusionary principle in that trial judges should have the power to admit hearsay evidence which is of probative value. The effect of this, he argued, would be to get rid of the exception and its technical manifestations. There is much to be said for this approach, after all, the judges have been given discretionary powers in most instances, and there is no real reason why they cannot be given the discretion to rule whether the hearsay evidence is admissible because of its probative value. Further, the trend of legislative intervention in this area appears to be in favour of the admissibility of such evidence, the **Criminal Justice Act** 2003 being the culmination of that approach.

The Law Commission had recognised the case for reform but its proposals did not go as far as some recommended by abolishing the rule. The approach taken in their Report 'Evidence in Criminal Proceedings: Hearsay and Related Topics' (No. 245, Cm 3670, 1997) was to preserve the rule but extend the range of exceptions alongside both an inclusionary and exclusionary discretion. One almost universally welcomed recommendation was that the decision in *Kearley* would be reversed. Implied assertions would not be hearsay. However, the overall cautious stance taken by the Law Commission which eventually led to legislation was criticised. Thus Jackson (1998, p. 187), commenting on the proposals, concluded that 'there are no functional reasons why the hearsay rule is needed in criminal proceedings any more than in civil proceedings'. He argued for an investigation code to govern police practice and for the defence to be given an opportunity to cross-examine an available witness on whom the prosecution depends by increased use of pre-trial procedures. He rightly stressed that in deciding admissibility 'the key issue is whether the police have discharged fair and accurate standards during the course of their investigation . . . rather than the technical question of whether out of court statements fall within the scope of the hearsay rule'.

Erosion rather than abolition is thus the current approach. The 2003 Act preserves the hearsay rule but increases the number of exceptions, particularly by the admissibility of oral statements, and also introduces an inclusionary discretion. The increased use of discretion creates more flexibility but also more uncertainty. Although often illogical in practice and at times defying common sense, the rule against hearsay has been long considered by many as contributing to the fairness of a trial. From this point of view current legislative changes allow oral first-hand hearsay, to extend the 'fear' exception to witnesses who are unavailable through fear of 'financial loss' and permit the, at least, theoretical possibility that a defendant could be convicted on hearsay evidence alone, which are some cause for concern. It is unlikely that the application of the **Human Rights Act 1998** means that hearsay evidence necessarily breaches art. 6(3)(a) of the European Convention on Human Rights (see *R* v *Gokal* **(1997) 2 Cr App R 266** and *Trivedi* v *United Kingdom* **(1997) EHRLR 520**. However, as Friedman (1998, p. 697) points out 'lurking within the rule against hearsay and often shrouded by its many excesses and oddities is a principle of magnificent importance, a principle first enunciated long before the development of the common law system but one that achieved its full development within that system. This is the principle that a person may not offer testimony against a criminal defendant unless it is given under oath face to face with the accused and subject to cross-examination.'

Zuckerman expresses here a common impatience and frustration with this ancient rule. However, an undue emphasis in this area on logic, even-handedness and flexibility may have the unfortunate result of further disadvantaging defendants at a time when, it is arguable, statutory changes are eroding long-standing principles such as the right to silence. After all, the biggest exception to the rule against hearsay, confessions, is clearly pro-prosecution. Reform of the rule against hearsay was long overdue but it is submitted that there is a case for accompanying any reform with a recognised right to confrontation, with the aim of assisting the innocent from wrongful conviction, ensuring procedural fairness and of improving the standards of police investigation.

However, it is arguable that in practice the change may not in practice be overwhelming since the courts may continue their cautious approach to the admissibility of hearsay and be wary of abuse. In *R v Mills* [2003] 1WLR 2931, the Court of Appeal quashed a conviction because, *inter alia*, a statement made to a police officer by a non-appearing witness had been wrongly admitted for the prosecution. It is of some interest to note that, under the **Criminal Justice Act 2003** provisions, if a non-appearing witness is put in fear by the parties, this may preclude admissibility of the statement the parties wish to tender. In *Mills* the allegation was that one police officer had warned the witness not to attend trial, illustrating that it is not only the defence who may carry out witness intimidation. Cross and Tapper point out (2007, p. 650) one difference from the old law is that under s. 116 the statement need no longer be one made to those investigating offences, and hence can clearly be applied to defence witnesses who become fearful, perhaps of the police, after providing an initial statement. Here too it is necessary to bear in mind the new environment in which the names and addresses of potential witnesses are required to be disclosed to the prosecution in advance.' The most important consideration, whatever the remaining technicalities of the law on hearsay, is that the question of fairness should be fully aired. This is explicitly reinforced by Article 6 as well as the provisions of **Criminal Justice Act 2003**. Choo (2006, p. 243) comments 'the provisions of the **Criminal Justice Act 2003**, largely following the recommendations of the Law Commission, maintain a "rule and exceptions" approach to hearsay doctrine, albeit that the specific exceptions are brought and there is an interests-of-justice exception'. He points out that Lord Justice Auld was critical of any reform which continued exclusionary rule and favoured 'making hearsay generally admissible subject to the principle of best evidence'. Choo convincingly suggests an alternative approach—that of maintaining a rule against hearsay but instead of recognising specific exceptions and an interests of justice exception, simply to have recognised the interests of justice exception as the only exception. Birch (2004, p. 572) regrets that the Auld reforms 'were not taken as seriously as they should have been' and predicts that 'it is more likely that judges will over time resort to the safety valve as a flexible weapon of choice'. She points out that 'if we did not have a safety valve, the judges would have to invent one, if only by dint of the process of "reading down" under the **Human Rights Act 1998** in order to admit crucial defence evidence'. She also argues that 'some breaking down of the traditional barriers of the adversarial system may help with difficult cases such as those involving third-party confessions and complainants who have withdrawn their complaints'. Dennis also speculated on the possibility of the interests of justice exception assuming greater importance. He questioned whether it will be 'a marginal sweeping-up power operating outside the statutory and preserved common-law exceptions in sections 116–118 or whether in practice it will be invoked in addition to, or even in substitution for, those exceptions' (2004, pp. 251, 252).

It appears under the **CJA 2003**, as before, that the hearsay rules are unlikely to fall foul of art. 6. In *R* v *Sellick* [2005] EWCA 651, the Court of Appeal held that the safeguards under the 1988 Act were sufficient to ensure compliance and there was 'still no absolute rule that, when a witness's statement was the sole or decisive evidence the admission in evidence of that statement would automatically lead to an infringement of the defendant's article 6 rights'. Following this approach the court held in *R* v *Imed-Al-Khawaja* [2006] 1 WLR 1078 that the admission of a witness statement of a complainant who had died prior to trial was not a breach of a defendant's right to a fair trial under the European Convention on Human Rights article 6. Jack J stated: 'where a witness who is the sole witness of a crime has made a statement to be used in its prosecution and has since died, there may be a strong public interest in the admission of the statement in evidence so that the prosecution may proceed . . . that public interest must not be allowed to override the requirement that the defendant have a fair trial. Like the court in *R* v *Sellick* we do not consider that the case law of the European Court of Human Rights requires the conclusion that in such circumstances the trial will be unfair.' Durston (2008, p. 289) comments: 'It is apparent that the courts are not lightly excluding hearsay evidence simply because of a potential breach of article 6. . .'

Doorson v *The Netherlands* (1990) was cited. The question was whether the proceedings as a whole were fair. In *R* v *Xhabri* [2006] 1 All ER 776 the court held that hearsay evidence adduced by the Crown satisfied the requirements of the **Criminal Justice Act 2003** s. 120 and was admissible under that provision, and alternatively the trial judge was entitled to exercise his discretion under s. 114 of the Act to admit the evidence on the basis that it was in the interests of justice. Article 6 (3) (a) did not provide a defendant with an absolute right to examine every witness whose testimony was used against him. In this case almost all the hearsay evidence derived directly or indirectly from the complainant, was available for examination. Thus although the current law is complex, it is arguably fair. The pragmatic approach taken by the courts on definitional matters suggests that the question of relevance will be crucial. Emson (2008, p. 126) comments, 'so long as a relevance can be established, the tribunal of law is entitled to adopt a "belt and braces" strategy if there is any uncertainty over the admissibility of an inferable statement. If the judge is of the view that the evidence is relevant and ought to be admitted, he will be able to rule that the exclusionary rule does not apply, by virtue of s. 115(3) of the Act and also rule, in the alternative, that if the hearsay rules does apply the evidence ought nevertheless to be admitted under the new discretion to admit inadmissible hearsay evidence (s. 114(1)(d)).' He cites *R* v *Tsichei* [2006] EWCA Crim 1815 in relation to an implied statement of identification during a telephone call as an example of this approach.

In the light of these decisions it is arguable that although the current law on hearsay is complex it is arguably fair in that it complies with the requirements of article 6 of the ECHR. Nonetheless leading scholars remain critical of the failure to abolish the rule by statute. Cross (2008, p. 644), for example, comments, 'Every human being deals with hearsay in his everyday decisions and judgments without undue difficulty, and it would seem to be much easier for a jury to apply such common skills than to engage in the convoluted reasoning induced by the inadmissibility of hearsay, under which evidence is to be accepted for some purposes but not for others, and against some people but not against others, which no-one would dream of adopting for any purpose at all outside the compulsion of the courtroom and which is capable of leading to illogicality, and demonstrably inconsistent conclusions.'

Question 4

Anna, Freda and Monisha are charged with robbery from Hendfield Building Society. Tracker dogs were used to trace them. Freda was discovered walking alongside the railway line a few hours after the robbery. She denied involvement and said she had been picking blackberries.

At an identification parade held a short time after the robbery, Anna was picked out as one of the robbers by Paul, the manager of the branch. As a result of a concussion later received in a road traffic accident, Paul is now suffering from amnesia and is unable later to remember what happened at the identification parade. However, Detective Inspector Daniels was present at the identification parade and is able to testify that Paul picked out Anna during the parade. Monisha was identified by Edmund, the assistant manager, who recognised her when he viewed the video-tape recording of Monisha during the robbery. The recording was accidentally deleted by Edmund shortly afterwards.

A few months after the arrest of Anna, Freda and Monisha, Gertrude spoke to her mother, just before she died, and confessed to having been one of the two persons who committed the robbery.

Advise as to the admissibility of the evidence.

Commentary

You need to discuss whether the evidence of the tracker dogs is admissible. Another issue is whether Detective Inspector Daniels is able to testify to what occurred during the identification parade. The problem with his testimony is that it may be hearsay. A further issue relates to the video recording and the identification of Monisha by Edmund and whether this infringes the rule against hearsay. The final point of the question requires a discussion as to whether an oral confession by a third party is admissible into evidence in view of the fact that it may infringe the hearsay rule and if so, whether any of the exceptions apply. Here you need to consider the possibility of the inclusionary discretion under s. 114. A statement not made in oral evidence in the proceedings is admissible as evidence of any matter stated if the court is satisfied that it is in the interests of justice first to be admissible. In deciding whether a statement is not made in oral evidence under this provision the court must have regard to the following factors (and to any others it considers relevant):

- how much probative value the statement has (assuming it is true) in relation to a matter in issue in the proceedings or how valuable it is for the understanding of other evidence in the case;
- what other evidence has been, or can be, given on the matter or evidence;
- how important the matter or evidence is in the context of the case as a whole;
- the circumstances in which the statement was made;
- how reliable the maker of the statement appears to be;
- how reliable the evidence of the maker of the statement appears to be;
- whether oral evidence of the matter stated can be given, and if not why it cannot;
- the amount of difficulty in challenging the statement;
- the extent to which the difficulty would be likely to prejudice the party facing it.

The court considered the application of the inclusionary discretion in *R* v *Xhabri* **[2006] 1 All ER 776**. It was stressed that the discretion granted by s. 114 was not restricted to the admission of a hearsay statement, the maker of which was not available for cross-examination. Note should be taken of the procedural requirements in the Criminal Procedure Rules 2005.

Answer plan

- Tracker dogs evidence—*R* v *Pieterson* (1995)
- Identification evidence avoids rule against hearsay—*R* v *McCay*, s. 120 **CJA 2003**
- Video-tape real evidence
- Admission by Gertrude inadmissible if *Blastland* followed–but see s. 114 **CJA 2003**

Suggested answer

The tracker dogs will have picked up the scent of the robbers and presumably their barking led to Freda being discovered. *R* v *Pieterson* [1995] 1 WLR 293 established that an account of the behaviour of tracker dogs will be admissible provided there is evidence of its reliability, which doubtless those handling the dogs could give. The Court stated:

> . . .if a handler can establish that a dog has been properly trained over a period of time the dog's reactions indicate that it is a reliable pointer to the existence of a scent from a particular individual then that evidence should properly be admitted.
>
> However it is important to emphasise two safeguards. First a proper foundation must be laid by detailed evidence establishing the reliability of the dog in question. Secondly the judge must, in giving his directions to the jury, alert them to the care

that they need to take and to look with circumspection at the evidence of tracker dogs, having regard to the fact that the dog may not always be reliable and cannot be cross examined.

In *R* v *Sykes* [1997] **Crim LR 752** the court stressed the importance of the judge directing according to these guidelines. Detective Inspector Daniels may be able to testify that he saw Paul identify Anna, as one of the robbers during the identification parade. Prima facie, it could be argued that this would infringe the rule against hearsay because '. . .[a]n assertion other than one made by a person while giving oral evidence in the proceedings is inadmissible as evidence of any fact asserted' (*R* v *Sharp* [1988] **1 WLR 7**) and therefore would be inadmissible into evidence.

The court may draw on the common law cases in deciding on admissibility. In *R* v *Osbourne; R* v *Virtue* [1973] **QB 678**, a witness could not recall what happened at an identification parade held some seven-and-a-half months earlier. A police officer who was present at the identification parade was permitted to testify that the witness picked out the accused. The Court of Appeal was of the view that the evidence was admissible as it sought to prove the fact of identification at the identification parade. The court did not deal satisfactorily with the point that the testimony of the police officer may be hearsay. It was suggested that the attitude of the Court of Appeal may have indicated that there was a new exception to the hearsay rule. However, Lord Morris in *Sparks* v *R* [1964] **AC 964** stated that there is no rule which permits the giving of hearsay evidence merely because it relates to identity. By analogy, in *R* v *Okorodu* [1982] **Crim LR 747**, a photofit picture which was constructed by a witness, who subsequently failed to pick out the accused at an identification parade, was admitted into evidence. The court was of the view that this should be admitted because where identification was in issue, the jury should have all relevant information available to them. Although this case is not strictly in point with the issue at hand, a parallel can be drawn with *Osbourne* in that the court appears to be prepared to admit evidence of identity even though it is technically hearsay. (*Okorodu* has now to be read in the light of *R* v *Cook* [1987] **1 All ER 1049**, where the Court of Appeal stated that sketches, photofit pictures and photographs were evidence which were in a class of their own. This type of evidence did not infringe the hearsay rule.)

The decision in *Osbourne* has to be compared with *Jones* v *Metcalfe* [1967] **1 WLR 1286** and *R* v *McClean* (1967) **52 Cr App R 80**. In these two cases, the issue revolved round whether a witness could refer to his conversation with another person as part of his testimony. It was held in both these cases that these were hearsay statements and therefore inadmissible. It is, however, likely that the court will be prepared to allow the testimony of Detective Inspector Daniels. If details of the identification parade had been written down, the position may be covered by the **Criminal Justice Act 2003** s. 117. The Courts generally take a liberal approach in admitting identification evidence; see *R* v *McCay* [1990] **1 WLR 645**. The common law provision on statements accompanying actions is preserved in s. 118(1)4(b). This is the principle which is applied in *R* v *McCay* [1990] **1 WLR 645**.

As regards the evidence of Edmund who identified Monisha from the video tape recording, it is clear that the video tape itself, if it was still available, would be admissible in evidence as original evidence: *Kajala* v *Noble* (1982) 75 Cr App R 149 and *R* v *Dodson* (1984) 79 Cr App R 220. However, in this case, it would appear that the video recording has been accidentally erased by Edmund. In *Taylor* v *Chief Constable of Cheshire* [1986] 1 WLR 1479, a video recording which was alleged to show the accused in the act of committing the offence was erased before the trial. The Court decided that it was proper for the police officers who had seen the recording to give oral evidence of the contents of the tape. Thus, it would appear that on the facts of the case, Edmund could give evidence of what he saw on the tape.

The final issue that has to be considered is whether the admission by Gertrude is admissible into evidence. Since she is unable to give evidence in court, her statement to her mother is clearly hearsay if adduced to suggest it is true. However, it could be argued that this evidence has probative value in that it may cast doubts on the prosecution's case that it was Anna and Monisha who committed the robbery. In *R* v *Blastland* [1986] AC 41, the House of Lords suggested that a confession by a third party that he committed the crime with which the accused was being tried, would be inadmissible because of the hearsay rule. The House of Lords in this case approved the earlier decision in *R* v *Turner* (1975) 61 Cr App R 67, where it was held that a confession by a third party who was not called to give evidence was inadmissible. The reason usually given for excluding this evidence is that it is not up to the courts to create new exceptions to the hearsay rule. That is a matter for Parliament.

On the assumption that Gertrude's confession is inadmissible because of the hearsay rule, the next question is whether it could be admitted under one of the exceptions to the hearsay rule. It may be possible to argue that Gertrude's confession amounts to a declaration against her interest. However, even if it applied this exception is not preserved in **CJA 2003**.

Other possible routes to admissibility are under s. 116 of the **Criminal Justice Act 2003**. This admits first-hand oral hearsay if there is a reason for not calling the witness. One of the possible reasons is that the witness is dead (s. 116(2)(a)). This would apply in the case of Gertrude. Finally, this statement may be admissible under the 'interests of justice' inclusionary discretion in s. 114.

Question 5

Tom is charged with sexually assaulting Harriet at a residential university summer school. He denies the charge and claims that Harriet made it up because he had spurned her advances. She did not report the incident until some time after it allegedly happened. Tom claims that in fact he was away from the summer school on the day in question on a bicycle trip. However, the computer records which list the bicycle hirings have no record of his name and no one else can substantiate his alibi. The college bursar, Graham, has a note on file on the day in question, based on information from Carol, gardener at the school. She claims to have seen a couple she identified as Tom and Harriet struggling in the grounds. They had not seen her and she did not intervene but saw Harriet run off with her clothes dishevelled. Having thought about the incident she went later and reported it to Graham, who made a note of it on his tape recorder and it was subsequently typed by his secretary, John. Carol is now working in Australia and has not been traced.

Discuss the admissibility of Carol's evidence and of the computer bicycle hire records.

Commentary

In this question you are asked to consider whether the items in question are hearsay and then whether they may be admitted under any of the statutory or common law exceptions preserved by statute. Bear in mind that you must first characterise the statements as hearsay or not on the basis of the common law definition. The bicycle records raise the preliminary matter of whether absence of a record is hearsay and you need not worry about acknowledging the uncertainty of the law in this area. In Carol's case you need to be familiar with the provisions of the **Criminal Justice Act** s. 117 and what is meant by acting in the course of trade, etc. Bear in mind the need to discuss whether the document was prepared for the purposes of a pending or contemplated criminal investigation.

Answer plan

- Definition of hearsay
- Graham's note and possible application of s. 116 or 117, **CJA 2003**
- Application of art. 6 to hearsay rule
- Negative hearsay—computer printout

Suggested answer

The rule against hearsay states that an assertion other than one made by a person while giving oral evidence in the proceedings is inadmissible as evidence of any fact charged, as the House of Lords confirmed in *Myers* v *DPP* [1965] AC 1001. Carol could give direct oral evidence of what she had seen and this would clearly be relevant to the facts in issue since Tom's defence is alibi and fabrication. Since she is not available, the only evidence of this is what she has told Graham. The question then arises as to whether the evidence is admissible by virtue of the exceptions for documentary hearsay under the **Criminal Justice Act 2003 (CJA)**.

Carol's statement may be admissible under ss. 117 and 121. Under s. 117 in criminal proceedings a statement contained in a document is admissible as evidence of any matter stated if:

- oral evidence given in the proceedings would be admissible as evidence of that matter,
- the requirements of subsection (2) are satisfied.

Subsection (2) is satisfied if the document was created or received by a person in the course of a trade, business, profession or other occupation, the person who supplied the information (the relevant person) had or may reasonably be supposed to have had personal knowledge of the matters dealt with and each person (if any) through whom the information was supplied from the relevant person to the person mentioned in paragraph (a) received the information in the course of a trade, business, profession or other occupation. The creator of the document may be the person who supplied the information.

Carol was acting in the course of a trade and might reasonably be expected to have had personal knowledge of the matters dealt with.

The general common law rule is that a party who wishes to tender evidence must prove any necessary preconditions by admissible evidence. Proof must be to the appropriate standard, namely proof beyond reasonable doubt in the case of the prosecution and proof on the balance of probability in the case of the defence.

Cross and Tapper point out (2008, p. 651) that it is far from clear why **CJA 2003** s. 133 cannot be employed for this purpose.

Some forms of documentary hearsay are admissible as an exception to the general hearsay rule. A 'document' by virtue of s. 134 **CJA** is 'anything in which information of any description is recorded'. Graham's tape-recorded note of what Carol told him is thus to be treated as a statement in a document. The admissibility of evidence in this situation is governed by s. 117 of the **CJA**. This provides that under certain specified circumstances a statement in a document can be admissible as evidence of any fact of which direct oral evidence would be admissible if the document was (i) created by a person in the course of a trade, business, profession or other occupation or as an office-holder; and (ii) the information was supplied by a person (whether or not the maker of the statement) who had personal knowledge of the matters dealt with.

Whether or not the tape recording is admissible, then, depends on Carol's and Graham's status. Carol had personal knowledge of the facts as she perceived them. Graham received the information in the course of his occupation as supervisor. The admission of the typed notes from Graham's recording is subject to the same principles as the tape recording. They are admissible also under s. 117 **CJA** because the typist, John, was acting in the course of business.

A statement prepared for the purposes of criminal proceedings or investigation, for example a witness statement, is not admissible under s. 117 **CJA** unless either one of the reasons for non-appearance of the witness in s. 116 **CJA** is met, or the maker of the statement (the 'relevant person') cannot reasonably be expected to have any recollection of the matters dealt with having regard to the time which has elapsed and all the circumstances (s. 24(4) CJA). This here is Carol. It is also necessary to consider the purpose for which the tape recording was made. In *R v Bedi* (1991) 95 Cr App R 21 the prosecution had been allowed to adduce evidence of bank reports concerning lost and stolen credit cards. The judge had not considered as he should have done the purpose for which the reports were prepared. Here, the Court of Appeal held they were business documents to which s. 24(1) CJA 1988 applied but that s. 24(4) did not. This was a matter of fact to be determined by the judge in the light of the surrounding circumstances. On the facts, it does appear unlikely that Graham made the statement for the purpose of criminal proceedings. In any case even if he did, Carol's absence probably is one of the acceptable reasons for non-appearance, following the Court of Appeal in *R v French and Gowhar* (1993) 97 Cr App R 421. In this regard in examining whether it was 'not reasonably practicable' to secure the attendance of Carol the court will question whether the prosecution have done their best to produce her as a witness. In *R v Gyima* [2007] EWCA 429 the Court of Appeal considered whether the prosecution should have employed a video link at the trial to enable a child witness to give evidence live from America. One of the factors was the expense. The court found 'the prosecution had proved that they had taken all reasonable steps to secure the witness' attendance'.

Section 124 of the Act enables the opposing party to test the credibility of the absent 'maker' of the statement. The purpose is to put the absent maker in as close a position as possible to a witness who testifies in person. Thus for instance with leave of the court the other side may call evidence that could have been put to the 'maker' in cross-examination as relevant to his credibility, as if he had given oral evidence.

The party seeking to rely on s. 117 CJA must satisfy the court that the requirements of the section have been met. Here it is the prosecution which wishes to use the statement and the criminal standard of proof will apply (see *R v Case* [1991] Crim LR 192). The judge must generally hear oral evidence in a voir dire. The Court of Appeal in *R v Minors* [1989] 1 WLR 441 held that 'the foundation requirements of s. 24 of the Act of 1988 will also not be susceptible of proof by certificate'. The court has a discretion to exclude the statement even if it is technically admissible under ss. 126(1) and 125, s. 78 of the **Police and Criminal Evidence Act 1984 (PACE)** and at common law.

Since Carol will not be available to be cross-examined on the identification, which is a fact in issue, it may be argued this would create unfairness to Tom. Section 120 is not available to the prosecution because this only applies to prior statements of witnesses who are called to testify.

The defence may try to argue that particular care must be taken since the statement involves evidence of identification. It will not necessarily be excluded, however. Much depends on the strength of the evidence. Thus in *R v Setz-Dempsey and Richardson* (1994) 98 Cr App R 23 the Court of Appeal held that statements ought not to have been admitted since medical evidence undermined the quality of the evidence and the evidence of identification might have been further undermined by cross-examination. However, in *R* v *Greer* [1998] **Crim LR 572** the evidence was admissible. It was held that the fact that there was other live identification evidence was not a reason for preventing the absent witness's evidence of identification from being read. Much will depend here then on whether the court is convinced that the defence is disadvantaged on the facts from being denied the opportunity to cross-examine Carol. It may be possible to take her evidence on commission. Thus in *R* v *Radak* **(1999) 1 Cr App R 187**, where the prosecution failed to do this it was held that the statement should have been excluded under s. 26 **CJA 1988**.

The defence will also argue that the court will have to take into account the provisions of art. 6 of the European Convention on Human Rights following the implementation of the **Human Rights Act 1998**. Art. 6(3)(d) of the Convention states that a person charged with a criminal offence has the right 'to examine or have examined the witnesses against him and to obtain the attendance and examination of witnesses on his behalf under the same conditions as witnesses against him'. The case-law suggests, however, that the provisions of the **CJA** are unlikely to be deemed incompatible with the Convention. In *Trivedi* v *United Kingdom* **(1997) EHRLR 520** the Commission decided that the provisions of ss. 23–26 of the 1988 Act were not contrary to art. 6. In **Gokal (1997) 2 Cr App R 266** the Court of Appeal considered that the rights of defendants under this statute were safeguarded by s. 26 and thus art. 6 was satisfied. It drew on *Kostovski* v *The Netherlands* **(1989) 12 EHRR 434** to illustrate that the purpose of art. 6 was not to regulate the domestic law of evidence but to ensure overall fairness of the trial.

The prosecution may wish to show the computer printout from the bicycle hirings to suggest that Tom's alibi is false. The first issue is whether it is hearsay. There was a conflict of authority on whether absence of a record constituted hearsay. In *R* v *Patel* **[1981] 3 All ER 94**, the Court of Appeal, while accepting that the Home Office records which did not contain the name of the alleged illegal immigrant were hearsay, would have allowed the officer responsible for their compilation to give evidence. In the subsequent case of *R* v *Shone* **(1982) 76 Cr App R 72** the Court of Appeal took the view that the absence of a record was non-hearsay, circumstantial evidence. The 'non-statement' here is in documentary form generated by a computer. Cross and Tapper (2007 at p. 605) consider that these cases may still apply under the new law. They point out that:

> Questions of implied assertion also arise when a negative is sought to be proved from failure to state a positive, in situations where one might be expected. In the old law the admissibility of such evidence was regarded as compatible with the exclusion of hearsay. It is envisaged that such evidence will continue to be admissible under the new statutory regime, even without explicit general provisions.

Under s. 129 where a representation of any fact is made otherwise than by a person but depends for such accuracy on information supplied (directly or indirectly) by a person, the representation is not admissible in criminal proceedings as evidence of the fact unless it is proved that the information was accurate.

Question 6

'Although the common law appears to regard some statements against interest as inherently more reliable than other hearsay statements, there appears to be no available exception in English common law to accommodate third party confessions.' (Jenny McEwan, *Evidence and the Adversarial Process*, 2nd edn, Oxford: Hart, 1998, at p. 243.) Discuss.

Commentary

Hearsay is an area which lends itself to essay questions where you will be expected to discuss the rationale and alleged absurdities of the rule. To answer such questions well you need to show your knowledge of the law and also make some references to the academic debates. There are a number of controversial aspects of the rule against hearsay. Here you are just asked to deal with one, namely the exclusion of third-party confessions. Be careful you do not stray over into making a general diatribe against the rule. Focus as always on the specific question set. However, the exclusion of third-party confessions, of course, is one aspect of the general principle that the rule applies equally to the defence as to the prosecution. The difficulty with broad questions of this sort is in imposing your own plan on the material. A suitable one here would be to discuss first of all whether the extract describes an existing state of affairs. If so (and it will presumably be so to some extent at least!) give examples of exclusion of third-party confessions. Then go on to discuss why this is so. You should then discuss finally whether there is a case for reform. Your essay thus falls into three parts, not forgetting of course a well-observed conclusion.

Answer plan

- Exclusion of third-party confessions one aspect of general principle that the hearsay rule applies to defence and prosecution
- Does the quote accurately explain the state of affairs?
- Examples of exclusion of third-party confessions—*R* v *Blastland*
- Case for reform, particularly in light of operation of s. 23 **CJA 1988**, replaced by s. 116 **CJA 2003**
- Effect of reforms under **CJA 2003**

Suggested answer

Here, McEwan is passing comment on the common law position in relation to hearsay evidence. This exclusionary rule operated to prevent admissions by third parties. That this is undoubtedly how the courts have interpreted the law is made clear in the House of Lords decision in *R* v *Blastland* [1986] AC 41. The Court of Appeal had refused to allow confessions made by M, whom the defendant B claimed had approached the victim after him; the court felt bound by the Court of Appeal decision in *R* v *Turner* (1975) 61 Cr App R 67, and also by *Myers* v *DPP* [1965] AC 1001, where the House of Lords held that it was for Parliament to create any new exceptions to the hearsay rule. This state of affairs raises the issues referred to in the question, namely is this an accurate assessment of the law, and if it is, is it desirable?

In *Turner*, the judge was held to have rightly refused to admit evidence that a third party, not called as a witness, had admitted that he had committed the robbery, with which the defendant was charged. The court rejected the view that any of the cases cited to it were authority for the proposition that hearsay evidence is admissible in a criminal case to show that a third party who has not been called as witness in the case has admitted committing the offence charged. The principle applies even if the third party is dead. Thus, in *R* v *Thomson* [1912] 3 KB 19, the Court of Appeal upheld the trial judge's exclusion of statements by a deceased woman that she had intended to carry out an illegal abortion on herself and that she had in fact done so.

In *R* v *Blastland* [1986] AC 41 the exclusion of two sets of statements was upheld by the Court of Appeal. One was a confession by the third party to the police and the other a statement by him on the night of the murder and on the following day in which his state of mind was revealed, in particular his knowledge about the murder at a time when it was not generally known. Leave was given to apply to the House of Lords only on the second statement, and, although not clearly dissenting from the Court of Appeal who held it was hearsay, the ratio of their decision was that the statement should be excluded because it was irrelevant.

The case-law suggests that the exclusion has primarily been applied to confessions made by third parties who are not called as witnesses, so arguably the evidence of their guilt is weak. However, as the above case-law suggests, there is nothing in the rule to indicate it should be confined to those cases. The case-law then does certainly affirm the existence of the rule to which McEwan refers. However, as she pointed out, it was at least theoretically possible for ss. 23 and 24 CJA 1988 to apply. This allowed documentary hearsay evidence to be admitted. A third-party confession could be admissible, if written or not oral. As regards first-hand documentary hearsay, it could have been admitted at the discretion of the court (under s. 25 CJA) provided the maker of the statement was unable to attend court as a witness for one of the reasons set out in s. 23(2), (3) CJA, namely, that he was dead or unfit to attend as a witness, that he was outside the UK and it was not reasonably practicable to secure his attendance, that he cannot be found, or that having made a statement to a police officer or an investigating officer he does not give evidence through fear or because he is kept out of the way. Furthermore, under s. 24 **CJA**, which covered multiple hearsay, business documents could may be admitted as long as each of the intermediaries was acting in the course of trade, business, etc. Thus theoretically a confession by a third person made, for example, to a teacher could be admitted as long as it is made in the form of a statement. Under the **Criminal Justice Act 2003** there are more possible statutory routes to admissible third-party confessions. First, s. 116 covers oral or written statements where there is a statutory reason for not calling the witness. Second, the inclusionary discretion under s. 114 may allow a statement to be admitted in the interests of justice. Finally the 'business' document exception under s. 117 mirrors that in the 1988 Act, so the arguments above apply.

One area of contention is whether a confession made by a co-defendant may be tendered by a defendant. Where there are two accused one defendant may want to make use of a confession by the other either because it supports his case or to cross-examine on any inconsistencies between the confession and the defendant's evidence at trial. If the confession is tendered by the prosecution this is possible but until recently there was conflict of authority in relation to confessions which either had not been used by the prosecution or had been excluded by the judge. Section 76 of **PACE** applies only where the confession is tendered by the prosecution. Clearly there is a potential conflict between the interests of the two defendants. The courts have gradually addressed this conflict. In *R* v *Rowson* [1986] **QB 174** the Court of Appeal held that the trial judge has no discretion to prevent counsel for the co-accused from cross-examining the maker of an inadmissible confession. Such questioning is for the purpose of attacking credibility by showing inconsistency. In *Lui-Mei Lin* v *R* (1989) 88 Cr App R 296 the Privy Council held that as long as the matter is relevant the right to cross-examine is unfettered. There was conflict of authority on whether the co-accused is able to use the confession as evidence of truth, for example where the confession exculpates him. In *R* v *Myers* [1998] **AC 124** the House of Lords resolved the conflict between *R* v *Beckford* [1991] **Crim LR 833** and *R* v *Campbell* [1993] **Crim LR 448**. Two defendants were jointly charged with murder. One made a statement which amounted to an admission that she had stabbed the victim but the statement was not preferred by the prosecution because of apparent breaches of the Code of Practice. The House of Lords held that the trial judge had rightly allowed the co-defendant to cross-examine about the statement and adduce it in evidence as relevant to his defence. Murphy (2007 at p. 324) comment on *Myers*:

> It follows from this decision that a co-accused may not only cross-examine the maker of the statement but may also cross-examine a police officer to whom the confession was made, if the maker does not give evidence, and that the judge has no discretion to prevent this.

The case shows a welcome inroad into the practice of exclusion of third-party confessions. However, the law still does not allow the admission of statements made by non-accused third parties'. Under the **Criminal Justice Act 2003** s. 128 a new s. 76A is inserted into **PACE** 1984 whereby a defendant may adduce a co-accused's confession if he can prove, on the balance of probabilities, that it was not obtained in violation of identical provisions as those in s. 76 **PACE**. *R* v *Johnson* [2007] EWCA Crim 651 shows the application of this provision. It shows that it applies where one defendant pleads guilty before the trial and is then permitted to change his plea. The co-defendant was allowed to adduce the earlier guilty plea, which had not been obtained by anything said or done which was likely to render any confession under these circumstances unreliable. This is thus a further inroad into the exclusion of third-party confessions.

Academic opinion generally has been critical of the exclusion of third-party confessions. Birch (1987) looks at *Blastland* in the light of the rule against hearsay generally. Referring to the House of Lords' refusal to create new hearsay exceptions, she argues that *Myers* v *DPP* [1965] AC 1001 (at p. 27) 'does not exclude the possibility of tinkering with existing exceptions'. She cites the common law exception most suitable to be amended as the declaration against interest, acknowledging that this exception identified by the House of Lords in the *Sussex Peerage Case* (1844) 11 Cl & Fin 85 must be against the proprietary pecuniary interest of the declarant and that the declarant must have died before the trial. However, Birch comes to the conclusion that it would be unrealistic to expect these obstacles to be overcome. She further argues that concern over letting in a third-party confession by the back door led the House of Lords to uphold a 'hearsay fiddle' by calling M's indirect evidence in *R* v *Blastland* of his 'state of mind' irrelevant.

Third-party confessions are excluded primarily because of the risk of a spate of false confessions. McEwan points out that the Lindbergh kidnapping in the United States resulted in over 200 confessions. Obviously, many such cases can be eliminated early on because the maker has insufficient knowledge of the details of the offence. But McEwan suggests that the adversarial system is ill-equipped to test the untrustworthiness of third-party confessions, although an inquisitorial procedure, not relying on oral evidence, could do so more easily.

There is thus a strong argument on grounds of lack of reliability for excluding third-party confessions. The weakness of this type of evidence is that of hearsay evidence generally, summarised by Tribe (1977, p. 959) as faulty perception, erroneous memory, ambiguity and insincerity.

With regard to declarations against interest then admissible as exceptions to the rule against hearsay, he points out that the sincerity problem is overcome by the assumption that a person is unlikely to make a statement adverse to himself unless it is true and ambiguity is avoided by admitting only statements that are sufficiently unambiguous that they can be found to be against the declarant's interest. He argues that defects of memory or faulty perception may apply. It could be submitted, however, that this is unlikely in the event of confession to a crime.

The question then arises, is there anything specifically at issue in third-party confessions which would argue for a new exception to be made to the hearsay rule? The major objection to the present state of affairs is that although it applies to prosecution and defence, obviously it most harms the defence (except in those cases where the third-party confessor is a co-defendant). Thus as Zuckerman (1989, at p. 184) points out, the rule violates the principle of protecting the innocent. He also adds (at p. 185) that it defies common sense. Arguably the non-admissibility of third-party confessions is all the more unfair to the defence since in *R* v *Hayter* [2005] UKHL 6, the House of Lords allowed a confession of one defendant to be considered by the jury as evidence against a co-defendant.

Clearly, confessions of defendants can be unreliable and psychologists have pointed out the many reasons for confessing other than truth. In fact, attempts to find general rationales are probably unwise. The question points to the desirability of an inclusionary discretion for hearsay evidence based on the strength and weight of evidence, not its form. The courts have taken very seriously the principle made in *Myers* that Parliament must make any radical changes on the rule against hearsay. But this principle is not universally applied in the law of evidence. Thus, in *R* v *Andrews* [1987] AC 281, the House of Lords made major changes to the common law res gestae exception to the rule against hearsay. There is a strong case to be made for a flexible, inclusionary discretion in relation to hearsay to avoid what Zuckerman (1989, p. 216) called 'an amount of casuistic sophistry' in the interests of a rule which is wider than its rationale requires. Parliament has now carried out a wholesale reform of the law on criminal hearsay in the **Criminal Justice Act 2003** and the routes for the possible admissibility of third-party confessions have increased. First, the scope for admitting oral hearsay is now much broader (s. 116), and second, the existence of an inclusionary discretion (s. 114) means the court may, in the interests of justice, admit statements which do not fulfil the statutory requirements. However, the courts will doubtless be influenced by common law jurisprudence in exercising this discretion.

Question 7

Henry is charged with causing grievous bodily harm to James. The prosecution case is that he attacked James with a knife after a row in a public house. James has been disfigured as a result of the wounding. Henry denies the attack, claiming he was elsewhere at the time and that he has never met James. James was taken to hospital by ambulance. As he travelled there he gave an account of the incident to PC Green. PC Green read it back to James and he nodded his agreement, not being able to sign because of the drips in his arm. After an operation he has not regained consciousness. Tom and Gerry were eyewitnesses to the incident and both made statements to the police which they subsequently signed. However, Tom has told the police he is too afraid to tell the court about what he saw and Gerry's mother has told police he also is too scared to give evidence. Freda, a Brazilian tourist, made a statement to Henry's solicitor after the incident that she was with Henry at the cinema at the relevant time. She has now returned to Brazil.
   Advise on evidence.

Commentary

You are presented in this question with several 'statements' and you are thus alerted that the **Criminal Justice Act 2003** ('**CJA**') may apply. You need to be aware of the recent case-law on the application of this statute. It is not enough simply to summarise the sections. In this question you need also to be aware of how the courts have interpreted these somewhat overlapping provisions and how their requirements can be proved. A failure to refer to the Court of Appeal decision **R** v **McGillivray (1992) 97 Cr App R 232,** for example, would be a weakness in an answer to this question. There is also some important case-law on what is meant by 'fear' in s. 23(3) **CJA**, now included in s. 116 **CJA 2003**. This question is an illustration of how evidential issues are closely related to procedural ones. Evidence courses vary in their emphasis on this area.

Answer plan

- James' statement to police—s. 116 **CJA 2003**
- **R** v **McGillivray**—statements to police
- Reason for non-appearance of Tom is fear—see s. 116(2)(e)
- Freda's statement—not reasonably practicable to call her—**R** v **Case (1991)**
- Discretion to exclude statements

Suggested answer

James makes a statement to a police officer but is not available as a witness at the trial because he is unconscious. Section 116 of the **Criminal Justice Act 2003** provides that a statement by a person is admissible in criminal proceedings as evidence of any fact of which direct oral evidence would be admissible. Thus 'first-hand' hearsay evidence is admissible provided certain conditions are met. Section 116 **CJA** rather than s. 117 **CJA** is arguably the appropriate section here, since the Court of Appeal held in **R** v **McGillivray (1992) 97 Cr App R 232** that s. 24 **CJA** did not apply to a statement made by a person subsequently deceased to a police officer. The court apparently took the view that s. 24 **CJA** was intended to apply to ordinary business transactions but not to 'police documents', although Smith (1994) disagreed with this interpretation. The maker of the statement must be unable to attend court as a witness for one of the reasons set out in s. 116(2).

Here, **CJA 2003** s. 116(2)(b) will apply, since the witness is unfit to attend. Further conditions are that the statement must be first hand hearsay and the person making it would be a competent witness. In **R** v **McGillivray** the Court of Appeal also held that an unsigned statement made by a deceased person to the police was admissible under s. 23 **CJA** provided that the deceased had clearly acknowledged by speech or otherwise that the statement was accurate. The victim who had been set alight made a statement to a police officer in hospital as a nurse confirmed. The court said the statement was admissible because the victim, who later died, had indicated it was accurate but he was physically unable to sign it. Section 116, unlike s. 23, admits first hand oral hearsay, so arguably Green can testify what James said to him.

With regard to Tom, the prosecution may seek to rely on s. 116(2)(e) that he does not give evidence through fear. There has been case-law on the interpretation of the predecessor to this section. In *R v Acton Justices, ex parte McMullen* (1990) **92 Cr App R 98**, the Divisional Court had to be satisfied that the witness was in fear as a consequence of the offence or of something said or done subsequently relating to it and the possibility of the witness's giving evidence. Furthermore, the same case held that it does not have to be proved that something has occurred since the commission of the offence to put the witness in fear so as to keep him out of the way. *McMullen* also established that the fear need not be a reasonable one, although the reasonableness might be a relevant consideration deciding admissibility. In addition, there was no requirement that the fear is linked to the offence. In *Martin* [1996] Crim LR 589 a silent stranger stood outside the witness's home and there was no obvious relation to the offence.

It may be difficult to prove that a witness who is not present in court is fearful. If the witness attends the fear may be visible (*R v Ashford and Tenteden Justices, ex parte Hilden* [1993] 96 Cr App R 92 and *R v James Greer* [1998] Crim LR 572). In *Neill v North Antrim Magistrates' Court* [1993] 97 Cr App R 121 there was an inadmissible third-hand hearsay statements. In *R v H.W. and M.* [2001] **The Times, 6 July** the evidence of fear was out of date, being based on an earlier statement for the police. It was recommended that the evidence of fear should be made available by video link or tape-recording.

Section 116(4) sets out the conditions under which the court may give leave for admitting these statements. Note that it refers to unfairness to the proceedings, not just the defendant. (*R v Cole* (1990) 90 Cr App R 478 was the leading case on the exercise of exclusionary discretion under **CJA 2008**).

A problem may arise if the jury asks why a witness was not called. In *R v Churchill* [1993] Crim LR 285, where the judge told the jury he had decided circumstances applied in which a crucial witness who claimed to be in fear need not give evidence, the Court of Appeal said the judge should have discussed with counsel how to handle the question. The judge's 'explanation had amounted to something in the nature of a pat on the back for a witness whose testimony had been disputed but had not been tested in cross-examination'. The jury might wrongly have inferred that the failure to testify could be a matter to the discredit of the accused. In the circumstances the judge should simply have said he could not answer the question. In *Neill v North Antrim Magistrates' Court* [1992] 1 WLR 1220, a case arising under a similar Northern Ireland provision, namely art. 3(3)(b) of the **Criminal Justice (Evidence, etc.) Northern Ireland Order 1988**, the House of Lords held that the fact that a witness was absent through fear had to be proved by admissible evidence. There, the evidence of the police officer as to what he had been told by the mother of the two youths about their apprehensions had been hearsay and could not be admitted under the exception to the hearsay rule that enabled the court to receive first degree hearsay as to state of mind. The House held (at p. 1229) that:

> Whatever may be the intellectual justification of the exception to the hearsay rule which enables the court to receive first degree hearsay as to state of mind . . . it cannot be stretched to embrace what is essentially a third hand account of the witness' apprehensions.

Accordingly, the statements of the youths should not have been admitted in evidence. *R* v *O'Loughlin* [1988] 3 All ER 431 was applied. The court held (obiter) that a statement by a witness who is afraid of appearing through fear would be admissible as a res gestae statement of present state of mind, the common law exception. Thus, the police officer may here give evidence of what Tom said directly to him but not what Gerry's mother told him, in explaining to the court why the witnesses will not give evidence. In *R* v *Rutherford* [1998] Crim LR 490 the Court of Appeal held that fear could be proved by a written statement from the witness. In *R* v *Sellick* the Court of Appeal held that a defendant's rights under art. 6(3)(d) of the Convention could not be infringed where he kept a witness away from a trial through fear as he was the author of his own inability to examine the witness and deprived himself of his only opportunity to do so. In such circumstances, provided that care had been taken to see that the quality of the evidence was compelling, firm steps had been taken to draw the jury's attention to aspects of the witness's credibility and a clear direction had been given to the jury to exercise caution, these precautions ensured fairness in compliance with art. 6(1); that even where a court believed to a high degree of probability, as opposed to being sure, that a witness was being intimidated on behalf of the defence or was sure that the witness could not be traced, there was still no absolute rule that where the witness's statement was the sole or decisive evidence the admission in evidence of that statement would automatically lead to an infringement of the defendant's art. 6 rights. The evidence of fear must not be second-hand.

The wording of this section is very similar to old law. It is the defence who will presumably try to rely on s. 116(2)(c) for Freda's statement. In satisfying the court that the requirements of the statute are met, the defence will only have to comply with the civil standard of proof as the Court of Appeal held in *R* v *Mattey and Queeley* (1995) 2 Cr App R 459. Freda's statement was presumably endorsed by her and the appropriate reason for not calling her appears to be that she is outside the United Kingdom and it was not reasonably practicable to secure her attendance. In *R* v *Case* [1991] Crim LR 192, the trial judge had admitted witness statements by two Portuguese tourists, including the victim. The Court of Appeal held that they had been wrongly admitted because the court should have been presented with other evidence on non-availability other than the contents of the statements. Thus, the defence must produce additional evidence that Freda cannot attend. The court must consider all the circumstances of the case. Following *R* v *Case*, the court may take account of the costs of Freda's travel in deciding what is reasonably practicable. In *R* v *Gonzales* [1992] **Crim LR 180**, the Court of Appeal held that the trial judge had been wrong in concluding that it was not reasonably practicable to secure the attendance of two booking clerks from Bogota. Further steps could have been taken, such as offering to pay their fares.

For all of these statements, even if these preliminary requirements are met, the court will only admit in the light of the discretion afforded under s. 126(1) **CJA**. With regard to Tom and Gerry's statements, the fact that Henry may have to give evidence to controvert them is not in itself unfair, as the Court of Appeal held in *R* v *Moore* [1992] **Crim LR 882**. In each case, the court must conduct a balancing exercise between the interests of the public as represented by the prosecution and the interests of the particular defendant. In *R* v *Cole* (1990) **90 Cr App R 478**, the Court of Appeal laid down guidelines for the exercise of this discretion under the **CJA 1988**. The court held that it was proper to have regard to the likelihood of it being possible to contradict the statement by the defendant giving evidence and calling witnesses. It may thus be unfair to admit the evidence of Tom and Gerry and not Freda's evidence because Henry may not have any other witness to back up his alibi. The defence is unlikely to succeed in arguing that the admission of documentary hearsay violates art. 6 of the European Convention on Human Rights, enshrined in English law by the **Human Rights Act 1998**. In *Gokal* (1997) **2 Cr App R 266** Lord Justice Ward stated that 'since the whole basis of the exercise of the discretion conferred by s. 26 is to assess the interests of justice by reference to the risk of unfairness to the accused, our procedures appear to us to accord fully with our treaty obligations'.

One final point of interest to note is that the Court of Appeal in *R* v *Montgomery* [1995] **2 All ER 28** confirms that a witness who does not give evidence through fear and whose evidence is admitted in documentary form may still be sentenced for contempt of court. So Tom and Gerry may be punished on those grounds.

Question 8

Mike, Tony and John are charged with stealing cash from the safe of a restaurant. The prosecution case is that the three acted in concert to break into the cafe, Mike and Tony breaking and entering and John driving the getaway car. When the police conduct a (lawful) search of Mike's flat they discover a piece of paper in his writing which states: 'John to get £1,000 for the car job, Tony and me to split the rest.' John's library ticket is found in a stolen car abandoned a few streets from the burglary, and a quantity of cash is found in a shed on an allotment which is shared by Mike and Tony. Tom, a vagrant, who often slept on the allotments, tells PC Jones that he had been sitting near the shed till late on June 19, the day of the burglary, and had seen the three defendants arrive together. He saw them put a bag in their shed and then leave. PC Jones makes a note of this information but does not ask Tom to sign it. Tom has now left the area and cannot be found. All three defendants deny the charges and say they have no idea how the cash came to be in the shed.

Advise them.

Commentary

A statement made in furtherance of a common purpose by one defendant may be admissible as evidence against the others. You need to consider this common law exception in relation to the note found in Mike's flat, or whether the **Criminal Justice Act 2003** (**CJA 2003**) should apply. The application of the statute should be considered in relation to Tom's evidence and in particular the implications of *R* v *Derodra* (**2000**) **1 Cr App R 41**. The library ticket may be also classed as a document overcoming the controversial implications of the decision in *Patel* v *Comptroller of Customs* **[1966] AC 356**.

Answer plan

- Statement of common purpose may be admissible against defendants in conspiracy or common enterprise cases—s. 118 **CJA 2003**
- Library ticket may be admissible under s. 118 **CJA 2003** or as real evidence
- Application of **Criminal Procedure and Investigations Act 1996**

Suggested answer

The prosecution are alleging that the three defendants acted together. The evidence of the note found in Mike's flat may be admissible as an exception to the rule against hearsay. The statement is in a document and therefore the question of s. 116 of the **Criminal Justice Act 2003** (**CJA 2003**) may be raised. However, in order for this to apply there has to be a reason not to call the maker of the statement and this will hardly apply in Mike's case since he will be at the trial as a defendant. Recent developments in the case-law have increased the likelihood of such statements being considered admissible under the common law and now included in s. 118 CJA 2003. A longstanding principle allowed the acts and declarations of one conspirator to be admissible against another as long as these were in furtherance of the conspiracy. In *Tripodi* v *R* [1961] 104 CLR 1 the High Court of Australia observed 'the combination or pre-concert to commit the crime is considered as implying an authority to each to act or speak in furtherance of the common purpose on behalf of the others'. It now appears that this principle has been extended beyond conspiracy cases. Thus in *R* v *Gray, Liggins, Riding and Rowlands* (1995) 2 Cr App R 100 it was held that in cases where there is no charge of conspiracy against two or more defendants where they are engaged in a common enterprise to commit a substantive offence or series of offences, the acts and declarations of one defendant in relation to their common enterprise are admissible against the others if they constitute evidence which shows the involvement of each in the offences. The facts in this question are similar to *R* v *Devonport and Pirano* **(1996) 1 Cr App R 221**, where a document showing the proposed division of the proceeds of a conspiracy to defraud was admissible against both accused because, *inter alia*, there was further evidence beyond the document itself that the accused were all involved. Here there is other evidence, including the finding of the cash. An important aspect of the decision in *Devonport and Pirano* was that the document was a record of the planned distribution of the proceeds, not a record of what had happened. Therefore Mike's statement is likely to be admissible against all three defendants. If the statement is admitted the judge will have to warn the jury that they should be satisfied that the evidence was that of an intention to split the proceeds of a crime they were planning to commit with a common purpose.

Section 118 preserves 'any rule of law under which in criminal proceedings a statement made by a party to a common enterprise is admissible against another party to the enterprise as evidence of any matter stated'. The Explanatory Note on the statute gives an example: 'if it is independently proved that A and B are involved in a joint enterprise to rob a jewellers', any incriminating statements made by A will also be admissible against B'.

The library ticket may be relevant evidence if it links John to the getaway car. If he denies having been in the car the prosecution may want to adduce it to undermine his defence. If the ticket has his name on it the question whether it is hearsay arises in that it constitutes an implied assertion that John was there. In *Patel* v *Comptroller of Customs* [1966] AC 356 a label bearing the inscription 'Produce of Morocco' was hearsay evidence. Here, however, the library ticket is not making an express assertion. It could be treated as a mark of identification rather than an assertion. In *R* v *Rice* [1963] 1 QB 857 an issue in the case was whether Rice had been a passenger on a particular flight to Manchester. An airline representative was allowed to give evidence that a ticket found in the file of those used on the flight had Rice's name on it. Winn LJ explained: 'The relevance of that ticket in logic and its legal admissibility as a piece of real evidence both stem from the same root, viz, the balance of probability recognised by common sense and common knowledge that an air ticket which has been used on a flight and which has a name upon it has more likely than not been used by a man of that name.' The ticket could be taken as real evidence, from which an inference could be drawn that John was in the car.

The decision in *Rice* has been much criticised. An alternative approach would be to see if the library ticket was admissible by virtue of s. 118 **CJA 2003**. A 'document' under the statute has the widest possible application of 'anything in which any information of any description is recorded'. The ticket with John's name on it was compiled presumably from information given by John, thus the information on his name was given by him, with personal knowledge of his identity to a person, the librarian, in the course of a trade, business, profession or other occupation. Since the document was not prepared in the course of criminal proceedings there is no need for a reason not to call the maker of the statement. Finally, the prosecution may want to rely on PC Jones' statement of what Tom had told him. If the statement was admitted at committal proceedings it would be admissible at trial by virtue of the **Criminal Procedure and Investigations Act 1996** subject to the right of the opposing party to object. The court may override an objection if it thinks it is in the interests of justice so to order. If it was not a formal deposition but information given by Tom to PC Jones at an early stage of the investigation it may be admissible by s. 116 **CJA 2003** if Tom had endorsed the statement or in some other way adopted it as his own. Alternatively it may be admitted as a first hand oral statement, as testified by Jones. There has to be a reason not to call Tom and on the facts we cannot tell whether an acceptable reason applies. Jones' statement may be admissible by virtue of s. 117 but since it was part of evidence-gathering again there has to be a reason for not calling the maker. Again there may be difficulties in applying an acceptable reason to Tom's absence. There is judicial discretion to exclude the statement even if it is admissible. The difference between real evidence and hearsay has proved difficult to distinguish. It is crucial in determining how the jury should be directed. This is illustrated in the recent case of *R* v *Nelson* [2004] **EWCA Crim 333**. The Court of Appeal considered the status of a statement which had been admitted. This was a record of a call made by the father of the defendant to the police shortly after an incident of stabbing. The defendant at trial claimed automatism in defence to the charge. The statement was original evidence to show that the father had been made aware of the stabbing by the defendant who was thus not suffering from automatism, but it was hearsay evidence if tendered to suggest he had carried out the stabbing. The jury should have been directed on this.

Additional Reading

Allen, J., 'The Working and Rationale of the Hearsay Rule and the Implications of Modern Psychological Knowledge' (1991) CLP 217.

Ashworth, A.J. and Pattenden R., 'Reliability, Hearsay Evidence and the English Criminal Trial' (1986) 102 LQR 292.

Birch, D., 'Hearsay Logic and Hearsay Fiddles: Blastland Revisited' in Smith P. (ed.) *Criminal Law: Essays in Honour of J.C. Smith* (Butternorth, 1987).

Birch, D., 'The Criminal Justice Act 1982. (2) Documentary Evidence' (1989) Crim LR 15.

Birch, D., 'Criminal Justice Act 2003. (4) Hearsay; Same Old Story, Same Old Song?' (2004) Crim LR 556.

Choo, A., 'The Hearsay Rule and Confessions Relied upon by the Defence' (1997) 1 E&P 158.

Choo, H., *Hearsay and Confrontation in Criminal Trials* (Oxford, 1996).

Dennis, I., 'The Criminal Justice Act 2003, Part 2' [2004] Crim LR 251.

Friedman, R.D., 'Thoughts from Across the Water on Hearsay and Confrontation' (1998) Crim LR 697.

Guest, S., 'The Scope of the Hearsay Rule' (1985) 101 LQR 385.

Hartshorne, J., 'Defensive use of a co-accused's confession and The Criminal Justice Act 2003' (2004) 8 E&P 165.

Jackson, J.D., 'Hearsay: the Sacred Cow that Won't be Slaughtered' (1998) 2 E&P 166.

Law Commission (Law Com. No. 245) *Evidence in Criminal Proceedings: Hearsay and Relevant Topics* (1997) www.lawcom.gov.uk/docs/lc245pdf (accessed 27/8/06).

Leng, R., and Taylor, R., 'Living with the Discretionary Admission of Written Hearsay in the Crown Court' (1997) 1 E&P 403.

Morgan, E.M., 'Hearsay Dangers and the Application of the Hearsay Concept?' (1948) 62 Harv LR 177.

Murphy, P., 'Hearsay: The Road to Reform' (1997) 1 E&P 107.

Ockleton, M., 'Documentary Hearsay in Criminal Cases' [1992] Crim LR 15.

Pattenden, R., 'Conceptual versus Pragmatic Approaches to Hearsay' (1993) 56 MLR 138.

Peysner, J., 'Hearsay is Dead. Long Live Hearsay!' (1998) 2 E&P 232.

Smith, J., 'Documentary Evidence in Criminal Proceedings' (1999) 149 NLJ 1550.

Spencer, J.R., 'Hearsay, Relevance and Implied Assertions' (1993) CLJ 40.

Tapper, C., 'Hearsay and Implied Assertions' (1992) 108 LQR 524.

Taylor, R., Wasik, M. and Leng, R., *Blackstone's Guide to the* Criminal Justice Act 2003 (OUP, Oxford, 2004).

Tribe, L., 'Triangulating Hearsay' (1974) 87 Harv LR 957.

6

Confessions
and the defendant's silence

Introduction

Confessions

This is an area in which your work will be improved if you read widely around the subject and do not approach it in a mechanical, overly technical way. In many trials the most cogent evidence available to the prosecution, on occasion the only evidence, will be a pre-trial confession by the accused. This is most frequently obtained by the investigating authority, generally the police, since the state acts as chief investigator as well as prosecutor. But while confessions have long been accepted as authentic evidence of guilt, they also posed certain risks, those both of unreliability and of violation of individual autonomy. On the one hand defendants may not be making a true confession, and on the other even if the confession was likely to be true it may have been obtained in ways that were the result of unacceptable pressure on the suspect, thus arguably sapping his free will. At the most extreme level this could be by torture.

Confessions as admissions of guilt have played an important part in the development of Western culture since the late Middle Ages and there is an intimate link between law and religion in this area. In 1215 the Roman Catholic Church, in the Fourth Lateran Council, made annual confession obligatory for all the faithful. The American academic Peter Brooks has made an extensive study of the cultural role of confessions. He writes (2001, p. 2):

> The confessional model is so powerful in western culture, I believe, that even those whose religion or non-religion has no place for the Roman Catholic practice of confession are nonetheless deeply influenced by the model. Indeed, it permeates our cultures, including our educational practices and our law. The image of the penitent with the priest, in the intimate yet impersonal, private and protected spaces of the confessional, represents a potent social ritual that both its friends and its enemies have recognised as a shaping cultural experience."

Thus the confession gives an absolution and is treated with reverence. Brooks continues, however, by explaining how the image of the confession is also one of deepest suspicion:

> Another image, though, is more regularly represented in our entertainments: the criminal suspect locked into the interrogation room, face to face with police detectives in a Spartan and sordid space where his confessions of guilt arise not from the spontaneous contrition of the aggrieved conscience, but from relentless interrogation. Only confession, the suspect is told, can bring release from interrogation. The interrogators are sure of his guilt. Denial will only make things worse. The process of rehabilitation and reintegration—if by way of punishment and expiation—can only begin when the suspect says those words, 'I did it.'

Brooks explores the different kinds of truths which are obtainable from confessions and illuminates the appetite for them in Western culture, but also their ambiguities and uncertainties.

Confessions may have contradictory outcomes—they make those who confess feel better rather than provide useful, objective evidence. In addition, the very process of interrogation, particularly when there is public pressure on the authorities to obtain a conviction, may lead to confessions which are the outcome of force, coercion or other exhibition of improper use of state power. From the seventeenth century in England force was less commonly used as a means of obtaining evidence. Sharpe (1998, p. 18) points out that gradually the 'status or authority of a confession made willingly and without violence was . . . distinguished in evidential terms from one made under duress'. As a result there has long been some legal control both over interrogation methods and admissibility of confessions at a later trial. Before the **Police and Criminal Evidence Act 1984**, however, this legal control was somewhat lightly applied. Common law specified that the admissible confession must be a voluntary one. The reasoning was primarily that one received under duress may be unreliable. The leading case was **Ibrahim [1914] AC 599,** where Lord Sumner stated: 'It has long been established . . . that no statement by an accused is admissible in evidence against him unless it is shown by the prosecution to have been a voluntary statement, in the sense that it had not been obtained from him either by fear of prejudice, or hope of advantage exercised or held out to him by a person in authority.' The subject of confession evidence and the companion issue of the privilege against self-incrimination have assumed new importance in the light of the implementation of the **Human Rights Act**. Increasingly, the courts are approaching these issues from the standpoint of the integral question of fair trial rights rather than an overly formal approach to procedural correctness.

The tables below give a very brief overview of some of the leading cases and statutes covering these areas: definition of confessions including statutory definition, 'mixed statements' and denials as confessions; the protective statutory regime including access to legal advice (s. 58 **PACE**) and the PACE Codes; exclusion by statute or common law; confessions challenged for authenticity; confessions and third parties.

Confessions play a large part in evidence examination questions just as they do in trials in real life. There are many cases on this subject, but the starting point is the **Police and Criminal Evidence Act 1984 (PACE)**, which includes both a definition of confessions (s. 82(1)) and a statement of the circumstances which would lead to their exclusion under rule (s. 76(2)(a) and (b)). You must distinguish this rule of exclusion from exclusion by exercise of the discretion by s. 78 on grounds of lack of fairness and by s. 82(3), which preserves the common law discretion. In determining whether the confession should be excluded or not, you will be called upon to see primarily if there has been a breach of the statute or the Codes of Practice. Exclusion is not automatic: you must assess the seriousness and the effect of any breach or other police malpractice, such as lies. You will therefore need to examine the facts systematically, listing possible transgressions and noting if they are deliberate or not. The courts have, in relation to s. 76(2)(a) and s. 78, stressed the importance of the state of mind of the investigating officers, whereas s. 76(2)(b) applies an objective test.

The Codes of Practice which accompany **PACE**, issued under s. 66, are very important in determining the admissibility of confessions, specifically Code C on Detention, Treatment and Questioning of Persons by police officers and Code E on the Tape-recording of Interviews. The current Code C contains a definition of a police interview (paragraph 11.1A) which was previously only defined in a Note for Guidance. The **Criminal Justice Act 2003** has introduced some important changes in relation to confessions and silence (see Tables 11, 12 and 13 below). Under s. 128 a new s. 76A **PACE** is created which applies s. 76 tests of admissibility for confessions made by a co-accused. One section which was brought into force in January 2004 increases the period of time that a person arrested on suspicion of an arrestable offence can be held to 36 hours (s. 7, amending s. 42(1) **PACE**).

Silence

Wide-sweeping changes were introduced in the **Criminal Justice and Public Order Act 1994** (CJPOA). These have implications for confessions because they make it proper for the court to draw inferences from the defendant's silence when questioned under caution under certain circumstances. The caution has been consequently reworded as follows: 'You do not have to say anything. But it may harm your defence if you do not mention when questioned something which you later rely on in court. Anything you do say may be given in evidence' (paragraph 10.5). You must be clear on the difference between s. 34 of the 1994 Act, which allows inferences to be drawn from the accused's silence after caution but is only activated if the accused or his counsel offers evidence in due course, which could have been provided in answers to earlier questions and sections 36 and 37 of the 1994 Act, which deal with silence on arrest whether or not the defendant offers an explanation at trial. Thus s. 36 of the 1994 Act allows inferences to be drawn from the failure of an arrested person to account for objects, substances or marks found on his person, his clothing or his footwear in his possession or in a place where he is at the time of arrest and s. 37 from his failure to or refusal to account for his presence at a place at or about the time of his arrest. (Section 35, which governs the defendant's refusal to testify, is covered in **Chapter 3**).

You will need to familiarise yourself with the Strasbourg cases in this area and also the increasing number of cases under the **Human Rights Act**; see particularly *Funke* v *France* (1993) **16 EHRR 297**, *Condron* v *UK* (2001) **31 EHRR 1**, *Brown* v *Stott* [2001] **2 WLR 817** and *Luckhof* v *Austria* (2008) **Crim LR 549**.

By s. 58 of the **Youth Justice and Criminal Evidence Act 1999**, ss. 34 and 36–38 of the **CJPOA** have been amended. The provisions are not operative if the accused was at an authorised place of detention and had not been allowed an opportunity to consult a solicitor prior to being questioned, charged or officially informed he might be prosecuted.

One final point to note is that silence itself may be admissible at common law as a confession if the defendant is on 'even terms' with his interrogator. This is discussed in *R v Webber* [2004] 1 WLR 404, paras 16, 17.

Tables 11, 12, and 13 give a summary of the main statutory provisions on confessions and on silence in the **CJPOA**, along with some notes on key cases.

Table 11 Confessions: s. 82(1) **PACE**—some key cases and statutory sections

Case/section	Principle
R v Sharp [1988] 1 All ER	'Mixed' statements admissible as truth of contents
R v Polin [1991] Crim LR 293	'Mixed' statement may be written or record of questions and answers in police interview
Section 118 **CJA 2003**	Preserves any rule of law of relating to the admissibility of confessions or mixed statements
Section 76 (1) **PACE**	Confession must be made by an accused person
R v Ward, Andrews, Broadley [2001] Crim LR 316	W's identification of himself evidence he was at scene and admissible as confession (?hearsay evasion)
R v Hasan [2005] 2 WLR 709	House of Lords overturned a Court of Appeal decision; s. 82 does not cover non-inculpatory statements which later are adverse to the maker, thus s. 76 did not apply, although s. 78 may confirmed *R v Sat-Bhambra* (1988) 88 Cr App R 55
Section 58 **PACE** amended by **Serious Organised Crime and Police Act 2005**˙	Enshrines principles of access to legal advice which may be delayed in cases of indictable offences (previously 'serious arrestable offences')
R v Samuel (1987) 87 Cr App R 232	S. 58 enshrines 'one of the most important and fundamental rights of a citizen'
R v Kirk [2000] 1 WLR 567	Suspect entitled to be told of seriousness of offence, otherwise s. 78 may apply
Section 76(2)(a) **PACE**	Misuse of power by authorities will lead to exclusion (see *R v Fulling* [1987] QB 426)
Section 76(2)(b) **PACE**	If anything said or done in the circumstances existing at the time that may render any confession unreliable it should be excluded
R v Harvey (1998) Crim LR 241	There is no need for police impropriety for s. 76(2)(b) to apply
R v Goldenberg (1988) 88 Cr App R 285	'Anything said or done is limited to something external to the person making the confession and to something which is likely to have some influence on him.'

Table 11 *(continued)*

R v *McGovern* **(1990) 92 Cr App R 228**	Confession given in a later properly conducted interview may be excluded since the way it was obtained may have been tainted by the earlier improperly conducted one
R v *Barry* **(1991) 95 Cr App R 384**	Test for applying s. 76(2)(b) • Identify the thing said or done • Query whether what was said or done was likely in circumstances to render unreliable a confession (objective test) • Query whether prosecution have proved beyond reasonable doubt that confession was not obtained in consequence of thing said or done (question of fact)
R v *Doolan* **[1988] Crim LR 747**	'Anything said or done' may include omissions, e.g. failure to caution and to keep a proper record
Section 78 **PACE**	Test is fairness to the proceedings
R v *Walsh* **(1989) 91 Cr App R 161**	'The main object of s. 58 and indeed of the code of practice is to achieve fairness to the accused or suspected person so as, among other things, to present and protect his legal rights; but also fairness to the Crown and its officers so that again, among other things, there might be reduced the incidence or effectiveness of unfounded allegations of malpractice.' (per Saville J)
R v *Armas-Rodriguez* **[2005] EWCA Crim 1981**	Significant and substantial breaches of Code C such as failure to caution, did not necessarily mean confession should be excluded under s. 78
R v *Mason* **[1988] 1 WLR 139**	Police deceit of a legal adviser an operative ground for exclusion under s. 78.
Thongjai v *R* **[1998] AC 54**	Whether a confession was made or not is a question of fact for the jury but if proof is difficult because of impropriety then it may also be a question of admissibility and a voir-dire held.
R v *Spinks* **(1981) 74 Cr App R 263**	Confessions are only evidence against the maker
R v *Myers* **[1998] AC 124**	Where there are two defendants D2 may adduce a confession by D_1 which is relevant to his defence even if it has been excluded as prosecution evidence under s. 78 **PACE**
Section 76(A) **PACE**	A defendant may adduce a co-accused's confession relevant to his defence if he can prove on the balance of probabilities that it was not obtained in violation of identical provisions to those in s. 76 **PACE**

Table 11 (*continued*)

R v *Mushtaq* [2005] 1 WLR 1513	Where the judge has ruled that a confession has not been obtained in breach of s. 76 the jury must be given the opportunity to decide for itself whether on its estimation of the facts the confession ought not to be taken into account
R v *Hayter* [2005] UKHL 6	Where there are co-defendants, the jury can use one defendant's confession in establishing his guilt and use that finding of guilt in deciding the guilt of the co-defendant

* **The Serious Organised Crime and Police Act 2005** has had an impact on the law on confessions. In particular it redefines the concept of an arrestable offence contained in s. 24 of the **Police and Criminal Evidence Act,** which was used as a basis for other extended powers, for example legitimising the extended periods of detention for questioning in the Police now have arrest powers for 'any offence' if the 'arrest conditions' prevail. The effect is that the delay of access to legal advice and extended detention without charge may now be triggered if the offence is an indictable one.

Table 12 Defendant's silence

s. 34	s. 36	s. 37
Suspect must have been given general caution Code C para. 10.4		
Suspect or his counsel at trial must offer explanation which might reasonably have been given earlier (s. 34(1))	Suspect must have been arrested and given the special warning (Code C para 10)	
	Suspect must be interviewed at police station unless the special conditions of Code C para. 11.1 apply, e.g., danger of interference with evidence	
If arrested, suspect at interview should be given opportunity to confirm/deny earlier silence outside police station	Suspect should be given opportunity at start of interview to confirm/deny earlier failure to account outside police station	
	Suspect must fail to account for objects, substances or marks	Suspect must fail to account for presence

Table 12 (*continued*)

Silence cannot be used as part of primary case against suspect	His failure to so account can be used as part of the primary case against him	His failure to so account can be used as part of the primary case against him

Suspect shall not be committed for trial or be convicted solely on silence, failure or refusal to account (s. 38(3))

Note 1. Where the accused was at an authorised place of detention at the time of the silence, failure or refusal to account the above sections does not apply if he had not been allowed an opportunity to consult a solicitor prior to being questioned, charged or officially informed he might be prosecuted.

Note 2. The court may draw inferences from D's failure to explain under s. 34 both after caution and before charge and on being charged.

Note 3. The court may draw inferences under ss 36 and 37 from failure of D to explain after arrest, after the effect of failure to explain has been explained to D.

Note 4. Section 34 covers questioning by a constable and also 'persons (other than constables) charged with the duty of investigating offences or changing offenders'. Sections 36–37 refer to questioning by police and Customs and Excise officers.

Table 13 Key cases on section 34

Cases	Principle
R v *Nickelson* [1999] Crim LR 61	Under s. 34 a fact which is not mentioned should be 'a fact which in the circumstances existing at the time [the suspect] could reasonably have been expected to mention'. A suspect would not be expected to give an explanation about evidence that he was not informed about at interview.
R v *Argent* [1997] 2 Cr App R 27	
R v *Webber* [2004] UKHL 01	D May be relying a 'fact' within the meaning of s. 34 not only where he gives evidence but also where he refused to testify but the fact is raised in cross-examination
R v *McGarry* [1999] 1 WLR 1500	If the judge decides that s. 34 does not apply the judge should direct that common law rules on silence may apply
R v *Betts and Hall* [2001] 2 Cr App R 257	Section 34 will not apply if D admits at trial a fact asserted by the prosecution, even if he did not mention it at interview
R v *Milford* [2001] 2 All ER 609; *R* v *Gowland-Wynn* [2001] EWCA Crim 2715 (disapproving earlier cases of *Gill* (2001) and *Mountford* (1999)	It is permissible for the judge to invite the jury to draw an inference from D's failure to mention a fact, even if this goes to the heart of his defence

The section has, as the above notes indicated, generated much case-law both in the national courts and at Strasbourg. It would be invidious to attempt to summarise this here but you should bear in mind the following key additional points.

Judicial Direction to the Jury

Failure to give correct directions to the jury may be grounds of appeal. The Strasbourg decisions have emphasised this: see *Condron* v *UK, Beckles* v *UK*. The Judicial Studies Board has set out specimen directions applying to the different sections of the statute: see **www.jsboard.com.uk**, Directions 38–45.

Silence on Legal Advice

This area has generated a huge amount of case-law. The fact alone that D relied on legal advice to remain silent is not enough to prevent the statute applying. Adjustments to advisable judicial directions on this have been made in the light of Strasbourg decisions. The history of the rulings is as follows:

- *Murray* v *UK* (1996) **22 EHRR 29**. The court found a breach of article 6 in the denial of the accused access to a solicitor. This decision led to **s. 58** of the **YJCEA 1999**, which amended the **CJPOA 1994** so that no inferences can be drawn if the accused was in police detention and did not have access to legal advice.

- *R* v *Condron* (1997). The Court of Appeal approved the trial judge's direction: 'You should consider whether or not he is able to decide for himself what he should do or having asked for a solicitor to advise him he would not challenge that advice.' This approach has now been changed in the light of the Strasbourg authorities.

- *Condron* v *UK* (2001) **31 EHRR 1**. There had been a violation of the applicant's Art. 6(1) rights since '. . . as a matter of fairness the jury should have been directed that it could only draw an adverse inference if satisfied that the applicants' silence at the police interview could only sensibly be attributed to their having no answer or none that would stand up to cross-examination'. See also *Beckles* v *UK* (2003) **36 EHRR 13** *Averill* v *UK* (2001) **31 EHRR 36** and *R* v *Betts and Hall* (2001) **2 Cr App R 257.**

- *R* v *Betts and Hall* [2001] **EWCA Crim 224**. The Court of Appeal stated that s. 34 should be interpreted as allowing adverse inferences only if the jury was satisfied that the suspect when questioned did not have an innocent explanation; see also *Beckles* v *UK* (2003) **36 EHRR**. Genuine reliance on legal advice meant adverse inferences could not be drawn.

- *R* v *Howell* [2003] **EWCA Crim 1** took a different approach from *Betts and Hall*. The suspect is expected to evaluate the legal advice. The court stated, 'There must always be soundly based objective reasons for silence, sufficiently cogent and telling to weigh in the balance against a clear public interest in an account being given by the suspect to the police.' These could include ill-health, shock or intoxication.

- *R* v *Knight* [2003] **EWCA Crim 1977** (obiter). *Howell* preferred to *Betts and Hall*.

- *R v Parchment* [2003] EWCA 2428. The Court of Appeal stated that the jury must be sure that the prosecution's case was so strong that it clearly called for an answer before drawing an adverse inference.

- *R v Hoare and Pierce* [2005] 1 WLR 1804. The Court of Appeal stated that decisions in *Howell* and *Knight* were not inconsistent with that in *Betts and Hall*. The court commented, 'Legal entitlement is one thing. An accused's reason for exercising it is another. His belief in his entitlement may be genuine, but it does not follow that his reason for exercising it is.' *Howell* and *Knight* approved.

- *R v Beckles* (No. 2) [2005] 1 WLR 2829 approved *Hoare*. If the accused genuinely relied on his solicitor's advice to remain silent, it was nevertheless permissible for the jury to draw an adverse inference if the jury considered it was not reasonable for him to do so.

- *R v Bresa* [2005] EWCA Crim 1414. The Court of Appeal held that the trial judge had failed to emphasise the defendant's legal professional privilege and had contained nothing about the jury having to be sure that the offender remained silent not because of the legal advice he received but because he had no answer to give in the interview. The court identified (para. 16) the key features of the Judicial Studies Board Specimen Directions, which should be followed and adapted to each case. They were: telling the jury of the defendant's rights and his choice whether to exercise them; making an accurate identification of the facts it is alleged he might reasonably have mentioned; a warning that there must be a case to answer; and finally a direction that the key question is, can the jury be sure he remained silent not because of any legal advice he received but because he had no satisfactory explanation to give. The court was here taking the same approach as in *Beckles*.

  Doak and McGourlay comment (2008, p. 108), 'Logically, it would appear to follow that if a defendant kept silent on legal advice, and not because he had no story to give or none that would stand up to scrutiny, then it does not matter whether the advice was well-grounded or not. From a due process perspective, where defendants genuinely rely on the advice of their legal representatives, they should not be penalised for doing so. If this were the case, what would be given by way of concession with one hand would effectively be taken away by the other.'

Other Statutory Provisions and the Defendant's Right to Silence

- *Saunders* v *UK* (1997). Use at trial of incriminating statements obtained from the defendant by DTI inspectors using their compulsory powers was oppressive. His right to silence was undermined by the pressure to cooperate. This case led to amendment of provisions, including s. 434 **Companies Act 1985**, which had rendered admissible in subsequent criminal proceedings evidence procured by compulsion during investigation; see also *Hertfordshire CC, ex parte Green Environmental Industries* [2000] AC 412.

- *Attorney-General's Reference (No. 7 of 2000)* [2001] **EWCA Crim 888**. Privilege against self-incrimination did not cover pre-existing documents obtained by compulsion but existing independently of the will of the D.
- *Brown* v *Stott* [2001] **2 WLR 817**. The Privy Council held that the use in evidence of the defendant's admission to driving at the time a traffic offence was committed did not violate Article 6. In *Luckhof* v *Austria* [2008] **Crim LR 549**, the strasbourg court found no violation of Article 6(1) in a case on similar facts.

Common Law and Silence

The common law provisions on the right to silence will still apply if the accuser and accused were on even terms (*Parkes* v *R* [1976] **1 WLR 1251**) and the accused had not been cautioned (see **Criminal Justice and Public Order Act**, s. 35(5)).

Question 1

'. . .a person who asks for legal advice may not be interviewed or continue to be interviewed until he has received it, unless delay has been lawfully authorised as described above. The result is that in many cases a detainee, who would otherwise have answered proper questioning by the police, will be advised to remain silent . . . it seems to us that the effect of s. 58 [of the Police and Criminal Evidence Act 1984] is such that the balance of fairness between prosecution and defence cannot be maintained unless proper comment is permitted on the defendant's silence in such circumstances. It is high time that such comment should be permitted together with the necessary alteration to the words of the caution.' (*R* v *Alladice* (1988) 87 Cr App R 380 at p. 385.)

Discuss in the light of subsequent developments.

Commentary

The right to silence remains a topical and popular question in current evidence examinations. Much opposition was expressed to the changes made in the **Criminal Justice and Public Order Act 1994**, six years after *R* v *Alladice*. You should be familiar with the relevant provisions of the 1994 Act with subsequent amendments to it, and with the academic and judicial controversy surrounding it. Be careful here to answer the specific question set, which is whether the availability of legal advice to the defendant gives such an advantage that comment on silence at interview is a suitable quid pro quo for the prosecution. The question is about relative advantages and disadvantages to the defendant rather than a request to recite all the arguments for and against abolition of the right to silence. You must deal with the details of the new provisions introduced in 1994 and also with the practical and principled arguments on this issue. As always in essay questions, some familiarity with the academic debates will raise your answer into the upper second if not first-class grade. Finally, be careful to avoid too much editorialising in such an answer. The examiner wants an analysis of the law, not a political diatribe.

Answer plan

- Does availability of legal advice to the defendant give such an advantage that comment on silence at interview is a suitable quid pro quo for the prosecution?

- Concentrate on advantages and disadvantages to the defendant rather than arguments for and against right to silence

- Section 58 is not an absolute right but protection has been improved—see revised Code C (Revised August 2004)

- Sections 34 to 38 of the **Criminal Justice and Public Order Act** contain safeguards and case-law has developed these

- The **Human Rights Act 1998** now enhances protection—see ***Murray*** v ***United Kingdom*** **(1996)** for the approach of the European Court of Human Rights but search for 'balance' may disadvantage defendants—see ***Stott*** v ***Brown*** **(2001)**

Suggested answer

The court here was expressing its exasperation with the practice of suspects refusing to answer questions at the police station. It suggested that because safeguards were provided for the suspect in the interview through the provision of legal advice, there should be some redress of the balance by allowing the suspect's silence to be made evidence at the trial. In fact Alladice's confession, made without a solicitor present, was held by the Court of Appeal to have been rightly admitted, thus the comment from Lord Lane, who delivered the judgment, did not arise from this specific example primarily. Alladice did not in fact exercise his right to silence. However, Lord Lane was expressing a more general unease felt by police, sections of the judiciary and the government. Despite recommendations over the past two decades by many bodies, such as the Royal Commission on Criminal Justice (Cm 2263, 1993) that the right to silence should be retained, the government has not accepted their validity. The **Criminal Justice and Public Order Act 1994** limited the pre-trial right of silence in several key areas. Inferences may now be drawn if the defendant relies on material in court which he did not divulge to the police while under caution (s. 34), or if he fails to account for objects, substances or marks on him at the time of arrest (s. 36), or fails appropriately to account for his presence at a particular place on arrest (s. 37). The caution and the Code of Practice were reworded. Lord Lane's invocation has thus been more than answered. Arguments have raged among academics, politicians and the legal profession for several decades. This essay will examine the procedural changes that have taken place since Lord Lane's comment made in 1988 and their implications for the 'balance of fairness'. It discusses the matters of principle involved.

The observation in the question suggests that s. 58 of the **Police and Criminal Evidence Act 1984** (PACE) gives the suspect such an advantageous position that there ought to be compensation for the prosecution. Under this section the suspect is given the right to request access to legal advice, although this may lawfully be delayed, in the case of an indictable offence, by a senior officer who has reasonable grounds for believing that if the right is exercised there may be interference with evidence, injury, alerting of suspects or hindrance in the recovery of property (s. 58(8) **PACE**). Thus, the right itself is not absolute and furthermore there are no automatic sanctions for its breach. To that extent, the suspect was, even before the 1994 changes, under some disadvantage. However, it is arguable that in their treatment of breaches of s. 58 **PACE** in cases where confessions were obtained, the courts protected the defendants. In *R v Samuel* [1988] QB 615, the Court of Appeal in holding that the confession should be excluded said that the task of satisfying a court that there were reasonable grounds for believing the consequences set out in s. 58(8) **PACE** applied will prove formidable. Thus, the scope for the police to deny access to a solicitor is restricted, particularly if the police act in bad faith, as the court acknowledged in *R v Alladice* itself.

Moreover, since 1988 access to legal advice has been improved. For example, a provision in the revised 1995 Code C accepted representations from the Law Society that the solicitor's role at the police station is 'to protect and advance the legal rights of his clients. On occasions this may require the solicitor to give advice which has the effect of his client avoiding giving evidence which strengthens a prosecution case.' On the other hand, protection for the defendant will be reduced under the **Criminal Justice Act 2003**, which will allow bad character of non-testifying defendants to be admitted.

The position at the time of *R v Alladice* was that under common law rules a suspect was not obliged to answer questions when interrogated by the police or others charged with investigating offences. This right derived in part from the privilege against self-incrimination and in part from the rules relating to the burden of proof. In *Director of SFO, ex parte Smith* [1993] AC 1 Lord Mustill (at p. 10) stated that the right was part of a disparate group of immunities, which differ in nature, origin, incidence and importance, and as to the extent to which they have already been encroached upon by statute. At common law the fact that a defendant exercises his right of silence in the specific context of a police interview is in general not evidence against him. One reason is that the parties are not on 'even terms', for the individual is faced with a person with power given by the state under orders to investigate offences. In the vast majority of cases a suspect in a police interview will not be on even terms with the investigating officers, although in *R v Chandler* [1976] 3 All ER 105 the Court of Appeal said that a detective sergeant and a suspect interviewed in the presence of his solicitor were speaking on even terms. It is arguable that this would still be the position before a caution since s. 34(8) of **CJPOA** preserves the existing law where the specific conditions set out in the Act do not apply. Although such a situation would be rare, it is important to stress that the application of the principle of the right to silence was never in the common law an absolute one.

Furthermore, the context in which Lord Lane made his remarks was one in which statutory provisions were significantly eroding the common law position. For example, a witness is obliged to answer questions put to him by Department of Trade inspectors under s. 434 of the **Companies Act 1985**, even if the answer might tend to incriminate him. At the end of 1988 the **Criminal Evidence (Northern Ireland) Order**, SI 1998 No. 1987, made provisions which became the model for changes in the **Criminal Justice and Public Order Act 1994**. Thus Lord Lane was to a large extent pushing against an already open door.

Despite these pro-defendant provisions, the Court of Appeal may in *R* v *Alladice* have expressed an unwarranted concern because the number who remained silent appears to have been small, although it does in fact appear that those who had legal advice did so more readily. The great majority of suspects in police stations did not exercise their right to silence. Zander (1994, p. 147) quotes a study in 1992 which showed 26% of suspects who had legal advice exercised their right, while 10% of those who had no legal advice did so. Also an ACPO study in 1993 found that 57% of suspects who had legal advice exercised their right while 13% of those who did not have a solicitor did so. Moreover, this has to be seen in the context of the report by the Legal Aid Board, also quoted by Zander, that only some 30% of suspects had legal advice in the police station either in person or over the telephone. One might argue then that even before the 1994 changes the protection afforded to silence was weak. The very nature of interrogation appears to compel cooperation. Two possible alternative views flow from this. If the protection for the defendant was illusory, why continue with the pretence? It would perhaps be better to concentrate on providing other safeguards. On the other hand, if there was no real problem with extensive exercise of the right, why was change needed to compensate the prosecution? On the latter point, the police argued that it was the small number of hardened criminals whom they were targeting. Galligan (1988 at p. 70) quotes the former Metropolitan Police Commissioner, Peter Imbert that the protection of silence has 'done more to obscure the truth and facilitate crime than anything else in this century'.

An examination of the CJPOA provisions, however, reveals that the changes actually brought in do not reflect completely the recommendations made in *R* v *Alladice*. The Court of Appeal there appeared to suggest that comment was appropriate on silence at the interview only. However, the new statute does not clearly preclude admitting silence outside of the police station. Thus s. 34 could on its wording, if further conditions apply, be activated on the giving of a caution, before arrest. Also Code C 11. 2 provides that at the beginning of an interview carried out in a police station, the interviewing officer, after cautioning the suspect, must put to him any significant statement or silence which occurred before the start of the interview. This is particularly significant in relation to ss. 37 and 36 of the 1994 Act, which deal with silence on arrest whether or not the defendant offers an explanation at trial. There is then fertile scope for appeal on whether the silence was properly obtained.

Another refinement of the statutory provisions is that s. 34 of the 1994 Act is restricted in its scope. This section does not allow inferences to be drawn from silence under caution per se but only from the giving of evidence in due course, which evidence could have been provided in answer form during earlier questioning under caution. The 'circumstances' referred to in the question there-fore are limited to those where an explanation is given at the trial. This still begs the question, however, as to the evidential worth of silence. Silence is necessarily ambiguous and might have been prompted by reasons other than guilt. None-theless defenders of the change advocated in *Alladice* would argue that refusal to answer questions is now, given the procedural safeguards, an informed and voluntary decision.

Furthermore, on this practical point s. 34(1)(b) of the 1994 Act allows infer-ences from silence when charged, not just when first interviewed. Enright (1995) suggested this provision led some solicitors to advise defendants to remain silent in interview but make a statement of their case at the charge stage. There were clear advantages for such defendants, since further questioning is precluded. He suggested also that juries will be less inclined to infer guilt from silence at the interview stage where the defendant has set out his position at the charge stage.

The 1994 Act has generated a significant amount of case-law illustrating that Lord Lane's enthusiasm for allowing comment on failure to respond to police questioning has in fact been more difficult to apply than his observation suggests. It is crucial that the jury is properly directed. In a judgment which underlined that there was no reason to distinguish between proper inferences which may be drawn under s. 34 and s. 35, the Court of Appeal limited the conditions under which the jury should be directed to draw an adverse inference. In *R v Cowan* [1995] 4 All ER 939 it held that it should only do so where it concludes the silence can only sensibly be attributed to the defendant's having no answer or none that 'would stand up under cross-examination'. The case-law illustrates that it is cru-cial for the jury to determine whether in the circumstances existing at the time the defendant could reasonably be expected to mention a fact. In *R v Argent* (1997) 2 Cr App R 27 it was made clear by the Court of Appeal that the court should not construe these circumstances in a narrow way. Relevant factors to bear in mind included the defendant's age, experience, sobriety, personality and legal advice. One protection was that the section could not be extended to matters which the defendant would not reasonably have been expected to mention, for example to explain something he was not asked to explain since it was only known about after the interview.

Michael Zander (1994 p. 149) observed 'the unknown quantity will be what streetwise solicitors advise clients'. He believed that the abolition of the right would make solicitors more, rather than less likely to advise the client to be silent. He suggested that if a suspect was silent on the basis of legal advice it could be put to the jury that no adverse inference should be drawn. The Royal Commission on Criminal Procedure (1993) pointed out that this was the case under comparable provisions in Scottish law.

However, the subsequent case-law showed that the court's attitude to legal advice was a much narrower one. It is now clear that the fact that a solicitor advised a client not to answer did not in itself prevent an adverse inference from being drawn. In *Condron and Condron* (1997) 1 WLR 827 the Court of

Appeal said that it was unlikely that the bare assertion that the defendant had not answered questions on the advice of his solicitor was by itself to be regarded as a sufficient reason for not mentioning matters. In *R v Roble* [1997] Crim LR 449 it was stressed that in order for the defendant to rely on legal advice to remain silent as operating to exclude adverse inferences he would have to indicate the reason for that advice since that would be a relevant circumstance for the jury to take into account in assessing the reasonableness of the decision to fail to give an explanation. In *Condron* the Court of Appeal stressed the importance of clear guidance to the jury. The judge should give the standard Judicial Studies Board direction as to what adverse inferences might be drawn and also direct along the lines set out in *Cowan*.

A further disadvantage suffered by the defendant who relies on the advice of a solicitor to remain silent is that if he goes beyond a mere statement of the advice to give reasons for it he has probably waived his legal professional privilege (*R v Bowden* [1999] 1 WLR 832). Furthermore, as the court pointed out in *R v Davis* [1998] Crim LR 659 in giving reasons for deciding not to answer questions the defendant was subject to the hearsay rule which might limit how he repeated what his solicitor had told him.

In some instances the courts have taken a stance protective of the defendant and thus no adverse inference from silence can be drawn where the accused calls no evidence and merely puts the prosecution to proof (*R v Moshaid* [1998] Crim LR 420) and the judge must so direct the jury (*R v McGarry* [1999] 1 WLR 1500). On the other hand, some judgments on s. 34 can be contrasted with the position under s. 35 of the 1994 Act in *Cowan*. Under s. 34 the judge is not required to direct the jury that it must find a case to answer before drawing any adverse inferences (*R v Doldur* [2000] Crim LR 178). The jury must consider both defence and prosecution evidence in the application of s. 34. The contrast between the earlier silence and later reliance on a fact may allow an inference to be drawn. As the above cases indicate, the enactment of Lord Lane's recommendation has resulted in a number of procedural and practical hurdles for defendants. However, specific protection for the defendant who is silent is provided by s. 38(3) of the 1994 Act which states that:

> . . .a person shall not have the proceedings against him transferred to the Crown Court for trial, have a case to answer or be convicted of an offence solely on an inference drawn from such a failure or refusal . . .

More controversial perhaps are the arguments over principles. The reference to 'balance of fairness' by Lord Lane just four years after the introduction of the elaborate balancing act of **PACE**, perhaps, was somewhat impatient. Furthermore, is it necessary for s. 58 **PACE** to be balanced at all? In *R v Samuel* [1988] QB 615 the Court of Appeal referred to access to legal advice as a fundamental right. Do such rights have to be compensated for?

The European Court of Human Rights has considered the operation of UK law in this area and it indicates that although the right to silence has not been regarded as an absolute Lord Lane's views expressed in *Alladice* did not evidence sufficient regard for the rights of the defendant. In view of the operation of the **Human Rights Act 1998** these cases assume greater importance. In *Saunders* v *United Kingdom* (1997) **23 EHRR 313** the Court said: 'Although not mentioned in art. 6 . . . the right to silence and the right not to incriminate oneself are generally recognised international standards which lie at the heart of the notion of a fair trial.' Here the Court held that Saunders had been deprived of a fair trial by reason of the use of statements obtained from him by the DTI inspectors, which counted to an unjustifiable infringement of the right to silence. True DTI investigations are not strictly parallel to the procedure contained in the **CJPOA** since in fraud cases suspects are subject to compulsion to give evidence.

In a Northern Ireland case the European Court of Human Rights again held that the right to silence was not an absolute. In *John Murray* v *United Kingdom* (1996) **22 EHRR 29**, the European Court of Human Rights determined that the right to remain silent under police questioning and the privilege against self-incrimination were generally recognised international standards which lay at the heart of the notion of fair procedure. But these immunities were not absolutes. Whether the drawing of adverse inferences from an accused's silence infringed art. 6 of the European Convention on Human Rights was a matter to be determined in the light of all the circumstances of the case, having particular regard to the situations where inferences might be drawn, the weight attached to them by the national courts in their assessment of the evidence and the degree of compulsion inherent in the situation. It could not be said that the drawing of reasonable inferences from the applicant's behaviour had the effect of shifting the burden of proof from the prosecution to the defence so as to infringe the principle of the presumption of innocence. The Court, however, determined on the facts that denial of access to legal advice for 48 hours did infringe the Article under the specific provisions of the 1988 order.

In the light of this decision the United Kingdom amended its laws, again illustrating that achieving the 'balance' indicated in Lord Lane's observation is problematic and may need to be subject to continual adjustment. By s. 58 of the **Youth Justice and Criminal Evidence Act 1999** ss. 34 and 36–38 of the **CJPOA** were amended. They are not to be operative if the defendant had not been allowed an opportunity to consult a solicitor prior to being questioned, charged or officially informed he was to be prosecuted. The potential for violation of art. 6(1) was also illustrated in *Condron* v *United Kingdom* [2000] **Crim LR 679**. The trial judge in that case was held to have violated art. 6(1) by failing to direct the jury that only if, despite the evidence or lack of it, the jury concluded that the failure to answer questions at interview could only sensibly be attributed to the accused's having no answer, or none that would stand up to cross-examination, they might draw an adverse inference. The Court of Appeal had accepted that there had been a misdirection but that nonetheless the guilty verdict should stand. The current position in relation to silence or legal advice is that the judge must direct the jury to apply a causal test. If the defendant relied on the advice s. 34 may not apply.

It is now clear that legal advice to remain silent will not preclude the possibility of adverse inferences being drawn. The jury must be directed that they must consider if it was reasonable to rely on the advice and if the accused remained silent because it suited his purpose (*R v Howell, R v Bresa*). This creates difficulties for defence solicitors. Cape (2006, p. 7) points out that '. . . solicitors should approach the issue of advising clients on "silence" with extreme caution, and where they do advise silence, should explain to the client that the fact that they are giving such advice will not necessarily prevent inferences from being drawn. Whilst solicitors must have proper regard for the decisions of the courts, if there are cogent reasons for silence solicitors must not flinch from advising accordingly, whilst ensuring that their clients are made aware of the risks of following that advice.' He points out that the jury will be asked to consider if there were soundly based objective reasons for the advice such as non-disclosure by the police or the defendant's ill health. The Specimen Direction of the Judicial Studies Board is as a result of these considerations are complex and Cross and Tapper (2007, p. 697) comment on the volume of case law it has generated, and the recommendation by the court of Appeal to restrict its use.

In *R v McGarry* [1999] 1 WLR 1500 the Court of Appeal had allowed an appeal by a defendant who had not relied in his defence on any facts he had failed to mention at police interviews because in these circumstances the judge could not leave to the jury the possibility of drawing adverse inferences from the defendant's failure to answer questions. The judge must positively direct the jury that they should not in any way hold the defendant's silence against him. The current very complex directions the judges must give are set out in Judicial Studies Board guidelines.

Other arguably liberal approaches are shown, for example, in *Bowden* where Lord Bingham CJ stated that since sections 34–38 'restricted rights recognised at common law as appropriate to protect defendants against the risk of injustice they should not be construed more widely than the statutory language requires'. Commenting on another case, *R v Knight* [2004] 1 WLR 340, Choo (2006, p. 73) points out that uncertainty surrounding prepared statements giving a full account of a defence later relied on has been resolved in favour of the defendant. Similarly in *R v Bresa* (2005) a conviction was overturned when the judge had failed to emphasise the importance of the defendant's right to privilege in relation to communications between him and his solicitor. The direction had contained nothing about the jury having to be sure that the offender remained silent not just because of the legal advice he received but because he had no answer to give in interviews. On the other hand, there are a number of restrictive decisions. For example, it is permissible for the judge to invite the jury to draw an inference from failure to mention a fact even if this goes to the heart of his defence (**Milford** [2001] 2 **All ER 609** and *Gowland-Wynn* [2001] EWCA Crim 2715; [2002] 1 Cr App R 569 disapproving earlier cases of *Gill* (2001) and *Mountford* (1999)). There is, however, some protection in s. 38(3): the accused cannot be convicted on failure to mention a fact alone. There has been a huge amount of case-law on the issue of legal advice and inferences from silence. The current position is enshrined in *R* v *Beckles* (2005), which sets out the need to follow the—frequently revised—Judicial Studies Board directions. In effect the jury is asked to consider the reasonableness of the decision of the defendant to act on the legal advice to remain silent. As Dennis (2007, p. 187) points out, '*Beckles* has probably settled the matter for the time being. It is unlikely that the Court of Appeal will wish to revert in a future case to either the *Betts and Hall* or the *Howell* approach'.

Thus although the Court of Human Rights in *Condron* identified the right to silence as a right which lay at the heart of a fair trial, it is clear that whether this right has been breached depends on the circumstances of each particular case. Academic opinion, however, does seem to suggest that an erosion of the right to silence has an adverse effect on the rights of the defendant. Zuckerman (1994, p. 117) stresses a fundamental claim to equality of treatment at the hands of officials. The principle of natural justice in the determination of charges, he says, requires the suspect to have full notice of the evidence against him and that the investigation of the charges takes place before an impartial tribunal. He should not be required to participate since he is unable to do so in a free and informed manner. This situation is not altered by the presence of his solicitor. In Zuckerman's view, the right way to deal with 'ambush' defences at trial is to institute a proper system of pre-trial pleading in which prosecution and defence set out in writing the essence of their cases. Zuckerman accepts (1994 at p. 139) that common sense in these circumstances might allow comment on silence. He argues:

> It is a matter of the most fundamental fairness that a person who has to answer a charge should be given adequate information about that charge. Until adequate provision is made for supplying suspects with such information, the process will not only be unfair but also dangerous, because it creates considerable scope for abuse. However, the courts have ample jurisdiction to ensure that comment on silence is allowed only where the questioning of the suspect has been fair. Once the courts have evolved parameters of fairness they would benefit not only the suspects who maintain silence but all suspects questioned by the police.

Not all commentators would agree with Zuckerman that comment on the suspect's silence may, given procedural safeguards, be acceptable. Galligan (1988) puts forward a justification for protecting the right to silence, basing it on the right to individual autonomy. He draws a distinction between privacy as to consciousness and privacy as to bodily parts, such as fingerprints: 'it is only privacy with respect to consciousness which is sufficiently fundamental to attract a blanket form of legal protection'. This is indeed a tenable position and one recognised by both the common law and statute; for example, the attempt to extend the right to silence to the defendant's refusal to give police a sample of his hair for forensic investigation. This position has been confirmed and strengthened by s. 62(10) **PACE**.

It is thus arguable that in an adversarial system in which the police are effectively a party, the way in which the investigation is conducted does have an impact on the legitimacy of the verdict. The conflict over the right to silence sets proponents of crime control against champions of due process. It is perhaps questionable whether the idea of 'balance' has any place where the state is confronting the individual. The parties are simply not and never can be on equal terms. Certainly, procedurally, suspects now have many more safeguards compared with pre-**PACE** days. However, given recent examples of lack of police integrity and the psychological fact that suspects may be silent for other reasons than guilt, perhaps as Zuckerman says (1994 at p. 139), any procedural changes may be insufficient if 'they do not address the principal causes of miscarriage of justice: police bias and witness suggestibility'.

A major issue in analysing the provisions on silence is the consequential complexity of the law in this area. The legislation has the objective of preventing the accused from inventing a defence at trial and encouraging early disclosure of evidence. These apparently simple aims have led to complex judicial directions to the jury. As the case of *R* v *O* [2000] **Crim LR 617** shows there may be a need for a s. 34 direction and in some cases a *Lucas* direction. The complexity of the law has led academics such as Birch (1999) to argue that the burdens outweigh the benefits. In *Bresa* the Court of Appeal also noted that where s. 34 is applied 'it seems to require a direction of such length and detail that it seems to promote the adverse inference question to a height it does not merit'. Another practical point is that there is now less likelihood of ambush defences, one of the reasons for the statutory erosion of the right to silence, in the wake of the disclosure provisions in the **Criminal Procedure and Investigations Act 1996**.

This question in short raises wider issues than the 'balance of fairness'. In any case the search for 'balance' appears never-ending. It is of concern to some commentators, such as Ashworth, that a consideration of the public interest may inhibit fairness. In *Stott* v *Brown* [2001] **2 WLR 819** the Privy Council held that the privilege against self-incrimination was not absolute and had not been balanced in this case against the clear public interest in enforcing drink-driving legislation. Section 172 of the **Road Traffic Act** allowed for the putting of one simple question subject to a moderate and non-custodial penalty for failure to answer. It was not incompatible with the Convention for the defendant's answer to be used against her at trial. Lord Lane in *Alladice* focussed on the pragmatic argument of achieving accuracy in decision-making. In summary it is argued that this stance has three major limitations. First, the search for balance is never-ending and piecemeal statutory amendments may cumulatively add up to overall imbalance. Thus, for example, the changes brought about in the **CJPOA** should be assessed alongside those in the **Criminal Procedure and Investigations Act 1996** where adverse inferences may be drawn as a result of the accused's failure to fulfil his obligations of disclosure. Second, it is submitted that there are other values, independent of rectitude, which should have a place in the criminal justice system. Trials are not just a matter of allocating liabilities or the balance of protection between prosecution and defence. As Galligan, citing Ronald Dworkin has argued, to take rights seriously is to understand that society cannot, if it wishes to be consistent, confer a right and then curtail it if there are social benefits in doing so. It is arguable that access to legal advice and the privilege against self-incrimination are both rights which should not lightly be tempered. Finally, it is not even self-evident that the legislation has achieved its aim (see Bucke *et al* (2000)). Balance remains an elusive goal. However, suspects are less likely to remain silent at the police station and more likely to testify (Jackson 2001). Overall the very complexity of the statute has led to what Dennis calls its 'marginalisation' and others doubt whether the impact of the **Human Rights Act 1998** has assisted significantly in this area to encourage a principled approach. As Choo and Nash put it (2003, p. 61) 'while effectively accepting that the privilege against self-incrimination is an implied right in the Convention, domestic courts have been willing to engage in vague balancing exercises to determine whether a prima facie breach of the privilege would lead to a breach of Article 6(1)'. As a result, as Choo (2006, p. 86) stresses, the right to remain silent 'has been substantially attenuated'.

This subject has occasioned fierce debate and there has been considerable academic opposition to the provisions, particularly in relation to the permissibility of the drawing of inferences from non-responses in police interrogation. Dennis has made a powerful critique of the law. He suggests (2007, p. 205) that 'the privilege is characterised not as a "human right", a notion that in an unqualified form begs some difficult questions, but as a functional device required in some context by the need of the criminal justice system to retain its internal coherence.' He states (p. 205–6) this view would lead to the conclusion that, 'the curtailment of the right to silence in the police station is objectionable because of the risk of abuse of state power associated with custodial interrogation. Section 34 of the **Criminal Justice and Public Order Act 1994** ought to be repealed as a matter of principle.' The same objection does not hold for inference from failure to testify at trial, where the procedural context of the accused's silence is wholly different. Section 35 of the Act is therefore supportable. Dennis' examination of the current law suggests that Lord Reid's recommendation therefore still causes unease some twenty years on.

Question 2

Darcy and Bingley are suspected of the murder of Mrs Bennett, Darcy's mother-in-law, who has disappeared in suspicious circumstances. They are both arrested, cautioned and taken separately into custody. On the way to the police station Bingley begins to sob and says, 'I'll miss the old bat, I should never have done it.' 'What do you mean? What have you done?' said PC Collins. 'Everyone knew she was an old cow but I'll never forget her face when we put the plastic bag over her,' replied Bingley. At the police station Bingley asks for a solicitor but the police refuse on the grounds that since the body has not yet been found other family members may be alerted to help conceal it. Bingley is questioned continually for nine hours, with only one break for tea and biscuits. The police then produce a skeleton which they have borrowed from a local medical school and tell Bingley they found it buried on his estate. He mistakenly thinks it is Mrs Bennett and says, 'Oh my God. She has been moved.'

The police claim that Darcy said, when they called at his house to arrest him, 'I'm glad you've come. I did us all a favour by finishing her off.' Darcy has, unknown to the police, a rare medical condition which requires frequent rest periods. He is denied a solicitor at the police station because the police fear the solicitor might advice him to remain silent. Anxious to get some sleep because he knows he will black out otherwise Darcy announces that he will cooperate with the questioning. He tells the investigating officer that he had killed Mrs Bennett and was proud of it. The confession is not recorded at the time but a note of it has been prepared by police to be read out at the trial. At the trial both plead not guilty and want to retract their statements at the police station. Darcy denies making the initial statement to the police at his house.

Advise Darcy and Bingley on evidence.

Commentary

You need to be careful to cover the rather specific issues in this question and not deal too generally with the law on confessions. Both Bingley and Darcy need to be advised whether their initial statements were made in the context of interviews as defined by the revised Code of Practice. Note that Darcy is in addition denying that he made the initial statement, not saying that it was improperly extracted from him. This is a question of fact not law and should arguably be tested by the jury. You need to discuss the possible breaches of **PACE** and the Code for each defendant and the implications of the trick played by the police on Bingley, as well as whether the earlier improperly conducted interview has tainted a subsequent one. With regard to Darcy you must consider whether his desire to end the interview and get some rest is self-induced and therefore since s. 76(2)(b) **PACE** has been interpreted in a restrictive way (see *R* v *Goldenberg* **(1988) 88 Cr App R 285**), whether it is applicable here.

Answer plan

- Are initial statements made by Bingley and Darcy made in interviews?
- Denial of statement by Darcy, question of fact
- Implications of possible breaches of the **Police and Criminal Evidence Act** and Code and of trick played by police
- Is Darcy's desire to end interview 'self-induced'?
- Does tainted first interview make even a properly conducted subsequent interview inadmissible?

Suggested answer

Bingley's arrest and the administration of the caution suggest that his treatment by the police at this point is correct. In the van he makes what could be taken to be an implied confession of responsibility for Mrs Bennett's death, according to the definition of a confession in s. 82(1) of the **Police and Criminal Evidence Act 1984** (PACE). The question arises as to whether it is an entirely spontaneous statement outside the context of an interview. Paragraph 11.1A of Code C defined an interview as 'the questioning of the person regarding his involvement or suspected involvement in a criminal offence or offences which, by virtue of paragraph 10.1 of Code C is required to be carried out under caution'. Such interviews should normally be conducted at a police station. In *R* v *Matthews* (1989) 91 Cr App R 43 the Court of Appeal adopted a broad approach to the definition of an interview but this has not always been followed. Thus, a conversation in a car between a defendant and police officers, where the defendant offered information and the officers only asked a few questions was not an interview: *R* v *Younis and Ahmed* [1990] **Crim LR 425**. Bingley has volunteered to open the discussion. The issue is the intention of the police officer in making the response, to secure either an admission or an innocent explanation. On the facts, the former seems more likely. If so, there have been breaches of the Code; the questioning was conducted away from the police station and no offer of free legal advice was made. There do not appear to be any special conditions here as set in paras 11.1 of Code C. The question then arises as to whether the statement is admissible. This is clearly not an instance of oppression under s. 76(2)(a) *PACE*. It is unlikely either that a submission under s. 76(2)(b) *PACE* would succeed since the courts appear to have confined its operation to those cases where something out of the ordinary has occurred, often in situations where the defendant is particularly vulnerable, for example in *R* v *Everett* [1988] **Crim LR 826**. Exclusion under s. 78 **PACE** is possible if the breaches are considered significant enough, as in *R* v *Canale* [1990] 2 All ER 187 or if the police acted with bad faith (see *R* v *Alladice* (1988) 87 Cr App R 380). However, there must be shown to be unfairness caused thereby to the proceedings to allow such a confession. If the defendant would have confessed anyway, as in *R* v *Alladice*, s. 78 **PACE** is not applicable. It is arguable here that Bingley was likely to have confessed unprompted.

At the police station the police are arguably acting correctly in the reason they give for delaying access to a solicitor. Murder is an indictable offence and the reason given for the delay appears to be within the scope of permissible reasons set out in s. 58(8) **PACE** as amended by **SOCPA 2003**. However, in *R* v *Samuel* [1988] QB 615, the Court of Appeal stressed that the prosecution has a formidable task in satisfying the court that there are reasonable grounds for such a belief. The questioning without a proper meal break is unlikely to amount to a breach of the Code justifying exclusion under s. 76 or 78 **PACE**. The courts have held that in order to consider excluding a confession under s. 78, breaches must be 'significant and substantial' (*R* v *Absolam* (1989) 88 Cr App R 332). In *R* v *Canale* [1990] 2 All ER

187 two police officers failed to record interviews contemporaneously because they thought it best not to do so. The Court of Appeal had said that the officers had shown a cynical disregard of the Code, which they had flagrantly breached. However, although the breach here in itself may be minor it has to be seen in the context of other more serious police malpractice. On the facts it appears that the police acted with bad faith with regard to the trick over the skeleton. It may be significant that it was the defendant and not his legal adviser who was tricked. In *R* v *Mason* [1988] 1 WLR 139 deceiving the solicitor was described by the court as a 'vital factor' in leading to exclusion. Thus, a confession obtained as a result of deception will be in danger of being excluded, but the particular circumstances of the case are important. Lord Lane said in *R* v *Alladice* that if the police had acted in bad faith the court would have excluded the confession under s. 78, if not s. 76 PACE. In *R* v *Walsh* (1989) 91 Cr App R 161, the Court of Appeal looked at several breaches of the statute and code and held that bad faith on the part of the police might make substantial or significant that which would not otherwise be so.

It is submitted that Bingley's confession is likely to be excluded under s. 78 PACE. There is a further consideration in that the fact that there have been breaches of the statute and/or Code in an earlier, initial interview may so taint subsequent interviews that they may affect the reliability of even a properly conducted interview. Here, the earlier possible breaches may render the second interview unreliable, irrespective of the breaches there outlined above. In *R* v *McGovern* (1990) 92 Cr App R 228, the Court of Appeal said that the question of whether a later interview should be excluded on these grounds is a question of fact and degree. However, in *R* v *Singleton* [2002] EWCA Crim 459 the Court of Appeal stated (at para. 10) '. . . where an early interview is excluded admission of a later interview must be a matter of fact and degree'.

In *McGovern* the accused, who had a very low IQ, confessed during two interviews. At the first interview her solicitor had not been present and there had also been breaches there of the Code C. The solicitor was present at the second interview. It was held there was a direct line of causation so that the breaches in the first interview tainted the second. In *R* v *Neil* [1994] Crim LR 441 the court held that if there were a series of interviews the questions to ask in order to decide whether to exclude on grounds of unfairness a later unobjectionable interview were, first, the objections to the earlier tainted interviews of a fundamental and continuing nature and, second, if so, were arrangements made for the accused to have sufficient opportunity to exercise an informed and independent choice as to whether he should repeat or retract what he said in the excluded interview or remain silent?

Darcy claims not to have made the initial statement. This is a question of fact and arguably should be put to the jury as the Privy Council held in *Ajodha* v *the State* [1982] AC 204. In *Thongjai* v *R* [1998] AC 54 the Privy Council developed the position on this. If the defendant claims that he did not make an alleged oral confession and also that he was badly treated by police before or at the time of the alleged confession, the court held that the judge should first decide whether, on the assumption that the alleged confession was made, it was admissible or not as a matter of law or discretion. Only if the alleged statement is admissible, on issue decided in a **voir dire**, should it be put to the jury to decide if it had taken place or not.

However, under paragraph 11.2A of the Code of Practice C, at the beginning of an interview carried out in a police station, the interviewing officer should put to the suspect 'any significant statement or silence' which occurred before his arrival at the police station and ask him if he confirms it. Thus Darcy's alleged statement on the doorstep should have been recorded and put to him for confirmation. If these provisions have been breached there would be grounds to challenge the admissibility of the alleged confession on a voir dire (*R* v *Sat-Bhambra* (1988) 88 **Cr App R 55**). It is arguable that Darcy's police station confession is potentially unreliable under s. 76(2)(b) because he made it in order to get out of the interview so that he could get some rest because of his concern over his medical condition. In *R* v *Goldenberg* (1988) 88 **Cr App R 285**, however, the 'something said or done' limb of the test was held not to be satisfied by the conduct of the maker of the confession. Thus, the confession of a heroin addict who confessed in order to get drugs, could not be excluded under s. 76(2)(b). However, there may be grounds for exclusion under s. 78 **PACE** since the police have refused access to a solicitor for an improper reason. In *R* v *McIvor* [1987] **Crim LR 409**, Sir Frederick Lawton sitting as a Deputy High Court judge in Sheffield Crown Court held that the police should not have refused access to legal advice on the grounds that the defendant would be advised to be silent. It is, however, not clear whether s. 76 or s. 78 was applied.

Question 3

Police are puzzled by a series of thefts of valuable greyhounds from a kennels and suspect the perpetrators are involved in a gambling scam. They call on Gerry and Cliff, noted professional gamblers, as part of their routine inquiries. Gerry invites them in and agrees to answer any questions, although he is clearly upset because he has just heard his mother is dying in hospital with cancer. As they are talking, Gerry's 14-year-old son, Tom, comes in and says: 'I hope they arrest you for cruelty to animals. It's horrible leaving that greyhound tied up in the shed. Grandma will cry her heart out when I tell her.' Gerry breaks down in tears and says: 'What a fool I have been. I said I'd mind the brute but I didn't know it was stolen. Cliff made me take it in.' He is arrested and cautioned and taken to the police station for questioning. There the custody officer asks him if he has his own solicitor. Gerry replies that he has but since he owes him money for arranging the sale of his house he doesn't like to call him. The police do not offer a duty solicitor and proceed to question Gerry further. Gerry tells them that he doesn't know any details of the thefts but the police persist in questioning him. The police then produce photographs of Tom on animal rights demonstrations and say to Gerry, 'You know we could take this further if you don't play ball.' Gerry then confesses that he, Cliff and several others had organised the thefts. He tells them that they had been forced to kill some of the dogs and they are buried on Hackney Downs. The police visit Cliff and ask him to come down to the station to help with their inquiries. He agrees but at the station asks for a solicitor. They reply that there is no need for that at this stage. They then leave him alone for about two hours. Cliff, who is 18 years old, suffers from claustrophobia and when they return is in a very distressed state. Cliff is cautioned and told he is under arrest; he begins to sob violently and admits that he had stolen the greyhounds. At the trial he argues that he was forced to make the confession due to his mental distress.

   Advise Gerry and Cliff.

Commentary

You must systematically list the circumstances relating to the admissibility of possible confessions by both defendants. In a question of this sort it is important not to miss any of the issues. The visit to Gerry is described as 'routine' initially, so you need to discuss if and when it becomes an 'interview', and thus whether the requirements of the statute and Codes of Practice apply. Is Gerry's 'mixed' statement a confession? It clearly is partly exculpatory and partly inculpatory. The information on legal advice given by the police to Gerry must be checked against the Code requirements. The confession in the police station is clearly obtained under some pressure and you must check whether s. 76 or 78 **PACE** can be applied to exclude it. Do not overlook the issue of the incriminating of a third party, namely Cliff and whether, even if the confession is inadmissible, the trial may still consider the discovery of real evidence which it prompted, the buried dogs. Cliff's treatment raises the question of whether the police should have treated it as an interview from the beginning since he was already under suspicion as a result of Gerry's statement. Consider finally his distressed state and the possible unreliability of the confession.

Answer plan

- Is the visit to Gerry an 'interview'?
- Status of Gerry's 'mixed' statement
- Is information on legal advice given correctly?
- Application of ss. 76–78 to confessions
- Confessions not evidence against third party
- 'Fruits of the poisoned tree'—discovery of real evidence as result of an inadmissible confession

Suggested answer

Gerry's initial statement in his house is clearly incriminating, although he is also trying to excuse himself. Since it is partly adverse to the maker it falls within the definition of 'confession' in s. 82(1) of the **Police and Criminal Evidence Act 1984 (PACE)**. If it is admitted the whole statement may be evidence of the truth of its contents, as the House of Lords held in *R* v *Sharp* [1988] 1 WLR 7. There is clearly no evidence of oppression here and therefore s. 76(2)(a) **PACE** is not applicable. However, it is necessary to consider the possible application of other sections of **PACE** and the Code of Practice. We are told the police are engaged in 'routine' inquiries, that is they are not conducting an interview, which is questioning of a person regarding his involvement in an offence, but rather questioning to obtain information. The state of mind of the police is the key question, but, on the facts as they are given, it seems the exchange was not an interview. The words uttered by Tom may amount to something said or done which was likely in the circumstances existing at the time to render unreliable any confession Gerry might have made. The Court of Appeal held that it is not necessary for the words or action to come from the police (*R* v *Harvey* [1988] **Crim LR 241**). There are two limbs to the test, first circumstances existing at the time and here Gerry's emotional state concerning his mother's condition may be applicable; see also *R* v *McGovern* (1990) 92 Cr App R 228. Second, as regards anything said or done, can Tom's words be sufficient? The main question is to find a causal connection between the words and the confession such as to make any confession in such circumstances unreliable. On the facts, there does not appear to be anything in Tom's remark which would have made any confession unreliable, unless it could be argued that Gerry confessed in order to stop Tom's tirade and painful remarks about his dying mother.

At the station, Gerry appears to have been properly cautioned but there may be inadequacies in the information given about access to legal advice which may, inter alia, render his confession inadmissible. Under s. 58 **PACE** and paragraph 11.2 of Code C, immediately prior to the commencement of any interview at a police station or other authorised place of detention, the interviewing officer must remind the suspect of his entitlement to free legal advice. It appears that, when Gerry is asked whether he has a solicitor and he replies that he is worried about owing him money, Gerry is not told of his entitlement to free legal advice. However, access to legal advice may be lawfully delayed for up to 36 hours in the case of indictable offences (s. 116 **PACE**). (The previous test referred to a serious arrestable offence, which included one which involves serious financial loss or gain so this may well have applied in the case of the greyhounds.) Thus, the failure in Gerry's case may well be permissible as long as the police can convince the court that they reasonably feared one of the contingencies referred to in s. 58(8) **PACE** would arise. In any case, a wrongly authorised delay in obtaining legal advice, does not render the confession automatically excluded under either s. 76 or 78 **PACE**. In *R* v *Alladice* (1988) 87 Cr App R 380, the court stressed that influential factors in excluding under s. 78 **PACE** were whether or not the police acted in bad faith and whether the presence of a solicitor would have made any difference, particularly to a seasoned offender.

However, there are arguably other pressing grounds to exclude the confession here under s. 76 **PACE**. Has this confession been obtained by oppression? Once the defence raises the issue and it is accepted by the judge as a possibility, the burden is on the prosecution to prove beyond reasonable doubt that it has not been so obtained. Does the implied threat to Tom amount to oppression of Gerry? Oppression is only partly defined in s. 76(8) **PACE** as including 'torture, inhuman or degrading treatment and the use or threat of violence whether or not amounting to torture'. Showing the photograph and the threat to 'take things further' probably does not fall within this partial statutory definition. However, in the leading case of *R* v *Fulling* [1987] QB 426 the Court of Appeal adopted the dictionary definition of 'exercise of authority or power in a burdensome, harsh or wrongful manner; unjust or cruel treatment of subjects, inferiors, etc., or the imposition of unreasonable or unjust burdens'.

In the court's opinion, it was difficult to envisage any circumstances in which oppression would not entail some impropriety on the part of the police. It is clear that Gerry here is being placed under psychological pressure as a result of the threat. The main requirement is misuse of power or authority. Thus, in *R* v *Paris* (1992) 97 Cr App R 99 the Court of Appeal held that it was oppressive within the meaning of s. 76(2)(a) **PACE** for police officers to shout at a suspect and tell him what they wanted to hear after he had denied the offence 300 times, so it is arguable that the treatment of Gerry amounts to oppression. Also s. 76(2)(b) **PACE** may be applicable in that in such circumstances any confession made by the defendant would be likely to be unreliable. This test is an objective one. Section 78 **PACE** is widely applied to confession evidence (*R* v *Mason* [1988] 1 WLR 139) and the combination of factors, particularly police bad faith over the threat, could lead to exclusion here. Even if the confession is excluded the court may still allow evidence of finding the greyhounds, although clearly their evidential worth will be less considering that it may not be possible to admit its source (s. 76(4) **PACE**). One final point is that even if the confession is admitted it will not be evidence against Cliff and should be edited at the trial. In *R* v *Silcott and Others* [1987] Crim LR 765 the interviews of some of the defendants implicated other co-accused. Hodgson J ruled that the references to names should be removed and initials were substituted. However, the prejudicial effect was not overcome since at the trial the prosecution were permitted to cross-examine over the meaning of the initials. Another solution is to order a separate trial, but this would be an extreme step and unlikely to happen here.

With regard to Cliff's position, it is arguable that the police were wrong not to treat their initial exchange with him as an interview under the definition in Code of Practice C paragraph 11.1A. There were already reasonable grounds to suspect him because of Gerry's confession. He should therefore have been cautioned and told of his right to free legal advice, although it is arguable that this is an indictable offence and access to a solicitor could be delayed on appropriate grounds. There is perhaps, a breach of the Code also in leaving him for two hours, since under paragraph 1.1 of Code C, persons in custody should be dealt with expeditiously. As someone not under arrest Cliff was free to leave but clearly had not appreciated this. There are possible grounds for unreliability given the 'something said or done' could be leaving him for two hours and the circumstances of his claustrophobia. For exclusion on grounds of s. 76(2)(b) **PACE**, there is no need for police impropriety. In *R v Crampton* **(1990) 92 Cr App R 369** according to the court it was a matter for those present at the interview to decide whether a drug addict was fit to be questioned in the sense that his answers could be relied upon to be true. The series of breaches could also, especially if bad faith was found, amount to exclusion on grounds of unfairness under s. 78 of **PACE**. Since *R v Ward* **[1993] 1 WLR 619** the courts have taken an increasingly open stance on allowing expert evidence of a psychiatrist or psychologist on the reliability of a confession if the accused was suffering from a mental disorder that fell short of mental illness. In *R v O'Brien* **[2000] Crim LR 676** the Court of Appeal stated that admissibility of expert evidence depended on the satisfaction of three conditions: first the disorder must be such that it would affect the reliability of the confession; second the accused's condition must depart significantly from the norm, and finally there must be an earlier history of his mental disorder. In that case expert evidence should have been admitted, since the accused's mental disorder was associated with the making of false confessions. Cliff might be able to rely on the case of *R v Blackburn* **[2005] EWCA Crim 1349**. The suspect was a vulnerable teenager, aged fifteen years, who did not have a mental disorder at the time of his interview when he made what was alleged to be a 'coerced compliant' confession. The Court of Appeal held that evidence of a forensic psychologist was admissible as relevant to the reliability of the confessions under s. 76(2)(b). The issue fell outside the jury's normal knowledge and experience. The court noted that the evidence of expert was that 'the key feature giving rise to a coerced compliant confession is fatigue, which, together with an inability to control what is happening, may induce the individual to experience a growing desire to give up resisting suggestions put to him'. It added, 'normal people, not suffering from any personality disorder or abnormal disorder, could be rendered compliant by prolonged interrogation'.

The defence will therefore have to examine whether the circumstances of the defendant's interrogation, combined with his claustrophobia and mental vulnerability and his age, make it arguable that an expert witness should be called.

Question 4

Arnold and Brenda are summonsed on charges of criminal damage of a wine shop in Boxfield High Street. The incident occurred at 3.00 a.m., when the window was smashed and the alarm sounded. Arnold was stopped shortly afterwards in the next street, where police suspicions are aroused because he is not wearing shoes. He is stopped and questioned in the street. He refuses to say why he was in the area at that time. He also refuses to explain why he is not wearing shoes. An abandoned pair of wine-covered sandals, which the police believe are Arnold's, are found near the scene of the burglary. Arnold is arrested and questioned about his where abouts and the absence of shoes in the police station. He has, on his request, a solicitor present on this occasion. His solicitor, however, considers that he is under the influence of drink and advises him not to answer questions at this stage. At the trial Arnold puts forward the explanation for his failure to respond to questioning that his solicitors had so advised him. He explains that he had not volunteered why he was in the area because he had been drinking with his girlfriend and did not want his wife to find out. He also says he had passed by the wine shop and seen the damaged window. Some wine from a broken bottle had spilt on his sandals. When he heard the police car coming he took off the sandals because he feared he would be implicated since he used to work at the shop. He denies involvement with the criminal damage. Brenda works at the wine shop and when she turns up for work next day and sees the debris, she asks the manager, 'What happened here?'. He replies, 'I think you know all about this don't you? Your friends and you smashed my window.' Brenda says nothing. She was interviewed by police with a solicitor present and again said nothing. At the trial Arnold and Brenda plead not guilty. She refuses to testify but her counsel cross-examines Arnold and asserts that it was Arnold who carried out the offence and that Brenda had nothing to do with it.

Advise on the evidence.

Commentary

The defendants here have acted in different ways in the face of questioning about their involvement in the offence. You will need to examine whether their reactions and behaviour amount to confessions; if so what is their evidential worth and if there are grounds to exclude them by rule of law or exercise of discretion. Arnold's behaviour raises several issues under the **Criminal Justice and Public Order Act 1994**, ss. 34, 36, 37 and 38. Brenda's situation involves a discussion of the law relating to silence in the face of questioning by the shop manager. You need therefore to discuss her behaviour in relation to common law provisions on silence. You are only given information about questioning outside the police station so do not speculate about other possible interviews.

Answer plan

- Admissibility of Arnold's silence when first questioned but not under arrest
- Applicability of **CJPOA**, ss. 34, 36 and 37 to interview at police station—Code C Annex C
- Directions to jury—see *Cowan, Condron,* JSB Specimen Directions
- Legal advice to remain silent—*Bowden;* effect on legal professional privilege.
- Admissibility of Brenda's silence—common law or **CJPOA**?
- Silence of Brenda at police interview—does s. 34 apply if she does not testify?

Suggested answer

The question involves an examination of the overlapping provisions of the **Criminal Justice and Public Order Act 1994**, which cover circumstances where a court may invite the drawing of inferences from an accused's silence. Section 34 applies after caution and up to charge, that is both before and after arrest. However, it only allows the court to draw inferences from silence if the defendant fails then to mention facts which he could reasonably have been expected to mention when questioned and which he relies on at trial for his defence.

The first question which arises is whether Arnold's silence when first questioned in the street is admissible. At this stage Arnold is not under arrest and ss. 36 and 37 are not applicable. The prosecution may try to argue that s. 34 does apply because Arnold gives an explanation at trial which he might reasonably have given when first questioned. It is unlikely that Arnold will be able to rely on s. 34(2A), in that he has not had an opportunity to consult a solicitor; that provision only applies if he was at an authorised place of detention at the time of the failure. He does give an explanation at trial for his whereabouts and his lack of shoes, so s. 34 may be engaged on those grounds. The prosecution will have difficulty, however, in successfully arguing that evidence from the interview 'at the scene of the crime' is admissible. A preliminary matter is that Arnold should have been cautioned (Code C, para. 10.4). Even if he had, it is doubtful that the failure to respond to police questions will be admitted.

Code of Practice C issued under the **Police and Criminal Evidence Act 1984 (PACE)** requires a police officer to caution the suspect before questioning him once there are grounds to suspect him of an offence. The caution now has been reworded and the suspect is warned of the possible consequences of his failure to mention relevant facts. It is unclear from the facts whether the police have reasonable suspicion of Arnold's involvement. His proximity to the scene of the crime and the lack of shoes do, however, appear to be significant. The issue is whether the questioning amounts to an interview. If it does then the statute and Code of Practice apply. The revised Code defines an interview as the questioning of a person regarding his involvement in an offence, but that questioning to obtain information or in the ordinary course of duty does not constitute an interview. This does leave some doubt, however, as to when questioning to obtain information turns into questioning about involvement in an offence. The case-law is primarily based on the admissibility of confessions, but is arguably relevant also to the suspect's silence. *R* v *Park* [1994] **Crim LR 285** upholds the principle that 'at the scene' interviews are not admissible. In that case, it was held that exploratory questions at a roadside could give rise in due course to a well-founded suspicion that an offence had been committed. So what started out as an inquiry could become an interview. However, the Court of Appeal upheld the judge's decision not to apply s. 78 **PACE** to exclude that part of the evidence: 'even if the roadside conversation should now be regarded as an interview . . . it was, as prosecuting counsel said, only just an interview . . .'.

In the instant case the police already know of the offence and so there might be more grounds for considering their questions to Arnold as an interview. Arnold will thus be advised that even if he has been cautioned it is possible that the prosecution cannot make use of his silence in the street, because he should not have been questioned away from the police station. It is, however, appropriate that 'emergency' provisions should be considered. He may be interviewed away from the police station if the consequent delay would be likely (a) to lead to interference with or harm to evidence connected with an offence or interference with or physical harm to other people; (b) to lead to the alerting of other people suspected of having committed an offence but not yet arrested for it; or (c) to hinder the recovery of property obtained in consequence of the commission of an offence. It does not appear on the facts that any of these do apply to Arnold and so it is unlikely his silence in the street will be admissible.

The prosecution may more successfully argue that ss. 34, 36 or 37 **CJPOA** may apply in the circumstances arising from the interview in the police station. Arnold is allowed access to a solicitor, so ss. 34(2A) and 36(4A) and 37(3A) are satisfied. He should in addition have been given an opportunity to confirm or deny his earlier silence outside the police station, and for ss. 36 and 37 to be operative he should have been given the special warning set out in Code C paras 10.10 and 10.11. The prosecution may seek to rely on ss. 34, 36 or 37, although Arnold may argue that s. 36 applied to the failure to account for the presence not absence of objects, namely his shoes. The plethora of case-law which has been generated in this area is applicable to all three sections (as well as s. 35, see *R v Cowan* [1996] QB 373). In *Argent* (1997) 2 Cr App R 27, the Court of Appeal set out the conditions which have to be met before a jury can draw an adverse inference. In particular it will be a matter for the jury to determine whether in the circumstances existing at the time the defendant could reasonably be expected to mention a fact. Relevant factors to be considered include the particular circumstances of the defendant and the state of his knowledge, including information from the police. Arnold is only expected to account or to mention facts he could reasonably have been expected to mention but it is certainly arguable that these included his absence of shoes and why he was in the area. The phrase 'in the circumstances' should not be construed restrictively, and references to 'the accused' must mean Arnold's actual qualities, knowledge, state of mind, etc. In *R v Kirk* [2000] 1 WLR 567 insufficient information given to a suspect before questioning meant the confession should have been excluded under s. 78. It is not necessary, however, that Arnold should be told the precise details of the alleged offence. *R v Compton* [2002] EWCA Crim 2835 also established that 'section 36, unlike section 34, invites no comparison between the statement in interview and the evidence at trial since section 36 contains no parallel to the question under section 34(1) of whether it was reasonable for the defendant to mention a particular fact: reasonableness usually being judged from the starting point of whether the fact was mentioned at trial'.

The standard Judicial Studies Board Specimen Direction No. 40 direction should be given and the jury should be directed that only if, despite the evidence or lack of it, they concluded that the failure to mention a fact or to account could only sensibly be attributed to the accused's having no answer, or none that would stand up to cross-examination, might they draw an adverse inference. Arnold may plead that under the **Human Rights Act 1998** the absence of such a direction is a violation of art. 6(1) of the European Convention on Human Rights (*Condron* v *United Kingdom* [2000] **Crim LR 679**). However, each case depends on its own specific facts.

Arnold may argue that he had remained silent on legal advice. That in itself is not sufficient to preclude the operation of ss. 34, 36 or 37 but it would be one of the circumstances that the jury should take into account (*Condron* v *UK* (2000)). Arnold should be warned that if he goes beyond a bare assertion of the solicitor's advice he risks breaching legal professional privilege (**Bowden [1999] 1 WLR 823**). It may not be necessary for the judge to direct the jury that they must find a case to answer against Arnold before drawing any adverse inference under ss. 34, 36, 37 (*R* v *Doldur* [2000] **Crim LR 178**).

What constitutes a proper inference for the court or jury in any particular case is a matter of fact. However, Arnold may gain some comfort from s. 38(3) of the 1994 Act, which provides that 'A person shall not have the proceedings against him transferred to the Crown Court for trial, have a case to answer or be convicted of an offence solely on an inference drawn from such a failure or refusal.' Here there does appear to be other circumstantial evidence, such as the finding of the sandals.

Brenda faces the possibility of her silences being admitted by common law or statute. First of all, is her failure to respond to the manager's allegation admissible? Under s. 82(1) **PACE** a confession includes any statement wholly or partly adverse to the person who made it, whether made to a person in authority or not and whether made in words or otherwise. The first question then is whether her silence is a statement made otherwise than in words. It is by no means clear that silence would fit such a definition. The common law rule is that a statement made in the presence of the accused is not evidence against him except in so far as he accepts what has been said (*R* v *Christie* [1914] **AC 545**). It may be that a reply or indignant rejection of the accusation could reasonably be expected from Brenda and thus her failure to do that may be an implied acceptance of the truth of the accusation. Thus in *Parkes* v *R* (1977) **64 Cr App R 25**, the defendant's silence when accused by a mother of stabbing her daughter was held by the Privy Council to have been properly admitted as evidence going to guilt. The courts have applied this principle to situations where the parties are on even terms. Brenda's accuser is her manager and she may have been quiet from considerations other than guilt. If her failure to reply is admitted, the jury should be directed to consider first whether the silence indicates acceptance of the accusation, and second whether guilt could reasonably be inferred from what she had accepted. A failure to leave both these issues to the jury led to the quashing of a conviction by the Court of

Appeal in *R* v *Chandler* [1976] 1 WLR 585. Section 34 of the **Criminal Justice and Public Order Act 1994** does not apply to Brenda because it is only relevant in relation to silence when being questioned by the police or others charged with investigating offences. The shop manager does appear to not fit this definition.

However, in relation to her silence at interview s. 34 may well apply. She has a solicitor present, thus satisfying one of the statutory requirements. Is she at trial relying on a fact she could have referred to earlier? Arguably this is the case since the defence that it was Arnold not her who committed the offence could have been known to her at the time of the police interview. It is no bar that the fact goes to the heart of her defence (*Milford* (2001)). Similarly, the fact that she presents the fact through her counsel does not per se preclude telling the jury that they may draw an adverse inference. In *R* v *Webber* (2004) the House of Lords held that the word 'fact' should be given a broad meaning. A party relies on a fact, for example, when his counsel conducts questioning in such a way that he puts a positive case to the witness.

The judge in the case of both defendants will have to follow Judicial Studies Board guidelines in giving clear directions to the jury in the summing-up.

Additional Reading—Confessions

Ashworth, A. and Emmerson B., 'Silence and Safety: The Impact of Human Rights Law' [2000] Crim LR 879.

Birch, D., 'The Sharp End of the Wedge: Use of Mixed Statements by the Defence' (1997) Crim LR 416.

Brooks, P., *Troubling Confessions* (University of Chicago Press, Chicago, 2001).

Choo, A., 'Confessions and Corroboration' (1991) Crim LR 867.

Choo, A, 'Corroboration of Disputed Confessions' (1991) 107 Law Quarterly Review 544.

Enright, S., 'Crime Brief' (1995) 145 New Law Journal 854.

Hirst, M. 'Confessions as Proof of Innocence' [1998] Cambridge Law Journal 146.

Mirfield, P., *Confessions and Improperly Obtained Evidence* (OUP, 1997).

Pattendon, R., 'Should Confessions be Corroborated?' (1991) LQR 317.

Sharpe, S., *Judicial Discretion and Investigation* (Sweet & Maxwell, London, 1998).

Additional Reading—Right to silence

Ashworth, A., *The Criminal Process*, 2nd edn (Oup, 1998).

Azzopardi, J. H., 'Disclosure at the Police Station, the Right to Silence, and *DPP* v *Arra*' (2002) Crim LR 295.

Birch, D.J., 'Suffering in Silence: a Cost-Benefit Analysis of s. 34 of the Criminal Justice and Public Order Act 1994' [1999] Crim LR 769.

Bucke, T., Street, R. and Brown, D., 'The Right of Silence: The Impact of the Criminal Justice and Public Order Act 1994', Home Office Research Study (London, 2000).

Cape, E., *Advising on Silence*, Criminal Practitioners' Newsletter, Law Society, January 2006.

Dennis, I.H., 'Miscarriages of Justice and the Law of Confessions: Evidentiary Issues and Solutions' [1993] PL 291.

Dennis, I.H., 'The Criminal Justice and Public Order Act 1994. The Evidence Provisions' [1995] Crim LR 4.

Dennis I.H., 'Silence at the Police Station: The Marginalisation of Section 34' (2002) Crim LR 25.

Easton, S., 'Bodily Samples and the Privilege Against Self-incrimination' [1991] Crim LR 18.

Enright S., 'Crime Brief' (1995) 145 NLJ 854.

Galligan, D.J., 'The Right to Silence Reconsidered' [1988] CLP 69.

Greer, S., 'The Right to Silence: A Review of the Current Debate' (1990) 53 MLR 709.

Jackson, John D., 'Silence and Proof: Extending the Boundaries of Criminal Proceedings in the United Kingdom' (2000) 5 E&P 145.

Jennings A., Ashworth A., and Emmerson B., 'Silence and Safety: the Impact of Human Rights Law' (2000) Crim LR 879.

Keogh, A., 'The Right to Silence—Revisited Again' (2003) 153 NLJ 1352.

Leng, R., 'Silence Pre-trial, Reasonable Expectations and the Normative Distortion of Fact-finding' (2001) 5 E & P 204.

Mirfield, P., *Silence, Confessions and Improperly Obtained Evidence* (OUP, 1997).

Munday, R. 'Inferences from Silence and Human Rights Law' [1996] Crim LR 370.

Seidmann, D.J., and Stein, A., 'The Right to Silence helps the Innocent: A Game-theoretic Analysis of the Fifth Amendment Privilege' (2000) 114 Harv LR 431.

Starmer, K., and Walker, C. (eds), *Justice in Error* (OUP, 1993).

Tain P., 'Non-police Station Interviews' (1995) 139 Sol Jo 299.

Williams, C.R., 'Silence in Australia: Probative Force and Rights in the Law of Evidence' (1994) 110 LQR 629.

Zander, M., 'Abolition of the Right to Silence 1972–1994' in Morgan, D, and Stephenson, G., *Suspicion and Silence. The Right to Silence in Criminal Investigations* (Blackstone, London, 1994), page 141.

Zuckerman, A.A.S., 'Bias and Suggestibility. Is there an Alternative to the Right to Silence?', in Morgan and Stephenson (eds) (sup cit), page 117.

7

Improperly obtained evidence

Introduction

Confessions apart, English law has in the past been notoriously unwilling to acknowledge the case for excluding evidence which is obtained in a way which involves the police acting improperly or even illegally. However, there is now a growing body of cases on a specific aspect of this, namely entrapment, whereby the police are arguably influencing the actual commission of the offence. Several cases have recently considered whether evidence obtained thereby should be excluded under s. 78 of the **Police and Criminal Evidence Act 1984 (PACE)**. You will need knowledge of the earlier common law position on this issue exemplified in *R* v *Sang* [1980] AC 402, a case which raised many academic hackles. There the House of Lords appeared to confine the discretion to exclude on grounds of impropriety to cases of confessions or those akin to confessions. The issue was seen to be based on the privilege against self-incrimination. Lord Diplock (at p. 436) explained it as follows:

> That is why there is no discretion to exclude evidence discovered as a result of an illegal search but there is discretion to exclude evidence which the accused has been induced to produce voluntarily if the method of inducement was unfair.

However, in principle, if not in practice, the courts now appear willing to apply s. 78 to improperly obtained evidence other than confessions, specifically that obtained by undercover police operations involving entrapment.

With regard to other non-confessional evidence such as evidence obtained as a result of a breach of the law the courts are rarely inclined to exercise the discretion to exclude. English law applies the rule that illegality does not affect the admissibility of evidence, or the 'fruit of the poisoned tree', as a matter of law. This principle influences the rationale of the exclusion of evidence by discretion.

The **Human Rights Act** 1998 and the Strasbourg case-law is having some impact in this area. In *Teixeira de Castro* v *Portugal* (1998) 28 EHRR 101 entrapment of a man with no previous connection with drug dealing was held to be a violation of art. 6. However, in *Khan* v *United Kingdom* (2000) 31 EHRR 45 the Strasbourg Court found no violation as a result of illegal police bugging of a suspect. Policy considerations of crime control versus due process come into play. As Lord Nolan commented in the House of Lords judgment in *R* v *Khan* [1997] AC 558 at p. 302, 'It would be a strange reflection on our law if a man who has admitted his participation in the illegal importation of heroin should have his conviction set aside on the grounds that his privacy has been invaded.'

The cases here form into two groups. First, there are those where there is some impropriety in the investigation which may amount even to illegality. An example is surveillance without following the proper procedures. The other group of cases are on entrapment. These operations may involve breaches of art. 6 and art. 8. You should be aware of the important case of *R* v *Looseley: Attorney-General's Reference No. 3 of 2000* [2000] 1 WLR 2060 and note that the House dealt more robustly with the question of staying the prosecution than with exclusion of evidence when the integrity of the criminal justice system is threatened. Choo (2006, p. 146) notes: 'what is notable about *Looseley* . . . , is that we have for the first time in England and Wales an articulate sustained and authoritative judicial consideration of entrapment of the sort that comparable jurisdictions have had for some years.' The Strasbourg case-law is important. Note particularly the case of *Allan* v *UK* (2002) 36 EHRR on the use of informers.

Finally, the increasing use of statute to regulate police investigations means a more bureaucratic approach to surveillance and undercover procedures. These are covered by the **Regulation of Investigatory Powers Act** 2000.

One issue which has aroused much controversy recently is that of 'intercept' evidence. Section 17 of the **Regulation of Investigatory Powers Act 2000** provides that 'no evidence shall be adduced, question asked, assertion or disclosure made or other things done in the, or for the purposes of or in connection with any legal proceedings which (in the end a manner) (a) discloses, in circumstances from which its origin in anything falling within subsection (2) may be inferred, any of the contents of an intercepted communications or any related communications data'. In its essence the purpose is to prevent the admission of a communication intercepted in the course of its transmission by means of a postal service or telecommunications system if the evidence might reveal the existence of a warrant. For policy reasons it is regarded as necessary to keep surveillance operations secret.

The Oxford academic Andrew Ashworth points out that the criminal justice system should protect defendants from abuse of state power:

> If a legal system declares certain standards for the conduct of criminal investigation—whether they are enshrined in a constitution, detailed in a comprehensive code or scattered in various statutes and judicial precedents—then it can be argued that citizens have corresponding rights to be accorded certain facilities and not to be treated in certain ways. If the legal system is to respect those rights, then it is arguable that a suspect whose rights have been infringed should not thereby be placed at any disadvantage: by 'disadvantage' is meant . . . that evidence obtained by investigators as a result of the infringement should not be used against the suspect (1977, p. 724).

Academic commentators have elucidated a number of principles which should inform the use of the discretionary judicial power to exclude evidence. These include upholding the suspect's rights, ensuring the reliability of the verdict, disciplining the investigative authorities, ensuring the legitimacy of the verdict and ensuring the integrity of the judicial process. Table 14 illustrates various stances the courts have taken to excluding evidence of secret police surveillance. Table 15 gives examples of cases on entrapment.

Question 1

(a) The police are concerned about a spate of burglaries from clothes shops on the Che Guevara estate where the perpetrators have not been caught. Inspector Hilary, a plainclothes policewoman, strikes up a conversation with a group of women suspects in the estate's launderette but does not say who she is. She expresses an interest in the attractive silk shirts they are washing. Alice, one of the women, agrees to get some for Hilary. They arrange to meet the next day and the shirts are exchanged for money. They turn out to have been stolen from Designer Modes, one of the shops on the estate. Alice is then arrested for dealing in stolen goods. Advise on evidence.

(b) Ronan and Olaf are suspected of dealing in stolen cars but the police are finding it difficult to get evidence against them. Ronan has a 'for sale' notice on a car outside his house and PC Henry in plain clothes knocks to inquire about it. He chats to Ronan for a while and then asks, 'Has the car been nicked some time ago?' Ronan replies, 'Only a few weeks.' Ronan is arrested and taken into the police station for questioning. Olaf is unaware of this but is separately asked to go to the police station to help with an investigation over a missing child. While he is there he sees Ronan in a room and asks if he can have a few words. The police superintendent agrees. Unknown to Olaf and Ronan the police have set up video and sound recording in the room. Olaf and Ronan converse and are recorded as admitting they had dealt in stolen cars. Both are charged. Advise on evidence.

Commentary

The police in these scenarios are engaged in undercover operations. The question turns therefore on the possibility of excluding evidence on the grounds that it has been obtained improperly. You must state the general rule of English law that the impropriety of the method of obtaining evidence generally bears no relevance to its admissibility, except in relation to confessions. The principle that there is no such rule of exclusion was set out by the Privy Council in *Kuruma* v *R* [1955] AC 197. However, although there is no rule of exclusion, there is a discretion to exclude if the admission of such evidence would be unfair. With regard to the common law discretion, the House of Lords in *R* v *Sang* [1980] AC 402 seemed to suggest that discretion to exclude evidence because it was illegally or improperly obtained only applied to confession evidence (or evidence analogous to confessions), unless its probative value was less than its prejudicial effect. *Sang* also held that there was a substantive rule that entrapment is no defence and that this could not be undermined by the use of an evidential discretion. Thus Alice, who is likely to argue she was tricked into committing the offence, cannot rely on the common law discretion. This common law discretion was limited in *R* v *Sang* to evidence obtained after the commission of the offence, so the common law is not applicable in the case of Alice if she argues entrapment. Cases of entrapment or the activities of an agent provocateur refer to those situations where the accused is either enticed or encouraged to commit an offence and is subsequently charged. However, s. 78 **PACE** has, in theory at least, now been acknowledged as of possible application in entrapment cases, although the courts have been slow to identify actual agent provocateurs. With regard to the discussion between Ronan and Henry you need to consider whether **PACE** Code C is being deliberately evaded. The surveillance of Olaf and Ronan raises the question of police bad faith and obedience to the proper precedents.

Answer plan

(a)

- Common law rule on improperly obtained evidence—*R* v *Sang* (1988)
- Fairness test applied by s. 78 **PACE** but no clear guidelines—see *R* v *Khan* (1996)
- Courts now accept that admitting evidence of entrapment MAY be unfair—see *R* v *Shannon* (2001)
- Section 78 and art. 6 arguably achieve same result—*Texeira* v *Portugal*
- Recent case of *R* v *Looseley* shows more robust approach to exclusion under s. 78 and to stay of proceedings

(b)

- Remarks by Ronan to PC Henry may be excluded if there was a deliberate attempt to circumvent Code—*R* v *Bryce* (1992); **RIPA 2000**

Suggested answer

(a) Tom and Alice may try to argue that the evidence against them should be excluded because it has been obtained improperly. Inspector Hilary did not reveal she was a police officer but appeared as a genuine purchaser and PC Henry was a trespasser when he gained the evidence of the confession. The general rule is that, as Crompton J put it obiter in *R* v *Leatham* [1861] 8 Cox CC 498, 'it matters not how you get it, if you steal it even, it would be admissible in evidence'. The test of admissibility is whether the evidence is relevant. Lord Fraser said in *Fox* v *Chief Constable of Gwent* [1985] 3 All ER 392, 397, 'the duty of the court is to decide whether the appellant has committed the offence with which he is charged and not to discipline the police for exceeding their powers'. However, although there is no rule of exclusion, it is open to the court as an exercise of discretion to exclude improperly obtained evidence if its admission would be unfair. In *R* v *Sang* [1980] AC 402 its exercise was limited to evidence obtained after the offence was committed. Thus the common law may apply to Tom because the questioning by

Table 14 Evidence obtained by covert police surveillance

Police secret recording operation	Authorised by regulation?	Police acting in bad faith?	Evasion of Code?	Comment outcome
R v *Khan* [1996] 3 WLR 162 (HL) listening device on flat, damaging property, drug dealing	There was then no statutory system to deal with covert listening devices	Police had trespassed and damaged property	No	Evidence admitted—gravity of offence outweighed possible breach of art. 8
Khan v *UK* (2000) 31 EHRR 1016 (EctHR)	Ditto	Ditto	No. Admissions were voluntary.	Violation of art. 8 not art. 6—national court had properly applied s. 78
R v *Mason* [2002] 2 Cr App R 628. Robbers bugged in cell (CA).	Non-statutory guidelines not complied with	No	No	Breach of guidelines insignificant—evidence admitted, art. 8 breached
Allan v *UK* (2002) 36 EHRR (ECtHR). Police coached informant to question A in cell and recorded conversation—murder charge.	No	Yes	Yes	Breach of art. 6 because of violation of suspect's privilege against self-incrimination—evidence should be excluded
R v *Grant* [2005] 3 WLR 437. Secret recording conversation of suspect and solicitor. (CA)	Not authorised	Yes	Yes	Trial stayed—breach of legal professional privilege
R v *Button* [2005] EWCA 516 suspect recorded communicating in cell. Murder charge. (CA)	Audio recording but not video authorised	No	No	Breach of art. 8 but fair to admit evidence

the undercover officer relates to past events. In practice, however, the common law discretion has given way to the application of s. 78 of the **Police and Criminal Evidence Act 1984 (PACE)**, which gives a statutory discretion to exclude evidence which would adversely affect the fairness of the proceedings. Thus the court has to consider the interests of the prosecution as well as the defence.

Table 15 Cases involving entrapment

Case	Outcome
Teixeira de Castro v *Portugal* **(1999) 28 EHRR 101 (ECtHR)**	Article 6(1) violated. Suspect had not been known to police and officers had gone beyond acting as undercover agents, they had incited offence. Evidence should have been excluded.
R v *Smurthwaite* **[1994] 1 All ER 898 (CA)**	Factors to be considered in excluding evidence listed. Evidence rightly admitted.
R v *Christou* **[1992] 1 QB 979 (CA)**	Code C inapplicable. Officers not acting as police officers. Evidence rightly admitted.
R v *Shannon* **[2001] 1 WLR 51 (CA)**	Need to distinguish situation where credibility and reliability of evidence is at issue from that where 'unfairness is more than a visceral reaction that it is in principle unfair as a matter of policy or wrong as a matter of law for a person to be prosecuted for a crime which he would not have committed without the incitement'. The latter is not in itself sufficient for exclusion. The abuse of process argument was not available since the entrapment was conducted by a journalist not 'the police (or someone acting on behalf of or in league with the police) and/or the prosecuting authority'. But see now *Council for the Regulation of Health Professionals* v *GMC* **[2007] 1 WLR 3091**. Sufficiently gross misconduct by a non-state agent may lead to use of the evidence being a breach of article 6.
R v *Looseley:* **Attorney General's Reference No. 3 of 2000, HL**	Useful guide is did police do no more than present defendant with unexceptional opportunity to commit a crime. Proper approach is stay of proceedings, but evidence may be excluded if trial has commenced. Stay of proceedings correct where officers had instigated the offence.[1]

[1]Choo (2006, p. 149) comments on this case, 'It is arguable that while not encapsulated in a statute, a reasonably coherent doctrine of entrapment is not, in the light of *Looseley* recognised in English law.' He suggests if stay is not justified, *Looseley* does now make clear the extent to which s. 78(1) may be applied to exclude evidence and that *Smurthwaite* and *Shannon* point in different directions, with *Smurthwaite* taking a more robust approach to exclusion.

There is nothing in the statute to suggest that the court should discipline the police. Statutory exclusion of confessions on the grounds of potential unreliability is confined to those made 'in consequence of anything said or done' during the interrogation. This does not apply here. However, the court may apply the discretion under s. 78 PACE. The courts will, in regard to confessions, look on bad faith on the part of the police as grounds for exercising the discretion (**R** v *Alladice* (1988) 87 CR App R 380), but the test is whether a trial containing evidence obtained as a result of a particular deceit would be fair. The approach is decided on a case-by-case basis. Thus, in *R* v *H* [1987] **Crim LR 47** evidence of secretly tape-recorded conversations between the complainant and the suspect in a rape case was excluded, whereas in *R* v *Jelen* (1989) 90 Cr App R 456, the Court of Appeal upheld the admission of tape recordings made in secret of two defendants in conversation. The Court of Appeal drew a distinction between the two cases, in that, in the latter, the police were at an early stage of their inquiries and the defendant had not been interviewed. A more recent example is *R* v *Khan* [1997] AC 558, where the police, following Home Office guidelines, placed an undercover listening device on the outside wall of a private house of a suspected heroin dealer. The police had caused criminal damage and were trespassing. The admissions so recorded were admitted. The House of Lords accepted as a factor in the case the gravity of the offence. Section 78 could in principle extend to the exclusion of evidence of the incriminating conversations. Thus exclusion was a matter of discretion not law, and art. 8 was also a relevant consideration. This was not, however, on the facts a suitable case for exclusion of the evidence. In this question Tom's offence of theft or receiving stolen goods is arguable less serious than that in *Khan*'s case. The test for admissibility lies in balancing the undermining of the defendant's privacy with the public interest in the prosecution of criminals. It is submitted that if Tom was not a suspect and had not been interrogated before, it is likely his admission will be allowed.

Alice may possibly argue that she would not have committed the offence if she had not been asked for the shirts by Hilary. In *R* v *Sang*, the House of Lords said entrapment is no defence and that this rule cannot be changed by exercise of discretion on admissibility of evidence. However, in recent years, the courts have shown a willingness at least to consider the exercise of s. 78 **PACE** in using its discretion to exclude evidence obtained by entrapment.

In *R* v *Smurthwaite* [1994] 1 All ER 898, the Court of Appeal accepted that s. 78 **PACE** had introduced some discretion to exclude evidence in such situations. It laid down guidelines to judges when exercising their discretion whether to admit the evidence of undercover police officers. The fact that the evidence had been obtained by entrapment does not of itself require the judge to exclude it unless it would have the adverse effect described in s. 78 **PACE**. However, factors to be taken into account were: was the officer enticing the defendant to commit a crime he would not otherwise have committed? What was the nature of the entrapment? Does the evidence consist of admissions to a completed offence or the actual commission of an offence? How active or passive was the officer's role in obtaining the evidence? Was there an unassailable record of what occurred or was it strongly corroborated? Reference was made to *R* v *Christou* [1992] QB 979, where the Court of Appeal said it was improper for police officers to adopt a disguise to enable them to ask questions without having to observe the Code, although they had not done so there in setting up a fake jewellery shop to take suspected stolen goods. The questions arose inevitably in the course of the exchange of goods. The **Human Rights Act** does not appear to have significantly changed the law in this area. In *R* v *Shannon* [2001] 1 WLR 51, the Court of Appeal considered that the approach of the Strasbourg Court in *Teixeira de Castro* v *Portugal* (1999) 28 EHRR 101 accorded with that in *Smurthwaite*.

Both Alice and Tom may be able to rely on the House of Lords decision in *Looseley* (2000) (**Attorney-General's Reference No. 3 of 2000**). This arose from two cases of 'entrapment' in one of which the undercover police officers had not abused their powers but in the other they had. The correct outcome was a stay of prosecution in the second case. As Lord Nicholls put it: 'Police conduct which brings out, to use the catch-phrase, state created crime, is unacceptable and improper. To prosecute in such circumstances would be an affront to the public conscience . . . Ultimately the overall consideration is always whether the conduct of the police or other law enforcement agency was so seriously improper as to bring the administration of justice into disrepute.'

The House agreed that a stay of prosecution for abuse of process was the only appropriate outcome of extreme cases of entrapment but suggested s. 78 could be brought into play where without the tainted evidence the trial could still proceed. In other words, in the wake of the enactment of the **Human Rights Act 1998** the courts take a more trenchant attitude to exclusion.

In Alice's case, the criteria set out in these cases are clearly relevant. In their light it would appear that evidence of the transaction of the shirts is probably admissible but not of any accompanying confession. Alice appears to have volunteered to get a shirt for Hilary without further prompting, so that the element of entrapment seems relatively minor. This appears to be one of those situations where the Inspector, Hilary, has been able to insert herself into a situation where the offence is already underway. She appears as willing to accept goods which might reasonably be expected to be stolen. Alice is presumably already in possession of the goods, so it is not a situation where, but for Hilary's intervention, the offence might not have been committed. Furthermore, the evidence relates to the actual commission of the offence, rather than to an admission to an already completed offence.

It thus seems likely that Alice had a crime in mind or was already knowingly in possession of the stolen shirts before Hilary appeared. Alice's chances of having the evidence excluded are very slim. Despite the acceptance in principle in *Smurthwaite* that evidence obtained by undercover operations before the commission of an offence could be excluded, in recent cases, the courts have not so acted. Alice has been deceived into producing evidence against herself but as the Court of Appeal said in *R* v *Christou* 'The trick was not applied to the appellants; they voluntarily applied themselves to the trick.' The defence will want to check whether the Code of Practice under RIPA has been observed. Paragraph 1.9 of the Code states that the proper authorisation of the undercover operation 'should ensure the suitability of such evidence under the common law, section 78 of the **Police and Criminal Evidence Act 1984** and the **Human Rights Act 1998**'.

(b) The questions here are how far Henry has adopted an undercover technique to circumvent the Code. On the facts as given it appears that the situation is similar to that in *R* v *Bryce* (1992) 95 Cr App R 320. However, it is not clear whether Ronan denies making the incriminating response to Henry. In *Bryce* the undercover police officer and the suspect had different versions of the offence. In that case the evidence of the effective confession was excluded on two grounds, the first of which may arguably apply here. The undercover officer in *Bryce* had asked two questions which were held to be a violation of Code C and had gone directly to the question of the suspect's guilt, unlike the position in *Christou* where the questions asked had been necessary to preserve the undercover officers' cover and had been indirect. In *Bryce* their questions were 'how warm' the car was and 'how long has it been nicked'. The second reason for exclusion, however, was that the suspect denied making the responses he was alleged to have made and since the code was not followed there was no authentic, contemporaneous record of what had happened. It followed that there was a risk of concoction. Ronan is advised therefore that he has grounds for the exclusion of his alleged confession on the basis that the code had been circumvented. If he has denied making the statements the case for exclusion is strengthened. The police undercover action in relation to Olaf and Ronan raises the questions of possible illegality and possible violation of art. 8 and art. 6. Article 8(1) ECHR provides that 'everyone has the right to respect for his private life'. However, Olaf and Ronan should be warned that even if a breach of art. 8 is found this does not necessarily mean that the evidence should be excluded under s. 78(1). Olaf and Ronan are entitled to challenge the use of the evidence and the trial judge should assess the effect of its admission on the fairness of the proceedings. More information is needed as to whether the secret recording was carried out according to the specifications of the **Regulation of Investigatory Powers Act 2000**. In *R* v *Button* [2005] EWCA Crim 516 the police had approval for covert audio surveillance, but not video. However, acting in good faith they had recorded by video and audio a discussion of two suspects in a cell. There was a breach of art. 8 but this was subsumed by the duty in art. 6 to ensure a fair trial. Through its obligation to ensure a fair trial in accordance with art. 6, the court was acting compatibly with the Convention. The court played no part in the interference with private life occasioned by the covert surveillance. The court's obligation was confined to deciding whether having regard to the way in which the evidence was obtained it would be fair to admit it. The court regarded the proposition that evidence obtained in breach of art. 8 should be excluded as a 'startling proposition, and one which we are pleased and relieved to be able to reject'.

The only countervailing point is that this does not appear to be a serious offence, unlike the murder charge in *Button*. Lord Steyn stated in *R* v *Latif* [1996] 1 WLR 104, '. . .the judge must weigh in the balance the public interest in ensuring that those that are charged with grave crimes should be tried and the competing public interest in not conveying the impression that the court will adopt the approach that the end justifies the means'. On the other hand, in *Looseley* the House of Lords gave greater weight to the consideration of whether the integrity of the criminal justice system was being consciously undermined. It is likely, however, that Olaf and Ronan will not be able to resist the admission of the conversation.

Question 2

'...Apparently reliable evidence may need to be excluded altogether if it carries significant risks of impairing the moral and expressive authority of the verdict.' (Dennis, I.H., *The Law of Evidence*, 2002, 2nd edn, Sweet & Maxwell at p. 45).

Discuss this statement in the light of the approach of the courts to the admissibility of evidence obtained by arguably improper means.

Commentary

You will be expected in this question to demonstrate appreciation of the extent to which, if at all, the introduction of s. 78 **PACE** and the **Human Rights Act 1998** have changed the law on the exclusion of improperly obtained evidence other than confessions. The question raises important issues of principle and asks you to discuss the argument that factual accuracy is not sufficient to found a court's verdict; the verdict must also have moral standing or legitimacy. This idea is very much associated with Ian Dennis and one advocated also by Roberts and Zuckerman (2004). You will need to give a brief outline of the law as it stood as a result of the House of Lords' decision in *R* v *Sang* [1980] AC 402. Robertson (1993, p. 805) argues that s. 78 **PACE** has effectively reversed the decision in *Sang*. The court should now consider excluding prosecution evidence by exercise of the discretion on the grounds of unfairness and there is no specification that such evidence is limited to that after the commission of the offence. Your answer should review the considerations which the courts bring to bear on exclusion of evidence obtained by police tricks such as entrapment and lies and contrast this with evidence obtained by breaches of primary or delegated legislation such as the **Road Traffic Acts** or the regulations on covert listening devices or Codes C and D of **PACE**. You should demonstrate your understanding of the terms of s. 78, which refers to 'the circumstances in which the evidence was obtained' as a ground for non-admissibility but only if it would have 'such an adverse effect on the fairness of the proceedings that the court ought not to admit it'. In other words, there has to be a causal connection between any impropriety and the trial proceedings (of course, the court may also exclude evidence which is not improperly obtained, but you are not asked about this here). There is much recent case-law on this issue and it is crucial also that you assess the impact of the **Human Rights Act 1998** in this area. Note that the question refers to 'use' of evidence obtained by arguably improper means. You should distinguish between those situations in which a stay of prosecution is appropriate and those in which the prosecution may go ahead but the evidence may be excluded.

Answer plan

- Has s. 78 reversed *Sang*?
- Improperly obtained evidence falls into two categories
- Consider entrapment, police traps
- Consider evidence obtained in breach of primary legislation

- Impact of **Human Rights Act**—*R* v *Looseley* contrasted with ***Attorney-General's Reference No. 3 of 1999***; whether stay of prosecution or exclusion of evidence appropriate
- Academic comment on pragmatic approach of courts

Suggested answer

At common law, courts have a general discretion to exclude evidence, albeit relevant, to ensure a fair trial. In *R* v *Sang* [1980] AC 402 the House of Lords acknowledged that this had two aspects, namely the exclusion of evidence if it would be likely to have a prejudicial effect outweighing its probative value, and a more limited discretion to exclude unfairly or illegally obtained evidence. This discretion took place in a context whereby the general rule of English law was that apart from confession evidence, impropriety in obtaining evidence has no relevance to admissibility. This is illustrated in cases such as *Kuruma* v *R* [1955] AC 197. Their Lordships in *Sang* limited the exercise of the discretion to exclude evidence obtained after the commission of the offence, likening the general exclusionary approach to that on unfairly obtained confessions based on the privilege against self-incrimination. A person should not be improperly led into giving evidence that could be used against him. In fact the courts rarely exercised the common law discretion to exclude. In *R* v *Christou* [1992] QB 979 Lord Diplock pointed out that the only case brought to their Lordships' attention in which the appellate court had actually excluded evidence on the ground that it had been unfairly obtained by a trick was *R* v *Payne* [1963] 1 WLR 637. Two 'strictures' therefore emerge from the pre-**PACE** position in *Sang*; first, that evidence obtained before the commission of the offence was not covered by the discretion and, second, that even with regard to evidence improperly obtained after the commission of the offence it would only rarely be appropriate to exercise discretion to exclude. It will be argued here that in both of these areas the post-**PACE** cases show that the judiciary has adopted a marginally more robust approach to exclusion and is slowly moving towards articulating a set of principles on which the discretion could be exercised.

In several early cases after the introduction of **PACE** the court took a restrictive approach. This shift could be perceived in *R* v *Christou* [1992] QB 979, where the Court of Appeal was prepared to consider the application of s. 78. Lord Taylor considered that the police trick in setting up a shop prepared to deal in stolen jewellery did not lead to unfairness to the proceedings but this implied that some tricks could. A more robust attitude was taken by the Court of Appeal in *R* v *Bryce* [1992] 4 All ER 567. Evidence of conversations between the defendant and undercover police officers should have been excluded because they concerned a fact in issue in the case, namely guilty knowledge of a stolen car. Here the evidence obtained was akin to a confession and was a deliberate attempt to circumvent Code C. In *R* v *Smurthwaite* [1994] 1 All ER 898 the Court of Appeal was prepared to accept that evidence obtained by entrapment would be excluded under s. 78 if it had the necessary adverse effect on the fairness of the proceedings. Thus the nature of the entrapment would affect the application of the discretion. This is a shift from the position in *Sang*, albeit not one which had led to actual exclusion of such evidence. It remained the position, as it does today, that entrapment was not a defence.

It is arguable that the guidelines set out in *Smurthwaite* do reveal a pragmatic approach, rather than a principled approach, to the exercise of the discretion to exclude. Factors to consider were:

(a) Was the officer enticing the defendant to commit a crime which he would not otherwise commit?

(b) What was the nature of the entrapment?

(c) Does the evidence consist of admissions to a completed offence or the actual commission of an offence?

(d) How active or passive was the officer's role in obtaining the evidence?

(e) Was there an unassailable record of what occurred or was it strongly corroborated?

(f) Had the officer abused his role by asking questions which ought properly to be asked at the police station and in accordance with the Codes?

A further factor, namely the seriousness of the offence charged, was added in *R* v *Latif* (1995) 1 Cr App R 270. In *R* v *Shannon* [2001] 1 WLR 51 at p. 69 d, the Court of Appeal upheld the trial judge's decision to admit evidence obtained when a journalist acted as an agent provocateur. Here the Court considered that the decision of the European Court of Human Rights in *Teixeira de Castro* v *Portugal* (1999) 28 EHRR 101 was 'not inconsistent with that of this court in *R* v *Smurthwaite* [1994] 1 All ER 898, 903'. The Strasbourg Court had, however, held that the use of entrapment evidence was a violation of art. 6: 'The use of undercover agents must be restricted and safeguards put in place . . . the right to a fair administration of justice nevertheless holds such a prominent place that it cannot be sacrificed for the sake of expediency.'

A number of commentators have deplored the approach taken by the English courts to evidence obtained by undercover activity. Robertson (1993) commends the more severe attitude to exclusion in Australia and Zuckerman (1989 at p. 357) was equally enthusiastic about the approach of the Canadian courts based as it is on what he calls the 'legitimacy principle', avoiding an absolute commitment to either exclusion or inclusion and approaching the issue as one of judicial integrity rather than a narrow pragmatism.

The reluctance of the courts to exclude evidence obtained by entrapment is paralleled by their approach to the admissibility of real evidence obtained after the commission of the offence. An early post-PACE case, *Matto*, appeared to herald a more principled approach to exclusion in a case where the police had illegally applied a breathalyser test to a motorist. The decisive fact, in the view of the Divisional Court, was that the police acted in bad faith. In the absence of bad faith it is rare for the discretion to exclude to be exercised in the case of improperly obtained evidence. In *R* v *Chalkley* [1998] QB 848 the Court of Appeal took a very narrow view of s. 78 and considered that it did not enlarge the common law. The trial judge had admitted evidence of secret tape recordings obtained in breach of **PACE** and the civil law of trespass, and in violation of art. 8 of the **European Convention on Human Rights**. Auld LJ in the Court of Appeal held that the balancing exercise undertaken by the trial judge was unnecessary considering that 'save in the case of admissions and confessions and generally as to evidence obtained from the accused after the commission of the offence there is no discretion to exclude evidence unless its quality was or might have been affected by the way in which it was obtained'. The tape recordings were highly probative of guilt and not affected by the unlawful police activity. This much-criticised decision suggests that there is thus no difference between the common law and *Sang*, and thus that it is hardly surprising that s. 78 is applied so narrowly.

However, this was not the view taken by the House of Lords in *Khan* [1997] AC 558. Although the House accepted here that the unlawfully obtained tape recordings were rightly admitted it did not rule out the possibility that the fairness of the proceedings might be compromised by impropriety in obtaining evidence even where the evidence is reliable. Sharpe commented (1997, at p. 222) '. . . the judiciary are refusing to utilise the unlimited discretion given to them under **PACE** to reverse the strictures of *Sang*'.

A review of the post-**PACE** case-law therefore does suggest that there is some truth in this comment that the discretion to exclude improperly obtained evidence was rarely applied. However, there are a number of complexities within this general observation. First, the courts are at least, as *Khan* and *Smurthwaite* show, prepared to consider excluding such evidence; *Chalkley*, where the sole test was reliability, is a somewhat anomalous case. Second, the courts are constrained by the wording of s. 78, which refers to 'fairness of the proceedings', rather than justice to the defendant, assuming a sort of equality of arms which is arguably not realistic. On the other hand, the House of Lords has now demonstrated that the spirit of *Sang* still lives in its interpretation of a statutory requirement. In *R* v *B* (*Attorney-General's Reference No. 3 of 1999*), [2001] 2 AC 91, their Lordships reversed an earlier judgment of the Court of Appeal. The Court of Appeal had held that the requirement under s. 64 of **PACE** to destroy DNA samples after an acquittal was mandatory and thus the sample could not be used in the subsequent trial of the same defendant on another charge. The House of Lords reversed this ruling and held such evidence was admissible, although there was a discretion to exclude under s. 78. Lord Hutton observed that the words of Lord Goddard in *Kuruma* set out the law clearly: 'In their Lordships opinion the test to be applied in considering whether evidence is admissible is whether it is relevant to the matters in issue. If it is it is admissible and the court is not concerned with how the evidence was obtained.' Thus the courts do show a pragmatic approach and one which arguably meets up with commonsense considerations, where evidence obtained, particularly real evidence, appears highly reliable and its exclusion could lead to the freeing of a clearly guilty person.

The issue, however, is not only one of the frequency with which s. 78 is used to exclude evidence but of whether it is possible and desirable to develop general principles with which to exercise this discretion. Here there are two opposing viewpoints. On the one hand there is the one put forward by Auld J in *Jelen and Katz* (1990) 90 Cr App R 456, at 465: 'the circumstances of each case are almost always different and judges may well take different views in the exercise of their discretion even where the circumstances are similar. This is not an apt field for hard case-law and well founded distinctions between cases.' This view finds perhaps surprising support in Strasbourg. Thus in *Khan* v *United Kingdom* [2000] Crim LR 684 the European Court of Human Rights found no violation of art. 6 in admitting the illegally obtained evidence, although there had been a violation of art. 8. The Court's approach was to accept that admissibility of evidence is a matter for the national courts and to be determined in the light of all the circumstances of the case.

In *R* v *Looseley* the House of Lords took a more robust approach on evidence obtained by entrapment. There an undercover police officer who had been given the defendant's name as a potential source of drugs arranged with him to exchange heroin for money. The defendant was charged with supplying or being concerned in supplying to another a class A controlled drug. The trial judge refused a preliminary request to exclude evidence or stay proceedings. The defendant pleaded guilty. In another case two undercover police officers offered contraband cigarettes for sale at a housing estate were introduced to the accused as a potential buyer. They sold him cigarettes and asked also if he could get heroin—at first the defendant hesitated and then agreed. He was also charged. The judge stayed the proceedings on the grounds that the police had incited the commission of the offence and that otherwise the accused would be denied his right to a fair hearing under art. 6(1). The stay was lifted, the prosecution offered no evidence and the accused was acquitted. The Attorney-General referred to the Court of Appeal the question whether in cases of entrapment the judicial discretion conferred by s. 78 of **PACE** and the power to stay proceedings as an abuse of process had been modified by art. 6(1) of the ECHR. The Court of Appeal held that it had not and that the trial judge had been wrong to stay the proceedings. The defendant in the first case appealed and reference was made from the Court of Appeal in the second. The House of Lords stated that the court must ask the central question which was whether the actions of the police were so seriously improper as to bring the administration of justice into disrepute. If there was an abuse of state power than the appropriate remedy was a stay of the indictment, rather than exclusion of evidence. The appeal of the defendant in the first case was dismissed since the undercover officer did no more than present himself as an ordinary customer to a drug dealer. The judge had been correct in the second case to stay the proceedings. The decision of the Court of Appeal was reversed in part. This judgment demonstrates strong judicial recognition of the dangers of excessive police behaviour in cases of entrapment. Lord Nicholls stated that *R v Sang* [1980] AC 402 had been 'overtaken' by statute and case-law.

The decision in *Looseley* has generally been applauded as indicating that the courts will take a robust approach to what they perceive as overly proactive policing. However, an alternative argument has been put by Squires (2006), who argues that the current law on entrapment is both incoherent and discriminatory. He writes (p. 353): 'We have moved from entrapment being irrelevant to criminal trials to it leading to proceedings being stayed, yet without clear articulation of why it ought to be regarded as so problematic.' Squires points out that there are real difficulties in assessing police practice, such as the meaning of an 'unexceptional opportunity' and what is meant by the police 'luring' the suspect. Squires refers to Lord Nicholls' statement in *Looseley* that 'ultimately the overall consideration is always whether the conduct of the police was so seriously improper as to bring the administration of justice into disrepute'. Squires observes that this is difficult to apply. The outcome, he argues, is that the courts distinguish between those who are criminally inclined and those who by social background, lifestyle, etc are not of such inclination. He writes (at p. 354), 'We are left with the courts apparently wishing to protect from prosecution those individuals who have been "caused" to commit crime, and such individuals are, in truth, those who the courts perceive not to be "real criminals" inhabiting a world of criminal temptations and opportunities.' This is in sharp contrast to the usual approach to criminal activities, which assumes free will on the part of the individual and does not consider background and disposition in relation to criminal liability. Squires argues (p. 374) that all 'opportunities to engage in crime are socially structured'. This is a persuasive argument, although the logical outcome of its adoption might be to give rise to more police-generated criminal activity. Many would argue that the beneficial effect of *Looseley* is to place restrictions on excessive policing.

English courts have been frequently criticised for not giving sufficient importance to the moral integrity of criminal proceedings (see, e.g., Choo and Nash (1997)). However, in recent years, particularly in *Looseley*, the judiciary has displayed a renewed emphasis on principle. Lord Lowry, for example, stated (at pp. 76, 77):

> [T]he court, in order to protect its own process from being degraded and misused, must have the power to stay proceedings which have come before it and have only been made possible by acts which offend the court's conscience as being contrary to the rule of law. Those acts by providing a morally unacceptable foundation for the exercise of jurisdiction over the suspect taint the proposed trial and, if tolerated, will mean that that the court's process has been abused.

It also demonstrates the somewhat different approach taken to stay of proceedings and exclusion of evidence. Emson (2006, p. 314) notes, 'it is therefore now clear (in the context of evidence other than confessions and analogous evidence) that the primary purpose of section 78(1) is to ensure forensic fairness in line with the scope of the general common law discretion. Generally speaking the subsection should be applied to exclude improperly or unlawfully obtained evidence only if that impropriety has so affected the reliability of that evidence (or has so undermined the accused's ability to challenge its reliability) that its admission would prevent the accused from receiving a fair trial.'

In practice, however, as Emson acknowledges, s. 78 may be applied to halt proceedings if the behaviour of the police or investigatory authorities undermines the trial's integrity. Since the improperly obtained evidence will usually be the only evidence, if the proceedings have not been stayed at the outset, consideration of s. 78 may lead to the same effect. This approach appears to be sanctioned by *Looseley*. Other academic writers such as Dennis (2002), Zuckerman (1989) and Robertson (1993), argue for an approach from principle. Dennis, for example, stresses the need to uphold the moral legitimacy of the verdict, which on occasion could mean that impropriety should lead to exclusion. He sees deficiencies in a number of other justifications for exclusion such as the possible deterrent effect on the police or the need to protect the accused. His arguments are persuasive and gain added strength under the provisions of the **Human Rights Act 1998,** which require a consideration of whether the defendant's Convention rights would be violated if the evidence were admitted. Roberts and Zuckerman (2004) also review the rationales for exclusion of improperly obtained evidence but observe that it is short-sighted not to take account of the fact that the evidence exists and that 'our knowledge of the world has changed forever and moral evaluation must take account of the realities of the situation' (at p. 153). They call for the development of 'principles of attribution specifying the circumstances in which the state is properly answerable for the activities of its servants and agents'. They see that a 'blanket rule of exclusion' (at p. 159) or an 'all purpose rule' would not be appropriate.

Ashworth (2000) argues for an underlying principle of fidelity to legal values which should guide the exercise of the exclusionary discretion. He stresses that the principle of integrity means that those who enforce the law should obey the law. This might mean that prosecutions should be dropped. He writes (at p. 659) 'where government officials have played a part in creating an offence, it seems appropriate to consider a procedural response that prevents a trial from taking place—notably, a stay of the prosecution on grounds of abuse of process'. He points out the importance of compliance with Convention rights under the **Human Rights Act.**

The **Human Rights Act,** however, maintains the doctrine of parliamentary sovereignty and it is always open to Parliament to amend the law so that police activity in a certain area has lawful authority. The police search in *Khan* would probably now be authorised by the provisions of Part III of the **Police Act 1997** or the **Regulation of Investigatory Powers Act 2000.** Thus any interferences with privacy may be in accordance with the law. Exclusion is still theoretically possible but even more unlikely. Whatever the rhetoric or theorising about exclusion of non-confession evidence obtained improperly, the courts will in all likelihood find circumstances in which it is justified to admit it. Defendants are on the whole not considered deserving of the exclusion of relevant evidence. In regard to entrapment and to other evidence obtained improperly this could be said to result in questionable procedures. As Sharpe (1994, at p. 796) points out 'there is arguably an abuse of process and resultant unfairness in upholding a conviction arising from incitement whoever initiates the conspiracy'. More generally there is a need for a clearer articulation of the theoretical basis on which the courts should approach the matter of improper police procedure.

It is arguable that the implementation of the **Human Rights Act 1998** has not meant an overly radical shift. In *R* v *P*, [2002] 1 AC 146, the House of Lords stressed the vital role of s. 78 as the means by which questions of admissibility are to be resolved. In this case, however, intercept evidence admissible in another country was admissible in the UK. Following *Khan* v *UK* they emphasised that the direct operation of Articles 6 and 8 of the European Court of Human Rights does not alter the role of s. 78 in this regard. The common criterion was that of fairness. Andrew Ashworth (2002, at p. 35) lists 'the right to be tried on evidence not obtained by violation of fundamental right' as one of the ten procedural rights for persons accused of potentially serious crime. He points out that 'whereas a breach of Article 3 [of the ECHR] will make it unfair to rely on a resulting confession, it seems that a breach of a defendant's Article 8 rights (for example by listening in to his conversations without authorisation to do so) will not necessarily render it unfair to rely on the resulting evidence' (at p. 36). He suggests that this departs from rule of law values. He asks, 'What moral standing would a court have, if it proceeded to a conviction on the basis of evidence obtained by a violation of a right that it purported to recognise as fundamental?' Recent case-law does suggest that English courts are now engaging with this moral dimension and have moved beyond the view that reliability is the only criterion for admissibility in relation to improperly obtained evidence. The approach evidenced in *Chalkley* [1998] QB 848 that factual guilt was sufficient seems shortlived. In particular it does seem that the law on entrapment has thus moved away from *Sang*. It is still not a defence but a more robust approach to exclusion or stay of prosecution is now taken, recognising that fair trial rights extend to pre-trial proceedings including police investigations. Ian Dennis, the author of the quotation in the question, has consistently argued that the law of evidence must be scrutinised in the context of how far it ensures the verdict in a criminal trial has moral legitimacy. This might trump factual accuracy. At one level, of course, this standpoint is undeniable. A court, for example, cannot accept even true evidence of a confession which was obtained by torture. This does also, of course, beg the question of the composition of legitimacy and who can decide what is legitimate. The House of Lords has ruled in a landmark judgment that evidence obtained by torture abroad is not admissible in English courts (*A* v *Secretary of State for the Home Department (No. 2)*, [2005] 3 WLR 1249). This case illustrates that the judicial process may be contaminated by the use of evidence obtained unlawfully or improperly by non-state actors.

Elected governments on the other hand, may argue that safeguarding the public is more important than insisting on certain rights for suspects, where these involve plans for mass murder. The issue perhaps is what Dworkin (2003) has called how 'to keep faith with our own humanity'. He argues, in apparent agreement with Dennis, that 'rights would be worthless—and the idea of a right incomprehensible—unless respecting rights meant taking some risk . . . of course we must sharpen our vigilance, but we must also discipline our fear. The Government says that only our own safety matters. That is a counsel of shame: we are braver than that, and have more self-respect.'

Should the discretion in its s. 78 be structured more formally? Ormerod and Birch (2004) review the move over the past 50 years from a position where 'the criminal courts claimed only modest discretionary powers to exclude evidence . . . to one in which the exclusionary discretion is the focal point of many trials'. They make the case for an overhaul of s. 78 'adopting not only a structure to the section by providing a catalogue of relevant criteria to be excluded, but also to guide the judge further by providing a presumption of exclusion for breach of specified rights' (p. 78). They acknowledge, however, that there may be judicial opposition to this potential fetter and that 'if 78, originally conceived as a limited control over the use of improperly obtained evidence, were to be reduced to a structured presumptive discretion such as that originally proposed by Lord Scarman in 1984, it would be necessary also to revisit the issue of discretionary control in every other aspect of that ubiquitous provision's current and much wider sphere of operation'. They warned that that might lead to a resurrection of the 'largely derelict domain of the preserved common law discretion'. The reform might thus be made nugatory.

Additional Reading

Ashworth, A., 'Excluding Evidence as Protecting Rights' [1977] Crim LR 723.

Ashworth, A., 'Should the Police be Allowed to Use Deceptive Practices?' (1998) 114 LQR 108.

Ashworth, A., 'Testing Fidelity to Legal Values: Official Involvement and Criminal Justice' (2000) 63 MLR 633.

Ashworth, A., 'Redrawing the Boundaries of Entrapment' [2002] Crim LR 159.

Birch, D., 'Excluding Evidence from Entrapment: What is a Fair Cop?' [1994] CLP 73.

Bronitt, S., and Roche, D., 'Between Rhetoric and Reality: Sociolegal and Republican Perspectives on Entrapment' (2000) 4 E&P 77.

Carter, P.B., 'Evidence Obtained by Use of Covert Listening Device' (1997) 113 LQR 468.

Choo, A., and Mellors, M., 'Undercover Police Operations and What the Suspect Said (or Didn't Say)' [1995] 2 Web JCLI.

Choo, A., and Nash, S., 'What Was the Matter with Section 78?' [1999] Crim LR 929.

Dennis, I., *The Law of Evidence*, 2nd edn (Sweet & Maxwell, London, 2002).

Dworkin, R., 'Terror and the Attack on Civil Liberties' (2003) New York Review of Books, vol. 50, no. 17, 6 November.

Heydon, J.D., 'Illegally Obtained Evidence' [1973] Crim LR 603.

Mirfield, P., 'Regulation of Investigatory Powers Act 2000. Evidential Aspects' [2001] Crim LR 91.

Ormerod, D. and Birch, D., 'Evolution of the Discretionary Exclusions of Evidence' [2004] Crim LR 138.

Ormerod, D., and Roberts, A., 'The Trouble with Texeira: Developing a Principled Approach to Entrapment' (2002) 6 E&P 38.

Robertson, G., 'Entrapment Evidence: Manna from Heaven or Fruit of the Poisoned Tree?' [1993] Crim LR 806.

Sharpe, S., 'Covert Police Operations and Discretionary Exclusions of Evidence' [1994] Crim LR 793.

Sharpe, S., *Judicial Discretion and Criminal Investigation* (Sweet & Maxwell, London, 1997).

Squires, D., 'The Problem with Entrapment' (2006) 26 OJLS 351.

8

Corroboration and identification

Introduction

This area is variously referred to in textbooks as hazardous evidence, supporting evidence or safeguards against unreliability and error. Thus it covers types of evidence which might intrinsically be of questionable reliability.

The scope of the law on corroboration has been substantially reduced by recent legislative and judicial reforms. There still remain the various categories of situations where corroborating or supporting evidence is required as a matter of law, i.e., where there can be no conviction in the absence of corroborating evidence. These are imposed by statute. Questions are not often asked about these in Evidence examinations. More important for your purposes is a category of what Murphy (2003, at p. 644) has called the 'quasi-corroborative rule', where additional evidence (not necessarily of the same type of evidence which is necessary for corroboration) is required before an accused person can, inter alia, be convicted or have a case to answer to. This relates to the limitation on the accused's right of silence under ss. 34 to 37 of the **Criminal Justice and Public Order Act 1994**. However, s. 38(3) of the 1994 Act makes it clear that the accused cannot have a case to answer, be committed for trial, or be convicted merely on the basis of this inference. This suggests that additional evidence is required before this can occur (see further **Chapter 6**).

The common law system has no general requirement for corroboration. A single piece of evidence is usually enough to convict. Prior to 1988, however, there were three categories of cases where although corroboration was not required as a matter of law, a corroboration warning was necessary. Failure to give such a warning was a valid ground of appeal. However, conviction was still possible without corroborative evidence. As long as the warning was given, the jury could convict in the absence of corroborative evidence. The three categories of cases were: evidence given by children of tender years on oath; evidence given by complainants in sexual cases; evidence given by accomplices on the prosecution's behalf. These provisions were criticised as being increasingly complex and technical.

The need for a corroboration warning for the first category was finally fully abolished by s. 34(2) of the **Criminal Justice Act 1988**. The last two categories where a corroboration warning was required were abolished by s. 32(1) of the **Criminal Justice and Public Order Act 1994**. There will still be cases where a corroboration warning may be required as a matter of discretion, for example, where the evidence of a witness is suspect for some reason specific to the case. If that is the case, the next question that arises is the type of additional evidence that can constitute corroboration. The classic definition of corroboration is that given by the Court of Appeal in *R* v *Baskerville* [1916] 2 KB 658. Lord Reading CJ (at p. 667) expressed the requirements as follows:

> . . .evidence in corroboration must be independent testimony which affects the accused by connecting or tending to connect him with the crime. In other words, it must be evidence which implicates him, that is which confirms in some material particular not only the evidence that the crime has been committed, but also that the prisoner committed it.

There were thus five limbs to the definition: the evidence had to be relevant, admissible, credible, independent of the witness to be corroborated and implicate the defendant in the commission of the offence.

The effect of the reforms of the **Criminal Justice and Public Order Act 1994** is to abolish the common law requirement for corroboration warnings in criminal trials. The case of *R* v *Makanjuola* [1995] 1 WLR 1348 considers the application of the new law. It emphasises that the old corroboration regime has been dismantled. The main areas now covered are identification evidence, evidence of lies made by the defendant and the current scope of broader discretionary warnings to the jury. Note that the leading cases are *R* v *Lucas* [1981] QB 720 and *R* v *Burge* [1996] 1 Cr App R 163. In the latter case, the Court of Appeal summarised 'the circumstances in which, in our judgement, a *Lucas* direction is usually required' (see Diagram 3).

As regards identification evidence, students will have to be familiar with the *Turnbull* guidelines or what Murphy has called 'the quasi-corroborative suspect witness direction'. Note also the new provisions on identification evidence in **CJA 2003** (see below page 211). Further, students may be expected to be familiar with Code D of the Codes of Practice of the **Police and Criminal Evidence Act 1984** (revised 2006), including the various annexes to it and how the identification evidence can be excluded if the Code is not followed, see also *R* v *Forbes* [2001] 1 AC 473. It is clear now that as a general, but not absolute, rule a suspect who disputes an identification has a right to a parade.

Code D specifies the procedures for cases of disputed information. If the suspect's identity is not known the witness may be taken to a particular neighbourhood or place to see if they can recognise the person they saw (para. 3.2). In other cases, the suspect may be known and available, meaning 'there is sufficient information known to the police to justify the arrest of a particular person for suspected involvement in the offence'. 'Such suspects are immediately available or will be within a reasonably short time and willing to take part in at least one of the following which it is practicable to arrange:

- video identification;
- identification parade; or
- group identification.'

The Code specifies that an identification procedure must be held if the suspect disputes being the person the witness claims to have seen unless it is not practicable or would serve no useful purpose in proving or disproving whether the suspect was involved in committing the offence. The Code specifies that a video identification parade should not be held unless there are specified reasons for doing so. If the suspect is known but not available, a video identification may be arranged using still images and finally if a video identification, an identification parade, and a group identification are all not practicable then the suspect may be directly confronted by the witness even if he does not consent (para. 3.23).

If the very detailed specifications of Code D are breached then s. 78 **PACE** may be applied to exclude the evidence. Code D para 3.12 states that a parade is to be held when 'the suspect disputes being the person the witness claims to have seen'. The leading case of *R* v *Forbes* [2001] 1 AC 473 makes it clear that this is to be strictly applied. Munday (p. 565) points out that 'forces reaffirmed the literal reading of Code D'.

In short, therefore, you should familiarise yourself with the two distinct ways that the reliability of identification evidence is enhanced: first, the judge should issue the *Turnbull* guidelines and second Code D should be followed in relation to identification procedures.

Diagram 3 Lies (non-hearsay) by defendant—*R* v *Burge* (1996)

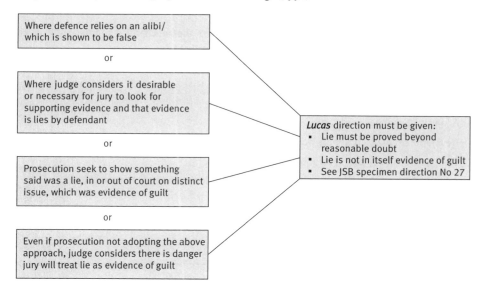

Where defence relies on an alibi/ which is shown to be false

or

Where judge considers it desirable or necessary for jury to look for supporting evidence and that evidence is lies by defendant

or

Prosecution seek to show something said was a lie, in or out of court on distinct issue, which was evidence of guilt

or

Even if prosecution not adopting the above approach, judge considers there is danger jury will treat lie as evidence of guilt

Lucas direction must be given:
- Lie must be proved beyond reasonable doubt
- Lie is not in itself evidence of guilt
- See JSB specimen direction No 27

Question 1

Does the concept of corroboration still have a place in Evidence law?

Commentary

This is a challenging question which requires you to take a critical view of recent changes to the law on corroboration. At a superficial level of course you might answer 'No' in the sense that formal law on corroboration has now been very largely abolished by s. 34(2) of the **Criminal Justice Act 1988** (concerning the evidence of children) and s. 32 of the **Criminal Justice and Public Order Act 1994** (concerning evidence of accomplices and of complainants in sexual cases). However, you are expected to take a broader view of the meaning of corroboration as supporting evidence and be aware particularly of the Court of Appeal ruling in **R** v **Makanjuola (1995),** which states that trial judges now have a broad discretion to issue warnings about witness testimony depending on the circumstances of the case. This discretionary approach of course pre-dated the reforms to the law on corroboration. The question will also test whether you have read beyond the standard textbooks in preparing for your assessment. Roberts and Zuckerman (2004), for example, make a very powerful theoretical case for maintaining the concept of corroboration as an aspect of what they call 'forensic reasoning'.

As with all essay questions there are many ways you can approach this. A possible outline would be as follows:

(a) *Introduction*: Meaning and history of corroboration. Arguments for changing the law.

(b) Remaining categories of hazardous evidence; *Turnbull, Lucas, Makanjoula*. Silence provisions **CJPOA 1994**.

(c) Theoretical arguments for maintaining concept of directing juries on how to assess quality of evidence.

(d) *Conclusion*: Comment on change from quantitative rather mechanical approach to fixed categories of witness towards an emphasis on the quality of the evidence.

Answer plan

- Analysis of changes made 1988 and 1994
- Development of discretionary warnings—identification
- Weaknesses in old law
- Critique of changes—concentration on quality of evidence and assessment of it rather than form of evidence and its admissibility

Suggested answer

English law, by contrast for example to Scots law, has never had a general requirement for evidence in criminal trials to be corroborated or supported. One piece of evidence, including the evidence of a competent witness, is sufficient for a finding of guilt. The general rule has been subject to a number of exceptions, both statutory and judge-made. As far as the former is concerned there are a tiny number of statutory provisions which require corroboration as a matter of law before guilt can be established. One example is s. 13 of the **Perjury Act 1911**. Such provisions are not controversial and do indicate that the term 'corroboration' still has significance. Another legislative approach is indicated by ss. 34–38 of the **Criminal Justice and Public Order Act 1994**, effectively requiring that the silence of a defendant is not sufficient to found a conviction but can be supporting evidence. Murphy has called this 'quasi-corroboration'.

More controversial over the years has been the judge-made law on corroboration which has been subject to statutory erosion over the past decade.

The most recent changes made in the law in this area, were those enacted in s. 32 of the **Criminal Justice and Public Order Act 1994**, which were as a result of a culmination of a decade of relaxation of this area of rigid rules. This statute abolished the need for a formal warning for complainants in sexual cases and for co-defendants testifying for the prosecution. The abolition of the third category where a corroboration warning was required, namely that of child witnesses, was completed by s. 34(2) of the **Criminal Justice Act 1988**. These statutory changes took place in a period of judicial activism in this area which had relaxed the law. The question calls for an examination of the necessity of these changes and whether further ones are needed.

The Law Commission report Corroboration of Evidence in Criminal Trials (1991, Cmnd 1620) (adopted by the Royal Commission on Criminal Justice; see Cm 2263, 1993) had described the law in this area as 'arcane, technical and difficult to convey'. It led to unnecessary formalism and unjustified categorisation of witnesses. Particular criticism was directed at the mandatory requirement of a corroboration warning for complainants in sexual cases, irrespective of the particular witness. Witnesses, it was contended, should be treated on their merits. The courts could of course always convict in the absence of corroboration but a failure to give the warning was likely to lead to the conviction being overturned on appeal. Of course, the statutory requirements of corroboration have not been affected by the abolition of the common law rules and there is little controversy on their application.

While the three main categories of cases requiring corroboration warning have been abolished by the 1988 and 1994 Acts, there is a case for maintaining a residual class of cases where some form of warning should be given because the testimony of the witness may be suspect or tainted for some reason. This could be because he or she may have a grudge against the defendant, or is malicious, or has some other purpose of his or her own to serve. It should be noted that there were some suggestions in some cases that where the evidence of a witness was suspect for a reason other than because her or she fell within the three categories discussed earlier, a discretionary warning was appropriate.

It has been submitted that where a witness has a substantial interest of his or her own to serve, there is a risk that false evidence might be given, and the full corroboration warning should be made. The courts have stated that where there is no basis for suggesting that a witness is a participant or in any way involved in the crime which is the subject-matter of the trial, there was no obligation to give the full corroboration warning. However, the courts did add that where there is evidence to suggest that the evidence of the witness is tainted for some reason, the judge should advise the jury to treat the evidence with more or less caution depending on the circumstances of the case.

In *R* v *Bagshaw* [1984] 1 WLR 477, the Court of Appeal stated that patients who were detained in a special hospital after conviction for an offence, who were witnesses at the trial of nurses who were charged with assaulting them, although not falling within the established categories where a corroboration warning had to be given, satisfied the criteria which justified the requirement of a full warning. The court went on to say that nothing short of the full warning would suffice. In *R* v *Spencer* [1987] AC 128, *R* v *Bagshaw* was overruled. The House of Lords decided that where the prosecution relied on the evidence of a witness who because of his mental condition and criminal background may give suspect evidence, the judge should warn the jury that it is dangerous to convict on the uncorroborated evidence of the witness. However, the House of Lords stressed that the judge need not give the full corroboration warning required in the established categories. It was important that the jury be made aware of the dangers of convicting on the uncorroborated evidence of the witness but the extent of the warning would depend on the facts and circumstances of the case. In other words the courts, although reluctant to extend the formal categories of witnesses requiring corroboration, have demonstrated that the concept of judicial warnings on the need to consider the strength of the evidence is a valuable one.

Another example of judicial acceptance of the need to temper the technical rules was *R* v *Chance* [1988] QB 932, where the Court of Appeal decided that where the only issue is one of identity in a rape case, only a *Turnbull* warning is required. In *R* v *Turnbull* [1977] QB 224 itself of course the Court of Appeal set 'guidelines' for identification cases rather than setting a requirement for a formal corroboration warning.

A major criticism of the corroboration rules had been the complex definition of corroboration, as set out by the Court of Appeal in the leading case of *R* v *Baskerville* [1916] 2 KB 658. As Bronitt (1991) pointed out, it concentrated on the quantity of testimony rather than its quality. By requiring 'independent evidence implicating the accused' rather than independent evidence that confirms the suspect witness is telling the truth, the definition concentrated on guilt rather than the witness's credibility. In *R* v *Hills* (1987) 86 Cr App R 26 the Court of Appeal held that cumulative corroboration was possible as a matter of principle, even though individually no one piece of evidence might fit the technical definition. The court thus took a welcome pragmatic view.

One question which remains, however, is whether the definition of corroboration is still needed. In the cases where the courts exercise discretion to issue a need for caution, will they rely on the technical definition of corroboration? The Law

Commission report anticipated not. In *R* v *Makanjuola* [1995] 1 WLR 1348, the Court of Appeal confirmed the Law Commission's view, rejecting the need for a 'full old style direction' in cases where the trial judge decided that some form of warning may be necessary. Lord Taylor CJ said (at p. 1351): '[i]t was, in our judgment, partly to escape from this tortuous exercise which juries must have found more bewildering than illuminating, that Parliament enacted section 32'.

As a result of *Makanjuola* trial judges have a wide discretion to warn about the testimony of witnesses depending on the circumstances of the case. This is arguably a welcome development and an improvement on the former rigid approach to corroboration. Since any warning is discretionary the Court of Appeal will only review the trial judge's decision if it is **Wednesbury** unreasonable. To give one example of the value of maintaining discretionary warnings, in *Pringle* v *R* [2003] UKPC 9 the Privy Council highlighted how, as Lord Hope put it, trial judges should consider this 'where an untried prisoner claims that a fellow untried prisoner confessed to him that he was guilty of the crime for which he was then being held in custody'. Some commentators are still uneasy about the current state of the law. As Choo (2006, p. 302) puts it '. . .There is a danger that trial judges may in fact be continuing to give strong warnings in relation to alleged accomplices testifying for the prosecution and complainants in sexual cases, even if a warning is not warranted in the circumstances of the particular case.' He points out that particularly in sexual cases there may be the danger of wrongful acquittals.

On the other hand, there may be occasions where judges should be more robust in issuing care warnings. One such is cell confessions. Guidance on this is given in *R* v *Stone* [2005] EWCA 105. In *Benedetto and Labrador* v *R* [2003] 1 WLR 1545 the prosecution case rested largely on a cell confession. The Privy Council stated that in these circumstances the prisoner would normally have an interest in providing information to the authorities and there would be safeguards in place. A judicial warning as to possible danger of relying on the confession was normally required.

The non-technical approach has been developed more fully and in a more rule-based way with regard to two particular kinds of evidence. A growing body of case law has indicated the sort of judicial directions which should be given in relation to evidence of a defendant's lies and to identification evidence. The leading case on the former is *R* v *Lucas* and on the latter *R* v *Turnbull*.

Clearly the law in this area is more flexible than the law on corroboration in the formal sense allows. It might therefore be said to support the proposition that the concept of corroboration in the wider sense is available, but there are also arguments against this. There is always a danger that the law will become too rigid. Thus Kennedy LJ in *Burge* and *Pegg* [1996] 1 Cr App R 163 stressed the danger of over-use of *Lucas* directions: 'If a *Lucas* direction is given where there is no need for such a direction (as in a normal case where there is a straightforward conflict of evidence) it will add complexity and do more harm than good.' In *R v Jefford* [2003] EWCA 1987 the Court of Appeal emphasised that the need for a *Lucas* direction was based on general principles, not technicalities. It stated 'the purpose of a **Lucas** direction is to guard against the forbidden line of reasoning that the telling of lies equals guilt. That may be true whether that lie is told in or out of court'.

The above comments have covered the generally welcomed erosion of the technical rules of corroboration. However, in some areas it might be arguable that a new category needs to be created. The Royal Commission on Criminal Justice (1993, Cm 2263), in spite of many calls for a requirement of corroboration of confessions, recommended only that it should be lawful for a jury to convict solely on the evidence of a confession, but the jury should be warned of the great care needed before doing so. In Scotland such a warning is required, but as confirmation of the essential facts of the case against the accused, not to confirm suspect testimony. In *Stone* the Court of Appeal again indicated reluctance to establish new categories of evidence requiring supporting evidence. 'Cell confessions' did not comprise a new special category where there would always need to be a cautionary warning. But as the comment in the Criminal Law Review on the case noted (2005, p. 571), the 'especially damning nature of the evidence' together with other dangers renders cell confessions 'a qualitatively more dangerous category of evidence in all cases'.

Not all commentators are convinced that the position in relation to identification evidence is satisfactory. This is a notoriously unreliable area. The Devlin Committee on Evidence of Identification in Criminal Cases (1976) found that misidentification is common and thus a possible source of miscarriage of justice. Even honest and independent witnesses may be mistaken. The committee was in favour of a rule subject to some exceptions that convictions should not rest solely on visual identification, even if more than one witness made it. Neither Parliament nor the courts have accepted this recommendation. The '*Turnbull* guidelines' remain then as an exhortation and, as the Court of Appeal demonstrated in *R v Hunjan* (1978) 68 Cr App R 99, if a warning is found to be insufficient, the conviction could be quashed on appeal.

However, Roberts and Zuckerman (2004, p. 495) although acknowledging that '**Turnbull** can hardly be said to have eliminated the risk of mistaken eye-witness identification leading to wrongful conviction', argued that the guidelines have 'probably achieved all that can be achieved in this regard without fundamentally rethinking the basic adversarial structure of English criminal procedure and trial practice'.

Overall these authors commend the new discretionary approach and argue (at p. 465) that 'corroboration retains great theoretical and practical significance . . . as the progenitor of what might be termed "post-quantitative" forensic reasoning rules—evidentiary rules structuring the jury's approach to reasoning about evidence'. They see the Strasbourg jurisprudence and the HRA as strengthening the non-technical concept of corroboration as 'supporting evidence'.

There has remained some pressure to extend the ambit of corroboration warnings in particular, as discussed above, to one of the most important pieces of evidence, the defendant's confession. Dennis points out (2007, p. 644) that 'There remains a good case for the introduction of such a warning requirement but to date no legislation has implemented this recommendation and the courts have shown no inclination to give effect to it.' The present tendency is to favour caution warnings which, as Dennis points out, are 'less formal and less technical'. Pattenden (1991) reviews the arguments for extending corroboration requirements to confessions. It should be noted that there is what Murphy (p, 593) calls a 'quasi-corroborative rule' applying to certain inferences under ss. 34–7 of the **Criminal Justice and Public Order Act 1994** covering the silence of the accused. Section 38(3) provides that:

> A person shall not have the proceedings against him transferred to the Crown Court for trial, have a case to answer or be convicted of an offence solely on an inference drawn from such a failure or refusal as is mentioned in section 34(2), 35(3), 36(2) or 37(2).

Murphy (p. 594) points out that this 'does not impose a requirement for corroboration, but does impose a requirement for additional evidence against the accused'.

The concept of corroboration does indeed still have a part to play alongside the overall objective of improving the quality of evidence and ensuring a fair trial. Perhaps the current controversy over flawed expert scientific testimony has given the concept a new lease of life. The cases of *R* v *Cannings* [2004] 1 WLR 2607 and *R* v *Clark (Sally)* (No 2) [2003] EWCA Crim 1020 stirred particular controversy over the flaws in the expert scientific evidence. In *Cannings* the Court of Appeal stated:

> . . .where a full investigation into two or more sudden unexplained infant deaths in the same family is followed by a serious disagreement between reputable experts about the cause of death, and a body of such expert opinion concludes that natural causes, whether explained or unexplained, cannot be excluded as a reasonable (and not a fanciful) possibility, the prosecution of a parent or parents for murder should not be started, or continued, unless there is additional cogent evidence, extraneous to the expert evidence . . . which tends to support the conclusion that the infant, or where there is more than one death, one of the infants, was deliberately harmed. In cases like the present, if the outcome of the trial depends exclusively or almost exclusively on a serious disagreement between distinguished and reputable experts, it will often be unwise, and therefore unsafe, to proceed.

However, the decision has been narrowly interpreted and did not apply in *R* v *Kai-Whitewind* [2005] EWCA Crim 1092, where there was a previously admitted urge to kill the infant. The new regime on corroboration is on the whole a welcome relaxation of an overly complex system which many commentators agreed served to confuse juries. The new flexibility of allowing judges to deal with cases on an individual basis is attractive, although it is of some concern that it may be more difficult to give equality of treatment to each defendant. However, perhaps the extent of the change has been over-emphasised. Murphy (2008 p. 601) comments:

> It is hard not to see a paradox (albeit a by no means undesirable one) in the re-emergence in a different guise of many of the principles developed at common law in relation to the corroboration rules. In a sense, the wheel has turned almost full circles, and corroboration has re-invented itself in a more contemporary posture. The courts have already come a long way, at least as a matter of practice, from the strict rejection of any semblance between corroboration warnings and suspect witness warnings in the substance of the matters dealt with in the directions to the jury. The difference lies in the absence of a strict legal requirement, although the dictates of practice are in many ways not as different as might be supposed. That is, it is submitted, simply a reflection of the realities of practice.

Murphy sees much to commend in the flexibility of the new regime and concludes, 'It is submitted that judges should not hesitate to give a warning in a case where the evidence seems suspect, even though the warning may in most cases be confined to a general note of caution.'

Question 2

Sam and Alan are charged with the attempted rape of Amy. The case against them is that Amy met Sam and Alan in the local wine bar and they started chatting. She had not known them before. After a short while Amy, who was feeling drunk, went outside to an alleyway for some fresh air. The alleyway was very dark at the time. Two men approached her and attempted to rape her. She thought she recognised one of them as one of the men in the wine bar but she is unsure. As a result of her screams the two men stopped and ran away. A passer-by, Mandy, saw two men running away and saw the face of one of them clearly under a street light. Mandy gave a description to the police and helped in constructing a photofit picture of the man she saw. Giles, a police constable, recognised the photofit picture as being that of Alan whom he had previously arrested on suspicion of criminal damage. Amy is taken to the wine bar the next day by police and picks out Sam, a customer, as one of the men who tried to rape her. The police had failed to take a description of the attackers from Amy before they took her to the wine bar. At first Sam claimed he was at work on the night of the alleged attempted rape but later admitted this was a lie and that he was in the wine bar with a girlfriend. He claims he lied to protect the girlfriend because she was married. Mandy was killed in a road traffic accident shortly after the alleged attempted rape. Both Sam and Alan deny any involvement in the attempted rape and demand that identification parades are held.

Evaluate the difficulties which the prosecution may face with the evidence.

Commentary

This question requires a discussion of the rules relating to the treatment of identification evidence in court and also the use of lies told by the defendant as prosecution evidence. As regards the victim's evidence, it is clear that because of her state of intoxication and the bad lighting conditions, a **Turnbull** direction will have to be given. The other issue revolves around the photofit picture and how the court should treat this evidence. Another difficulty that will be encountered is with regards to the identification of Alan by Giles. The basis of Giles's recognition of Alan and whether that is admissible in evidence will have to be considered. There is also the point in relation to corroboration in this case in that it needs to be made clear that no corroboration warning is required as a result of the **Criminal Justice and Public Order Act 1994**.

Answer plan

- Identification evidence and **Turnbull** direction—s. 78, **PACE**
- Revised Code D **PACE**—identification parades—see *R* v *Forbes* **(2001)**
- Sam's lie—consider *Lucas* (1981)
- Mandy's testimony and possibility of admissibility of photofit
- Giles' identification of Alan—not permitted to say why he knew Alan
- No need for corroboration warning

Suggested answer

The problems faced by the prosecution counsel start with the identification of Sam by the victim, Amy. In effect, her identification evidence is weak both because of her intoxicated condition and the bad lighting conditions. In *R* v *Turnbull* [1977] QB 224, the Court of Appeal laid down guidelines for the treatment of identification evidence where the case depends wholly or substantially on the correctness of the identifications. The guidelines state, inter alia, that the judge should warn the jury of the special need for caution, before convicting the accused in reliance on the correctness of the identification evidence which the defence alleges to be mistaken. The judge should draw the jury's attention to the possibility that an error was made and should invite them to examine closely the circumstances in which the observation took place. The guidelines go on to provide that the jury should also examine closely the conditions under which and the length of time for which the observation took place. Factors such as whether the witness knew the accused, or whether there was any particular reason for the witness to remember the accused, or how soon after the event did the witness give a description to the police should also be considered. The guidelines make it clear that the judge should remind the jury of any weaknesses in the identification evidence and that where the identification evidence is weak, the judge should withdraw the case from the jury unless there is any other evidence which will support the identification evidence.

It has been made clear by the Court of Appeal in *R v Oakwell* [1978] 1 WLR 32, that the *Turnbull* guidelines are not to be interpreted inflexibly. It is thus clear that on the facts of the present case, the judge will need to draw the jury's attention to the weaknesses present in Amy's identification evidence, namely that it was dark, that she was intoxicated, and the fact that she may have remembered him because of the time spent talking to him in the wine bar. If the judge considers that the quality of the identification is good then he may allow the case to proceed in the absence of any other evidence supporting the identification, as long as he delivers the *Turnbull* warning in the summing-up. On the other hand, if the judge is of the opinion that the quality of Mandy's or Amy's identification is poor but sees there is other evidence which could support the two identifications then he should point this out to the jury. It is for the jury to decide whether the evidence does support it. He should also warn the jury about any evidence which, it is felt, they might wrongly believe is supportive. The possible supporting evidence is Sam's admitted lie (see below).

The defence may suggest that the police should have held a parade rather than take Amy to the wine bar for the identification. However, it may be argued that they had no information whereby they could make an arrest of Sam. Code D of **PACE** governs the procedure for obtaining identification evidence. Code D 3.2 provides that where the identity of a suspect is not known a police officer may take a witness to a particular neighbourhood or place to see whether he or she can identify the person allegedly seen on the relevant occasion. Before doing so however, and, where practical, the police should take a record of any description given by the witness of the suspect (D 3.2(a)). Here the police have failed to do this. Arguably admission of Amy's identification would have an effect on the fairness of the proceedings and the judge may use his discretion to exclude the evidence under s. 78 **PACE**. If, however, the identification evidence is admissible it may be used to go to the consistency of the witness in identifying Sam in court.

The demand for identification parades is significant. The Court of Appeal in *R v Popat* (1998) 2 Cr App R 208 had held that an identification parade is not obligatory but only one factor to be taken into account. Breaches of the Code may thus lead to exclusion of identification evidence because the latter may be less reliable. The police should comply with the procedures of the Code in order to prevent unfair prejudice to the defendant. It should be noted, however, that in *R v Kelly* [1998] 162 JP 231 the Court of Appeal held that not all breaches of the Code would lead to non-admissibility of the evidence. In *R v Forbes* [2001] 1 AC 473, the House of Lords held that an identification parade was mandatory where the suspect disputed the identification and consented to the parade. It was held that paragraph D–2.3 (now 3.12) clearly specified that a parade was to be held whenever a suspect disputes an identification. This therefore was a mandatory requirement and the section should be read literally. It is arguable therefore that one should be held here. If one is held and Amy cannot recall at the trial who she identified the accompanying police officer may give details of her identification evidence (*R* v *McCay* [1990] 1 WLR 645). The common law exception to the rule against previous consistent statements allowed evidence of out-of-court identification to be given by the witness or a third party who had witnessed the identification. The **Criminal Justice Act 2003** extends this exception. Section 120(4) and (5) allow a witness's previous statement which 'identifies or describes a person, object or place to be admissible of any matter stated if the witness indicates that to the best of his belief he made the statement, and that to the best of his belief it states the truth'.

The identification evidence against Sam is arguably weak and the prosecution may seek to rely on his admitted lie as supportive evidence of his guilt. If they do so the judge will have to warn the jury about the dangers of relying on this evidence. In *R* v *Goodway* (1994) 98 Cr App R 11 Lord Taylor CJ stated that '...where lies told by the defendant are relied on ... as support for identification evidence, the judge should give a direction along the lines indicated in *Lucas* [1981] QB 720'. In *R* v *Burge and Pegg* (1996) 1 Cr App R 364 the Court of Appeal summarised the circumstances in which a *Lucas* direction should be given. Sam has admitted the lie so it is therefore unnecessary for the judge to direct that the jury must find it proved beyond reasonable doubt. The lie can support the prosecution case only if the jury is sure Sam did not lie for an innocent reason. There is thus a significant amount of case-law on the issue whether lies told by the defendant can be supporting evidence. It is likely therefore that the judge will warn the jury along the lines set out in *Lucas* and *Burge and Pegg*. The jury must be satisfied that there is no innocent motive for the lie, as here there may be. It may be that Sam lied to protect his girl-friend. On the facts as given this does not appear to be the sort of case where a direction would be otiose, in that to reject Sam's account would all but leave the jury with no logical alternative but to convict.

Mandy does not appear to have seen Sam but only Alan. Since the evidence against Sam is so weak and in view of the *Turnbull* guidelines, it is possible that the judge will withdraw the case against Alan and direct the jury to acquit him. If, however, there was another eye witness who saw Alan running away, albeit in a fleeting glimpse-type situation, whilst the judge may leave the evidence to the jury, he would need to give the *Turnbull* warning and direct them specifically that even a number of honest persons can be wrong: *R* v *Weeder* (1980) 71 Cr App R 228 and *R* v *Breslin* (1984) 80 Cr App R 226.

The other difficulty that the prosecution may have with the evidence is Mandy's testimony. If Mandy was still alive and gave testimony in court, her testimony would be subject to the *Turnbull* direction, as it could be argued that her evidence falls within the situation which the *Turnbull* guidelines were intended to cover. Again, arguably an identification parade should have been held, although clearly

Mandy's death was unforeseen. However, now that she is dead the question is whether the photofit is admissible into evidence. In *R v Smith* [1976] **Crim LR 511**, a photofit picture was held not to offend the rule against hearsay. However, the Court of Appeal in *R v Cook* [1987] **1 All ER 1049** went a step further. The Court of Appeal decided that photofit pictures were in a class of evidence of their own. Neither the rule against hearsay nor the rule against previous consistent statements had any application to such evidence. The photofit pictures are, according to the Court of Appeal, manifestations of the seeing eye, translations of vision onto paper through the medium of a police officer's skill of drawing or composing which a witness does not possess. The Court of Appeal's approach in drawing an analogy between a photofit or sketch and a photograph is arguably surprising in view of the acknowledged differences between them. Nonetheless, the decision in *Cook* has been followed by the Court of Appeal in *R v Constantinou* (1989) **91 Cr App R 74**. Thus, on the facts of this case, it is clear that the photofit picture would be admissible in evidence notwithstanding that Mandy is not able to give evidence.

However, in view of the fact that Mandy's identification originally was as a result of a fleeting glance situation, it seems probable that the judge will have to give the *Turnbull* direction with respect to this evidence and may have to withdraw the case from the jury unless there is some other evidence to support.

The third problem with the evidence is with regards to Giles's identification of Alan. Whilst it is likely that he can say that he identified Alan from the photofit picture, he is not allowed to say why he knew Alan. It is not permissible to tell the jury that the reason why Giles recognised Alan was because he had previously arrested Alan for criminal damage. The only exception to that is where the evidence came within what was known as Similar Fact evidence (*DPP v Boardman* [1974] **3 All ER 887** and *DPP v P* [1991] **2 AC 447**), now covered by the **Criminal Justice Act 2003**. As this does not appear likely, the evidence of the previous arrest of Alan by Giles is not admissible in evidence.

It should be noted that a corroboration warning is no longer necessary, even though this is a case involving a sexual offence: s. 32(1), **Criminal Justice and Public Order Act 1994**.

Thus, on the facts of the present case, it is likely that the case against Sam will be withdrawn from the jury and the *Turnbull* direction will, at the very least, have to be given with respect to the identification of Alan. It is not altogether clear whether the case against Alan will be withdrawn or not. This would depend on whether there was any other evidence available to support it.

Additional Reading

Birch, D., 'Corroboration in Criminal Trials. A Review of the Law Commission's Working Paper' (1990) Crim LR 667.

Birch, D., 'Corroboration: Goodbye to All That?' (1995) Crim LR 524.

Choo, A., 'Confessions and Corroboration: A Comparative Perspective' [1991] Crim LR 867.

Cutler, B.L., and Penrod, S.D., *Mistaken Identification—The Eyewitness, Psychology and the Law* (Cambridge University Press, Cambridge, 1995).

Dein, J., 'Non Tape Recorded Cell Confession Evidence' [2002] Crim LR 630.

Dennis, I., 'Corroboration Requirements Reconsidered' [1984] Crim LR 316.

Jackson, J.D., 'Credibility, Morality and the Corroboration Warning' (1988) CLJ 428

Law Com No. 202 *Corroboration of Evidence in Criminal Trials* (London, 1991).

Mirfield, P., 'Corroboration After the 1994 Act' (1995) Crim LR 448.

Ormerod, C.A., 'Sounds Familiar—Voice Identification Evidence' (2001) Crim LR 595.

Pattenden, R., 'Should Confessions be Corroborated?' (1991) 107 LQR 317.

Roberts, A., 'Does Code D Impose an Unrealistic Burden on the System of Summary Justice?' (2001) 165 JP 756.

Roberts, A, 'The Problem of Mistaken Identification' (2004) 8 E & P 100

Tinsley, Y., 'Even Better than the Real Thing? The Case for Reform in Identification Parades' (2001) 5 E&P 99.

Twining, W., **Rethinking Evidence** (OUP, Oxford, 1990).

9

Opinion evidence

Introduction

This area of Evidence law is dominated by the question of expert witness evidence and the extent to which flawed testimony has led to miscarriages of justice. When experts are mistaken the consequences can be very serious—as illustrated, for example, by Professor Frank Scuse and Home Office forensic scientists in relation to the Birmingham Six, Maguire Seven and Judith Ward cases. It should be stressed, however, that expert evidence is now commonplace in both criminal and civil trials and the courts and Parliament have developed procedures to try to ensure that such evidence is of a high quality. However, these procedures are a somewhat eclectic mix of common law and statute. Their development to some extent reflects the growing importance of scientific expertise in society as a whole.

Students should be aware of recent developments in civil and criminal law. The former includes the **Civil Evidence Act 1995** and the **Civil Procedure Rules 1998**. As far as criminal law is concerned this is mainly a case-law subject, but you should be familiar with s. 30 of the **Criminal Justice Act 1988** as far as expert evidence and hearsay is concerned and s. 35 of the **Criminal Justice Act 2003** requiring notice by the defence of the intention to call expert witnesses. The **Criminal Justice Act 2003** has made some changes in this area. Section 118(8) preserves the common law rule under which in criminal proceedings an expert witness may draw on the body of expertise relevant to his field. Section 127 relates to the preparatory work of experts. The Explanatory Note provides that it addresses the problem which arises where information relied upon by an expert witness is outside the personal experience of the expert and cannot be proved by other admissible evidence. The new statutory provision is based on the intention that rules about advance notice of expert evidence will be amended so as to require advance notice of the name of any person who has prepared information on which the expert has relied. In effect, an expert's opinion may be based on statements not prepared by him if:

- the statement was prepared for the purposes of criminal proceedings;
- the person who prepared the statement had, or may reasonably be supposed to have had, personal knowledge of the matters stated.

Your course may have touched on the law on expert witnesses in the United States, in particular **Frye v US (1923)** and *Daubert* v *Merrell Dow* (1993), where the jurisprudence has been rather more developed. More recent cases involving controversial expert evidence are those of *R* v *Clark* [2003] EWCA Crim 1020 and *R* v *Cannings* [2004] EWCA Crim 01. You may also be expected to be familiar with the elements of probability theory. Of course, ideally evidence students should be mathematically literate, although it is comforting, if worrying, that judges or juries are not always necessarily equipped with those same skills—any more than expert witnesses are generally well-versed in criminal or civil justice principles.

In answering a question in this area, you must be familiar with the differences between expert and non-expert opinion evidence. Be clear on when and in what circumstances both types of evidence are admissible and the questions that can be asked of the expert whilst giving evidence. The specific approach that should be taken after that depends on whether the question relates to civil or criminal trials.

Question 1

'An expert's opinion is admissible to furnish the court with scientific information which is likely to be outside the experience and knowledge of a judge or jury. If on the proven facts a judge or jury can form their own conclusions, without help, then the opinion of an expert is unnecessary.' *R* v *Turner* [1975] QB 834, per Lawton LJ, at 841.

Critically examine the application of the approach outlined here in relation to the role of expert opinion evidence in criminal trials.

Commentary

This appears to be a relatively straightforward question. However, you should avoid the temptation to give a narrative account of the law and instead display your analytical knowledge of some of the controversies in this area, such as whether criminal trials should move towards court-appointed experts as in civil cases and whether the law in the area needs codifying. Recent cases about flawed expert evidence have shone the spotlight on this area of law, particularly on the question of whether the distinction between fact and opinion is a meaningful one.

Answer plan

- *Turner* illustrating traditional approach of courts, separating expert witness evidence and ordinary witnesses
- In practice distinction difficult to draw; and courts influenced by public opinion on what areas are acceptable for expert evidence—e.g. difficulty over psychiatric evidence

- Arguably many witnesses give opinion evidence to some extent—the issue is to what extent scientific as opposed to eye-witness evidence is verifiable
- Liberal approach of English courts to scientific expertise—contrast more jurisprudential approach in US
- Assessment of reform arguments—court-appointed experts; scientific education for courts; stress that even scientific evidence cannot attain certainty

Suggested answer

Expert opinion evidence is of growing importance in criminal trials. The Runciman Royal Commission's Crown Court Study (1993) found that in about one-third of all disputed trials scientific evidence played a part. Fifteen years later the numbers have doubtless increased, particularly in the wake of the development of DNA profiling. As Roberts and Zuckerman put it: 'It is no exaggeration to regard DNA technology as the most revolutionary contribution to criminal investigation and forensic proof since the introduction of fingerprinting a century earlier' (2004, at p. 291). The overall picture in relation to the use of expert evidence has changed since the landmark case of *Turner* quoted in the question, but the judicial approach to the admissibility of such evidence is still as expressed there. This expression, although accurate, indicates also the limitations of the current approach—some of which will be examined here. Lawton CJ points out here that expert evidence is only to be admitted on matters where a judge or jury cannot form their own conclusions. The essay will suggest that the distinction is not so easy to draw, particularly in certain scientific areas such as psychology. Further it will be argued that admissibility is only one aspect of the problematic nature of expert evidence, another being the way the courts, including the jury, handle such evidence. Finally the contribution of expert evidence to miscarriages of justice will be examined.

The general rule is that a witness can only testify with respect to those matters which he or she actually observed or perceived. The witness is not entitled to give his or her own opinion on the matter. It is for the jury in a criminal trial to draw inferences from the evidence as the trier of fact, not the witness. There are a number of exceptions to this general rule. Munday (2007, p. 349) identifies four in addition to expert opinion. In the following areas a non-expert witness may give opinion evidence: identity, a witness's feelings, handwriting proved by a non-expert (see **Criminal Procedure Act 1865**, s. 8), and matters of impression and narrative.

The major exception to this general rule is in the case of expert witnesses. With regards to those matters for which the judge or jury may require assistance, the opinion of experts on those matters may be admissible. Examples of where the judge and jury may require assistance include scientific, medical and forensic evidence. The weight to be given to such evidence is a matter for the jury. It is apparent that this type of evidence is admissible because the jury would not be able to draw the appropriate inferences and form proper opinions from the facts requiring expert opinion: *Buckley* v *Rice Thomas* (1554) **Plowd 118**.

Before an expert witness can give opinion evidence relating to any particular issue, it is for the judge to decide whether that particular witness is an expert. This would be dependent on whether the witness had undergone a course of study giving the requisite expertise in that area or whether his experience is such as to make him an expert. It is not essential that in all cases the expert possess formal qualifications. In *R* v *Silverlock* [1894] **2 QB 766**, opinion evidence from a solicitor was admitted, by the Court for Crown Cases Reserved, with respect to handwriting even though he did not possess any formal qualification in it but merely studied it as a hobby. The courts' liberal approach to expertise is illustrated more recently in *R* v *Hodges* [2003] **2 Cr App R 247**, where the Court of Appeal allowed a police officer experienced in drug crime to give evidence as to the price and general supply procedure for heroin in the specific area. It is arguable that what is at issue here is not the rather simplistic distinction between expert and lay opinion suggested in *Turner*, but the more fundamental test of whether the evidence of the proposed witness is relevant. The Court of Appeal has set out the principles involving the admissibility of expert opinion evidence:

> For expert evidence to be admissible two conditions must be satisfied: first, that study the more experience will give a witness's opinion an authority which the opinion of one not so qualified will lack; and secondly the witness must be so qualified to express the opinion . . . . If these two conditions are met the evidence of the witness is admissible, although the weight to be attached to his opinion must of course be assessed by the tribunal of fact. (*R* v *Lutrell* [2004] **EWCA Crim 1344**)

Choo (2006, p. 252) summarises the two conditions as 'necessity and reliability' and adds 'the extent to which the twin issues of necessity and reliability are adequately accounted for in the law on the admissibility of expert opinion evidence is a question which ought to underlie any consideration of the law in this area' (p. 253).

Expert opinion evidence is not admissible per se in all criminal trials. Where the issue is one for which the jury is able to decide and does not require the assistance of experts, no opinion evidence from experts is admissible. The reason is because such evidence is usually unnecessary and irrelevant. In *R* v *Chard* (1971) **56 Cr App R 268**, evidence from an expert with regards to the alleged inability of the accused to form the necessary mens rea of the offence was disallowed by the Court of Appeal. The Court emphasised that where there was no issue of mental instability or illness, it is inappropriate to allow evidence from a medical witness as to the state of the accused's mind. Likewise in *R* v *Turner* [1975] **QB 834** itself, where the accused's defence was one of provocation, the Court of Appeal excluded evidence from a psychiatrist because there was no issue as regarded his mental state. The issue of provocation was one for which the jury could decide. Lawton LJ stated in that case that the fact that an expert witness possessed impressive scientific qualifications did not necessarily make his opinion on matters of human nature any more helpful. These were matters for which the jury was competent to decide.

The restriction on the admissibility of expert evidence on matters for which the jury requires no assistance includes a restriction on expert evidence on the credibility of a witness or the accused save in exceptional circumstances: *Lowery* v *R* [1974] AC 85. Although, in **Lowery**, such evidence was admitted, Murphy (at 2008 p. 371) regards this decision as applying only to the specific facts of the case rather than a general exception to the usual rule. This approach appears to be correct in the light of *R* v *Rimmer* [1983] **Crim LR 250**, where the trial judge refused to allow the evidence of an expert on the basis that this related only to the credibility of the accused. Murphy points to the case of *R* v *Weir*, *R* v *Somanathan* **[2006] 1 WLR 1885**, to illustrate the difficulty of applying the principle advocated here by Lawton CJ that expert evidence should not be allowed on issues within the jury's everyday knowledge, in particular that relating to he credibility of a witness. The case also illustrates that 'science' may be widely defined and that experts may be called to give evidence on social science, here, arguably, anthropology or religious studies. The case concerned the rape of a female member of his congregation by a Tamil Hindu priest. A professor of Hinduism was called as an expert witness by the prosecution to give evidence on how difficult it was for such a victim to make an allegation against a priest. The Court of Appeal held that the evidence was rightly admitted. Kennedy LJ stated (at para 49) that counsel '. . . did not ask the witness to express a view about the truth or falsehood of the allegation, and he did not purport to do so, but the jury was entitled to know from an expert whether or not within the Hindu community an allegation of this kind was unusual'.

Murphy comments (at p. 372), 'With respect, whether or not the allegation was unusual (and whether or not it required courage, etc) was irrelevant to the case except insofar as it tended to confirm the credibility of the complainant. Thus the only basis on which the court might have sought to defend the admissibility of the evidence was that the jury would be unable to assess the complainant's credibility without expert assistance. This would involve the proposition that the reluctance of a Hindu woman to accuse a priest of rape is a concept beyond the ordinary experience of most jurors, and so justifies a departure from the general rule expounded in *Turner*.'

Lawton LJ's observation in *Turner* correctly indicates how the courts call on experts for evidence on 'scientific information which is likely to be outside the experience and knowledge of a judge or jury'. However, it does not indicate how such areas can be identified. In practice the courts have had to consider the difficult question of at what point modish discoveries become a new science. In the United States for a long period the test set by *Frye* v *US* (1923) was that of 'general acceptance in the particular field to which it belongs'. English law did not have the same preoccupation with mainstream branches of science. Bingham LJ stated in *R* v *Robb* (1991) 93 Cr App R 161 that opinion evidence may be given in a wide range of areas, some 'far removed from anything which could be called a formal scientific discipline'. In *Robb* evidence of a voice identification technique was held to be properly admitted.

Another criticism made of *Turner* is that jurors might indeed welcome evidence within their broad general knowledge, such as human behaviour. In fact in practice this does happen. In **R v Stockwell (1993) 97 Cr App R 260** the Court of Appeal allowed evidence from an expert about identifying a suspect by looking at video footage, which might be taken to be an everyday activity.

In effect admissibility often turns on whether in society as a whole there is an acknowledgement of the importance of experts in a particular area. Some 'experts' such as psychiatrists are treated with more scepticism than others. One area of controversy that has generated recent case-law is that of facial-mapping, illustrating that new areas of recognised expertise are continually developing. In **R v Mitchell [2005] EWCA Crim 731** the court accepted that a facial-mapping expert can give an opinion, although this had been doubted in **R v Gray [2003] EWCA Crim 1001**. Ear print evidence is another contested area. It is important to realise that no evidence is infallible and that even fingerprint evidence may have a rate of error. As the **New Scientist (2005)** noted, 'fingerprint matching is undoubtedly a valuable tool for catching criminals but it suffers from one major flaw: nobody knows how often fingerprint examiners make a wrong call'. In **R v Gilfoyle [2001] 2 Cr App R 57** the court held that evidence of a 'psychological autopsy' for the purpose of determining whether an alleged murder victim had in fact committed suicide was not admissible. Such autopsies did not have real scientific basis. (At the time of writing this case has been referred to the Criminal Cases Review Commission.)

At one time expert opinion evidence was inadmissible on the ultimate issue in the case. This was because the expert would be usurping the function of the jury: *M'Naghten's Case* (1843) 10 Cl & F 200. However, it is clear that whilst the rule is still referred to, in practice expert evidence on the ultimate issue is allowed. In *DPP v A & BC Chewing Gum Ltd* [1968] 1 QB 159, 164, Lord Parker CJ in the Divisional Court stated that:

> Those who practise in the criminal courts see every day cases of experts being called on the question of diminished responsibility, and although technically the final question 'Do you think he was suffering from diminished responsibility?' is strictly inadmissible, it is allowed time and time again without objection.

Section 3 of the **Civil Evidence Act 1972** abolished the ultimate issue rule in civil proceedings. The position in criminal proceedings is that an expert can give his opinion on an ultimate issue within his area of expertise. In **R v Stockwell (1993) 97 Cr App R 467** the Court of Appeal stated that evidence on the ultimate issue is admissible. This case also raises, however, a matter which is not covered in Lawton LJ's statement. What is the status of expert opinion evidence? In *Stockwell* the court said that the judge must make it clear that the jury must decide the issue and may reject the expert's evidence. This is the general rule. However, in *R* v *Tilly* [1981] 1 WLR 1309 the Court of Appeal overturned a guilty verdict where the expert evidence was unchallenged and clearly suggested the verdict was unsustainable. In other words on occasion the expert evidence may determine the case.

It seems however that juries are on the whole more inclined to accept prosecution expert opinion evidence. Edmond (2002, p. 58) points out that 'Scientific evidence is an important component of most high profile miscarriage of justice cases.' He points out (at p. 59) that a 'common concern is that excessive reliance is placed on scientific evidence: that its potential fallibility is not recognised'. This is all the more significant in view of the 'meagre resources' available to the defence to challenge such prosecution evidence.

It should be acknowledged that the current status of expert opinion evidence is by no means settled. A number of practical and theoretical issues demand attention. Some arguments have been put that a system of court-appointed experts (perhaps as well as party-appointed experts) should be established in criminal cases. Court-appointed experts were introduced in civil cases by the Woolf reforms in 1997/1998. But there are a number of difficulties. The criminal trial paradigm is still an adversarial one, with the search for a conclusion based on the conflict between two sides, and society is arguably not ready for trial by experts. In addition, it is a fallacy to think that there is necessarily only one version of scientific evidence. The question is most often that of probabilities, not certainties. As Howard (1991, at p. 101) points out, 'It is slightly mysterious that it should be thought that experts are venal mountebanks when engaged by the parties but transformed into paragons of objectivity when employed by the court.'

What is undeniable is that there is increasing public attention and some unease about the treatment of expert evidence in criminal cases. In March 2005 the House of Commons Science and Technology Committee published a report entitled *Forensic Science on Trial*. The conclusions noted:

> 189. While we recognise that the number of miscarriages of justice associated with expert evidence may be relatively low, we are extremely concerned by the lack of safeguards to prevent such miscarriages of justice from happening, and the complacency of the legal profession in regard to these matters. The complexity and role of forensic evidence are ever increasing and we have not seen evidence to reassure us that the criminal justice system has kept pace with these developments, or will be able to do so in the future. We have made a number of recommendations that we believe could improve the quality and treatment of expert evidence and decrease the potential for miscarriages of justice due to flawed expert evidence. These include greater scientific input and oversight through the establishment of both a Scientific Review Committee within the Criminal Cases Review Commission and a Science and the Law Forum, increased use of pre-trial hearings (in line with the Criminal Procedure Rules), and forensic and process training for all those involved in the criminal justice system as a condition of the role.

However, the committee was anxious that any failures should be recognised as systems failures and that 'focusing criticism on the expert has a detrimental effect on the willingness of other experts to serve as witnesses and detracts attention from the flaws in the court process and legal system which, if addressed, could help prevent future miscarriages of justice'.

The law on opinion evidence 20 years after *Turner* is thus still evolving. Education in science for juries and legal personnel is one way forward but as the court in *Adams* [1996] 2 Cr App R 467 stressed, trials are about common sense, not mathematical or scientific reasoning. Thus Bayes' theorem[1] was not appropriate for use in jury trials. Some look longingly at the more theoretically coherent approach in the United States, as seen in *Daubert* v *Merrell Dow* and Federal Rule of Evidence 702 (see *R* v *Dallagher* [2002] EWCA Crim 1903). Perhaps the impetus for change will come from miscarriages of justice based in part on misconceptions about scientific opinion evidence. The Court of Appeal in *R* v *Clark* (2003) laid down clearer guidelines about procedure where there is dispute about scientific evidence and the case rests largely or entirely on this. In *R* v *Cannings* [2004] 1 WLR 2607 the Court of Appeal Criminal Division addressed the problem of disagreement between experts on the cause of infant deaths. It stated that, in such a situation, where death by natural causes could not be ruled out 'the prosecution of a parent or parents for murder should not be started or continued unless there is additional cogent evidence, extraneous to the expert evidence . . . which tends to support the conclusion that the infant, or where there is more than one death, one of the infants, was deliberately harmed'. However, in *R* v *Kai-Whitewind* [2005] 2 Cr App R 31 Judge LJ stated (at pp. 84–5), '. . . the logical conclusion of what we shall describe as the overblown Cannings argument is that where there is a conflict of opinion between reputable experts, the expert evidence called by the Crown is automatically neutralised. That is a startling proposition, and is not sustained by Cannings. In Cannings there was no evidence beyond the inferences based on coincidence which the experts for the Crown were prepared to draw.'

Roberts (2008, p. 443) points out that 'the principal weakness in the English law concerning the reception of expert evidence is that its development has been based on pragmatism rather than principle'. He deplores the way the courts draw 'vague analogies with approaches taken in other jurisdictions' and suggests the 'development of a judicial gate-keeping function in English civil procedure'. He argues that 'a central concern of any proposal for reform ought to be how best to address a lack of technical or scientific expertise on the part of those responsible for determining the admissibility of expert testimony'. Roberts recommends 'the adoption of pre-trial procedures which provide for direct involvement of experts in the gate-keeping process'. In short, there is a growing pressure for reform of the law in this area.

---

[1] Bayes' theorem provides a way of calculating the conditional probability of an event. If there are two events A and B, the probability of A given B (written as P(A|B) in statistical shorthand, and always expressed as a positive number between 0 and 1) can be derived from the formula $P(A|B) = P(B|A)P(A)/P(B)$.

Question 2

Sarah (a minor) is suing Henfield Health Authority for damages for pain and suffering and loss of earnings as a result of negligent treatment she received as a patient in Henfield Hospital. It is alleged that the surgeon who operated on her was negligent in that what was supposed to be a simple surgical procedure resulted in partial paralysis of her left side. Her solicitors have sought the opinion of Dr Williams, who produced a written report concluding that in his opinion, the surgeon had not followed proper practice. The defence wishes to call evidence of Joan Soap, a psychiatrist, to the effect that Sarah is not to be trusted to speak the truth.

   Advise the parties.

Commentary

This question requires a consideration of the application of the **Civil Evidence Act 1995**. This replaced and repealed Part I of the **Civil Evidence Act 1968** and ss. 2(1), (2) and (3)(b) of the **Civil Evidence Act 1972** and provides for the making of new rules governing the admissibility of expert opinion evidence. A working knowledge of the procedural rules governing the admissibility of expert reports under the **Civil Procedure Rules 1998** will need to be shown.

Answer plan

- Admissibility of expert evidence in civil cases
- Application of section 3(1) Civil Evidence Act 1972 which allows evidence on ultimate issue, applied in *Re M and R (Minors)* (1996)
- Judge must establish expertise of Dr Williams and Joan Soap
- Experts may rely on work of others, see *R* v *Abadom* (1983)
- Application of *Civil Procedure Rules,* rule 35.1

Suggested answer

The general rule is that a witness cannot give his or her opinion on a fact in issue. To allow a witness to do so would be to usurp the function of the court, which is to draw an inference from the facts put before it. A witness should therefore only be allowed to give evidence of facts and that which he or she has observed. However, there are exceptions to this and the important exception that applies here is the admissibility of expert opinion evidence where it would assist the court in reaching its decision.

   First, it should be noted that the expert evidence is admissible even though it may give an opinion on the ultimate issue. On the facts of the present case, it is arguable that Dr Williams, by concluding that the surgeon was negligent, is offering an opinion as to the ultimate issue. The difficulty faced in criminal trials is not present here. This is because s. 3(1) of the **Civil Evidence Act 1972** provides that where any person is called as a witness, his opinion on any relevant matter (which by subsection (3) includes an issue in the proceedings in question), on which he is qualified to give expert evidence, is to be admissible in evidence.

Jane Soap's evidence raises more difficult issues. In *Re M and R (Minors) (Sexual Abuse: Video Evidence)* [1996] 4 All ER 239, Butler-Sloss LJ held that a suitably qualified expert could give evidence as to the credibility of a child witness who had given evidence by way of a videotaped interview. The expert evidence fell within the ambit of s. 3 of the **Civil Evidence Act 1972**. Murphy (2008, at p. 369) argues that this analysis is inaccurate but can be defended on the basis that this was expert psychiatrist and psychologist's evidence. He points out that the 'ultimate issue in such a case is not whether the child's evidence is credible but whether the alleged abuse occurred (though obviously the question of the child's credibility is of great importance in resolving the ultimate issue)'. He goes on, however, to point out that the decision in the case can be defended on the basis that although expert opinion is not admissible on the issue of credibility since that is a lay matter, it is 'within the province of psychiatrists and psychologists to form an opinion about credibility because their diagnoses and recommendations for treatment or therapy are often based on the factual accounts given to them by their patients and clients'. Murphy suggests that 'the fact that such an expert witness believed what he was told is a fact which is essential to explain the formation of his opinion and can be admitted on that basis without considering the ultimate issue rule'. Murphy's approach suggests that expert psychiatric and psychological witnesses may be in a different position to that of other experts. The issue for the defence is relevance. If Sarah's testimony is disputed then arguably her credibility is a collateral issue and evidence may be taken on it.

It will be necessary to establish that Dr Williams and Joan Soap have the requisite expertise in the area in order to give their opinions on these matters: *R* v *Silverlock* [1894] 2 QB 766. This will be a question for the judge to decide prior to allowing the evidence to be admitted.

Another point to note is that both experts are entitled to rely on the work of others in reaching his conclusion. This was made clear in *R* v *Abadom* [1983] 1 WLR 126 (although a criminal case, the principle is likewise applicable here), where the Court of Appeal held that the expert opinion evidence was admissible although the expert had relied on statistics supplied by the Home Office Research Establishment. The Court decided that the expert was entitled to rely on this research in forming his opinion and that this did not violate the rule against hearsay. In fact in civil proceedings hearsay statements are admissible under the **Civil Evidence Act 1995** since, with certain provisos, such statements are admissible as 'any representation of fact or opinion however made'.

The **Civil Procedure Rules 1998** have made fundamental changes as to the admissibility of expert evidence in civil cases. Rule 35.1 of the 1998 Rules restricts expert evidence to that which is reasonably required to resolve the proceedings.

One of these fundamental changes that the Rules have made is that in accordance with r. 35.3 the duty imposed on the expert is to assist the court on those matters in which he has expertise. The fact that the expert is employed by one of the parties is dealt with by the rule that makes it clear that the duty to the court overrides any obligation to the person who instructed him. This is reinforced by the fact that the written expert reports must be addressed to the court. This requirement of objectivity, and the duty owed to the court, had been previously stressed by the court in *Vernon* v *Bosley* (No. 1) [1997] 1 All ER 577.

The 1998 Rules have also made changes as to how the expert evidence is presented to the court. Rule 35.5 provides that expert evidence shall be given by way of a written report in all cases unless the court orders otherwise. For cases that are on the fast-track the court will not permit oral expert evidence unless the interests of justice requires such oral testimony. Rule 35.10 states that the report should contain a statement that the expert understands his duty to the court and has complied with it. It must also verify that the facts and opinions stated in the report are true and correct. The court will have to be satisfied that the experts are independent—in other words that although they are retained by the parties they give opinions in an objective and fair way and place their duty to the court beyond that to the parties. Rule 35.3 of the **Civil Procedure Rules 1998** provides: '(1) it is the duty of an expert to help the court on the matters within his expertise. (2) This function overrides any obligation to the person from whom he had received instructions or by whom he is paid.' In *Liverpool Roman Catholic Diocese Trustees Inc* v *Goldberg (No. 2)* [2001] 4 All ER 950 the court held that a QC should not act as an expert witness on behalf of a member of his chambers. The latter was a defendant in an action for professional negligence and the proposed expert witness had expressed his sympathy for his colleague.

As regards whether the expert can be called to give evidence (for cases not on the fast track), this is governed by r. 35.4. This provides that no party shall call an expert without the court's permission. When permission is sought from the court, the party must identify the field in which he wishes to rely on the expert evidence and, where practicable, the expert in that field on whose evidence he wishes to rely.

In the present case, before the evidence of Dr Williams and Joan Soap can be adduced, permission will have to be obtained from the court and the way the evidence will be presented will be by way of a written report. If the parties wished to call experts to give oral testimony, then permission of the court has to be obtained and would depend on the circumstances of the case as to whether the court will allow such testimony to be given. Each can also appoint their own expert but the two experts will then have to meet to agree the reports to the court.

In civil cases there are strict rules about advance notice of expert evidence (see **Civil Evidence Act 1972**, s. 2(3)). Under the **Civil Procedure Rules 1998** (CPR) a party who fails to disclose an expert's report may not use the report at trial or call the expert as witness without the court's permission (r. 35.11).

Both Sarah and the Henfield Health Authority should be warned that they should be certain they want to use the experts' reports before disclosing them to the other side. Under the CPR any party to whom such a report is disclosed can put it in evidence, legal professional privilege being lost at that point (see **Chapter 11**). CPR, r. 35.7(1) states that 'where two or more parties wish to submit expert evidence on a particular issue, the court may direct that the evidence on that issue is to be given by one expert only'. It may well be the case that the parties wish to call evidence on these issues and if they cannot agree on the expert the court may select an expert from a list submitted by the parties or give directions on how the expert should be selected. Once selected each party can instruct the expert, although they must send copies of the instructions to the other side. Finally, both parties can expect the judgment to reflect the reasons why the views of the expert have been accepted. Lord Phillips of Worth Matravers MR stated the positions where two or more experts have been called as witnesses. The judge should:

provide an explanation as to why he has accepted the evidence of one expert and rejected that of the other. It may be that the evidence of one or the other accorded more satisfactorily with facts found by the judge. It may be that the explanation of one was more inherently credible than that of the other. It may simply be that one was better qualified, or manifestly more objective, than the other. Whatever the explanation may be, it should be apparent from the judgment. (*English* v *Emery Reimbold and Strick Ltd* (2002) 3 All ER 385)

There may be grounds of appeal if the judge prefers lay opinion to uncontradicted expert opinion on a matter on which expert opinion is appropriate (*Re B (A Minor)* [2000] 1 WLR 790).

Additional reading

Alldridge, P., 'Scientific Expertise and Comparative Criminal Procedure' (1999) 3 E&P 141.

Bernstein, D., 'Junk Science in the United States and the Commonwealth' (1996) 21 Yale J Int Law 123.

Edmond, G., 'Judicial Representations of Scientific Evidence' (2000) 63 MLR 216.

Edmond, G., 'Constructing Miscarriages of Justice: Misunderstanding Scientific Evidence in High Profile Criminal Appeals' (2002) 22 OJLSI 53.

Graham, M.H., 'The Daubert Dilemma: at last a Viable Solution?' (1998) 2 E&P 211.

House of Commons Science and Technology Committee 7th Report. *Forensic Science on Trial* (2005) HL96–1 http://www.publications.parliament.uk/pa/cm200405/cmselect/cmsctech/96/9602.htm

Howard, M.N., 'The Neutral Expert: A Plausible Threat to Justice?' [1991] Crim LR 98.

Mackay, R.D., and Colman, A., 'Excluding Expert Evidence. A Tale of Ordinary Folk and Common Experience' [1991] Crim LR 800.

New Scientist, 'The Myth of Fingerprints', 17 September 2005, 3.

O'Brian, E. Jr, 'Court scrutiny of expert evidence: Recent decisions highlight the tensions' [2003] 7 EXP 172.

Ormerod, D., 'Sounds Familiar—Voice Identification Evidence' [2001] Crim LR 595.

Pattenden, R., 'Expert Evidence based on Hearsay' (1982) Crim LR 85.

Pattenden, R., 'Conflicting Approaches to Psychiatric Evidence' [1986] Crim LR 92.

Redmayne, M., *Expert Evidence and Criminal Justice* (OUP, Oxford, 2001).

Roberts, A., 'Drawing on Expertise: Legal Decision-making and the Reception of Expert Evidence' (2008) Crim LR 443.

Roberts, P., 'Forensic Science Evidence after Runciman' (1994) Crim LR 78.

Spencer, J.R., 'Court Experts and Expert Witnesses. Have we a Lesson to Learn from the French?' (1992) CLP 213.

Wilson, A., 'Expert Testimony in the Dock' (2005) 69 JCL 330.

10

Issues in the course of trial

Introduction

This topic generally deals with the type of questions that can or cannot be asked in examination-in-chief or cross-examination in criminal trials.

Evidence courses vary in how they group the various aspects of the law of Evidence. In some courses competence and compellability (see **Chapter 3**) is covered along with other issues concerned with witness examination. That area overlaps considerably with criminal procedure and Evidence courses vary in the topics they cover. The areas covered in this chapter are:

Examination in Chief

- refreshing memory;
- rule on previous consistent statements and exceptions;
- hostile witnesses;

Cross-examination

- rule on previous inconsistent statements;
- rule of finality to answers to collateral questions and exceptions;
- special rule for cross-examination of complainants in sexual offence cases;
- non-defendent's bad character.

One important aspect of this topic is the weight to be put on testimony which has been proven to be inconsistent with the previous statement of the witness, i.e., whether it is evidence of the facts stated therein or whether the inconsistent testimony is to be disregarded. It is in this regard that the nature of the trial is important. Generally, the inconsistent testimony is disregarded in criminal trials, whilst it is evidence of the facts stated therein in the case of civil trials.

Another important aspect of this topic deals with the questions that can be asked about the complainant's sexual history in the case of a trial involving a sexual offence.

For example, can the complainant be asked whether she is or was a prostitute? This will be considered in the light of s. 41 of the **Youth Justice and Criminal Evidence Act 1999**.

The House of Lords in *R* v *A* (**No. 2**) **[2001] 2 WLR 1546** considered whether the rape shield provisions of this section were compatible with the right of trial guaranteed under art. 6 of the European Convention on Human Rights. The House was asked to consider the following question:

> May a sexual relationship between a defendant and a complainant be relevant to the issue of consent so as to render its exclusion under s. 41 of the [1999] Act a contravention of the defendant's right of fair trial?

The House made it clear that it will be for the trial judge in each case to determine whether or not the evidence is sufficiently probative to justify admission. The House then went on to interpret s. 41 in a manner compatible with the demands of the **Human Rights Act**. Ordinary canons of statutory interpretation did not allow such a construction, so the House applied s. 3 of the **Human Rights Act,** which requires that 'so far as it is possible to do so primary legislation . . . must be read and given effect in a way which is compatible with the Convention rights'.

Students must be familiar with this important case. Other procedural changes in the **Youth Justice and Criminal Evidence Act** restrict the accused's right to cross-examine vulnerable witnesses in person.

The **Criminal Justice Act 2003** (**CJA 2003**) made considerable changes in this area.

Changes in CJA 2003 on Witness Testimony

(i) Refreshing memory ss. 139–141

139—Use of documents to refresh memory

(1)—A person giving oral evidence in criminal proceedings about any matter may, at any stage in the course of doing so, refresh his memory of it from a document made or verified by him at an earlier time if—

> *(a) he states in his oral evidence that the document records his recollection of the matter at that earlier time, and*

> *(b) his recollection of the matter is likely to have been significantly better at that time than it is at the time of his oral evidence.*

(2)—Where—

> *(a) a person giving oral evidence in criminal proceedings about any matter has previously given an oral account, of which a sound recording was made, and he states in that evidence that the account represented his recollection of the matter at that time,*

> *(b) his recollection of the matter is likely to have been significantly better at the time of the previous account than it is at the time of his oral evidence, and*

> *(c) a transcript has been made of the sound recording, he may, at any stage in the course of giving his evidence, refresh his memory of the matter from that transcript.*

The law relating to refreshing memory before giving evidence is unchanged.

Note that s. 120(3) deals with the evidential status of documents referred to in refreshing memory procedure. Under the common law the document is only evidence of the credibility of the maker. Under s. 120(3) these statements will be evidence of the truth of the matters stated.

(ii) Rules on previous consistent and inconsistent statements

Sections 119 and 120 affect the evidential status of previous consistent and inconsistent statements which now become further exceptions to the rule against hearsay. In particular s. 120(7) makes a wide sweeping development of the common law on 'recent complaint', which only applied in sexual cases.

Key sections are as follows:

120—Other previous statements of witnesses

(1) . . .

(2) If a previous statement by the witness is admitted as evidence to rebut a suggestion that his oral evidence has been fabricated, that statement is admissible as evidence of any matter stated of which oral evidence by the witness would be admissible.

(3) . . .

(4) A previous statement by the witness is admissible as evidence of any matter stated of which oral evidence by him would be admissible, if—

    (a) any of the following three conditions is satisfied, and

    (b) while giving evidence the witness indicates that to the best of his belief he made the statement, and that to the best of his belief it states the truth.

(5) The first condition is that the statement identifies or describes a person, object or place.

(6) The second condition is that the statement was made by the witness when the matters stated were fresh in his memory but he does not remember them, and cannot reasonably be expected to remember them, well enough to give oral evidence of them in the proceedings.

(7) The third condition is that—

    (a) the witness claims to be a person against whom an offence has been committed,

    (b) the offence is one to which the proceedings relate,

    (c) the statement consists of a complaint made by the witness (whether to a person in authority or not) about conduct which would, if proved, constitute the offence or part of the offence,

    (d) the complaint was made as soon as could reasonably be expected after the alleged conduct,

    (e) the complaint was not made as a result of a threat or a promise, and

    (f) before the statement is adduced the witness gives oral evidence in connection with its subject matter.

(8) For the purposes of subsection (7) the fact that the complaint was elicited (for example, by a leading question) is irrelevant unless a threat or a promise was involved.

Section 120(6) does not have any precedent at common law and will limit the occasions on which 'memory refreshing documents' are needed.

Note that an exculpatory statement made on accusation is not included in this list, and so is only evidence of consistency if admitted.

(iii) Bad character of non-defendants

Section 100 (which is not yet in force) allows proof of bad character of non-defendants to be admissible in certain circumstances. Section 98 defines 'bad character' and s. 99 abolishes the common law rules on bad character.

100—Non-defendant's bad character

(1) In criminal proceedings evidence of the bad character of a person other than the defendant is admissible if and only if—

   (a) it is important explanatory evidence,

   (b) it has substantial probative value in relation to a matter which—

   (i) is a matter in issue in the proceedings, and

   (ii) is of substantial importance in the context of the case as a whole, or

   (c) all parties to the proceedings agree to the evidence being admissible.

(2) For the purposes of subsection (1)(a) evidence is important explanatory evidence if—

   (a) without it, the court or jury would find it impossible or difficult properly to understand other evidence in the case, and

   (b) its value for understanding the case as a whole is substantial.

(3) In assessing the probative value of evidence for the purposes of subsection (1)(b) the court must have regard to the following factors (and to any others it considers relevant)—

   (a) the nature and number of the events, or other things, to which the evidence relates;

   (b) when those events or things are alleged to have happened or existed;

   (c) where—

   (i) the evidence is evidence of a person's misconduct, and

   (ii) it is suggested that the evidence has probative value by reason of similarity between that misconduct and other alleged misconduct, the nature and extent of the similarities and the dissimilarities between each of the alleged instances of misconduct;

   (d) where—

   (i) the evidence is evidence of a person's misconduct,

   (ii) it is suggested that that person is also responsible for the misconduct charged, and

   (iii) the identity of the person responsible for the misconduct charged is disputed, the extent to which the evidence shows or tends to show that the same person was responsible each time.

(4) Except where subsection (1)(c) applies, evidence of the bad character of a person other than the defendant must not be given without leave of the court.

This is a major change from the previous position. It applies to witnesses for the defence or prosecution.

Question 1

Daniel, a police constable, in response to a call on his radio, went to investigate an alleged burglary at Henfield Road. As he drove up to the scene of the crime, he saw Henry dressed in a T-shirt and running shorts and carrying a holdall on his back, running in the opposite direction. Daniel chased after him but soon lost him. Daniel made a note of what he had seen in his notebook, but did not do so until nearly six months later, just before the trial. Just after the incident, Henry went voluntarily to the police station and was interviewed. He said that the reason that he was in the area at the material time was because he had been out jogging, as he was training for the London Marathon and that the holdall contained bricks to weigh him down. Henry is charged with burglary. Advise on the following evidential matters:

(a) Can Daniel refresh his memory from his notebook outside court before giving evidence? If Daniel then gives evidence for the prosecution without referring to the notebook can the defence cross-examine him as to the contents of the notebook?

(b) Can Daniel refresh his memory from his notebook in court? And if so, can it be put in evidence?

(c) What use can the defence make of Henry's statement at the police station?

Commentary

This is a straightforward question concerning the witness refreshing his or her memory both inside and outside the court room and the use that the opposing counsel may make of the statements or documents used by the witness to refresh his or her memory. Part **(d)** concerns the issue of the accused's reaction on being confronted with incriminating facts.

Answer plan

- Refreshing memory—relevant case-law (1996); new **CJA 2003** provisions—*R* v *McAfee* **(2006)**
- Cross-examination and inspection permissible—see *Owen* v *Edwards* **(1983)**
- Conditions for refreshing memory—**CJA 2003**
- Inadmissibility of previous consistent statement unless falls within exceptions **CJA 2003**
- Arguable that exception applies as statement made at scene of crime

Suggested answer

(a) On the facts of the case, it would appear that Daniel will be called as a witness for the prosecution. The question that arises is whether he can refresh his memory from his notebook outside the court before giving evidence. It should be noted that it is common for witnesses to look at written statements which they have made, in order to refresh their memory, before testifying on the witness stand. This practice was recognised by the Court of Appeal in *R v Richardson* [1971] 2 QB 484. In any event, even if there was a rule prohibiting such action, the rule would be unenforceable.

In *Richardson*, four prosecution witnesses were given their statements prior to their testimony. The statements were not sufficiently contemporaneous for them to be used to refresh their memory in court. The accused argued on appeal, that as the statements were not contemporaneous for the purpose of the rule on refreshing memory in court, their evidence should not have been admitted. The Court of Appeal rejected this argument and approved the dicta in *Lau Pak Ngam* v *R* [1966] Crim LR 443. In that case, the Supreme Court of Hong Kong stated that if witnesses were deprived of the opportunity of checking their recollection beforehand by reference to statements or notes made near to the time of the events in question, testimony in the witness box would be no more than a test of memory, rather than of truthfulness. Further, refusal of access to the statements would create difficulties for honest witnesses, but would not hamper dishonest ones. The approach of the court in *Richardson* was later applied in the case of *Worley* v *Bentley* [1976] 2 All ER 449.

Subsequently, the court made it clear in *R v Da Silva* [1990] 1 All ER 29, that the judge has a discretion to allow a witness to withdraw from the witness stand in order to refresh his memory from a statement made near or at the time of the events in question. The judge has this discretion even where the statement is not contemporaneous with the events. Before he exercises his discretion, the judge must be satisfied that the witness cannot recall the events in question because of lapse of time, that the witness had made a statement near the time of the event representing his recollection of them, that he had not read the statement before testifying and that he wishes to read the statement before he continues to give evidence. In *R v South Ribble Magistrates' Court, ex parte Cochrane* (1996) 2 Cr App R 544, the Divisional Court made it clear that *R v Da Silva* did not lay down a rule of law that all four conditions must be satisfied. The court had a discretion whether to permit a witness to refresh his memory from a statement which was made non-contemporaneously.

Thus, it would appear proper for Daniel to refresh his memory from his notebook outside the court before testifying on oath. Even if it is unclear that Daniel made the note of the events contemporaneously with the events in question, this would not necessarily be fatal.

The next issue is whether the defence can cross-examine Daniel as to the contents of the notebook if he consults it before trial. The Court of Appeal in *R* v *Westwell* [1976] 2 All ER 812 decided that if the prosecution counsel is aware that his witness has refreshed his or her memory outside the court, it was 'desirable but not essential' that the defence should be informed of this fact. Failure to do so would not be a ground for acquittal. Once the defence is aware that Daniel has refreshed his memory from his notebook outside the court, they are entitled to inspect the notebook, and cross-examine Daniel on the relevant matters contained in it. This was so held by the Divisional Court in *Owen* v *Edwards* (1983) 77 Cr App R 191.

However, the court in *Owen* v *Edwards* made it clear that if the defence counsel cross-examines a witness on material in the notebook or statement, which has not been used by the witness to refresh his memory, they run the risk of the notebook or statement being put in evidence. The court applied by analogy the rule applicable where the witness refreshes his or her memory in court. Section 120(3) of the **Criminal Justice Act 2003** provides that if a witness's memory-refreshing statement becomes admissible as a result of cross-examination then it is admissible evidence of any matter stated of which oral evidence by the witness would be admissible.

Thus, provided the defence cross-examines Daniel on the part of the notebook which he has used to refresh his memory, the notebook will not be put in evidence. If the defence was to go beyond that, the notebook may be put in evidence.

(b) Daniel may be entitled to refresh his memory by referring to his notebook in court provided the pre-conditions are satisfied. This is now covered by the **Criminal Justice Act 2003**, s. 139. The common law test specified that a memory-refreshing document requested by a witness giving oral evidence had to be contemporaneous. The new test allows a witness to consult a document if it was made when his recollection is likely to have been 'significantly better' when he made or verified it. In other words, the court will look at the quality of the evidence in the notebook rather than the time it was made. However, as Choo points out (2006, p. 403) the previous rule was 'liberally interpreted'. In *R* v *McAfee* (*John James*) [2006] EWCA Crim 2914 the Court of Appeal examined the question of what is meant by the witness's recollection being 'significantly better' when they make their note. The defence may argue that a note made shortly before the trial and many months after the incident would not satisfy this provision. The court noted that contemporaneity was not required and that the trial judge was best placed to pronounce on whether a witness's memory when he made the statement was likely to have been significantly better then when testifying. In this case the court approved the trial judge's decision to allow the memory-refreshing police document made four-and-a-half months after the incident. The court stated that it would not lightly interfere with the first instance judge's decision. They also stated that, 'A judge must have a residual discretion to refuse a section 139 application even if the statutory conditions are met. But there were no good reasons for doing so in this case. The prosecution were entitled to present their best case to the jury. That is the object of many of the provisions in the 2003 Act.' It is likely therefore that Daniel will be able to refresh his memory from his note.

The notebook should be handed to the defence counsel or the court so that it may be inspected and the witness cross-examined on its contents. The defence counsel can request that the jury be shown the notebook if it is necessary for the determination of an issue: *R* v *Bass* [1953] 1 QB 680.

Under the common law rule, which survives the **CJA 2003**, the notebook could not be evidence in the case. But it should be available for inspection by the defence. *R* v *Sekhon* (1987) 85 Cr App R 19 sets out guidelines whereby memory-refreshing documents may be shown to the jury to help them follow the cross-examination. If the cross-examiner only refers to parts of the document which the witness used in refreshing his memory then the party calling the witness cannot require that the document becomes evidence. If, however, the cross-examination uses other parts the witness has not relied upon then the party calling the witness may insist that the document becomes evidence (*Senat* v *Senat* [1965] **p. 172**). Daniel should be advised that s. 120(3) of the **Criminal Justice Act 2003** would then apply and the document would be evidence not only of consistency, as under the common law, but of the truth of its contents. However, under s. 122 **CJA 2003** the document must not accompany the jury when they retire to consider their verdict unless all parties to the proceedings agree or the judge gives his permission. The risk is the jury will attach disproportionate weight to what is a hearsay statement. In *R* v *Hulme* [2007] 1 Cr App R 26 the Court of Appeal held that the judge had been wrong to allow a witness statement to be taken into the jury room.

(c) The general rule is that a witness may not give evidence, during examination-in-chief, of a previous consistent statement. The out-of-court statement may be excluded for two reasons: first, the rule against hearsay and second, the rule against narrative. The reason for the rule is that it can be easily manufactured; it adds nothing to the witness's testimony and is usually self-serving: *Corke* v *Corke and Cook* [1958] P 93 and *R* v *Roberts* [1942] 1 All ER 187. Although there are a number of exceptions to the general rule, the only one which may apply here is where the accused has made a statement on being accused of the crime. Where the accused makes an admission on being accused of the crime, this is admissible in evidence of the facts stated therein. Where the accused denies the charge, the statement, whilst it may be admissible in some circumstances, for instance to show the accused's reaction when taxed with incriminating facts, is admissible only to show consistency of the accused's testimony and goes only to credit. It is not evidence of the facts stated therein: *R* v *Storey* (1968) 52 Cr App R 334 and *R* v *Pearce* (1979) 69 Cr App R 365. The **CJA 2003** has not affected this exception to the rule against narrative.

One issue is whether Henry's statement is taken to be exculpatory, inculpatory or mixed (see **Chapter 6**). It is assumed here that the defence is arguing that the statement is an exculpatory one. However, Henry's statement may alternatively be admissible as evidence of the truth of its contents under s. 114(1) (d) of the **Criminal Justice Act 2003** if the 'interests of justice' test is satisfied. However, Henry should be warned that not all previous consistent exculpatory statements will be admitted. In **R v Tooke (1989) 90 Cr App R 417** a written statement was not admitted since it did not add to a previous oral statement. Again, in **R v Lowe** [2003] EWCA Crim 3182 the Court of Appeal held that a statement which was made over four months after arrest was not admissible since it could not have been evidence of reaction to the accusation. On the facts, however, it is likely that the court may allow Henry to give evidence of his prior statement which he made in the police station, as evidence of his reaction when confronted at the police station. The statement is not evidence of the facts stated in it. However, Henry's statement may alternatively be admissible as evidence of the truth of its contents under s. 114(1)(d) of the **Criminal Justice Act 2003** if the 'interests of justice' test is satisfied.

Question 2

Frank is prosecuted for dangerous driving after he knocked down a pedestrian, Jennice. Jennice alleges that as she was crossing Middlefield Road, Frank hit her with his car, causing a fracture of her left leg. She states that Frank was driving his car at an excessive speed and without due care and attention. Frank's defence is that Jennice lurched out onto the road suddenly and he was unable to avoid her. He admits that the accident took place and the injuries suffered by Jennice. Advise Frank on the following evidential matters:

(a) Dr Lee gives evidence for the prosecution that when he examined Jennice in the casualty department where she was brought after the accident, there were no signs of recent intoxication. Can he be cross-examined on the fact that he had told Lisa, a nurse at the hospital the next day, that Jennice appeared to be drunk when she was brought into the hospital? Can evidence in rebuttal be called if Dr Lee denies the conversation?

(b) Herbert, an eyewitness to the accident, has given evidence that he saw Frank driving erratically immediately prior to the accident. Can he be cross-examined that he was convicted of perjury seven years ago?

(c) Before the trial, Paul, the manager of Toasters, a wine bar, has given a written statement to Frank's solicitor. In the statement, Paul said that he served Jennice three to four Singapore Slings, a cocktail, an hour before the accident. When testifying for the defence, he states that Jennice came into the wine bar to use the ladies room and did not have anything to drink. What use can be made of his written statement?

Commentary

(a) The issue here is whether a witness can be cross-examined as to a previous inconsistent statement and the evidential value to be put on such a statement.

(b) This part of the question involves the issue as to the admissibility of the previous convictions of a witness and the effect that it has on his testimony.

(c) This relates to the question as to what the defence can do where the witness called by him does not come up to proof and the value of the testimony or the previous statement made by the witness.

Answer plan

- Admissibility of previous inconsistent statement and its evidential value—ss. 4 and 5 **Criminal Procedure Act 1865** and s. 119 **CJA 2003**
- Admissibility of previous convictions of a witness—s. 6 **Criminal Procedure Act 1865** and s. 100 **CJA 2003**
- **Application of Rehabilitation of Offenders Act 1974** to criminal trials
- Witness does not come up to proof
- Position of 'hostile witnesses'—s. 3 **Criminal Procedure Act 1865**; s. 119 **CJA 2003**; *Joyce* v *Joyce* (2005)

Suggested answer

(a) The issue here is whether Dr Lee's conversation with Lisa, which is inconsistent with his present testimony, can be admitted into evidence. This is governed by s. 4 of the **Criminal Procedure Act 1865** setting out the procedure to be followed. This states that if a witness is asked during cross-examination about a prior statement (whether oral or written) made by him which is inconsistent with his present testimony, and does not admit that he had made such a previous inconsistent statement, the cross-examining party may adduce evidence of that inconsistent statement. Before the inconsistent statement can be adduced into evidence, the procedure laid out in s. 4 has to be complied with, namely, the circumstances in which the previous inconsistent statement was made must be put to the witness and he must then be asked whether he had made such a statement.

Thus, in this case, if Dr Lee denies making such a statement, evidence of the prior inconsistent statement can be adduced. This may take the form of calling Lisa as a rebuttal witness. If, on the other hand, Dr Lee admits making the statement, then the normal practice would be to ask him whether he still wishes to stand by his previous testimony. In most instances, when faced with such a situation, it is unlikely that the witness will stand by his previous testimony.

The next question is the value to be placed on the previous inconsistent statement. On the facts of this case, the previous inconsistent statement will help the defence's case that Jennice lurched suddenly onto the road, possibly because she was intoxicated. This would be the case if the previous statement is admissible as evidence of the facts stated in it. The **Criminal Justice Act 2003**, s. 119(1) provides that a prior inconsistent statement which is admissible into evidence, is admissible as evidence of the facts stated therein and is not merely evidence of the consistency or inconsistency of the witness. Thus the statement by Dr Lee to Lisa would then be admissible as evidence of the fact that Jennice was intoxicated when she received treatment in the hospital.

(b) Frank should be advised that under s. 6 of the **Criminal Procedure Act 1865**, a witness may be questioned as to whether he or she has been convicted of any felony or misdemeanour, and if he or she denies it or does not admit that fact, or refuses to answer the question, evidence can be adduced to prove such a conviction. Although the **Rehabilitation of Offenders Act 1974** does not apply to criminal proceedings, the court will take into account the length of time since the conviction. The court does retain a discretion not to allow the cross-examination of a witness regarding his or her previous spent conviction. The judge in considering whether to exercise his or her discretion should weigh the degree of relevance of the spent conviction against the prejudice it may cause against the witness. An unfair degree of prejudice may lead to an unfair trial.

Thus, whether Herbert can be questioned about his conviction for perjury would depend in part on whether it is a spent conviction under the 1974 Act and whether, if it was a spent conviction, the court would be prepared to allow the cross-examination about it on the basis that justice could not otherwise be done. That is a question for the court to decide. However, bearing in mind that the conviction is for perjury, even if it is spent, it is likely that the court may allow the cross-examination of Herbert regarding it.

It should also be noted that it is a matter of judicial discretion how far the cross-examination of a witness may go about his or her previous conviction under s. 6 of the **Criminal Procedure Act 1865**. If Herbert does deny the previous conviction, this can be proved by a certificate from the court of the conviction under s. 73 of the **Police and Criminal Evidence Act 1984**.

However, Frank should be aware that cross-examination of witnesses in criminal proceedings is also now limited by ss. 100 and 101 of the **Criminal Justice Act 2003**. Section 101(1) provides that in criminal proceedings the bad character of a person other than the defendant is admissible if and only if it is important explanatory evidence, it has substantial probative value in relation to a matter which is a matter in issue in the proceedings and is of substantial importance in the context of the case as a whole or all parties to the proceedings agree to the evidence being admitted.

It is arguable that the perjury conviction would only be admissible if Frank denied that he was driving erratically and then it has substantial probative value in relation to an important issue.

In *R* v *Weir* [2006] 1 WLR 1885 the Court of Appeal held that the trial judge had erred in admitting evidence of a previous caution administered to a witness since it did not have substantial probative value in relation to the witness's credibility. However, in the light of a very strong summing-up on the defendant's convictions the conviction was not unsafe.

Thus an application to have Herbert's convictions admitted would have to be made to the court. Here it is arguable that the perjury conviction has 'substantial probative value' and is admissible under s. 100(1)(b) in that it is of 'substantial importance in the context of the case as a whole'.

(c) In this situation, Frank should be advised that his witness, Paul, is not coming up to proof. The general rule is that a party may not impeach his own witness. This means that Frank cannot call evidence from another source to show that Paul is lying, forgetful or mistaken. He can, of course, call other witnesses who may be able to testify as to what Jennice drank at the wine bar, if there were any. The court must be satisfied that Paul is a hostile witness and not one who does not give evidence through fear (*R* v *Honeyghon and Sayles* (1999) Crim LR 221). On this see **Chapter 5**.

There are, however, exceptions to this general rule. In order for the exceptions to apply, it is necessary to determine whether Paul is merely an unfavourable witness or a hostile one. In the former case, the witness is one who is not coming up to proof whether because they are mistaken, foolish or forgetful. In such a case, the witness cannot be attacked as to his credit or challenged as to his previous inconsistent statement. However, if the witness is regarded as a hostile witness, at common law the previous inconsistent statement can be put to him and leading questions to test his memory and perception may be asked. A witness is regarded as hostile when he is not desirous of telling the truth at the instance of the party calling him.

In view of the fact that his previous statement to the solicitor is clear and unambiguous, it is possible that Paul may be treated as a hostile witness. However, this is a matter for the judge to decide. The procedure in such a situation is for counsel to make an application to the judge, to treat the witness as hostile. The judge can decide whether the witness is hostile by looking at the prior statement, the witness's demeanour and attitude.

If the judge decides that Paul is a hostile witness, then he may be asked leading questions and may be cross-examined by the defence as to his previous inconsistent statement (see *R* v *Thompson* (1976) 64 Cr App R 96) under s. 3 of the **Criminal Procedure Act 1865** (which applies only in cases of hostile witnesses; see *Greenough* v *Eccles* (1859) 5 CBNS 786, a case on the identically worded s. 22 of the **Common Law Procedure Act 1854**), before the defence can prove that

Paul made a previous inconsistent statement, he must be reminded of the circumstances of the previous statement sufficient to designate the particular occasion and must be asked whether or not he has made such a statement.

If Paul refuses to admit making such a statement, s. 3 of the 1865 Act allows the party calling the witness, the defence in this case, to prove that such a statement was made by the witness. The Act sets out the procedure for cross-examining a hostile (described here as 'adverse') witness on 'a statement inconsistent with his present testimony'. This will apply whether Paul gives testimony that differs from the earlier statement or says nothing at all (**R v Thompson (1976) 64 Cr App R 96**). Paul may then be cross-examined on the earlier statement. Section 4 deals with proof of 'contradictory statements of adverse witnesses' and s. 5 with cross-examination on a previous statement in writing.

The prosecution should be reminded that cross-examination is only allowed on previous inconsistent statements on matters relevant to facts in issue—not to those on credibility (*R v C & B* **[2003] EWCA Crim 29**).

In **Joyce v Joyce [2005] EWCA Crim 1785** the Court of Appeal considered the impact of s. 119 of the **Criminal Justice Act 2003,** which allows previous inconsistent statements to be admissible as evidence of the truth of any matter stated. This is a change from the previous law, which only allowed such statements to be evidence of lack of credibility. The case involved eye witnesses who had given pre-trial statements identifying the accused. However, they retracted their statements at trial and became hostile witnesses. The judge sanctioned the admission of their pre-trial identification under s. 119 as evidence of their truth, on which the jury could decide. The Court of Appeal upheld the decision that the jury could 'evaluate, separately and together the quality of the three witnesses' oral evidence and to be able to rely, if they thought fit on the terms of the original statement'.

Question 3

John is charged with the attempted rape of Patricia. He denies the offence and claims that he was chatting innocently to the girl about her dog. He claims that she invented the attempted rape.

(a) Advise on the likely admissibility of evidence from Patricia's flatmate that Patricia came home sobbing and when asked what was the matter said she had been 'interfered with'.

(b) When first arrested John makes the claim that he stopped Patricia simply to chat about her dog when she was out walking. He says he had an identical breed of dog. The prosecution accuse him of having made this up.

(c) The defence wish also to call evidence that Patricia had made previous allegations of sexual assault which turned out to be fabricated.

Commentary

This question involves the types of questions that the prosecution and the defence can ask either in examination-in-chief or in cross-examination in a rape trial. In part **(a)**, it will be necessary to discuss the general rule with respect to the admissibility of prior consistent statements and the exception to that rule in cases involving sexual offences. In the next part of the question, the discussion is centred around the question as to whether evidence can be given of John's immediate reaction and his subsequent admission. Students, especially for part **(c)**, would have to be familiar with s. 41 of the **Youth Justice and Criminal Evidence Act 1999**.

Answer plan

- Admissibility of previous consistent statement
- Exception for recent complaints by certain witnesses and conditions of admissibility—s. 120, s. 114 **CJA 2003**
- Admissibility of John's statement to rebut allegation of recent fabrication
- Permissible cross-examination of rape victims on previous sexual history and previous false allegations
- **Youth Justice and Criminal Evidence Act**, s. 41

Suggested answer

(a) The general common law rule is that a witness may not be asked in examination-in-chief whether he or she had made a prior statement, either oral or written, consistent with his or her testimony. The reason for the rule is that it can be easily manufactured, it adds nothing to the witness's testimony and is usually self-serving: *Corke* v *Corke and Cook* [1958] P 93 and *R* v *Roberts* [1942] 1 All ER 187. There are a number of exceptions to this general rule. It may therefore be possible for evidence to be given of Patricia's statement to her flatmate under one of these exceptions in statute or common law.

In cases involving sexual offences, evidence of a recent complaint by the victim could be given even though this may be a self-serving statement: *R* v *Osborne* [1905] 1 KB 551. It was suggested by Holmes J in *Commonwealth* v *Cleary* (1898) 172 Mass 175, the reason this exception is permitted is because of the '. . . survival of the ancient requirement that a woman should make hue and cry as a preliminary to an appeal of rape'. The recent complaint could be oral or written and includes a note given by mistake to a friend: *R* v *B* [1997] Crim LR 220.

In order for the complaint to be admissible, it had to have been made voluntarily (i.e., it should not have been elicited by questions of a leading and intimidating nature) and at the first reasonable opportunity that offers itself. Whether these conditions are satisfied is a question of fact depending on the circumstances of the case. This would include the character of the complainant and the relationship between the complainant and the person to whom she might have complained. In *R* v *Valentine* (1996) 2 Cr App R 213, the Court of Appeal recognised that some complainants might find it impossible to complain to the first person they encounter after the alleged attack. It is likely that if the statement was made by Patricia within a week of the alleged incident it will be admitted. (In *R* v *Birks* [2002] EWCA Crim 3091 a complaint made from six months to a year after the final attack in a series of sexual assaults was too long.) The requirement that the complaint has to be made voluntarily does not rule out the complaint being procured by questioning, but only where the questions are of a leading and intimidating manner. Thus questions such as 'Why are you crying?' would be permitted but not 'Did A sexually assault you?'. In *R* v *Osborne*, a complaint by a girl of 13 of an indecent assault to a friend was permitted where she was asked 'Why are you going home?'. This area is now covered by s. 120 of the **Criminal Justice Act 2003**. Section 120(4)(b) admits a statement which consists of a complaint made by a witness (whether to a person in authority or not) about conduct who claims to be a person against whom an offence has been committed. The statement must consist of a complaint made by the witness about conduct which would, if proved, constitute the offence or part of the offence, the complaint was made as soon as could reasonably be expected after the alleged conduct, it was not made as a result of a threat or a promise and before the statement is adduced the witness gives oral evidence in connection with its subject-matter. The section thus incorporates the common law approach on admissibility of recent complaints by alleged victims in sexual cases but extends it to all offences. Whilst giving evidence the witness must indicate that to the best of his belief he made the statement, and that to the best of his belief it states the truth.

On the facts of the present case, prima facie, it would appear that Patricia's complaint to her flatmate would be admissible, provided that it was made at the first reasonable opportunity that offers itself. There is nothing in the facts to suggest otherwise. The prosecution may rely on *R* v *Xhabri* [2005] EWCA Crim 3135. In this case the complainant alleged she had been raped and forced to work as a prostitute. She had made an number of telephone calls to her parents and others about her plight and the question was whether the evidence of the receivers of the calls could be received. At trial the judge allowed them in under s. 120(5) (previous identification), s. 120(6) (a fresh statement when the witness could not be expected to recall) and s. 120(7) (recent complaints).

The court held that s. 120(7) was rightly applied but not s. 120(5) and (6). The court also noted that the evidence could have been admitted under s. 114(1)(d). There was no conflict with art. 6. The hearsay provisions under the statute applied to both defence and prosecution and so the principle of the equality of arms was upheld. Article 6(3)(d) did not give a defendant an absolute right to examine every witness whose testimony was adduced against him. The touchstone was whether fairness of the trial required that in the present case almost all the hearsay evidence derived directly or indirectly from the complainant. She was available for cross-examination and so this satisfied the requirements of art. 6(3)(d).

In *R* v *O* [2006] 2 Cr App R 27, the Court of Appeal held that s. 120(7) allows more than one complaint to be admitted. It also stated that 'this is no longer a question of considering whether a complaint is made as soon as could be reasonably expected after the alleged complaint, which is a different test'. The complaint if admitted will be evidence of the truth of its contents, as an exception to the rule against hearsay.

(b) The first question to address is whether the prosecution is simply arguing that John should not be believed or whether it is alleging he has just made up this explanation. If it is the latter then the rule against the admissibility of previous consistent statements applies. In *R* v *Oyesiku* (1971) 56 Cr App R 240 it was held that a previous statement may be admissible to disprove the accusation. The purpose of bringing in the statement is to suggest that the prosecution is wrong to say that John had just made it up. The statement is not evidence of the truth of its contents but of the credibility of the witness (*R* v *Y* (1995) Crim LR 155). This area of law, however, has been changed by s. 120(2) **Criminal Justice Act 2003**. Admissibility is not affected. That is a matter for the judge. However, this status of the evidence is changed. It now becomes evidence 'of any matter stated of which oral evidence by the witness would be admissible'.

(c) The defence is also claiming that the complainant is making a false allegation and that she has made it before. Here s. 41 does not apply since making a false allegation is not 'sexual behaviour'. This was established in *R* v *MH* [2002] **Crim LR 73**. The Court of Appeal set out guidelines for questioning on false allegations in *R* v *C & B* [2003] EWCA 29. The defence should establish that the previous allegations were made and were false and that there is an evidentiary basis for the claim.

Then there is the question of whether the proof of falsity of the previous allegation is supported by evidence other than previous sexual behaviour. If proof of falsity requires questions on sexual behaviour, then s. 41 would apply. In *R* v *H* [2003] **EWCA Crim 2367** the court observed: 'However, it has been established that the fact that a complainant has fabricated allegations of sexual conduct in the past would not be prohibited by section 41(4) as the questions would not be about "sexual behaviour" but about lies.'

The court also referred to the danger of abuse:

> With regard to questioning about other complaints, *R* v *T and H* [2001] EWCA Crim 1877 indicates that, absent any basis for suggesting that such complaints were false, such questioning falls to be regarded as being 'about [the] sexual behaviour of the complainant'. The rationale, as we see it, must be that, if evidence is adduced about complaints which cannot properly be challenged as false, then the intention must be to elicit the other sexual behaviour or experience, the subject of such complaints, and so to deploy it in one way or another to the complainant's discredit,

e.g., by arguing that it has been wrongly transposed and attributed to the present defendant in the complainant's account . . . in order to get to first base to keep outside the section with regard to previous inconsistent statements defence counsel has to produce material that justifies cross-examining at all.

In *R* v *E* [2004] EWCA Crim 1313 there was held to be no evidential basis for cross-examination on previous allegedly false allegations. However, in *R* v *Garaxo (Shino)* [2005] EWCA Crim 1170 the Court of Appeal held that the trial judge should have allowed cross-examination on two previous allegations of sexual assault made by the complainant. Although the judge held there was insufficient evidence that these were untrue the Court of Appeal noted that, depending on the answers given by the complainant, a jury could have concluded the allegations had been false. If the defence wish to cross-examine on previous false allegations they may have to satisfy the conditions of s. 100 **Criminal Justice Act 2003**.

Thus whether s. 41 applies or not depends on the circumstances of the previous complaints which the defence claim have been made by Patricia. Section 41 of the **Youth Justice and Criminal Evidence Act 1999** provides that if at trial a person is charged with a sexual offence no evidence can be adduced nor questions asked in cross-examination about any sexual behaviour of the victim without leave of court. Section 41(2) makes it clear that the court will not grant leave unless it is satisfied that the evidence is of the kind specified in s. 41(3) which applies where the issue is other than consent, as is the case here. In *R* v *F* [2005] 1 WLR 2848 the Court of Appeal held that if the criteria for admissibility of evidence under s. 41 are found the judge has no discretion to exclude it.

Questions on Patricia's previous sexual history will not be allowed if the purpose of the proposed questioning is an attack on her credibility, s. 41(14). However, in *R* v *M* (2004) All ER (D) 103 the Court of Appeal held that if the purpose of the questions was supporting the denial of the offence as well as undermining the complainant's credibility, such questioning would not be excluded.

Question 4

Critically evaluate the extent to which s. 41 of the Youth Justice and Criminal Evidence Act 1999 addresses the shortcomings of s. 2 of the Sexual Offences (Amendment) Act 1976.

Commentary

Essay questions are not usually set on issues in the course of trial. One possible question however on this subject relates to the effect of the new s. 41 of the **Youth Justice and Criminal Evidence Act 1999,** which replaced s. 2 of the **Sexual Offences (Amendment) Act 1976**. Before attempting this question, students would be expected to be familiar with the background relating to both the Acts, including some knowledge of the Heilbron Committee Report of the Advisory Group on the Law of Rape (Cm 6352, 1975). It is important that students are able to demonstrate to the examiner a clear understanding of the Act and the courts' approach to this statutory provision. You should assess whether the **Human Rights Act 1998** has had an impact in this area.

Answer plan

- Background to operation of s. 2 **Sexual Offences (Amendment) Act 1976**
- Examination of *R* v *Viola* **(1982)**
- Academic comment, e.g., Temkin
- Analysis of s. 41 **YJCEA 1999**
- Judicial creativity—*R* v *A*
- Difficulty of achieving balance between rights of defendant and victim
- Effect of **Human Rights Act 1998**

Suggested answer

Section 2 of the **Sexual Offences (Amendment) Act 1976** was introduced as a result of the recommendations of the Heilbron Committee, which considered the issue of rape trials in 1975 (Report of the Advisory Group on the Law of Rape, Cm 6352, 1975). In this report the Heilbron Committee was critical of the use of sexual history evidence at common law, which allowed the victim to be cross-examined on her previous sexual relationships and evidence called to contradict her. This was especially so where it was alleged that the victim was a prostitute or was a person who was 'notorious for want of sexual chastity' or who had had prior consensual sexual relationships with the accused. The Committee recommended that limitations be put on this, which resulted in s. 2 of the 1976 Act. Parliament introduced a distinction between questions or evidence of the victim's sexual relationship with the accused and that of other men. In the latter, leave of court had to be obtained before the victim could be asked such questions.

Amongst the shortcomings in s. 2 of the 1976 Act, was that it allowed questions about the victim's sexual experience, where it was relevant to an issue at trial. An example of this is on the issue of consent: *R* v *Lawrence* [1977] **Crim LR 492** and *R* v *Viola* [1982] **3 All ER 73**. Temkin ([1993] Crim LR 3) criticised *Viola* in that it allowed evidence of sexual history, which she argues is scarcely relevant. She is of the view that the Court of Appeal in *Viola* attributed too much relevance and undue significance to such evidence. Further, the court's approach to s. 2 and the issue of leave was not necessarily consistent: *R* v *Barton* (1987) **85 Crim App R 5**, compared with *Viola*. In *Barton*, the court suggested that the judge's decision whether to grant leave was an exercise of the judge's discretion but in *Viola*, the court suggested that it was an exercise of the court's judgment. A significant body of comment (for example, Sue Lee's *Carnal Knowledge: Rape on Trial* (London, Penguin, 1996)) criticised the operation of s. 2 of the **Sexual Offences (Amendment) Act 1976**. Research showed that the cases which were the most difficult to prove were those where there had been some prior relationship between the complainant and the accused. A Home Office Research Study (Jessica Harris and Sharon Grace, 'A Question of Evidence? Investigating and Prosecuting Rape in the 1990s') showed that out of a sample of 500 complainants only 6% resulted in conviction for rape or attempted rape. There was a significant increase in the number of acquaintance and intimate rapes.

Section 2 of the 1976 Act has now been replaced by s. 41 of the **Youth Justice and Criminal Evidence Act 1999**. It applies to all sexual offences, not just rape as in the earlier law. This introduced broader provisions to this area of law and applies to any sexual offence as defined in s. 62 of the 1999 Act. It provides that if at trial a person is charged with a sexual offence, no evidence can be adduced nor question asked in cross-examination about any sexual behaviour of the victim except with the leave of the court. Section 41(2) makes it clear that the court will not grant leave, unless it is satisfied that the evidence is of a kind specified in s. 41(3) or (5), and a refusal of leave might render unsafe a conclusion of the jury on any relevant issues in the case. This is a very high test. Section 41(3) deals with evidence relevant to an issue in the case and a distinction is drawn between issues that are issues of consent and those that are not. Issues of consent essentially means the question as to whether the victim consented to the sexual conduct to which the accused is being tried. Subsection (5) relates to evidence that rebuts or explains any evidence adduced by the prosecution about any sexual behaviour of the victim.

There are two main differences between s. 41 of the 1999 Act and s. 2 of the 1976 Act. The first is that it does not draw a distinction between questions relating to the victim's sexual relationship with the accused and other men. The new statutory provision imposes a general prohibition against either type of evidence but allows such evidence to be adduced with leave of the court. The emphasis of s. 41 is on the relevance of the evidence in order for leave to be granted. Regardless of this, in most cases, the previous sexual relationship with the accused is arguably relevant to the issue of consent, whilst her relationship with other men will generally only be relevant in cases of false accusations or misidentification.

It is clear that s. 41(3)(b) and (c) has the effect of reversing the decision in *R* v *Riley* (1887) 18 QBD 481. Leave will be unlikely to be granted in rape cases for evidence to be adduced of the victim's sexual behaviour merely because there had been previous voluntary sexual intercourse between the accused and the victim. The complainant in a sexual case is protected further from the bad character provisions of s. 100 **Criminal Justice Act 2003** (see **Chapter 4**). The section 112(3)(b) provides that the statute doesn't affect the exclusion of evidence under s. 41 **YJCEA**.

Section 41(3) provides that where the issue is consent and s. 41(2) is satisfied, leave to adduce or cross-examine on previous sexual behaviour may be allowed in situations where it occurred at or about the same time as the event or is so similar to the event which forms the basis of the charge against the accused. Alternatively, such evidence is allowed because it is so similar to any behaviour which took place at or about the same time as the behaviour which is the subject-matter of the charge that it cannot be explained on the basis of a coincidence. The purpose of this is clearly to restrict evidence, which is relevant to the issue of whether there was consent. Section 41(4) clearly specifies that 'For the purposes of subsection (3) no evidence or question shall be regarded as relating to a relevant issue in the case if it appears to the court to be reasonable to assume that the purpose (or main purpose) for which it would be adduced or asked is to establish or elicit material for impugning the credibility of the complainant as a witness.' But it is not always possible to draw a clear distinction between relevance to an issue and relevance to credit. If the courts interpret these provisions literally then there is a danger that it may exclude evidence that is relevant.

The second main distinction is that s. 41 does not apply only to rape offences. The term 'sexual offence' as defined by s. 62 includes rape or burglary with intent to rape, unlawful sexual intercourse, indecent assault, forcible abduction, indecent conduct towards children and other offences. Thus, s. 41 will apply to cases where there is no issue of consent.

It should be noted that where leave of the court is granted for evidence of the victim's sexual history to be adduced, s. 41(6) makes it clear that only evidence of specific instances of sexual behaviour can be adduced. This prevents evidence of the victim's reputation for sexual behaviour from being brought in, thereby removing one of the excesses of the common law which allowed such evidence to be adduced.

One aspect of s. 41 where it is arguable that the court should be prepared to grant leave is in cases where s. 41(5) applies. This is where evidence of the victim's sexual history has been adduced by the prosecution. In such a case, the accused should be given leave to rebut or explain the evidence, although such instances where such evidence would be adduced by the prosecution would be rare.

One other aspect of s. 41 that is important is that s. 41(4) prevents evidence of sexual behaviour of the victim as a means of impeaching the credibility of the victim. This is clearly a welcome change to s. 2 of the 1976 Act, which was an issue that the court had difficulty in dealing with in *Viola*.

The changes introduced by s. 41 have been welcomed in many respects and they resolve a number of the problems prevalent in s. 2 of the 1976 Act. What remains unclear is whether the prohibition on the accused in adducing evidence of the victim's previous sexual behaviour contravenes the **Human Rights Act 1998**. It has been argued that the prohibition contained in s. 41 as well as the specific prohibition on cross-examination by the accused in person (ss. 34–39) contravenes the accused's right to a fair trial. This has yet to be resolved by the courts and developments in this area are awaited. The Government claimed that it had taken account of the Canadian case of *R* v *Seaboyer* [1991] 2 SCR 577, where a provision which allowed sexual history evidence only in limited and pre-determined circumstances was held to be a violation of the right of the accused to a fair trial. Many critics, however, are not convinced that the new sections will survive a challenge under art. 6 of the **European Convention on Human Rights**. The rape-shield provisions have now been reviewed by the Court of Appeal and the House of Lords.

In interpreting the new provisions the Court of Appeal has identified the difficulty of drawing the distinction between evidence of previous consensual sexual activity between the parties adduced to demonstrate that the complainant in fact consented to sexual intercourse and evidence going to the defendant's belief in the complainant's consent. This quite artificial distinction is a consequence of s. 41. The Court of Appeal came close to ridiculing this provision in *R* v *Y (Sexual offence: Complainant's sexual history), The Times,* 13 **February 2001**. It took the view that if the section required the judge to sum-up on the basis that evidence was admissible as to the defendant's belief in the complainant's consent but inadmissible as to whether she had in fact consented, his remarks would have more the flavour of Lewis Carroll than a rehearsal of matters of jurisprudence. The court also took issue with the view that previous recent sexual intercourse between complainant and defendant in a trial for rape was irrelevant as to whether the complainant had consented to intercourse in the alleged rape. It was common sense that a person, whether male or female, who had previously had sexual intercourse with the defendant might, on the occasion in dispute, have consented to sexual intercourse with the defendant. The Court did not accept that such an approach stemmed from a sexist view of women. It seemed to reflect human nature. The trial process would be unduly distorted if the jury were precluded from knowing, if it were the case, that the complainant and the defendant had recently taken part in sexual activity with each other and it might be that a fair trial would not be possible if there could not be adduced in support of the defence on consent, evidence as to the complainant's recent sexual activity with the defendant.

Arguably, the statute is an instance where the desire to balance the rights of defendants and victims has tipped the scales too heavily and jeopardises the integrity of the criminal trial.

The issue was referred to the House of Lords (see *R* v *A (No. 2)* [2001] 2 **WLR 1546**). Lord Steyn pointed out that, 'The genesis of the problem before the House was that s. 41 imposed identical exclusionary provisions in respect of a complainant's sexual experiences with the accused as with other men.' This posed 'an acute problem of proportionality'. The House concluded that it was a matter for the trial judge in each case to actually determine whether or not the evidence was sufficiently probative to merit admission. In a judgment which showed the impact of the **Human Rights Act,** it declared that since ordinary canons of statutory interpretation of s. 41 did not allow admission of such evidence, the section should be interpreted in the light of s. 3 of the **Human Rights Act 1998** to allow compliance with the provisions of art. 6.

In a unanimous judgment a number of the speeches indicated that excluding such evidence might jeopardise the fairness of the trial. Lord Steyn declared that evidence may be 'so relevant to the issue of consent that to exclude it would endanger the fairness of the trial'. It is indeed the case that relevance depends on context and that legislating too narrowly on it may be unwise. The House of Lords addressed the problem by stretching the interpretation of s. 41(3)(c) to allow questioning on the previous sexual encounter. They applied s. 3 of the **Human Rights Act 1998,** which as Lord Steyn put it 'requires the court to subordinate the niceties of the language of s. 41(3)(c) and in particular, the touchstone of coincidence, to broader considerations of relevance judged by logical and common sense criteria of time and circumstances'.

Kibble (2005 p. 263) sees judicial discretion as the core issue. He writes: 'A cornerstone of much critical discussion in this area has been the argument that judicial discretion to admit evidence of prior sexual history is the core of the problem and the demand that as far as possible such discretion be eliminated.' He points out that the non-discretionary approach has been rejected in other jurisdictions and argues that 'a reasonable measure' of judicial discretion must be preserved.

Thus while Temkin, by contrast, calls for a more purist approach to s. 41, others see the provisions as too mechanical, although *R* v *A* went some way to allow judicial discretion to include prior sexual history of the complainant.

As Roberts and Zuckerman suggest (at p. 272) 'Prevailing wisdom among commentators and even according to senior members of the judiciary is that s. 2(1) of the 1976 Act was an abject failure.' But they said 'it would be cavalier revisionist history to write off the whole exercise as an unmitigated disaster'. The experience of the reformed law suggests that the changes may have addressed some problems but also generated new ones. The court's approach has been criticised as unprincipled by a number of commentators (see McEwen (2001, p. 257)). Some commentators suggest that the reasoning is tortuous and that a declaration of incompatibility would have been preferable. Others, such as Cook, argue that the purpose behind the Act is undermined to the detriment of complainants. The main problem is that the defence must convince the court to allow leave to question about any previous sexual behaviour of the complainant. There is a high test for admissibility, since the court must be convinced that the evidence is relevant within the terms of the Act or probative enough that a failure to admit it might result in a miscarriage of justice. In practice the courts appear to have applied *R* v *A* in a well-reasoned way. Thus in *R* v *Richardson* [2003] EWCA Crim 2754 the Court of Appeal held that a narrow interpretation of s. 41(3)(c) would be unfair and quashed a conviction where the trial judge had not permitted cross-examination about a continuing sexual relationship between the complainant and defendant.

Thus, in conclusion, although arguments in favour of s. 41 may be understandable it is arguable that a heavy-handed interference with judicial discretion on such a key issue as relevance is inimical to justice. An alternative approach might be to continue to enhance procedural protection for vulnerable witnesses (as in Special Measures Directions, which do not take away rights from the defendant).

Kelly, Temkin and Griffiths, in the Home Office Report on the operation of this law, give some figures on applications under s. 41. Defence applications were made in one-quarter of the trials studied and two-thirds were granted. More applications were made where a pre-existing relationship between the complainant and the defendant is claimed and these applications were granted more often.

Dennis (2006, p. 869) comments, 'Defence lawyers do not generally come well out of this report; they are accused at various points of evading the legislation by not making necessary applications, or flouting the judges' rulings, or of using devious ploys to attack the complainant's credibility in contravention of s. 41(4). Such judgments will inevitably be contested.' Dennis acknowledges, however, that 'there is clearly still scope for improvement, even if one does not support the authors' recommendations for further tightening of the section'.

It remains to be established that the evidential changes in sexual cases have produced the increase in convictions which their supporters anticipated.

Additional Reading

Adler, Z., *Rape on Trial* (Routledge, 1987).

Birch, D., 'A Better Deal for Vulnerable Witnesses' (2000) Crim LR 223.

Birch, D., 'Rethinking Sexual History Evidence: Proposals for Fairer Trials' (2002) Crim LR 531.

Cook, K., 'Sexual History Evidence: The Defendant Fights Back' (2001) 151 NLJ 1133.

Dennis, I., 'Sexual History Evidence: Evaluating Section 41' (2006) Crim LR 869.

Durston, G., 'Cross-examination of Rape Complainants: Ongoing Tensions Between Conflicting Priorities in the Criminal Justice System' (1998) 62 J Crim Law 91.

Durston, G., 'Previous (In)Consistent Statements' [2005] Crim LR 206.

Hoyano, L.C.H., 'Striking a Balance between the Rights of Defendants and Vulnerable Witnesses: Will Special Measures Directions Contravene Guarantees of a Fair Trial?' (2001) Crim LR 948.

Kelly, L., Temkin, J., and Griffiths, S. (2006); 'Section 41: An Evaluation of New Legislation Limiting Sexual History Evidence in Rape Trials', Home Office Online Report 20/06, London: Home Office.

Kibble, N., 'The Sexual History Provisions: Charting a Course Between Inflexible Legislative Rules and Wholly Untrammelled Judicial Discretion' [2000] Crim LR 274.

Kibble, N., 'Judicial Perspectives on the Operation of s. 41' [2005] Crim LR 190, 263.

McColgan, A., 'Common Law and the Relevance of Sexual History Evidence' (1996) 16 OJLS 275.

McEwan, J., 'In Defence of Vulnerable Witnesses: The Youth Justice and Criminal Evidence Act 1999' (2000) 4 E&P 1.

Mirfield, P., 'Human Wrongs?' (2002) 117 LQR 20.

Naffine, N., 'Possession: Erotic Love in the Law of Rape' (1994) 57 MLR 10.

Temkin, J., *Rape and the Legal Process* (OUP, 1987).

Temkin, J., 'Prosecuting and Defending Rape: Perspectives for the Bar' (2000) 27 Journal of Law and Society 219.

Young, G., 'The Sexual History Provisions in the Youth Justice and Criminal Evidence Act 1999—A Violation of the Right to a Fair Trial' (2001) 41 Med Sci Law 217.

11

Privilege and public policy

Introduction

You will have realised by now that a great deal of the law of evidence deals with the exclusion of material from court. Thus, the rule against hearsay excludes evidence primarily because of the fear of adducing inferior albeit relevant evidence. This chapter deals with evidence which is excluded for wider public interest considerations. A party or witness or even a non-participant in the proceedings may refuse to disclose information, papers or answer questions even though such material may have a high degree of relevance and reliability.

Exclusion on the basis of privilege should be distinguished from that based on a broader public policy justification, generally called public interest immunity. There are several privileges to consider, though you may take comfort from Murphy's observation (2008, at p. 447) that they are 'few and limited'. They are: the privilege against self-incrimination; legal professional privilege; 'without prejudice' statements; and a limited privilege for journalists' sources. Not all of these are taught in all Evidence courses. The existence of the privilege means that a person is not in contempt of court for refusing to disclose information coming under this head and no adverse inferences may be drawn. These species of private privilege only exist if they are claimed by the party or witness seeking to rely on them. They may be waived accidentally or purposely by the party but not by the court. The latter will, however, consider whether the privilege exists and the appropriate extent of it. The courts accept that abrogation of these privileges can only be made by statute, but nonetheless there is considerable scope for judicial definition of limits.

The areas which are most likely to occur in Evidence courses are privilege against self-incrimination and legal professional privilege. The former includes the right to silence of the defendant (see **Chapter 6**) and the compellability of witnesses (see **Chapter 3**). The privilege against self-incrimination generally is upheld by common law. In *R* v *Director of the Serious Fraud Office, ex parte Smith* [1993] AC 1, at p. 30, Lord Mustill identified the constituent parts of the privilege and it may be helpful for you to remind yourself of this clear account:

(1) A general immunity, possessed by all persons and bodies, from being compelled on pain of punishment to answer questions posed by other persons or bodies.

(2) A general immunity, possessed by all persons and bodies, from being compelled on pain of punishment to answer questions the answers to which may incriminate them.

(3) A specific immunity, possessed by all persons under suspicion of criminal responsibility whilst being interviewed by police officers or others in similar positions of authority, from being compelled on pain of punishment to answer questions of any kind.

(4) A specific immunity, possessed by accused persons undergoing trial, from being compelled to give evidence, and from being compelled to answer questions put to them in the dock.

(5) A specific immunity, possessed by persons who have been charged with a criminal offence, from having questions material to the offence addressed to them by police officers or persons in a similar position of authority.

(6) A specific immunity (at least in certain circumstances, which it is unnecessary to explore), possessed by accused persons undergoing trial, from having adverse comment made on any failure
   (a) to answer questions before the trial, or
   (b) to give evidence at the trial.

In *Derby Magistrates Court, ex parte B* [1996] AC 487, 507, Lord Taylor of Gosforth CJ stated the rationale for the privilege:

> The principle which runs though all these cases, and the many other cases which were cited, is that a man must be able to consult his lawyers in confidence, since otherwise he might hold back half the truth. A client must be sure that what he tells his lawyer in confidence will never be revealed without his consent. Legal professional privilege is thus much more than an ordinary rule of evidence, limited in its application to the facts of a particular case. It is a fundamental condition on which the administration of justice as a whole rests.

In a later decision of the House of Lords, in *Re L (a Minor)* [1996] 2 WLR 395, *Ex parte B* was distinguished on the basis that what was decided in that case about the absolute nature of legal professional privilege related only to legal advice privilege. Controversially, the House decided that care proceedings under Part IV of the **Children Act 1989** were 'essentially non-adversarial in their nature' and so litigation privilege did not apply.

Lord Taylor there outlined the public interest in the privilege:

> But it is not for the sake of the applicant alone that the privilege must be upheld. It is in the wider interests of all those hereafter who might otherwise be deterred from telling the whole truth to their solicitors. For this reason I am of the opinion that no exception should be allowed to the absolute nature of legal professional privilege, once established.

In *Three Rivers District Council* v *Bank of England (No. 6)* [2004] UKHL 48 the House of Lords made it clear that legal advice has a broad definition. The issue was the relationship of any communication to the relevant legal complex.

The importance of legal professional privilege has been acknowledged in a number of cases. In *General Mediterranean Holdings SA* v *Patel* [2000] 1 WLR 272 the House held that it overrode rule 48.7(3) of the **Civil Procedure Rules 1997,** which covers evidential issues determining a wasted costs application. The argument, however, that fair trial rights are maintained even where the accused was denied access to another person's privileged material has been questioned. Emson writes (p. 363), '. . . there can be little doubt that to deny the accused access to cogent (and otherwise admissible) evidence on the ground that it is privileged will on occasion result in a violation of article 6(1)'.

You should note that the privilege is subject to a number of statutory exceptions, although some statutes put limits to the use to which any information revealed may be put in criminal proceedings and this is influenced also by the requirements of Article 6 ECHR. Legal professional privilege is primarily a case-law subject. It is also implied into Article 6 of the ECHR.

As Murphy points out (2008, p. 410):

> The privileges against self-incrimination and compelled disclosure of confidential communications between lawyer and client are recognised generally in common law jurisdictions, including England. But in other respects English law maintains an illiberal attitude to confidential communications. The law has failed to accord recognition to other privileges which American common law has generally upheld, for example the privileges against compelled disclosure of confidential communication between doctor and psychotherapist and patient.

He points out that, on the other hand, Article 10 of the ECHR has had some effect on this area, allowing a limited privilege for journalists with respect to their sources of information (**Contempt of Court Act 1981**, s. 10).

Exclusion of evidence on grounds of public interest immunity arises where the court, not the parties or witnesses, accepts a duty of non-disclosure for the public good. Primarily, the issue is one of non-disclosure of documents rather than oral testimony. The original objection to the disclosure may be made by the court itself or by any person or body including government departments, even though not taking part in the proceedings. The court will itself scrutinise the claim. There is some conflict of authority on whether the immunity can be waived, though the prevailing view seems to be that this depends on the nature of the document. Those whose disclosure would endanger national security, for example, probably fall outside the category of those that can be waived, whereas those protecting confidentiality in order to promote candour, could fall inside. In fact, public interest immunity claims are more often made in civil litigation. The *Matrix Churchill* trial highlighted the difficulties of applying the doctrine in criminal cases.

Commentators generally agree that the law has been unsatisfactory. Even after the Attorney General's guidelines publication of the disclosure was in the hands of the prosecution, the court did not usually make a ruling, and the defence were often unaware of what had not been disclosed. *R* v *Ward* [1993] 1 WLR 619 was a very important decision. As a result the prosecution, if it sought to claim public interest immunity, had to give notice so the court could be asked to rule on the legitimacy of the claim (see also *R* v *Davis* (1993) 1 WLR 613, which modified *R* v *Ward*). Disclosure was put on a statutory footing in the **Criminal Procedure and Investigations Act 1996**, amended by the **Criminal Justice Act 2003**.

Non-disclosure on grounds of public interest immunity may be requested by the parties or by the court. Non-disclosure has been ordered on the grounds that the document falls into a particular 'class' which should not be revealed. The Report of the Inquiry into the Export of Defence Equipment and Dual-Use Goods to Iraq and Related Prosecutions (the Scott Inquiry) criticised the use of class claims even in relation to national security. As a result in 1996 the Lord Chancellor issued a statement that government departments would no longer seek non-disclosure simply on the grounds that the documents fell into a particular class. One controversial recent development is the use of special counsel in cases where it would be against the public interest to disclose details of application to the defendant; see *R* v *H* [2004] 2 WLR 335 and *Edwards and Lewis* v *UK* (2005) 40 EHRR 24. The **Freedom of Information Act 2000** contains a number of exemptions from the general duty of disclosure analogous to public interest immunity circumstances. Examples of areas where public policy may require non-disclosure of evidence in court include: national security; defence and foreign policy; the identity of police informers; protection of children; and confidential records held by public bodies. You should have at least an outline knowledge of the procedure for non-disclosure of documents. In civil cases it is covered by rule 31.19 (1) of the **Civil Procedure Rules** and in criminal cases the common law was incorporated into statutory rules under the **Criminal Procedure and Investigations Act 1996** and is now to be found in the **Criminal Procedure Rules 2005**.

Question 1

Emily is suing Heathcliff Translation Services for failure to deliver the translation of her novel. Rochester, a Heathcliff employee, is refusing to respond to interrogatories because he fears his involvement in submitting invoices for work that had not been done may expose him and his wife to fraud charges. Rosa, Rochester's wife, worked as a secretary for Heathcliff. At the same time Heathcliff is subject to investigation by the (imaginary) Translators Regulatory Body (TRB), an organisation set up under statute. The TRB argue that Heathcliff do not comply with their minimum standards. The TBA has statutory powers for their inspectors to examine documents and records. Carlye, the owner of Heathcliff, at first refuses to allow an inspection, claiming his privilege against self-incrimination, but he then allows, he search to go ahead. Inspectors examine Carlyle's computers and find evidence of both child pornography and fraudulent business practices. Carlyle asks his lawyer for advice on whether he can prevent the material being handed to the police. James, who works in the lawyers' offices, and who is Emily's brother, sends her a copy. Emily wants to use aspects of the document as part of her case against Heathcliff.
    Advise the parties.

Commentary

You have a clue that this question involves privilege in the reference in the question to refusing to give evidence. A more complex question is refusal to allow inspection of documents. This area has a close affinity with that covered in Chapter 6 in relation to inferences drawn from silence, but here we are looking at the privilege in relation to civil proceedings. The issue has aroused some recent controversy, which makes it a likely examination question. The second part of the question deals with another head of privilege, namely legal professional privilege between lawyer and client: you need to trace carefully the stages whereby privilege may be threatened but then possibly reclaimed.

Answer plan

- Privilege against self-incrimination in civil proceedings— see *R* v *Director of the Serious Fraud Office, ex parte Smith* (1993); *C Plc* v *P (Attorney-General intervening)* [2007] 3 **WLR** 437
- Does application of privilege deprive the claimant of her remedy?—see *AT&T Istel* v *Tully* (1993)
- Impact of **Human Rights Act 1998**— **Saunders** v **UK**
- Legal professional privilege may apply to note of discussion between Carlyle and company lawyer but does not apply to copies
- Possibility of *Asburton* v *Pape* (1913) injunction

Suggested answer

These are civil proceedings and Rochester and Carlyle are seeking to exercise the privilege against self-incrimination. The privilege is based on common law and is acknowledged in s. 14(1) **Civil Evidence Act 1968**. This states: '(1) The right of a person in any legal proceedings to refuse to answer any question or produce any document or thing if to do so would tend to expose that person to proceedings for an offence or for the recovery of a penalty—. . .(b) shall include a like right to refuse to answer any question or produce any document or thing if to do so would tend to expose the husband or wife of that person to proceedings for any such criminal offence or for the recovery of any such penalty.'

The privilege which they seek to exercise is the second of the six aspects identified by Lord Mustill giving the House of Lords judgment in *R* v *Director of Serious Fraud Office, ex parte Smith* [1993] AC 1, 30: 'A general immunity, possessed by all persons and bodies, from being compelled on pain of punishment to answer questions the answers to which may incriminate them.' The justification for the existence of the privilege, according to Lord Templeman in *AT&T Istel Ltd* v *Tully* [1993] AC 45, is first that it discourages the ill-treatment of a suspect and second that it discourages the production of dubious confessions.

The scope of the privilege was set out by the Court of Appeal in *Blunt* v *Park Lane Hotel* [1942] 2 KB 253, 257 per Goddard LJ:

> The rule is that no one is bound to answer any question if the answer thereto would, in the opinion of the judge, have a tendency to expose the deponent to any criminal charge, penalty or forfeiture which the judge regards as reasonably likely to be preferred or sued for.

Its scope was limited in civil proceedings by the **Civil Evidence Act 1968**, which provides by s. 14(1) that:

> The right of a person in any legal proceedings other than criminal proceedings to refuse to answer any question or produce any document or thing if to do so would tend to expose that person to proceedings for an offence or for the recovery of a penalty— (a) shall apply only as regards criminal offences under the law of any part of the United Kingdom and penalties provided for by such law.

Dealing first with the refusal to respond to interrogatories, it is for Rochester to persuade the judge that the privilege should apply because his answers might expose him and Rosa to criminal proceedings. Thus in *Rank Film Distribution Ltd* v *Video Information Centre* [1982] AC 380, the House of Lords upheld the claim for privilege because there was a real danger of a criminal charge of conspiracy to defraud against the defendant.

A consideration which will be relevant to Hardacre is how far the application of the privilege may restrict the recovery of money or property by Emily. The House of Lords in *AT&T Istel Ltd* v *Tully* [1993] AC 45 established that there is no reason to allow a defendant in civil proceedings to rely on it, thus depriving a claimant of his rights, where the defendant's own protection can be secured in other ways. As Lord Templeman said (at p. 53):

> It is difficult to see any reason why in civil proceedings the privilege against self-incrimination should be exercisable so as to enable a litigant to refuse relevant and even vital documents which are in his possession or power and which speak for themselves.

Referring to the defendant, Lord Templeman said:

> . . .Mr Tully would be entitled to rely on [the privilege against self-incrimination] if but only if and so far as compliance with the order of Buckley J would provide evidence against him in a criminal trial. There is no reason why the privilege should be blatantly exploited to deprive the plaintiffs of their civil right and remedies if the privilege is not necessary to protect Mr Tully.

In that case a plaintiff was making a claim for damages and repayment of money obtained by fraud. At the same time, a police investigation was set up. The plaintiffs were granted orders requiring the defendants to disclose all dealings concerning the money. The order contained a condition that it would not be used in the prosecution of a criminal offence. The order was later varied and the plaintiff appealed against the variation. The House of Lords varied the order after the Crown Prosecution Service gave an informal assurance that it would not seek to use the divulged material. Thus, if here the judge were assured that the answers would not be relied on in criminal proceedings, there might be no obstacle to the requirement that Rochester answer the questions.

If no such undertaking had been given by the Crown Prosecution Service, Rochester's failure to answer questions involves then a clash between two principles, namely the duty to testify and the privilege against self-incrimination. Ng (2008 p. 152) points out that 'When we examine claims to privilege we start with the primary assumption that there is a general duty to give what testimony one is capable of giving and that any exception is a derogation from he general rule. This is in line with the legal proposition that the privilege attaches to a witness rather than to the evidence itself.' The question then arises as to whether Emily will succeed in getting an order to compel Rochester to answer, violation of which would be contempt of court. There is no indication that the statute in this case has abolished the privilege. The privilege, therefore, if it applied here, would also cover answers to questions which might tend to implicate Rosa.

In *Versailles Trade Finance Ltd* v *Clough* [2001] **EWCA Civ 1509** the court stressed the need to bear in mind the interests of the claimant, as well as the potential unfairness to the reluctant witness should a criminal trial take place. Whether Rochester was ordered to respond or not would therefore depend on the likelihood of his facing a criminal trial and the extent of the potential prejudice should he do so.

Carlyle and Rochester should be aware, however, that the privilege has been subject to judicial criticism. In *Tully* Lord Templeman stated (at p. 53): 'I regard the privilege against self-incrimination exercisable in civil proceedings as an archaic and unjustifiable survival from the past when the court directs the production of relevant documents and requires the defendant to specify his dealings with the plaintiff's property or money.'

Recent case-law suggests that Carlyle may be on particularly weak ground in resisting disclosure of the material found as a result of the search. In *C Plc* v *P* (*Attorney-General intervening*) the Court of Appeal drew a distinction between response to questions and 'independent' evidence. In this case a search order issued to discover materials relating to copyright infringement unexpectedly revealed child pornography. The court stated (at p. 34): 'The privilege can be invoked to refuse to answer interrogatories or to refuse to disclose matters which are ordinarily discoverable; those matters may be documents or other "things", but independent matters coming to light in the course of executing a proper order of the court are in an altogether different category.'

The pornography could therefore be handed to the police. Carlyle is likely to be the subject of a police investigation.

The third issue in the problem involves the note of the discussion between Carlyle and the company lawyer. Legal professional privilege attaches to certain communications between lawyer and client provided the purpose of the consultation is not the furtherance of crime. Though it is a common law privilege, its scope is authoritatively said to be summarised by s. 10 of the **Police and Criminal Evidence Act 1984**. The House of Lords so held in *R* v *Central Criminal Court, ex* *parte Francis & Francis* [1989] AC 346. Carlyle is seeking immunity for communications with the lawyer for the purpose of giving or receiving advice. The fact that the lawyer is employed by the company does not exclude his communications from the scope of the privilege. However, copies of the communications are not privileged: *Calcraft* v *Guest* [1898] 1 QB 759. But until they are actually before the court, Carlyle could be granted an injunction to restrain the use of the documents, which were clearly obtained in breach of confidence as the Court of Appeal held in **Lord Ashburton** v **Pape** [1913] 2 Ch 469. However, Carlyle may not need to apply for an injunction. Rule 31.20 of the **Civil Procedure Rules 1998** allows such documents to be used only with permission of the court. Hence, when Emily seeks to use the document, Carlyle may be able to object to its use on the ground of privilege.

Question 2

Brenda is charged with unlawful possession of pornographic photographs discovered after a legally conducted police raid on her flat. Her defence is that they were sent through the post to her unsolicited and she, although disgusted and puzzled, had put them on one side and had forgotten to destroy them. She noted that they purported to be from an organisation called the Partners Exchange. She recalls that her neighbour Archie who had made several unwelcome sexual advances to her had mentioned that he belonged to the Partners Exchange, which he said arranged 'interesting introductions'. Having spurned his advances she thought no more of the matter but now she suspects that Archie, who was known to the police as a drug user, may have sent the mail and then informed on her.

Advise Brenda.

Commentary

English law has long protected the anonymity of informants in matters relating to public prosecutions, or civil proceedings arising from them. There is clearly a public interest in protecting such sources because the information might otherwise dry up. There is a presumption of non-disclosure and it is for the accused to show there is good reason, arising from the defence case, to breach it. In these instances the court must, as in all cases involving public interest immunity, balance the rights of the accused against any countervailing public interest in protection of sources. In this question, as in all practical questions, you should state the basic rule, citing if you can authority to back up your point. Then you look at possible exceptions to the principle of protection and consider the question of fact in this case, namely would disclosure help the defendant's case?

Answer plan

- Rule on naming informers— *Marks* v *Beyfus* (1890); *Conway* v *Rimmer* (1968)
- Duty of disclosure— *R* v *Ward* (1993)
- **Criminal Procedure and Investigation Act 1996,** as amended by the **CJA 2003**
- Issue is will identity of informer contribute to issue before the jury? See *R* v *Slowcombe* (1991)
- Article 6 case-law

Suggested answer

A long-established rule prevents witnesses being asked, or answering, questions about the names of informers or the nature of the information given. The rule applies to criminal proceedings. It has been acknowledged that in criminal proceedings the identity of police informers may be excluded if the public interest requires it. This applies as long as the information is not necessary to establish guilt. Lord Esher MR stated in *Marks* v *Beyfus* (1890) 25 QBD 494, at p. 498: 'If upon the trial of a prisoner the judge should be of the opinion that the disclosure . . . is not necessary or right in order to shew the prisoner's innocence, then one public policy is in conflict with another public policy and that which says that an innocent man is not to be condemned when his innocence can be proved is the policy that must prevail.' The rationale of the rule was explained by Lord Reid in *Conway* v *Rimmer* [1968] AC 910, 953: 'The police are carrying on an unending war with criminals many of whom are today highly intelligent. So it is essential there should be no disclosure of anything which might give any useful information to those who organise criminal activities.' However, *R* v *Ward* [1993] 1 WLR 619 placed the prosecution under an obligation to disclose to the defence all the material on which the prosecution is based. In *R* v *Horseferry Road Magistrates' Court, ex parte Bennett (No. 2)* [1994] 1 All ER 289 the Divisional Court set out the procedure the Crown should follow for voluntary disclosure of documents in criminal cases. This area is now covered by the **Criminal Procedure and Investigation Act 1996**. Section 21(2) preserves the common law rules as to whether disclosure is in the public interest. It is for the courts to decide what should not be disclosed. The prosecution must thus assert a claim to public interest immunity if evidence of the identity of informers is to be excluded.

Under the **Criminal Procedure and Investigations Act 1996** primary disclosure must be made under s. 3(1)(a) of any prosecution material which has not previously been disclosed to the accused and which in the prosecutor's opinion might undermine the case for the prosecution against the accused. Secondary disclosure under s. 7(2)(a) is to be made following delivery of a defence statement, of previously undisclosed material which might be reasonably expected to assist the accused's defence. The **Criminal Justice Act 2003** amended s. 3(1)(a) so as to require primary disclosure of any previously undisclosed material 'which might reasonably be considered capable of undermining the case for the prosecution against the accused or of assisting the case for the accused'.

The prosecution is placed under an obligation to reveal first any evidence that might undermine the prosecution case and, later, information which assists the defence case. The **Criminal Justice Act 2003** has changed the pre-trial disclosure regime, making new demands on defence and prosecution. The procedure differs according to the sensitivity of the material. The judge may hear an application for disclosure either **inter partes,** or in extremely sensitive cases **ex parte.** On the facts this would appear not to be a situation which required the defence counsel to be present. A procedure introduced under the **Special Immigration Appeals Commission Act 1997** allows for the appointment of an independent special counsel, who will be shown the disputed evidence but may not communicate it to the defendant or his legal advisers. This way of dealing with the awkward problems posed by disclosure is likely to become more widespread, though its unsatisfactory nature is obvious enough.

Where the revelation of the existence of an informer would otherwise require the abandonment of the prosecution, application can be made *ex parte* by the Crown without notice to the defence: *R* v *Davis* **[1993] 1 WLR 613.** The court will normally exclude evidence of an informer's identity, but where the judge is of the opinion that disclosure is necessary to establish the accused's innocence, it is a rule of law that the judge must allow the question to be asked and require an answer: *Marks* v *Beyfus* **(1890) 25 QBD 494.** It is for the accused to show that there is good reason to expect that disclosure is necessary to establish his innocence. This should normally be done before the trial in proceedings to set aside a witness summons or subpoena for the appropriate Crown witness: *R* v *Hennessy* **(1978) 68 Cr App R 419.** Brenda may rely on *R* v *Agar* **(1989) 90 Cr App R 318,** where it was held on appeal that disclosure of the name of an informer in a drugs case was necessary where the defendant claimed to have been set up by the informer and the police acting together. In reaching its decision whether to allow disclosure, the court can take into account the informer's willingness to be named, but this is not conclusive: *Savage* v *Chief Constable of Hampshire* **[1997] 1 WLR 1061.**

Here, Brenda is claiming that Archie framed her and not just that he informed. In *R* v *Slowcombe* **[1991] Crim LR 198,** where the identity of the informer would have contributed little or nothing to the issue before the jury, disclosure was refused. If Brenda is able to put up some evidence that Archie did set the police onto her, the jury may well conclude that her story may be true, so her counsel should be permitted to ask the police whether Archie was the informant. The association with the Partners Exchange may well be relevant evidence and lead to an inference of Archie's involvement. If Archie was not the informer, the police would not be required to name the informer, however, and the jury would be asked to believe Brenda's case without that knowledge.

Brenda may find some support in the principle of the right to a fair trial enshrined in Article 6(1) ECHR. The Strasbourg Court had discussed the issue in a number of cases, including *Rowe* and *Davis* v *UK* (2000) 30 EHRR 1, *Jasper* v *UK* (2000) 30 EHRR 441 and *Fitt* v *UK* (2000) 30 EHRR 480. In *Fitt* v *UK* (para. 45) the following observation was made:

> The entitlement to disclosure of relevant evidence is not an absolute right. In any criminal proceedings there may be competing interests, such as national security or the need to protect witnesses at risk of reprisals or keep secret police methods of investigation of crime, which must be weighed against the rights of the accused. In some cases it may be necessary to withhold certain evidence from the defence so as to preserve the fundamental rights of another individual or to safeguard an important public interest. However, only such measures restricting the rights of the defence which are strictly necessary are permissible under Article 6(1). Moreover in order to ensure that the accused receives a fair trial, any difficulties caused to the defence by a limitation on its rights must be sufficiently counterbalanced by the procedures followed by the judicial authorities.

Brenda may be assisted by the House of Lords ruling in *R* v *H*, *R* v *C* [2003] **UKHL 3,** where the House set out the procedure to be followed when the prosecution refuses to disclose evidence on the grounds of public interest. It held that: 'In considering any disclosure issue the trial judge had to constantly bear in mind the overriding principle that derogation from the principle of full disclosure had always to be the minimum necessary to protect the public interest in question and must never imperil the overall fairness of the trial.' It considered also the possibility of partial disclosure and the option of discontinuing the prosecution in order to avoid making a disclosure.

Question 3

The social services department of the Henfield Borough Council have applied to the court for an order placing Gertrude's children into care. She wishes to bring into evidence a tape recording of a meeting held at the Henfield Borough Council's Family Unit attended by Gertrude and a number of other parents. She argues that the tape recording demonstrates that the children were happy when they were with her. Henfield Borough Council refuses to allow the tape to be admitted into evidence on the grounds of public interest immunity. The council want to call Gertrude's husband, Fred, to give evidence at the hearing.

Advise Gertrude.

How would your advice differ if Gertrude is facing criminal charges arising from the same facts?

Commentary

This is straightforward question about public interest immunity (PII). It is important that you show that you are aware that public interest immunity can also apply to bodies other than government bodies. As Lord Hailsham remarked in **D** v **NSPCC** **[1978] AC 171**, 'the categories of public interest are not closed and must alter from time to time whether by restriction or extension as social conditions and social legislation develop' (at p. 230). You should also explain the different approaches of the courts according to whether the proceedings are civil or criminal. The reference to the calling of Fred requires you to consider the privilege against self-incrimination in relation to spouses.

Answer plan

- Difference between Public Interest Immunity and other types of privilege
- Rules on disclosure
- Confidentiality and tape-recording—see **Campbell** v **Tameside** (1982)
- Public Interest Immunity in criminal cases
- Art. 6 consideration—see **Rowe and Davis** v **UK** (2000)

Suggested answer

Certain types of evidence, though relevant, are not admissible because their disclosure is held to infringe a public interest. The so-called public interest immunity differs from other types of privilege. The judge of his own motion can exclude the evidence if he thinks the public interest so demands: *Conway* v *Rimmer* [1968] AC 910. The court made it clear that in reaching this decision, it had to balance the interests of the parties in order to decide whether to withhold or to compel disclosure. Public interest immunity can apply where the party concerned is not a central government department, as the House of Lords held in *D* v *NSPCC* [1978] AC 171.

A party seeking disclosure must show that he or she has a legitimate interest in seeking disclosure. Under r. 31.6 of the **Civil Procedure Rules 1998** a party must disclose all relevant documents. Under r. 31.17(3), an order for disclosure can be made only where the documents or the evidence, in relation to which disclosure is sought, are likely to support the case of the applicant or adversely affect the case of one of the other parties. Further, the disclosure must be necessary to fairly dispose of the claim or to save costs.

There is no doubt that the tape recording of the meeting is capable of being subject to public interest immunity. The argument for non-disclosure is likely to be that the workings of the social services department should be kept secret so that people will deal with them in confidence. There appears to be less force in the argument here, because the tape records a meeting in which Gertrude herself took part, but the Council may be worried that future participants may not want to take part if the tape recordings may be admitted as evidence. In *Campbell* v *Tameside MBC* [1982] QB 1065, the Court of Appeal was presented with an application for public interest immunity concerning records of a local education authority, but upheld their disclosure since they were necessary for the plaintiff's case. The records here concerned children and the courts have frequently held such records to be protected from disclosure because there is an important public interest in keeping confidential this sensitive work. It is possible that the interests of the children rather than those of Gertrude will be paramount. However, even if the courts acknowledge on inspection that public interest immunity applies, it is arguable that it is open to them to accept a waiver, although there is no clear authority on this. In *Campbell* v *Tameside MBC*, Lord Denning, obiter, said there was a difference between claims affecting documents which should be kept secret on grounds, for example, of national security and those of a lower level of confidence. Immunity should, in the latter, be capable of being waived. Thus, the local authority could agree to submit the tape recording.

In criminal cases, the court is generally the final arbiter of the question as to whether the evidence should be excluded on the basis of public interest immunity: *R* v *Davis* [1993] 1 WLR 613. The Court of Appeal in *Davis* stated that the prosecution should make disclosure of all relevant material and inform the defence that an application to withhold evidence which they regard as being subject to public interest immunity would be made. The defence would have a right to be heard when the application is being considered. In exceptional cases, an ex parte application can be made without the defence being informed. This decision can be reviewed by the judge during the trial. The guidance in *Davis*, as well as the decision in the case of *R* v *Ward* [1993] 1 WLR 619, are now incorporated in the **Criminal Procedure and Investigations Act 1996**. This introduced rules in respect to pre-trial disclosure of evidence in criminal cases and treatment of sensitive material, including evidence subject to public interest immunity. It should be stressed that the court, not the prosecution, must decide on the claim to withhold evidence, otherwise a failure to do so would be a violation of the accused's right to a fair trial: *Rowe and Davis* v *United Kingdom* (2000) 30 EHRR 1.

In assessing whether the evidence ought to be withheld on the grounds of public interest immunity in criminal cases, the balance of competing interests should be made. In the present case there is clearly a need to afford greater protection to Gertrude, as an accused, than as a party to civil proceedings. The courts must balance the public interest and the rights of the individual affected. In *R* v *Governor of Brixton Prison, ex parte Osman* [1991] 1 WLR 281, the weight to be attached to the interests of justice was very great where the documents were necessary to the defence in a criminal case. However, Lord Taylor in *R* v *Keane* [1994] 1 WLR 746 at p. 751 commented in the Court of Appeal, that the right answer must result from 'performing the balancing exercise not from dispensing with it'. He said 'if the disputed material may prove the defendant's innocence or avoid a miscarriage of justice then the balance comes down resoundingly in favour of disclosing it'.

The position thus seems to be that a public interest immunity claim may be made in criminal cases. Murphy comments (2008, p. 421): 'The withholding of evidence, especially evidence which might assist the defence, is a serious step and one which should be taken only where a strong public interest in withholding it clearly outweighs the general obligation of disclosure.' Significantly, the Court of Appeal allowed the appellants' appeal against conviction in the light of the judgment of the Strasbourg Court in *Rowe and Davis* v *United Kingdom*, [2000] Crim LR 584. The failure to allow judicial scrutiny of material sought to be withheld under public interest immunity had violated the right to a fair trial. As was stated in *ex parte Osman*, the public interest in the administration of justice will weigh very heavily in the balance if the liberty of the defendant is at stake, particularly here where there is no question of national security.

Leigh (1995) pointed out that British procedures in this area are a 'patchwork' and suggested it would be 'better to introduce a comprehensive code integrating the safeguards, such as the **US Classified Information Procedures Act**, 18 USC app 1– 18 (1982)'. The House of Lords has given attention to the problem of PII in criminal trials in *R* v *H* (2004) although for Choo (2006, p. 160) it was 'disappointing' that the House 'did not take the opportunity to dispel uncertainty in this area'. He acknowledged, however, that the House strongly implied that the material in question in a criminal case must be inspected by the judge. The House also anticipated that special counsel may be appointed in rare cases. It set out detailed guidance for making PII claims in criminal cases.

With regard to Fred's position as a witness to the civil hearing the parties will need to take note of the **Children Act 1989** s. 98. This provides that in proceedings concerning the care of children a person cannot refuse to answer questions on the grounds either that the person or his or her spouse would be incriminated. The welfare of the children is of paramount importance. However s. 98(2) protects Gertrude if she faces criminal charges. Any evidence in the care proceedings is not admissible in subsequent proceedings except perjury. One controversial issue is whether pretrial statements are protected as well as evidence in the proceedings. The answer in *A Chief Constable* v *A County Council* [2002] EWHC 2198 Fam appears to be 'yes'.

Question 4

Mr X is suing the Rural Retreat nursing home for negligently causing the death of his wife. He alleges that Gloria, a nursing auxiliary, administered a drug overdose. He wishes to adduce in evidence a letter and a report for the home's insurers made after the death of Mrs X in preparation for a health and safety inquiry in which other staff gave evidence that there was lax management in the home and bottles were often mislabelled. The report and papers were also sent to the nursing home's lawyer. Jane, Mr X's neighbour, works as a clerk for the lawyer. She took a secret photocopy of the papers and sent them anonymously to Mr X. Advise on the report's admissibility, along with correspondence between the lawyers and the nursing home.

Commentary

The specific questions here on legal professional privilege are: How far does it stretch to correspondence with third parties? What is the status of copies? If the privilege is lost can use of the document be restrained by an injunction on grounds of confidentiality? How does the **Civil Procedure Rules 1998** affect this?

Answer plan

- Legal professional privilege and third parties
- Status of copies
- 'Inadvertent' inspection
- Conduct of third party
- **Civil Procedures Rules, r. 31.20**

Suggested answer

The report contains cogent evidence of the state of affairs in the home at the time of Mrs X's death and would clearly be useful to Mr X in the litigation.

Third-party or litigation privilege is directed at communications with potential witnesses and covers communication between the party and a third party, or communications between the party's lawyer and a third party.

However, it may be argued in answering this question that the home would have been entitled to claim legal professional privilege for the report by its insurers. The House of Lords in *Waugh* v *BRB* [1980] AC 521 held that this would be so provided the report was compiled with a view to pending or contemplated litigation with the dominant purpose of obtaining legal advice. In that case the defendants were sued under the **Fatal Accidents Act 1976**. The plaintiff's husband had died in a railway collision. The widow asked for discovery of an internal report by the defendants submitted to the railway inspectorate and the ministry. However, the report was also intended to give details to the Railway Board's solicitor so he could give advice. There was no privilege because the intended or contemplated litigation was not on the facts 'at least the dominant purpose' of creating the document.

The fact that it was sent to the home's legal department would not confer on the report legal professional privilege which it did not already possess (otherwise every litigant could protect embarrassing documents merely by sending them to his legal representatives, as the Divisional Court held in *R* v *Peterborough JJ, ex parte Hicks* [1977] 1 WLR 1371). In *Ventouris* v *Mountain* [1991] 1 WLR 607 the Court of Appeal held that legal professional privilege could not attach to original documents which did not come into existence for the purposes of the litigation but already existed before the litigation was contemplated or commenced. Each case will turn on its facts but it appears here that the likelihood is that the insurers were anticipating legal proceedings and that is the dominant purpose for which the papers came into being.

Mr X should be advised that the courts have taken a strict view on what amounts to legal proceedings. In *Re L (A Minor) (Police Investigation: Privilege)* [1997] AC 16 the House of Lords decided that legal professional privilege applies only in adversarial proceedings and therefore would not apply to advice concerning investigations and inquiries. It may be argued here that the communication was in anticipation of a public inquiry. In *Re L* the majority of the House of Lords held that while legal professional privilege in the form of communication between lawyer and client was absolute it did not apply to confidential communications with third parties in relation to proceedings brought under the **Children Act 1989**. One issue was the use of the document in possible criminal proceedings against a mother who had communicated confidentially with an expert. However, the rule in *Re L* has been criticised by Murphy (2003, at p. 494) as being 'a judicial creation' which undermines the basic rights of the parties.

The correspondence between the lawyers and nursing home management are also privileged if they are for the purposes of legal advice. The courts interpret this to mean 'dominant purpose' (see *Three Rivers District Council* v *Bank of England (No. 5)*).

However, the privilege extends only to the original document. The contents of a privileged document can be proved by secondary evidence, including the production of copies, following the Court of Appeal decision in *Calcraft* v *Guest* [1898] 1 QB 759. This rule was explained in *Lord Ashburton* v *Pape* [1913] 2 Ch 469 by Cozens-Hardy MR, as arising from the fact that the court in an action where it is sought to prove the contents of a privileged document from secondary sources, is not trying the circumstances under which the document was produced. But that rule, as he pointed out, had no bearing on a case where the whole subject-matter of the action is the right to retain the copy of a document which is privileged. **Ashburton** established the availability of equitable relief to restrain the use of copies of documents which were subject to a duty of confidence and possession of which it had been wrongfully obtained. Despite some attempt to reconcile these principles, uncertainty arises as to the result in such cases. This has now been simplified by the **Civil Procedure Rules 1998**.

Rule 31.20 of the 1998 rules provide that where a party inadvertently allows a privileged document to be inspected, the party who has inspected the document may use it or its contents only with the permission of the court. The consequence of this is that a party seeking to restrain the use of a privileged document, whether a primary or secondary copy, does not have apply for an injunction to restrain its use. Under this rule the court can of its own motion or on the application of a party to the case order the return of the document which is privileged without separate proceedings from being commenced. It should be noted that this rule does not affect the question as to how the court decides whether a document is privileged.

The difficulty is that the court must decide whether the document has been 'inadvertently' inspected. There remains the question as to whether this applies to cases where the document has been obtained by fraud or trick. At common law, the court took the view that how the document was obtained was not relevant and the issue was whether the party claiming its return was entitled to have it: *Goddard* v *Nationwide Building Society* [1987] QB 670.

The Court of Appeal in *Derby & Co Ltd* v *Weldon (No. 8)* [1990] 3 All ER 362 emphasised that no balancing exercise is required when a party seeks to vindicate privilege in documents mistakenly disclosed. As Dennis (2002, at p. 354) comments, 'It is clear that the conduct of the third party is not a critical issue . . . some innocent recipients of privileged documents disclosed by mistake may be restrained from using them in the same way as a party who acquired them by fraud.' It should be noted that under r. 31.20 of the **Civil Procedure Rules** (CPR), if a party inadvertently permits a privileged document to be inspected it may only be used with the permission of the court by the party who has inspected it.

It is clearly the case here that Jane, the clerk, is subject to the duty of confidence as against her employer. She has broken her obligation of secrecy in passing the document to Mr X, even if the documents had been obtained without any reprehensible conduct. The home could ask for the return of any privileged documents when Mr X seeks leave of the court to use the document under CPR r. 31.20. Mr X should be warned that the courts have taken a rather strict approach since the CPR were introduced (see *USP Strategies* v *London General Holdings* [2004] EWHC 373 Ch). Mr X's counsel may be under ethical restraints under the Code of Conduct for the Bar, which may prevent him using communications that have come into Mr X's hands by such unorthodox means.

Question 5

Alice, the four-year-old daughter of Mrs Y is badly injured in a playground incident at Treasure Island Nursery. Mrs Y is suing the nursery. An internal report has been prepared by the Department for Education as part of its routine inspection of private nursery schools. In this report the Department indicates concern about management procedures and lack of proper vetting of staff at Treasure Island Nursery. The Department claims that the report is covered by public interest immunity because to disclose it would prejudice the conduct of future inspections in that it would deter witnesses from giving evidence. A 'mole' in the department sent a photocopy of key sections of the report to the pressure group Childwatch which is helping Mrs Y and they have offered to let her have a copy.

Advise on the admissibility of the report.

Commentary

A straightforward question about public interest immunity. Note that public interest immunity attaches to copies of documents, unlike the position in relation to legal professional privilege, which only extends to an original document.

Answer plan

- General rule on public interest immunity
- **Civil Procedure Rules 1998**, r. 31.6
- Tape-recording of meeting may be subject to public interest immunity on grounds of confidentiality in the public service
- Court in criminal cases is arbiter of whether evidence should be admitted

Suggested answer

Public interest immunity protects the nation or the public service against the harm which can arise by disclosure of certain documents. It is not material to the claim that the party making it is not a party to the proceedings as here. It is also irrelevant here that the report is in the form of a copy. The argument of the Department for Education is that staff and owners of nurseries would in future be less candid with their inspectors if they knew their statements were likely to be used in litigation. The Crown is not a party to the proceedings here, so should give notice that it intends to contest the production of the report. Under r. 31.19 of the **Civil Procedure Rules 1998** any person, including the Crown, may apply for an order that he is entitled to withhold a document on the ground of public interest immunity.

The application to exclude should be supported by evidence. Under r. 31.19(6) of the 1998 Rules, the court may require that the documents or evidence be produced for its inspection so it can decide where the public interest lies. The claim can be either on a 'class' or a 'contents' basis, saying either that the document belongs to a class of documents whose production is not in the public interest or that its production is objectionable because of its specific contents. Although in the wake of the Scott Report the Lord Chancellor announced in 1996 that the government would not attempt to justify withholding documents on a class basis, this does not apply to non-governmental organisations although, as Murphy (at p. 477) points out, 'it is to be hoped [they] will follow suit'.

The claim here appears to be of the 'class' type but Lord Reid in *Conway* v *Rimmer* [1968] AC 910, indicated that courts are likely to be more sympathetic if the claim is of the 'contents' type. The court has power to inspect the documents and in a class claim is likely to do so. The courts are not obliged, since *Conway* v *Rimmer* abrogated the rule in *Duncan* v *Cammell Laird* [1942] AC 624, to accept without question the minister's certificate. Mrs Y in this case would have to show that the report was 'necessary either for disposing fairly of the cause or matter or for saving costs', which is not a difficult hurdle on the present facts: see *Air Canada* v *Secretary of State for Trade (No. 2)* [1983] 2 AC 394. In addition, the application for disclosure should not be a 'fishing expedition', though plainly that does not apply in the present case. The argument that if it became known that confidential reports might be disclosed for the purposes of private litigation, the elements of frankness and candour in their preparation might be lost, carries less weight after *Conway* v *Rimmer*. In *Science Research Council* v *Nassé* [1980] AC 1028 that reasoning was rejected by Lord Salmon. Lord Fraser saw the need to prevent disclosure as only a private interest of the individuals who prepared the documents. But the need for candour was strongly defended by Lord Wilberforce (dissenting) in *Burmah Oil Co. Ltd* v *Bank of England* [1980] AC 1090, so might still have some foundation.

Mrs Y can clearly argue that the report is relevant. She may be able to rely on waiver by the witnesses. In *Alfred Crompton Amusement Machines Ltd* v *Customs and Excise Commissioners* [1974] AC 405 the documents in question were business documents submitted by third parties to the Commissioners as part of a valuation of the plaintiff's machines. In this case, the balance of interests fell evenly and the House was inclined to hold in favour of the claim for public interest. However, Lord Cross thought that a person for whose benefit the objection was made could waive the immunity, although this was doubted by Lord Simon in *Rogers* v *Home Secretary* [1973] AC 388. The authorities thus conflict on this point of the availability of waiver.

Finally, it might be difficult to argue here that there is a public interest in non-disclosure since revealing the weakness in the nursery's procedures may well assist the wellbeing of children more than anonymity for whistleblowers.

Question 6

Jane has been the victim of an unlawful drugs raid although no charges were preferred after it. She was badly hurt in the raid. She believes the raid occurred as a result of an article she wrote after an interview with a Mr Big detailing the extent to which drug dealers were plying their wares among school children. Jane is considering suing the police, having already made a complaint to the Independent Police Complaints Commission (successor to the Police Complaints Authority), which it has investigated. She wonders if she will be able to obtain copies of the investigation and is worried that at the trial she may be forced to disclose the name of Mr Big since she had promised him anonymity.

Advise Jane of her legal position.

Commentary

You should not attempt this question if you are not reasonably familiar with the landmark decision in *R* v *Chief Constable of the West Midlands, ex parte Wiley* [1995] AC 274. Otherwise, there is a real danger you will be citing overruled authorities. This is an instance when it is vital to check that your textbook and lecture notes are up to date. In this case judicial review had been sought of the refusal of Chief Constables to give undertakings that material relating to complaints against the police would not be used to prepare defences to civil claims on police misconduct. The House of Lords decided that no class immunity applied to police complaints procedure documents and cases which held otherwise were overruled. It was acknowledged that in some cases a 'contents' claim might be appropriate and that there may be a 'class' claim for subgroups of documents. Subsequently, this latter view was accepted for reports of officers investigating a complaint in *Taylor* v *Anderton (Police Complaints Authority Intervening)* [1995] 1 WLR 447. The other part of the question deals with journalists' sources, and whether or not you are allowed to take a statute book into the examination; you must be reasonably familiar with the text of the **Contempt of Court Act 1981**, s. 10.

Answer plan

- General rule on PII
- Difference between class and content claims
- PII and police complaints—see *ex parte Wiley* (1995)
- Modification made in *Taylor* v *Anderton* (1995)
- s. 10 **Contempt of Court Act 1981**

Suggested answer

The House of Lords in *R* v *Chief Constable of the West Midlands, ex parte Wiley* [1995] AC 274 overruled previous authorities and decided that it was no longer necessary to impose a general class public interest immunity on documents generated in the course of an investigation by the Police Complaints Authority of a complaint against the police. What has to be decided is whether the particular documents in this case are covered by public interest immunity. This is a matter for the court hearing Jane's civil action for assault. Jane's case will not be helped by *Taylor* v *Anderton* [1995] 1 WLR 447, where the Court of Appeal held that a 'class' immunity applied to a sub-group of documents, namely reports of officers investigating a complaint. Any immunity which does attach to any of the documents is limited to the disclosure of the documents or their contents rather than the use of knowledge obtained from them. Jane may be refused sight of the documents on grounds of public interest immunity, namely that preserving the confidentiality of the reports outweighed the public interest in disclosure in that they were not necessary for fairly disposing of the case or saving costs. The important point is that it is for the court to inspect the documents and decide accordingly whether or not to admit them, following the current civil procedure rules.

Jane is also worried that she will be forced to disclose the identity of Mr Big. The courts have been very reluctant to acknowledge privileged confidential relationships apart from that between a lawyer and client. One area of concern has been confidentiality between journalists and their sources. The attempt to assert a general journalistic immunity based on public policy, protecting, for example, dissemination of information by granting sources anonymity, failed in *British Steel Corporation* v *Granada Television Ltd* [1981] AC 1096. The House of Lords, recognising the importance of protecting certain confidences while also recognising that it had a discretion to order disclosure, ordered Granada to disclose the identity of an informant. In this case, the majority felt Granada's conduct was irresponsible in using the 'leaked' confidential reports on the national steel strike. The House agreed, with Lord Salmon dissenting, that although the courts had a wish to respect journalistic sources, no public policy immunity existed which would override the public policy of making relevant evidence available to the court. British Steel Corporation had a worthy case. Disclosure of the source of information contained in a publication is now governed by statute.

Section 10 of the **Contempt of Court Act 1981** provides that:

> No court may require a person to disclose, nor is any person guilty of contempt for refusing to disclose, the source of information contained in a publication for which he is responsible, unless it be established to the satisfaction of the court that disclosure is necessary in the interests of justice or national security or for the prevention of disorder or crime.

Parliament, according to Murphy (2008, p. 481), 'took the most remarkable step of introducing a new statutory privilege'.

The section will thus give Jane as a journalist a presumption against disclosure of the identity of Mr Big. The police if they wish disclosure will have to convince the court that one of the four reasons in the section applies, the two most likely being necessary either in the interests of justice or the prevention of crime. As regards the former, the majority of the House of Lords in *Secretary of State for Defence* v *Guardian Newspapers* [1985] AC 339 held it to mean technically the administration of justice in the course of legal proceedings in a court of law, tribunal or other such body. However, Lord Bridge in *X* v *Morgan-Grampian (Publishers) Ltd* [1991] 1 AC 1 did not think resort to actual legal proceedings was required. In any case, it will be difficult for the police to establish that they need Mr Big's identity either for their defence against Jane or to exercise another legal right. The court may, however, consider that the police require the identity for the prevention of crime. It will then have to balance the interests of a free press in non-disclosure of sources against the police contention. This approach was followed by the Court of Appeal in *Camelot Group plc* v *Centaur Communications Ltd* [1998] 1 All ER 251. However, the European Court of Human Rights came to a different conclusion in *Goodwin* v *United Kingdom* (1996) 22 EHRR 123 at p. 436. This aspect of s. 10 was considered in **Re an Inquiry under the Company Securities (Insider Dealing) Act 1985 [1988] AC 660.** Inspectors carrying out a criminal investigation contended that disclosure of the sources of a journalist's article about insider dealing was 'necessary in the interests of the prevention of . . . crime'.

This area of law has been influenced by the **Human Rights Act 1998.** In *Ashworth Hospital Authority* v *MGN Ltd* [2001] 1 WLR 515 the Court of Appeal held that the interpretation of s. 10 should accord with Article 10 of the European Convention on Human Rights and set out an overall test. Murphy (at p. 508) comments, 'it may be that if *Ashworth Hospital* v *MGN Ltd* is to be taken as the leading post-**Human Rights Act** authority, the law of England may be brought more into line with the Convention jurisprudence than was the case in the older authorities'.

Three aspects of the House of Lords ruling are relevant to Jane's concern: first, s. 10 applied to all types of proceedings; second, the 'prevention of crime' could refer to crime in general, and third, 'necessary' meant somewhere between 'indispensable' and 'expedient'. (On the last point it is arguable that the definition reduces the standard enacted by Parliament.) If the police decide that Mr Big's identity is necessary for their general investigations into drug dealing, then Jane may be ordered to disclose it.

Additional Reading

Allen, T.R.S., 'Abuse of Power and Public Interest Immunity: Justice Rights and Truth' (1985) 101 LQR 200.

Allen, T.R.S., 'Legal Privilege and the Principle of Fairness in the Criminal Trial' (1987) Crim LR 449.

Auburn, J., *Legal Professional Privilege: Law and Theory* (OUP, 2000).

Brown, Sir Simon, 'Public Interest Immunity' [1994] PL 579.

Forsyth, C., 'Public Interest Immunity: Recent and Future Developments' [1997] CLJ 51.

Leigh, I., 'Reforming Public Interest Immunity' [1995] 2 Web JCLI. http://webjcli.ncl.ac.uk/articles2/leigh2.html

Leng, R., 'Losing Sight of the Defendant: The Government's Proposals on Pre-trial Disclosure' (1995) Crim LR 704.

Newbold, A.L.E., 'The Crime/Fraud Exception to Legal Professional Privilege' (1990) 55 MLR 472.

Newbold, A.L.E., 'Inadvertent Disclosure in Civil Proceedings' (1991) 107 LQR 99.

Scott, Sir Richard, Report of the Inquiry into the Export of Defence Equipment and Dual-Use Goods to Iraq and Related Prosecutions (1996) HC 115.

Spencer, M., 'Bureaucracy, National Security and Access to Justice: New Light on *Duncan v Cammell Laird*' (2004) NILQ vol 55, no. 3277.

Sprock, J., 'The Criminal Procedure and Investigations Act 1996. (1) The Duty of Disclosure' (1997) Crim LR 308.

Tapper, C., 'Privilege and Confidence' (1972) 35 MLR 83.

Tapper, C., 'Prosecution and Privilege' (1996) 1 E&P 5.

Taylor, C., 'In the Public Interest. PII and Fair Trials' (1999) 63 JCL 67.

Tomkins, A., 'Public Interest Immunity after Matrix-Churchill' [1993] PL 650.

Tomkins, A., 'Public Interest Immunity: Freedom of Information and Judicial Discretion' in *Administrative Law. The Future: Old Constraints and New Horizons* (eds P. Leyland and T. Woods, London 1997).

12

Mixed questions

Introduction

Examination questions in evidence papers frequently cover several issues. There is no way you could anticipate any particular combination of topics so the questions will be a test of your skill in identifying what specific areas of knowledge will be needed. Obviously, you will not be able to cover each area in the same depth as the single issue questions. The skill lies in identifying the relevant areas and you will lose marks if you ignore one. It is most important therefore that you spend some time in listing the various matters which raise a point of law, then specify the appropriate statute or case-law and finally apply the law to the facts in the question.

The skill lies in identifying all the relevant areas—you will lose marks if you ignore one. A well-crafted question will not contain any redundant information, so you should be prepared to comment on all parts of the question. You are not generally being asked in these questions to evaluate or criticise the law as it is, but to identify the legal issues in the narrative as you are given it and apply the law to each of them. However, it may be appropriate to refer to academic commentary, particularly in new areas of law. It might be useful to have a mental checklist to ensure that you have not missed some obvious issue when you answer a mixed question. A key preliminary point is to see if the question involves criminal or civil law or a mixture of both. Here are some outline pointers to frequently recurring areas:

- Relevance is the pre-condition of admissibility. It may be appropriate to show your powers of logical analysis and fact management by explaining why a particular piece of evidence is relevant to the trial.

- Burden and standard of proof are always in the background and you are generally expected to say something about them. You might be given an extract from a statute, including an imaginary one, which refers to the need to 'prove' and be expected then to construe the wording in the light of the changes brought about by the **Human Rights Act 1998** to the allocation of legal and evidential burdens.

- Does the question involve a confession or silence when interviewed on the part of the defendant? Bear in mind that confessions can be made to non-state agents, may be ambiguous and could even, under the common law, involve silence if the parties are on 'even terms'. Only apply CJPOA if the silence is in the face of questioning by state officials charged with this task.

- Is there any indication that evidence was improperly obtained? Any suggestion of impropriety or illegality by, e.g., the police?—s. 78 **PACE** then may apply.

- References to spouses, children, reluctant witnesses, witnesses who refuse to testify or fail to come up to proof all indicate that competence and compellability may be in issue.

- Examination and cross-examination. The special rules relating to vulnerable witnesses such as alleged victims in sex cases are most significant here. If your course has covered Special Measures Directions then bear those in mind.

- Corroboration/supporting evidence. The formal rules here have now been either abolished or simplified but you should still be prepared to comment on the desirability of supporting evidence, particularly in relation to identification evidence, lies told by the defendant and silence.

- Character evidence. Be aware that what used to be called Similar Fact evidence is now covered in the **CJA 2003** and that the rules on admissibility of character evidence by a non-defendant witness are also covered by that Act.

- When there is a reference to an out-of-court oral or written statement, including one made by a witness who is testifying, think hearsay. But bear in mind that the important question is not the **form** the statement is in but the **purpose** for which it is being tendered in evidence. Note the radical changes to hearsay in the **CJA 2003**.

- References to communication with a lawyer may raise legal professional privilege. In civil cases communications with a third party may also be privileged if there is pending litigation.

- Public interest immunity will usually only come up in criminal cases in relation to police informers.

- Opinion evidence is a topical issue and easily recognised. The grey areas include the admissibility of expert evidence in relation to human behaviour.

Once you have listed the issues you recognise in the question you should work systematically to cover them, dealing with the facts of the question, not generalities about the law. If you are asked to advise the parties it is usually best to include a short concluding paragraph summarising your advice. You should make good reference use of the excellent new texts in this area which discuss the cumulative impact of recent changes to the law of evidence, such as Choo (2006).

Question 1

Jones and Watkins are both accused of the murder of Simpson. Both blame the other for the offence. Jones has three previous convictions for disorderly behaviour, while Watkins has five previous convictions for robbery, in two of which he had been part of a gang which had used knives and pick-axes and had threatened their victims. Freda was a witness to the killing of Simpson and she gave a statement to the police but also claimed that Jones afterwards threatened to harm her if she told what she had seen. Jones denies this. Watkins' counsel wishes to adduce evidence that Jones had pleaded not guilty to all the previous charges of disorderly behaviour on which he had been convicted. Watkins had previously worked as a security guard in a college. The prosecution wish to call evidence of an internal college disciplinary hearing over an allegation of assault on a student. As a result, Watkins had been dismissed. At the investigation stage Jones had refused to answer police questions but his solicitor read out a prepared statement. Freda has a conviction for shoplifting. She states she is too afraid to give evidence at trial. Jones had pleaded not guilty to the previous charges on which he was convicted.

   Advise on evidence.

Commentary

The question covers three areas. You need to consider the application of the new character provisions of the **Criminal Justice Act 2003**, the provisions on silence in the **Criminal Justice and Public Order Act 1994** and the special provisions relating to witnesses who claim they are afraid to give evidence.

Answer plan

- Jones and Watkins (co-defendants) and Freda as witness—various instances of criminal convictions and behaviour not leading to a criminal charge are given (the assault on the student and the alleged threats to Freda). Do these fall within the definition of bad character in **CJA 2003** s. 98?

- Freda is a non-defendant—what are the provisions relating to the admissibility of her bad character? See s. 100 **CJA 2003**. If Jones or Watkins adduce this consider s. 101(1)(g)

- Watkins and Jones operate a 'cut throat' defence. Consider the operation of s. 101(1)(e), *R* v *Randall* [2003] UKHL 69, *R* v *Robinson* [2005] EWCA Crim 3233 and *R* v *Lawson* (2006) LTL 25/8/2006

- Watkins' previous offences are arguably of the same nature as the current charge—are they admissible under s. 101(1)(d)?

- Freda is afraid to give evidence—operation of s. 116 **CJA 2003**; current law on anonymous witnesses

- Jones refuses to answer police questions–consider s. 34 **CJPOA 1994** and *R* v *Knight* [2004] 1 *WLR* 340
- Finally, it will be necessary to consider how the judge should direct the jury in relation to any evidence which is admissible

Suggested answer

The two co-defendants, Jones and Watkins and the witness, Freda, have previous convictions and/or instances of reprehensible behaviour. Before examining whether these are likely to be admissible at trial it is necessary to examine whether they fall within the sort of behaviour which is covered by s. 98 **CJA 2003**. The definition covers evidence of, or a disposition towards, misconduct. The term 'misconduct' is further defined in s. 112 as the commission of an offence or other reprehensible behaviour. The Explanatory Note to the Act specifies that, 'This is intended to be a broad definition and to cover evidence that shows that a person has committed an offence, or has acted in a reprehensible way (or is disposed to do so) as well as evidence from which this might be inferred'. Thus the definition is likely to cover all the behaviours cited, namely the previous convictions and the disciplinary charge. However, with regard to the alleged threat made by Jones, para. 357 of the Explanatory Note makes it clear that this evidence is likely to be regarded as evidence relating to the facts of the offence and so does not come within s. 98. It reads, 'Evidence that the defendant had tried to intimidate prosecution witnesses would also be admissible outside this scheme [s. 98] as evidence of misconduct in connection with, as appropriate, the investigation or the prosecution of the offence, as would allegations by the defendant that evidence had been planted.'

Jones and Watkins should be aware that the **CJA 2003** applies in relation to the admissibility of their bad character whether they give evidence or not.

To take first the position of Freda, the non-defendant, the first question is whether evidence of her shoplifting offence is admissible. Section 100 **CJA 2003** specifies that evidence of the bad character of a person other than a defendant is not to be given without the permission of the court (s. 100(4)) and this can only be given if it meets one of three conditions: They are:

- it is important explanatory evidence;
- it is of substantial probative value to a matter in issue and that issue is one of substantial importance in the case; or
- the prosecution and defence agree that the evidence should be admitted.

Here we are told that there is a dispute between Jones and Freda as to what happened. It is arguable therefore that if Jones' counsel applies to have the evidence admitted under the second head above the court may give permission. Jones should then be aware, however, that it may be arguable that he has now 'attacked the character of another person' and that the prosecution may seek to have his previous convictions admitted under s. 101(1)(g). This is dealt with below.

Freda is frightened to give evidence. This may bring into play s. 19 of the **Youth Justice and Criminal Evidence 1999**, which covers special measures for the giving of evidence by fearful witnesses. As Cross and Tapper (2004, p. 247) point out, 'Since the adversarial system, with its underpinning of orality, is still fundamental to the system of criminal trial, it is important to encourage witnesses to testify, both by the provision of support and information before trial and by the amelioration of stress and fear at trial.' The judge may consider the use of video linkage or screens. An alternative approach is for Freda's pre-trial statement to be admitted under the hearsay provisions of the **CJA 2003**. Section 116(2) sets out a procedure which may apply where 'through fear the relevant person does not give (or does not continue to give) oral evidence in the proceedings, either at all or in connection with the subject matter of the statement, and the court gives leave for the statement to be given in evidence'. Fear is to be 'widely construed'. The fear need not be reasonable (see **R** v ***Acton Justices, ex parte McMullen*** (1990) **92 Cr App R 98**). The admissibility of Freda's evidence in this way will depend upon the exercise of the court's discretion, which will include a consideration of fairness in view of the impossibility of cross-examining Freda. The prosecution must prove the existence of Freda's fear by non-hearsay admissible evidence (see ***Neill*** v ***North Antrim Magistrates' Court*** [1992] **1 WLR 1220**. The court may exercise its discretion not to allow this hearsay evidence since Freda will not be cross-examined, thus arguably undermining the defence. Evidence of Freda's lack of credibility may be given even if she does not appear.

It is unlikely in the light of the House of Lords' landmark decision in ***R*** v ***Davis*** [2008] **3 WLR 125** that Freda will be allowed to give evidence anonymously. The House of Lords reversed the Court of Appeal's ruling that three frightened witnesses could give evidence anonymously. At the trial protective measures had been imposed whereby the witnesses' addresses and personal and identifying particulars were withheld from the defendant and his legal advisers. The defendant's counsel was not permitted to ask any question which might enable their identification, they gave evidence under pseudonyms behind screens so that they could be seen by judge and jury but not by the defendant, and their natural voices, although heard by the judge and jury, were subject to mechanical distortion so as to prevent recognition by the defendant. The testimony of the witnesses was decisive and the defendant was convicted. The House of Lords held that it was a long-established common law principle that a defendant in a criminal trial should be confronted by his accusers so that he might cross-examine them and challenge their evidence. The majority (Lords Bingham, Rodger, Brown and Mance) held that, although witness intimidation had been a serious threat to the administration of justice, there had been no departure from the rule until the courts' recent authorisation of witness anonymity. This practice was irreconcilable with the common law rule and incompatible with the ECHR. Any revision was a task for Parliament. The case was remitted to the Court of Appeal. Parliament speedily passed the **Criminal Evidence (Witness Anonmity) Act 2008** which will apply to the retrial.

Jones and/or the prosecution may try to have Watkins' previous convictions admitted as evidence. The prosecution may argue that they are admissible under s. 101(1)(d) as relevant to an important matter in issue between the defendant and prosecution. The test for admissibility has been set out in *Hanson*:

1. Does the history of conviction(s) establish a propensity to commit offences of the kind charged?

2. Does that propensity make it more likely that the defendant committed the offence charged?

3. Is it unjust to rely on the conviction(s) of the same description or category; and, in any event, will the proceedings be unfair if they are admitted?

In this case the previous convictions arguably show a propensity to violence if not to murder, but the Court of Appeal in *Hanson* stressed that 'In referring to offences of the same description or category, section 103(2) is not exhaustive of the types of conviction which might be relied upon to show evidence of propensity to commit offences of the kind charged. Nor, however, is it necessarily sufficient, in order to show such propensity that a conviction should be of the same description or category as that charged.' Even if the judge decides the offences are eligible to be considered under this head she must apply her discretion under s. 101(3): 'The court must not admit evidence under subsection (1)(d) if on an application by the defendant to exclude it, it appears to the court that the admission of the evidence would have such an adverse effect on the fairness of the proceedings that the court ought not to admit it.' She must also consider s. 103(3), which refers to 'the length of time since the conviction or for any other reason, that it would be unjust for it to apply in this case'. If the evidence is admissible under this head then Jones may make use of it also to try and establish his innocence. In *R* v *Randall* (2003) Lord Steyn stated 'For the avoidance of doubt I would further add that in my view where evidence of the propensity of a co-accused is relevant to a fact in issue between the Crown and the other accused it is not necessary for the trial judge to direct the jury to ignore that evidence in considering the case against the co-accused. Justice does not require such a direction to be given. Moreover such a direction would needlessly perplex juries.'

However, even if the court ruled the convictions and the disciplinary charge inadmissible for the prosecution under this section it would still be open to the co-defendant Jones to put in an application to have the character of Watkins put in evidence. The relevant section is s. 101(1)(e). Under this, evidence must have substantial probative value in relation to an important matter in issue between the defendant and the co-defendant. Since each blames the other for the offence it is likely that Jones will argue that Watkins' previous convictions and the reason for his dismissal demonstrate a propensity to violence which he, Jones, does not have. *Murdoch* v *Taylor* [1965] AC 574 gives guidance on the meaning of evidence against a co-defendant under the CEA 1898. However, it is to be noted that the CJA 2003 more readily admits bad character evidence. Only if the evidence is evidence of propensity to untruthfulness is it a precondition that the defendant has undermined the co-defendant's defence.

With regard to the evidential value of the bad character evidence, in *R v Randall* the House of Lords made it clear that where two defendants were jointly charged with a crime and each blamed the other for its commission, one accused could rely on the more significant criminal propensity of the other in order to prove his innocence. In that case the co-defendants were charged with murder and each claimed the other had killed the victim. The evidence of the antecedents of the co-defendant was relevant not only to lack of credibility but also to the issue of which of them was more likely to have committed the offence. That case was decided upon under the **Criminal Evidence Act 1898,** but it was relied upon in *R v Dennis Robinson* under the CJA 2003. There the Court of Appeal held that the judge had been entitled to direct the jury to consider all the evidence, including evidence adduced by one of the co-defendants as to the bad character of her co-accused. The exclusionary discretion in relation to s. 101(3) does not apply to s. 101(1)(e).

Jones' convictions arguably do not show a propensity to extreme violence and so may not be admissible under the above heads. Jones may decide to put his conviction in evidence on the basis that they do not demonstrate a propensity to such violence. This would be covered by s. 101(1)(b). Alternatively, the evidence may be admissible by the prosecution under s. 101(1)(g) since Jones has adduced Freda's convictions. In this case the court has discretion not to admit the evidence under s. 101 (3). The explanatory note on s. 101(1)(g) states that such evidence 'will primarily go to the credit of the defendant'. However, it adds 'Currently a jury would be directed that evidence admitted in similar circumstances, under the 1898 Act, goes only to credibility and is not relevant to the issue of guilt. Such directions have been criticised and the new statutory scheme does not specify that this evidence is to be treated in such a way. However, it is expected that judges will explain the purpose for which the evidence is being put forward and direct the jury about the sort of weight that can be placed on it.' Depending on how the evidence is treated in the trial it is possible that even if it is not admitted under s. 101(1)(e) that Watkins' counsel may be able to cross-examine Jones on it. In a controversial decision the Court of Appeal held in *R v Highton* [2005] EWCA 1985, 'Once evidence of bad character became admissible through one of the "gateways" in the **Criminal Justice Act 2003** the use to which it could be put depended upon the matters to which it was relevant rather than upon the gateway through which it was admitted. Accordingly, evidence of an offender's bad character admitted under s101(1)(g) could be used, if relevant, to show the offender's propensity to commit offences of the kind with which he was charged.'

However, it may be that Watkins can argue that the fact that Jones pleaded not guilty in the previous trials is of substantive probative value to the matter in issue between the two defendants. The issue is which is telling the truth. Section 104 further explains 'matter in issue between the defendant and a co-defendant'. It states that 'Evidence which is relevant to the question whether the defendant has a propensity to be untruthful is admissible on that basis under section 101(1)(e) only if the nature or conduct of his defence is to undermine the co-defendant's defence.' That seems to be the case here. In *R v Hanson* the Court of Appeal considered the meaning of 'propensity to untruthfulness', which was 'not the same as propensity to dishonesty'. It stated (para. 13),

> It is to be assumed, bearing in mind the frequency with which the words honest and dishonest appear in the criminal law, that Parliament, deliberately chose the word untruthful to convey a different meaning, reflecting a defendant's account of his behaviour, or lies told when committing an offence. Previous convictions, whether for offences of dishonesty or otherwise, are therefore only likely to be capable of showing a propensity to be untruthful where, in the present case, truthfulness is an issue and, in the earlier case, either there was a plea of not guilty and the defendant gave an account on arrest, in interview, or in evidence, which the jury must have disbelieved, or the way in which the offence was committed shows a propensity for untruthfulness, for example by the making of false representations.

Thus, further information is needed to assess whether the earlier not guilty pleas indicate that degree of untruthfulness on the part of Jones. In *R v Lawson* the Court of Appeal held that a judge was correct to allow the prosecution to adduce bad character evidence in order to establish a defendant's propensity as to truthfulness where there were inconsistencies between the defences of the two co-accused and the evidence was of substantive probative value. Here the bad character evidence was a previous conviction for unlawful wounding. It was noted in *R v Campbell* [2007] EWCA Crim 1472 that as a result of the CJA 2003 it has been much more common for evidence of the accused's bad character to be admitted at trial. However, in that case a restrictive stance was taken to s. 103(1)(b). It held that to suggest that a propensity for untruthfulness makes it more likely that a defendant has lied to the jury is not likely to help them. If they apply common sense they will conclude that a defendant who has committed a criminal offence may well be prepared to lie about it even if he has not shown a propensity for lying, whereas a defendant who has not committed the offence charged will be likely to tell the truth, even if he has shown a propensity for telling 'lies'. It followed that a propensity for untruthfulness will not normally be of assistance in assessing guilt.

Finally, with regard to Jones' refusal to talk to the police at interview and his submission of a statement, Jones may rely on *R v Knight*, where the Court of Appeal discussed what was meant by the defendant's failure to mention at interview facts later relied on for his defence under s. 34 CJPOA 1994. It held that the failure was not meant to be that of refusing to answer questions. Accordingly a statement given to the police at the time of the refusal to answer questions and put later in evidence read out by the judge in the summing-up meant that inferences could not be made under s. 34. As Choo (2006, p. 73) comments, 'In sum any uncertainty surrounding prepared statements that provide a full account of the defence later relied on has now been resolved in favour of the defendant. The Court of Appeal has taken a pragmatic approach to the interpretation of section 34 on this point, paying due attention to the rights of the defence and clearly acknowledging that the right to silence is not to be interfered with lightly.'

Question 2

Alerted by a burglar alarm, police from a nearby station arrive at a house in Meadow Way at 9.00 p.m. on Thursday night. They find a smashed window and while two officers search the house a third searches the street for suspects. Meanwhile the owner of the house, Jack, is pursuing someone running down the street. He sees Wayne running several yards away, catches up with him and grabs him. 'You rat,' Jack shouts, 'you've tried to burgle my house.' Wayne says nothing but tries to shake Jack off. Wayne is arrested and cautioned. At the police station he is questioned in a series of interviews beginning at 4.00 a.m. on Friday 2 April. He is cautioned before all the interviews. Before the first interview Wayne requests access to a solicitor, but this is denied by Inspector Brown on the grounds that they suspect Wayne had an accomplice who could be alerted by calling a solicitor. At the first interview, Wayne refuses to cooperate with the questioning. At the second interview Wayne is again denied a solicitor, but offers to 'tell what he knows', if the police promise to put in a good word for him to the judge. The Inspector nods his assent. Wayne then says that he was out playing football with his friends on the night in question and when making his way home he kicked the ball through the window of Jack's house. He ran off because he was scared. The second interview ends at 12 noon on Saturday. He is given no food. Wayne is later charged with attempted burglary. At trial the prosecution put it to him that Jack had had an affair with his wife.
    Advise on evidence.

Commentary

Among the issues you must consider here are whether fleeing can constitute adverse evidence and what is the evidential value of silence in the face of questioning both by persons in authority and an ordinary citizen. You must recall both the common law rules and also the new provisions under ss. 34 and 37 of the **Criminal Justice and Public Order Act 1994**. In addition, you will have to deal with the possibility of breach of s. 58 of the **Police and Criminal Evidence Act 1984** (**PACE**) and the Codes of Practice. The Codes are very comprehensive and you will obviously not be able to remember all the details, but you must touch on the main points, considering possible breaches in the period of detention and the related question of whether the offence here is an indictable offence. The circumstances of the obtaining of Wayne's statement, and whether it is inadmissible under ss. 76 or 78 of **PACE** should be considered. You must identify the various legal issues first and then in turn consider the relevant law in relation to the narrative of events. In these questions it is useful to prepare a plan for your answer to ensure your coverage is comprehensive.

Answer plan

- Implied assertion by conduct—is 'fleeing' a statement or the circumstances of the alleged offence?

- Evidential value of silence in face of questioning by persons in authority and ordinary citizens—CJPOA 1994 and common law

- Possible breaches of s. 58 **PACE** 1984 and Codes of Practice (revised periodically)

- Investigate whether an earlier silence at interview when replaced by an explanation is admissible; no solicitors present—Code C Annex C

- Wayne's statement 'mixed'—*R* v *Sharp* (1988); possible exclusion under s. 76 or 78 **PACE**

- Wayne presented with prosecution fact of wife's affair—s. 34 apply?

Suggested answer

The case concerns the question of whether various items of evidence are likely to be admissible for the prosecution. This essay takes each issue in turn.

Wayne is seen fleeing from the scene of the crime. Does this have evidential significance? A confession is defined in s. 82(1) of the **Police and Criminal Evidence Act 1984 (PACE)**. It '. . . includes any statement wholly or partly adverse to the person who made it whether made to a person in authority or not and whether made in words or otherwise'. It is arguable that this definition is wide enough to include an admission by conduct. The Criminal Law Revision Committee in its 11th Report (1972, Cm 4991) gave as an example, a possible admission by conduct, a nod of the head. But that is clearly an express statement by conduct. It is unlikely that an implied statement by conduct such as running away will be accepted as a confession. In *Preece* v *Parry* [1983] **Crim LR 170** the Divisional Court held that violent behaviour on arrest was capable of being a confession. This is generally regarded as an unusual case.

Clearly, however, the fact that Wayne is running away along the street is part of the circumstances of the alleged offence and is therefore relevant as an integral part of the events forming part of the basis of the charge. It would arguably be admissible under s. 98(a) **CJA 2003** as evidence which 'has to do with the alleged facts of the offence with which the defendant is charged'. See also s. 101(1)(c).

Wayne's silence in the face of accusations from Jack is more likely than his fleeing to amount to an admission. The common law rule is that a statement made in the presence of the accused cannot amount to evidence against him, except in so far as he accepts what has been said, as the House of Lords held in *R* v *Christie* [1914] **AC 545**. However, if in certain circumstances a reply or rebuttal would reasonably be expected, silence can be taken to be a confession. The test of admissibility of this type of silence is whether the parties are speaking on even terms: see *R* v *Mitchell* (1892) 17 Cox CC 503 and the Privy Council decision in *Parkes* v *R* (1977) 64 Cr App R 25. The court will thus have to decide first whether Jack and Wayne were speaking on even terms, which does seem likely. Thus, any direction by the judge that the silence could amount to a confession is arguably proper. The judge, however, must be careful to direct the jury to consider, first, whether the silence does indicate acceptance of what Jack said and, if so, whether guilt could reasonably be inferred from what he had accepted. It was the failure of the judge to leave these two issues to the jury and his suggestion that the defendant's silence could indicate guilt which led the Court of Appeal to quash the conviction in *R* v *Chandler* [1976] 1 WLR 585.

This common law principle is not affected by s. 34 of the **Criminal Justice and Public Order Act 1994,** which covers questioning under caution by a police constable. Section 34(5) of the 1994 Act provides that the section does not:

> prejudice the admissibility in evidence of the silence or other reaction of the accused in the face of anything said in his presence relating to the conduct in respect of which he is charged . . . or preclude the drawing of any inference from any such silence or other reaction of the accused which could properly be drawn apart from this section.

Under the **PACE** Code of Practice C paragraph 11.1, following a decision to arrest, the suspect must not be interviewed except at a police station unless the 'emergency' exceptions apply. It appears Wayne's treatment accords with this. Furthermore, Wayne should take account of paragraph 11.4, which provides that at the beginning of an interview carried out in a police station the interviewing officer, after cautioning him, is to put to the suspect any 'significant statement or silence' which occurred before the start of the interview. Wayne should be given an opportunity to confirm or deny any pre-interview silence or statement.

In addition, European Human Rights law must now be considered under the **Human Rights Act 1998.** The right to a fair trial under Article 6 extends to pre-trial as well as trial proceedings. Evidence obtained at interview may be excluded if it affects the fairness of the proceedings. The Strasbourg Court has placed much emphasis on the right of access to legal advice specifically in relation to the admissibility of silence as evidence, leading to changes in UK legislation (*Murray* v *UK*).

Some possible procedural flaws arise in relation to Wayne's interviews at the police station. Wayne maintains silence at first and then makes a statement. It is necessary to consider the application of ss. 34 and 37 of the 1994 Act, Wayne's failure to account for his presence in the street at the initial interview may be admissible under s. 37, since the court is permitted to draw inferences, whether or not the accused gives another version of events at trial. The investigating officer must give the additional special warning set out in para. 10.10 of Code C. Section

34, on the other hand, does not allow inferences to be drawn from silence, per se, but only when the accused for his defence in later proceedings relies on evidence, which evidence could have been provided in answer form during earlier questioning. The statute in fact does not make it clear whether an earlier silence in an early interview albeit replaced by an explanation at a later one is admissible, although it would seem rather harsh to interpret the statute against the defendant in this way. The evidential value of silence which is shortly replaced by an explanation, as is the case here, must be low. For s. 34 to apply there must be *inter alia* a 'fact' relied on by Wayne at trial which he could reasonably have been expected to have raised earlier. The purpose of the legislation is to prevent 'ambush defences' or concocted evidence in situations where the prosecution will not have been able to properly mount a challenge. It does not apply to situations where the new fact is true. Presumably the prosecution wishes to imply a motive of revenge on the part of Wayne and make a possible defence of accidentally breaking the window less likely. If Wayne simply accepts the prosecution evidence at trial that Jack was having an affair with his wife he is probably not running the risk of having an inference of guilt drawn from his failure to mention it at interview. It is the case that under s. 34 a fact may be relied upon by the defendant which is not put in evidence on his behalf (see *Chenia* [2002]). However, in *Betts and Hall* [2001] 2 Cr App R 257 the Court of Appeal held that if the defendant simply admits at trial a fact asserted by the prosecution even if he failed to mention it at interview that in itself should not lead to s. 34 applying. Note also that no inference should be drawn if the fact relied on is true (*Webber* [2004] UKHL 01). However, the most significant consideration is that s. 34 should not apply here in any case since there has apparently been a serious breach of criminal procedure in the failure to allow access to requested legal advice. Silence at interview is admissible only if, inter alia, the suspect has been given the opportunity to consult a solicitor (s. 34(2A)). It appears that this has been wrongly denied to Wayne so the silence may be inadmissible.

Wayne's statement takes a form which is partly exculpatory and partly inculpatory in that he accepts he was at the scene but not that he was attempting to burgle. Following the House of Lords decision in *R v Sharp* [1988] 1 WLR 7, such mixed statements are admissible as evidence of the facts related. However, the confession is evidence against Wayne and not Dan and the jury must be so warned, following the decision of the Court of Criminal Appeal in *R v Gunewardene* [1951] 2 KB 600. Confessions may also be edited. In *R v Silcott* [1987] Crim LR 765 at first instance, the trial judge ruled that the names of co-defendants implicated in a confession should be replaced by initials. However, in *R v Jefferson* (1994) 99 Cr App R 13, the Court of Appeal said it was a matter for the discretion of the trial judge whether to edit such interviews.

It is possible, however, that the whole statement itself should be excluded. Confessions may be excluded under several provisions of **PACE**. The grounds are oppression under s. 76(2)(a); unreliability under s. 76(2)(b), both of which operate as a rule of law; and unfairness under s. 78, which operates as the exercise of discretion. There appear to be no grounds of oppression here, but s. 76(2)(b) **PACE** may be appropriate. Arguably, Wayne has been induced to confess by a promise of a favour. In *R* v *Barry* (1991) 95 Cr App R 384, the promise of bail led to a confession being held potentially unreliable by the Court of Appeal. It must be shown that there is a connection between what was said or done and the confession. It is arguable that Wayne was induced to confess by the indication of favourable treatment by the Inspector. Thus the 'something said or done evidence' is the possible inducement. The 'circumstances' are arguably the absence of a solicitor with whom Wayne could discuss the offer (*R* v *Mathias* (1989) Crim LR 64). If the judge accepts this as an arguable proposition, then the burden of proof is on the prosecution to prove in a voir dire beyond reasonable doubt that the confession was not so obtained. The test is an objective one of whether any confession obtained in such circumstances would be likely to be unreliable.

Even if s. 76(2)(b) **PACE** is not applicable there may be sufficient breaches of other sections of the statute and the Code to warrant exclusion under s. 78 **PACE** by the exercise of the court's discretion. The circumstances in which the statement was obtained reveal a number of possible breaches of the statute and Codes of Practice.

First, Wayne has his access to a solicitor denied. Delay in obtaining legal representation is only permissible under s. 58 **PACE** if the offence is an indictable offence. Following the introduction of the **Criminal Justice Act 2003** detention without charge is permitted for up to 36 hours for indictable offences without reference to a magistrate. The reason for delaying legal advice given by the police, namely fear of alerting another suspect, does appear to comply with s. 58(8)(b) **PACE** but the police must put up cogent evidence to justify such a fear (see *R* v *Samuel* [1988] QB 615). (Prior to the 2003 Act the court had to determine whether the attempted burglary amounted to a serious arrestable offence. Further information would have been needed on the relative status of the victim and perpetrator, to determine whether the offence would cause serious financial gain or loss.) As the offence does constitute an indictable offence, the reason for delay in access to a solicitor appears appropriate, as long as the delay has been authorised by a senior officer. Further, Wayne should have been allowed eight hours' rest in any 24 hours free of questioning, with breaks for refreshment and periodic checks during the questioning.

The courts appear to take the attitude that to justify exclusion under s. 78 **PACE**, the breach or breaches must be 'significant and substantial', as the Court of Appeal held in *R* v *Keenan* [1990] 2 QB 54. A key issue is whether the police acted in bad faith: *R* v *Alladice* (1988) 87 Cr App R 380. In *R* v *Canale* [1990] 2 All ER 187 the Court of Appeal held that the officers had shown a cynical disregard of the Code, which they had breached flagrantly. The Court held that the confession should have been excluded under s. 78 **PACE**. Section 76(2)(b) **PACE** was not appropriate since the accused had been in the Parachute Regiment and was not therefore in the position of a vulnerable defendant in the face of police questioning.

Here, there also appear to be breaches of the conditions of detention. In the absence of bad faith, the court will be concerned to look at whether the breaches were operative in leading to potential unreliability under s. 76(2)(b) **PACE** or unfairness to the proceedings under s. 78.

Thus Wayne's silence in the face of the accusation from Jack is probably admissible. The cumulative effect of the possibly wrongful denial of legal advice, the apparent inducement and breach of the statute and Code C are together likely to lead to Wayne's initial silence at interview and his partly inculpatory statement being held inadmissible.

Question 3

John is an inmate of a hostel for young stablehands employed by Harry, who trains horses. Harry has set up and owns the hostel, to provide accommodation for his staff. Ann, the residential care worker at the hostel has, unknown to Harry, been allowing the residents to watch 'pirate' videos she has bought in a car-boot sale. A quarrel breaks out in the hostel recreation room one evening while students are watching a violent video which Ann has brought in. John, sickened by the violence, wants the video to be turned off so he can play snooker but Ann refuses. A scuffle breaks out and John is poked in the eye by Fred, another employee who is holding a snooker cue. It later becomes apparent that John has been blinded in one eye. After the incident, the snooker table is removed from the residents' lounge. At the same time Harry offered John £5,000 compensation 'without prejudice', but John rejected this as too low. Harry writes to Sally, his solicitor, after the accident and sends Fred's job application, which reveals that he had been sacked from a previous post at a residential hostel after allegations of violence against the inmates. Harry also sends the snooker cue to the solicitor for 'safe keeping'. John is suing Fred and Harry as being vicariously liable for the incident and for assault. The case is set down for trial. Ann is refusing to answer questions on the issue or to appear as a witness.

Discuss the evidential issues involved, not the matters of substantive law.

Commentary

You are not told what the evidential issues are so you must be careful to identify the relevant ones. You are clearly warned not to discuss the matters of liability in negligence, even if you feel you could shine in that area! This is a civil case in which you would be quite justified in referring to the burden and standard of proof as a basic question of evidence. The refusal of Ann to appear prompts you to dwell on the compellability of witnesses and since there is a suggestion of criminal activity on her part, you need to bear in mind the privilege against self-incrimination on which there has been some recent case-law under the **Human Rights Act**. You also need to consider whether the removal of the snooker table after the incident is a relevant piece of evidence. Explicit questions uniquely on relevance are rare but you should not ignore a possible part-question. The exchange with the lawyer raises the issue of legal professional privilege, both in relation to the correspondence and the sending of the snooker cue. As for Harry's without prejudice offer of compensation, you need to consider whether this can be disclosed in court. The approach you should adopt is to list the issues in the order in which they appear in the question and work systematically through them.

Answer plan

- Ann's refusal to appear—compellability as witnesses—possible privilege against self-incrimination
- Relevance of removal of snooker table after incident
- Exchange with lawyer—legal professional privilege—correspondence and sending of snooker cue
- Can without prejudice offer of compensation be disclosed?
- Burden of proof in civil cases
- Fred's earlier sacking—consider Similar Fact in civil cases

Suggested answer

All admissible evidence must be relevant, although not all relevant evidence is admissible. The removal of the snooker table is arguably not relevant to the facts in issue. To qualify for admission it should increase or diminish the probability of the existence of a fact in issue. Reciding on relevance is a matter of drawing generalisations from experience. Does the removal of the table make it more or less probable that Harry was vicariously liable in negligence or that Fred had assaulted John? Relevance is a matter of logic not law, but it may be appropriate to cite *Hart* v *Lancashire and Yorkshire Railway Co.* (1869) 21 LT 261. There, a runaway engine ran into a stationary train on a branch line, injuring the plaintiff. He sued the railway company and used as evidence the fact that the company had subsequently changed the points system. On appeal, the evidence was held to be wrongly admitted since, as Bramwell B said (at p. 263):

> People do not furnish evidence against themselves simply by adopting a new plan in order to prevent the recurrence of an accident.

It is therefore likely that the removal is not legally relevant.

In this civil case John has the legal burden of proof on both suits (*Miller* v *Minister of Pensions* [1947] **2 All ER 372**). There is an issue as to whether the standard of proof in these two suits of negligence and assault is the same. In *Hornal* v *Neuberger Products* [1957] **1 QB 247, CA**, a case of fraudulent mis-representation, Denning LJ said, 'The more serious the allegation the higher the degree of probability that is required.' The case-law does seem to suggest that the more serious the allegation, the more cogent is the evidence required to overcome the unlikelihood of what is alleged and thus to prove it. However, the standard of proof is still the balance of probabilities. In *Re Dellow's Will Trusts* the issue in the civil case was whether the husband had been killed unlawfully by the wife. Ungoed Thomas J stated, 'there can hardly be a graver issue than that'. The standard of the balance of probability was applied. In *Re H and Others* [1996] **AC 563** a majority of the House of Lords held that there was no third standard in some civil cases. With regard to the assault charge therefore, the gravity of the issues is part of the circumstances which the court has to take into consideration in assessing the balance of probabilities.

Ann is reluctant to appear as a witness possibly because she is afraid that evidence of her wrongdoing, namely showing pirate videos, may be revealed. These in themselves are relevant to the suits in that they were the cause of the quarrel. Their criminal origin is not relevant. In *Blunt* v *Park Lane Hotel* [1942] **2 KB 253** Goddard LJ expressed the scope of the common law rule, that no one is bound to answer any question if the answer thereto would, in the opinion of the judge, have a tendency to expose the deponent to any criminal charge, penalty or forfeiture which the judge regards as reasonably likely to be preferred or sued for. In practice, of course it is only the exposure to possible criminal charges which is of concern. The right is referred to in the **Civil Evidence Act 1968**, s. 14(1)(a), which provides that if the claim is made in civil proceedings the offence must be provided for by law of any part of the UK. If the pirate videos are held to be relevant to the proceedings and counsel wish to pursue a line of questioning on this, Ann may be permitted to refuse to answer (*Rank Film Distributors Ltd* v *Video Information Centre* [1982] **AC 380**). If a witness is wrongly compelled to answer a question in breach of the privilege against self-incrimination, the answer will be inadmissible in subsequent proceedings against him (*R* v *Garbett* (1847) **1 Den CC 236**). In *At & T Istel* v *Tully* [1993] **AC 45** Lord Templeman (at p. 53) condemned the privilege against self-incrimination in civil proceedings as archaic and unjustifiable. That case involved the disclosure of documents rather than the appearance of witnesses, but it does suggest that the judiciary will not apply the privilege too readily. As Lord Griffiths said (at p. 57) the law was in need of 'radical reappraisal'. However, the House of Lords conceded that any abrogation of the privilege in such cases could only be made by statute.

There is clearly a public interest in speedy settlement of civil litigation and the law does offer some protection to communications which are aimed at achieving this. Obviously, there is a danger that an offer of settlement may be later interpreted as an admission of liability. Because of this, communications between parties, namely Harry's offer of settlement, may not be ordered to be disclosed on discovery and will not form part of the documents placed before the court, as the House of Lords held in *Rush & Tompkins Ltd* v *Greater London Council* [1989] AC 1280. The privilege is that of the parties, so it only applies if Harry requests it. However, although without prejudice correspondence may not be admissible on the issue of liability, it may be admissible on other grounds such as costs, where delay or unreasonable refusal to settle may be material (see RSC Order 22 r. 14). This rule applies the proposal made by Cairns LJ in *Calderbank* v *Calderbank* [1976] Fam 93.

It is a common law rule that communications passing between lawyer and client about materials prepared for the purpose of litigation are privileged. In this question, the first aspect of legal professional privilege applies, namely, that communications between lawyer and client made in the course of seeking and giving advice within the normal scope of legal business are privileged if the client seeks the privilege. Thus, any advice that Sally gave to Harry could not be disclosed (*Minter* v *Priest* [1930] AC 558). Section 10 of the **Police and Criminal Evidence Act 1984 (PACE)** gives statutory recognition to legal professional privilege. However, Harry cannot claim the privilege for material objects so the snooker cue is not covered, nor can there be a claim of privilege for Fred's job application, since these did not arise in the course of his relationship with the lawyer (*R* v *King* [1983] 1 WLR 411). In that case, the court expressed doubts about the earlier decision, *Frank Truman Export Ltd* v *Commissioner of Police for the Metropolis* [1977] QB 952, where Swanwick J held that pre-existing documents which might be relevant in evidence against the plaintiff, were privileged in the hands of the plaintiff's solicitor to whom they had been delivered for his consideration in relation to likely criminal charges. The job application is likely to be highly probative and admissible as 'Similar Fact' evidence (*Mood Music Publishing Co. Ltd* v *de Wolfe* [1976] Ch 119). In that case, Lord Denning MR, after referring to what was then Similar Fact evidence in criminal cases, stated,

> In civil cases the courts have followed a similar line but have not been so chary of admitting it. In civil cases the courts will admit evidence of similar facts if it is logically probative, that is if it is logically relevant in determining the matter which is in issue: provided that it is not oppressive or unfair to the other side: and also that the other side has fair notice of it and is able to deal with it.

The House of Lords reconsidered this area of law in *O'Brien* v *Chief Constable of South Wales Police* [2005] 3 All ER 931. The House stressed the difference between the civil and criminal tests for the admissibility of previous misconduct to show propensity. The latter has been now changed in the **Criminal Justice Act 2003**. Lord Phillips stated,

> I would simply apply the test on relevance as the test of admissibility of similar fact evidence in a civil suit. Such evidence is admissible if it is potentially probative of an issue in the action.

He went on, however, to acknowledge that the 'policy considerations that have given rise to the complex rules . . . in sections 100 to 106 of the 2003 Act' may have a part to play and referred to the objective of dealing with cases justly in CPR r 1.2. The court will consider, therefore, whether the prejudicial effect of admitting the earlier allegations of violence against Fred will generate unfairness. In *O'Brien* earlier evidence of impropriety on the part of a chief constable was admitted in a suit for misfeasance in public office and malicious prosecution.

Question 4

Tanya witnessed an attempted break-in of an off-licence and claims she saw a car speed away from the scene. She phoned the police and dictated the car registration number to PC Ford, who wrote it down in his notebook. Tanya also wrote down the number in her diary. PC Ford found a cigarette lighter with the initials RS at the scene of the crime. The car is traced to a Richard Smith, who claims it was taken without his permission by his neighbour Harold and that he had nothing to do with the crime. He claims Harold has been waging a vendetta against him. Richard has been seeing a psychiatrist who has diagnosed him as suffering from a mental condition whereby he can sometimes not tell fact from fiction. The prosecution intend to call Dr Wong to give expert evidence on Richard's mental state. Richard claims Harold told him that he, Harold, had used Richard's car on the night of the burglary. Harold denies he said this.

Advise on evidence.

Commentary

This question requires the student to consider a number of different evidential issues. The first part requires a discussion on whether a witness can refresh his or her memory from a number of possible sources. There is also a need to consider whether this infringes the rule against hearsay. The cigarette lighter as evidence should be considered and the status of Harold's statement as possible hearsay. Finally, a discussion of the admissibility of expert opinion evidence will be necessary in relation to Dr Wong's testimony.

Answer plan

- Can witness refresh memory when in witness box—**CJA 2003**
- Application of hearsay rule to PC Ford's statement to Richard—**CJA 2003**
- Admissibility of lighter and initials—real evidence
- Admissibility of Dr Wong's testimony as expert opinion evidence

Suggested answer

The first issue relates to the admissibility of Tanya's statement to the police. It is clear that whilst testifying in court, Tanya is unable to remember the registration number and it is therefore necessary for Tanya to be able to refresh her memory by using PC Ford's notebook or her own diary. One issue is whether Tanya verified Ford's entry. In *Jones* v *Metcalfe* [1967] 1 WLR 1286, the Divisional Court refused to allow a police officer's testimony regarding the registration number of a lorry which had been told to him by an eyewitness. This was because the statement was hearsay and since the police officer had failed to read the number back to and have it verified by the witness, it could not also be used to refresh the eyewitness's memory. Section 139 CJA 2003 now replaces the common law provisions on memory-refreshing documents. In effect Tanya may refresh her memory from a document while giving oral evidence providing she confirms that the document represents her recollection at the time she made it and her recollection was likely to have been significantly better at that time than it is while she is giving oral evidence. It is likely that she can rely on either the extract from the notebook entry if she had verified it, or her diary. If the defence inspect these documents and cross-examine her on parts not relied on to refresh her memory then the party who called the witness may have the document admitted (*Senat* v *Senat* [1965] 1 WLR 981). Under s. 120(3) CJA 2003 the document then is evidence of any matter stated of which oral evidence would be admissible.

The entry in the diary should ideally have been made at the first practicable opportunity at a time when the events were still fresh in Tanya's mind. The earlier common law provision applied the principle of contemporaneity but the wording of the CJA does not indicate such a strict approach.

The diary or notebook should be handed to the defence counsel or the court so that it may be inspected and the witness cross-examined on its contents. The defence counsel can request that the jury be shown the notebook if it is necessary for the determination of an issue: *R* v *Bass* [1953] 1 QB 680. Finally, the document should be the original. However, if the original has been lost, it seems that a verified or accurate copy can be used (see *R* v *Cheng* (1976) 63 Cr App R 20).

With respect to the finding of the cigarette lighter, it is submitted that this is a piece of real evidence, which should be admitted into evidence for the jury to draw their own inferences. The difficulty is whether this may be inadmissible because of hearsay. It is unclear whether the identifying marks, names or initials on the item make any statement as to identity. In *R* v *Rice* [1963] 1 QB 857, the Court of Criminal Appeal allowed into evidence an airline ticket bearing the accused's name. The court rejected an argument that the airline ticket should not be admitted because it was hearsay. It was of the view that the ticket was admissible as relevant albeit circumstantial evidence to show that a person with the name of the accused had flown at the time and date stipulated on the air ticket. If *Rice* is correct then the cigarette lighter would be admissible provided that the court can be convinced that it was relevant to the facts in issue. This is supported by *R* v *Lydon* (1986) 85 Cr App R 221, where a piece of paper bearing the accused's first name, found near a gun which had been used in a robbery, was held to be admissible evidence to link the accused to the gun. Presumably, if the lighter had the appearance of just being lost, then there is a strong argument for its admission into evidence. However, if it appears that the lighter had been lost some time ago, then it is unlikely to be admitted because it may be irrelevant. The argument is that it could have been lost at the same place as the scene of the burglary sometime prior to the commission of the offence.

Can Richard give evidence of what Harold allegedly told him? The purpose of adducing the statement would be to suggest it was true; that is, that it was Harold who committed the offence. It would thus arguably fall within the definition of hearsay in s. 114 **CJA 2003**. It may, however, be admitted under one of the statutory exceptions, the most likely being s. 114(1)(b), the common law exception of *res gestae*. The prosecution may argue that the statement is a third-party confession and that the courts have shown reluctance to admit such statements on the grounds of inadmissible hearsay or irrelevance. In *R* v *Blastland* the House of Lords took a restrictive view of relevance in ruling that what an absent third party said to a number of individuals which if true would have tended to exonerate the accused was inadmissible because it was evidence of a state of mind and emotion which was irrelevant to the facts in issue. Here it seems the defence is arguing that Harold was the perpetrator. If he is called as a witness he could be cross-examined and if he denies taking the car his alleged previous inconsistent statement to Richard could be put to him under the procedure set out in s. 4 **Criminal Procedure Act 1865**. The statement may be evidence of the truth of its contents following s. 119 **CJA 2003**.

With regards to the evidence of Dr Wong, it may be possible that this evidence is admissible for the prosecution on the basis that it relates to a matter for which the judge or jury may require assistance, namely whether Richard's version of events is to be believed. The weight to be given to such evidence is a matter for the jury. It is arguable that this type of evidence is admissible because the jury would not be able to draw the appropriate inferences and form proper opinions from the facts requiring expert opinion: *Buckley* v *Rice Thomas* (1554) Plowd 118. Before an expert witness can give opinion evidence relating to any particular issue, it is for the judge to decide whether that particular witness is an expert. It is not essential that in all cases the expert possess formal qualifications: *R* v *Silverlock* [1894] 2 QB 766.

However, expert opinion evidence is not admissible per se in all criminal trials. Where the issue is one on which the jury is able to decide and does not require the assistance of experts, no opinion evidence from experts is admissible. The restriction on the admissibility of expert evidence on matters for which the jury requires no assistance includes a restriction on expert evidence on the credibility of a witness or the accused save in exceptional circumstances: *Lowery* v *R* [1974] AC 85, although, in *Lowery*, such evidence was admitted. The Court of Appeal in *R* v *Turner* [1975] QB 834 regarded this decision as applying only to the specific facts of the case rather than establishing any general principle. This approach appears to be correct in the light of *R* v *Rimmer* [1983] **Crim LR 250**, where the trial judge refused to allow the evidence of an expert on the basis that this related only to the credibility of the accused. Of course, the precondition of the admissibility of Dr Wong's evidence is that Richard's disorder is relevant. Admissibility will first be dependent on the statements from Richard being put in evidence or of the defence putting forward this evidence in some way.

On the facts of the present case, it may then be argued that Dr Wong's evidence is relevant and admissible because it relates to an issue with which the jury may need assistance, namely Richard's mental condition and the effect of such an illness. The question is whether the latter falls 'within the limits of normality' referred to in *Turner* (at p. 841). Sections 118(1) and (2) **CJA 2003** set out the requirements whereby experts giving evidence may draw on the words of others and not violate the rule against hearsay. Generally this is allowed but with an 'interests of justice' proviso (s. 127(4)).

The prosecution should be warned that it is possible this evidence will not be admitted. The courts are very reluctant to admit expert evidence on witnesses' mental states. In *Gilfoyle* [2001] **2 Cr App Rep 57** the court stated that the jury did not need the evidence of a psychologist to inform them how ordinary people react to the stresses of life. To succeed the prosecution will need to convince the court that Richard's alleged abnormality is significant (*O'Brien, Hall and Sherwood* [2000] **Crim LR 676**).

Question 5

Fred is charged with sexual assault on Amanda, his colleague at work. He denies the assault took place. He denies he was at her flat on the night in question. He accepted that he had been there earlier in the week and said Amanda had pestered him for sex and that when he declined she had threatened to make things difficult for him at work. He also alleges that she told colleagues she had made up claims of sexual assault earlier. He also says that she had a grudge against him because he had been promoted at work and that she had had affairs with a number of male colleagues.

Paul, a prosecution witness, will give evidence that when he arrived at Amanda's place, a short while after the rape was alleged to have taken place, he saw someone rush out of the door. As it was already dark at the time, Paul only managed to see his face when he ran past a street light outside Amanda's house. He later identified Fred as the man at an identification parade held a week later.

Fred has a previous conviction for sexual assault on a female co-worker, five years ago. He is considering whether to testify.

Discuss the evidential issues.

Commentary

This is a typical evidence examination question consisting of a mixture of several different topics in one question. The issues here include the questions that can be asked in cross-examination and whether if a denial is made, evidence in rebuttal is admissible. It is also necessary to consider the effect of the accused's previous conviction, i.e., whether the prosecution can introduce that into evidence either under **CJA 2003**. There is the further problem of weak identification evidence, which will necessitate the giving of the **Turnbull** direction. Further, there is the issue of the falsity of the alibi. It is also important to note that a corroboration warning is no longer required, although this is a case of sexual assault.

Answer plan

- Is Amanda's denial of making allegation out of malice a collateral issue—and therefore answer would be final? Possible exception of bias
- Can Amanda be cross-examined on alleged sexual encounters with third party and on alleged threats against Fred? s. 41 **Youth Justice and Criminal Evidence Act 1999**
- Identification of Fred—**Turnbull** direction
- Fred's previous conviction—effect of provisions in **CJA 2003** and recent case-law
- Failure to testify—s. 35 **Criminal Justice and Public Order Act 1994**
- *R* v *Becouarn* [2005] UKHL 55
- No need for corroboration warning

Suggested answer

There are a number of evidential issues to be considered here and it may be simplest just to take each one of them in turn. The first issue relates to whether Fred's counsel can cross-examine Amanda on the basis that she made the allegation out of malice because Fred had previously spurned her advances. It is clear that Fred's counsel can ask the question but that if she denies it, the general rule is that since this is a collateral issue, her answer would be final: *R* v *Burke* (1858) 8 Cox CC 44. Fred's counsel can continue to cross-examine her about the matter but is not allowed to bring in evidence to contradict her. However, there are exceptions to the general rule and the exception that may apply here is that of bias. In *R* v *Shaw* (1888) 16 Cox CC 503, the defence was allowed to call evidence in rebuttal of a witness's denial that he had a grudge against the accused. Thus, it is likely that in this instance, if Amanda was to deny that she made the allegation out of malice, Fred's counsel could not only cross-examine her on the matter, but also call evidence to rebut her testimony on that issue.

The next evidential issue is whether Amanda can be cross-examined on previous sexual history. The ability of the defence to ask the victim questions of her sexual history is now restricted by s. 41 of the **Youth Justice and Criminal Evidence Act 1999**. These provisions must now be interpreted in the light of the **Human Rights Act** (see *R* v *A* (2001)).

Fred is making two allegations: first, that Amanda is promiscuous; and second, that she had made false allegations before. As far as the first is concerned it seems likely that the court would refuse cross-examination under s. 41. Where sexual behaviour is with third parties there would have to be very special facts before cross-examination would be permitted and in particular those facts would have to relate to specific instances of alleged sexual behaviour. The issue here does not appear to be consent and so s. 41(3)(b) and (c) do not apply. Under s. 41(4) no evidence or question will be regarded as relating to a relevant issue in the case if it appears to the court reasonable to assume that the purpose (or main purpose) for which it would be adduced or asked is to establish or elicit material for impugning the credibility of the complainant as a witness. However, Fred may rely on the recent case of *R* v *Martin* [2004] EWCA Crim 916. In that case the Court of Appeal held that s. 41 did not preclude questions which did not solely go to credibility but which supported the defendant's contention that the allegations against him were false. The court may permit cross-examination of Amanda about the incident earlier in the week in question when she had allegedly pestered him for sex and he had refused. Fred may be assisted by recent case-law under **CJA 2003**. In *R* v *V* [2006] EWCA Crim 1901 the Court of Appeal held that the appellant who had been charged with sexual offences against his daughter should have been allowed to cross-examine her about a sexual allegation that she had previously made where there was evidence to show that it was false; however, that failing did not render his convictions unsafe. In that case there was sufficient evidential base to suggest that an earlier allegation made by the daughter to her friend had been untrue. The test for leave to bring in the bad character evidence of a non-defendant under s. 100 **CJA 2003** was passed and s. 4 of the **1865 Criminal Evidence and Procedure Act** should have been employed if the daughter had denied admitting the falsity of the allegation. It is likely, therefore, that Fred's counsel will be allowed to cross-examine Amanda on the allegation.

A further issue relates to the identification of Fred by Paul. In *R* v *Turnbull* [1977] QB 224, the Court of Appeal laid down guidelines for the treatment of identification evidence where the case depends wholly or substantially on the correctness of the identification. The guidelines state, inter alia, that the judge should warn the jury of the special need for caution, before convicting the accused in reliance on the correctness of the identification evidence. The judge should draw the jury's attention to the possibility that an error was made and should invite them to examine closely the circumstances in which the observation took place. It was made clear in *R* v *Oakwell* [1978] 1 WLR 32, that the *Turnbull* guidelines are not to be interpreted inflexibly. Thus in this case, the judge will have to warn the jury that the identification evidence may be weak in that it was dark that night and Paul only had a quick glimpse of Fred's face whilst the latter was passing a street light. These factors should be drawn to the jury's attention. The judge will have to be satisfied that in the event that the identification evidence is weak, there must be other evidence to support the correctness of the identification. This will be for the judge to decide looking at all the evidence available. Furthermore, the identification parade should have been held in accordance with Code D issued under **PACE 1984**. If not, evidence may be excluded under s. 78 of that Act.

There is also the problem of Fred's previous conviction for sexual assault on a female co-worker five years ago. This conviction may be admissible under the provisions on bad character in the **CJA 2003**. As a conviction it satisfies the test of bad character under s. 98 and Fred may have triggered its admissibility under two heads and these considerations will apply whether he testifies or not. First, the prosecution may argue that the conviction is admissible under s. 101(1)(d) as being relevant to an important matter in issue between prosecution and defence. This section equates to the earlier common law provisions on similar fact, although it is clearly the intention of the new Act that more of such evidence will be admitted (see *R v Hanson* [2005] 2 Cr App R 21). The current test for admissibility is set out in *Hanson*. The court should consider three matters:

- Did the history of the convictions establish a propensity to commit offences of the kind charged?
- Did that propensity make it more likely that the defendant had committed the offence charged?
- Was it just to rely on the conviction(s) of the same description or category; and in any event would the proceedings be unfair if they were admitted? Sections 101(3) and s.103(3) allow the court an exclusionary discretion. One factor would be how long ago the offence was.

Fred's conviction of a sex offence appears to fall into the same category of offence as the current charge, although the current **Categories of Offences Order** (SI 2004 No. 3346) issued under the **CJA** lists only offences of dishonesty and sexual offences against children. In *Hanson* the Court of Appeal stated that 'In referring to offences of the same description or category, section 103(2) is not exhaustive of the type of conviction which might be relied upon to show evidence of propensity to commit offences of the kind charged' (see also *R v Weir*). The prosecution will rely on recent case-law which does indicate a low threshold for admissibility. In particular, where the offence is a sexual one previous sexual behaviour seems almost routinely to be admitted. In *R v Weir* the Court of Appeal held that evidence of an earlier caution for taking an indecent photograph of a child was rightly admitted in a trial where the defendant was charged with sexually assaulting a 13-year-old girl. It is not fatal to the prosecution's application that Fred has only one previous conviction, especially since this is a charge of sexual offence. In *Hanson* the Court of Appeal stated, 'There is no minimum number of events necessary to demonstrate such a propensity. The fewer the number of convictions the weaker is likely to be the evidence of propensity. A single previous conviction for an offence of the same description or category will often not show propensity. But it may do so where, for example, it shows a tendency to unusual behaviour or where its circumstances demonstrate probative force in relation to the offence charged' (compare *DPP* v *P* [1991] 2AC 447 at 460E to 461A).

If the prosecution do succeed in this application it may be that the evidence will be admissible under s. 101(1)(g) 'attacks another person's character'.

Fred has attacked the character of Amanda. As Doak and McGourlay (2008, p. 290) put it 'This is a continuation of the tit for tat rule which applied under s1(3)(b) of the **Criminal Evidence Act 1898** under which the shield against cross-examination was lost if a defendant cast imputations on the character of the prosecution, prosecution witnesses or the deceased victim.' It now applies, however, even if Fred does not testify. The discretion to exclude evidence of the defendant's bad character under s. 101(3) applies to this section. Although evidence admitted under this head goes mainly to credibility, following *R* v *Highton* it may also be evidence of propensity (see also *R* v *Randall* [2004] 1 WLR 56).

If Fred chooses not to give evidence, it should be borne in mind that s. 35 of the **Criminal Justice and Public Order Act 1994** allows the court or the jury to draw such inferences as appear proper from the accused's failure to give evidence without good cause. Thus there is a risk that the jury may draw adverse inferences from his failure to give evidence in court (see *R* v *Cowan*). Under s. 35(5) a failure to answer questions is presumed to be 'without good cause' unless the accused is entitled under statute not to answer particular questions or enjoys a legal privilege not to answer them or alternatively the court grants discretion not to answer. The judge should follow the Judicial Studies Board Guidelines on Fred's non-appearance to testify. The directions follow those in *Cowan* and are different from those under ss. 34, 36, 37. In particular the jury is restricted to considering the prosecution's case in deciding whether it should draw an adverse inference. The points covered should remind the jury of the following: the burden of proof was on the prosecution; the defendant had a right to silence; silence alone could prove guilt; the jury must first consider whether there was a case to answer and if the answer was 'yes' then ask if the defendant had an answer would he not have gone into the witness box. In *Birchall* (1999) Lord Bingham CJ stated: 'Inescapable logic demands that a jury should not start to consider whether they should draw inferences from a defendant's failure to give oral evidence at his trial until they have concluded that the Crown's case against him is sufficiently compelling to call for an answer.'

In *R* v *Becouarn* [2005] UKHL 55 the House of Lords held that the Judicial Studies Board specimen direction was sufficiently fair to defendants. The jury could be directed that they could draw an adverse inference if they considered the accused to have no answer to the prosecution case, or none that would stand up to cross-examination, even though an additional reason might be that he would have his criminal record revealed if he testified. The House rejected any direction along the lines of *Lucas* pertaining to lies by the defendant that there might be other reasons for the defendant's silence. (This situation, of course, is less likely to arise now since criminal record may be revealed in certain circumstances even if the defendant does not testify.)

Finally, it should be noted that by virtue of s. 32(1) of the 1994 Act, there is no longer any necessity for the judge to give the jury a corroboration warning in a case involving a sexual offence.

Question 6

Jeremy, Harold, Christine and Joan are on trial for supplying illegal drugs. They share a flat in which the police find quantities of heroin, £50,000 in used banknotes, and a large quantity of designer clothes. The defendants claim that they had won the money at horse-racing. They claim that the heroin must have been left by a student they had put up for the night, who has now disappeared. At the investigation stage they all have the same solicitor, Good & Co. Before the trial Christine changes solicitor. Jeremy pleads guilty and gives evidence for the prosecution. Christine's counsel has sought leave to produce a statement that Jeremy had made to Good & Co. which is inconsistent with evidence he gives in court and which would help Christine's defence. Harold had made a confession of his responsibility for the drug dealing in a statement to the police, in which he said that Christine was not involved in the offence. Harold's confession is, however, excluded by the trial judge beforehand in a voir dire. At the trial, in giving evidence, Harold claims that he had seen Christine selling drugs outside a school. Christine's counsel wishes to question him on his statement to the police. Joan refuses to answer a number of questions at a police interview with a solicitor present. She does say, however, she was not a user of drugs. She claims at trial that she was a user, not a supplier of drugs.

Advise on the admissibility of Jeremy's statement with Good & Co. and whether Christine's counsel is likely to be able to question Harold on his pre-trial statement.

Commentary

You will need to show first, an awareness of recent case-law dealing with legal professional privilege when it appears to conflict with the interests of a defendant. The question also requires an appreciation of the tricky situation arising when a defendant wishes to adduce a co-defendant's confession or to cross-examine a co-defendant on a confession which has already been ruled inadmissible as part of the prosecution's case. This question requires familiarity with the concept of relevance and in particular a knowledge of case-law on the relevance of 'life-style' in drugs cases.

Answer plan

- Relevance of 'life-style' evidence in drug offences
- Legal professional privilege will apply to Jeremy's statement—see *R* v *Derby Magistrates' Court, ex parte B* (1995)
- Counsel for co-accused may cross-examine maker of inadmissible confession to undermine credibility
- Excluded confession may be available to co-defendant—*R* v *Myers*, CJA 2003
- Joan's statement at trial—whether inference may be drawn from earlier silence; **Lucas** direction on lies

Suggested answer

All evidence must be relevant, although of course not all relevant evidence is admissible. The test for relevance is a matter of experience and common sense. Recently a number of cases have shown the application of the concept of relevance in connection with drug dealing. In *R* v *Wright* **[1994] Crim LR 55** the Court of Appeal held that the finding of a large quantity of cash was capable of being relevant to the issue of whether the accused was supplying drugs to others. It is clear, however, that the judge must direct that the jury must not treat that evidence as evidence of propensity. In *R* v *Grant* **(1996) 1 Cr App R 73** guidelines for directions to the jury were set out. In order for the finding of the £ 50,000 to constitute evidence the jury would have to reject the explanation that it was a result of success at the races and accept that there was no other innocent explanation. If the jury were to conclude that the presence of the money indicated not only past dealing, but an ongoing dealing in drugs, then finding the money together with the drugs in question would be a matter which they could take into account in considering whether the necessary intent to supply had been proved. £50,000 is likely to be considered a large enough amount to be relevant but the admissibility of the evidence of designer clothes is less certain. Further information is needed to establish how exclusive they are (Nike, Gap or Versace?). It has in any case been held that evidence of lavish lifestyle will only rarely be relevant to an issue of intent to supply (*R* v *Halpin* **[1996] Crim LR 112**). In the controversial case of *R* v *Guney* **(1998) 2 Cr App R 242**, on the other hand, the Court of Appeal said that whether evidence is relevant depends on the particular circumstances of each case. Evidence of cash and lifestyle might even be relevant to possession, but more likely to intent to supply. In that case the Court of Appeal held that the evidence of finding nearly £ 25,000 in the accused's bedroom near to the drugs was admissible relevant evidence on the question of possession. The accused had claimed the drugs were planted on him. The court stated, however, that evidence of a lavish lifestyle or possession of large sums of cash was not without more proof of possession.

There is no general privilege attached to confidential statements made between professional people and their clients. However, the major exception to this is legal professional privilege, which covers certain types of correspondence between a lawyer and his or her client and certain communications between a lawyer and/or client and third parties. The privilege belongs to the client, who can insist on non-disclosure by the lawyer or third party in question. The scope of the privilege is given in s. 10 of the **Police and Criminal Evidence Act 1984 (PACE)**. This section, however, does not regulate its use in general but sets limits on police powers to search for and seize evidence. Jeremy can thus claim legal professional privilege for his statement to Good & Co. He may waive this if he wishes. However, if he fails to it will be impossible for Christine to challenge it successfully in the light of a House of Lords ruling. Christine might reasonably argue that a refusal to disclose harms her defence and in the case of *R v Ataou* [1988] QB 798, that claim w as heard sympathetically by the Court of Appeal. However, in *R v Derby Magistrates' Court, ex parte B* [1996] AC 487, the House of Lords overruled *Ataou* and the earlier case of *R v Barton* [1972] 2 All ER 321. The House held that '. . . no exception should be allowed to the absolute nature of legal professional privilege once established'. The House also held that the privilege is the same whether it is sought by the prosecution or the defence and the 'refusal of the client to waive his privilege, for whatever reason, or for no reason, cannot be questioned or investigated by the court'. The court considered that 'if a balancing exercise was ever required in the case of legal professional privilege it was performed once and for all in the 16th century'. In that case a witness, B, who had previously been acquitted of a murder, could not be compelled to produce a confession made in the presence of his solicitor in a subsequent trial of his stepfather for the same offence. This decision has been much criticised. Choo, for example (2006, p. 188) comments that it 'is open to criticism on the ground that it overlooks the importance of the need to protect the innocent from wrongful conviction'. The House of Lords limited its scope in *Re L (A minor)* [1996] 2 WLR 395 when it held that it was confined to legal advice privilege and did not apply in care proceedings. It is assumed that Jeremy's statement concerns legal advice privilege. Christine is unlikely to succeed in obtaining the document.

Evidence of Harold's confession is clearly relevant to the trial since it conflicts with his evidence in court. He had previously absolved Christine but now he is implicating her. Christine's counsel is advised to apply to present Harold's confession not as to the truth of its contents but in order to demonstrate the inconsistency of Harold's testimony and thus to undermine his credibility. In *R v Rowson* [1986] QB 174 the Court of Appeal held that a trial judge did not have a discretion to prevent counsel for a co-accused from cross-examining the maker of an inadmissible confession. Such questioning is for the purpose of showing that the witness has made a previous inconsistent statement and thus undermining his credibility. The judge must make it clear to the jury that any evidence of the confession is not evidence of guilt. The only pre-condition is that the evidence be relevant, as the Privy Council held in *Lui-Mei Lin* v *R* (1989) 88 Cr App R 296. The right to cross-examine is thus unfettered. An alternative, and perhaps better approach, however, would be an application to sever the indictment. This is illustrated by *R* v *O'Boyle* (1991) 92 Cr App R 202, where a joint trial would be harmful to the defendant subject to such cross-examination, whereas a separate trial would not harm the co-defendant and the prosecution.

In *R* v *Myers* [1998] AC 124 the House of Lords went further and held that a confession excluded by s. 78 **PACE** might still be available to a co-defendant. A defendant in a joint trial has the right to ask about a voluntary statement made by a co-accused outside court even though it is not relied on by the prosecution as long as it is relevant to the party who wishes to rely on it. This would not be the case if the confession was excluded by s. 76(2) **PACE**. Thus Christine may be allowed to cross-examine Harold and the officer to whom he made the confession. The evidence adduced would be relevant both to credibility and the facts in issue. The judge would have no discretion, as between co-accused, to exclude it. Further information is required as to whether Harold's confession is excluded under s. 78 **PACE** or s. 76 **PACE**. Section 76A(1) **PACE** now states that 'in any proceedings a confession made by an accused person may be given in evidence for another person charged in the same proceedings (a co-accused) in so far as it is relevant to any matter in issue in the proceedings and is not excluded by the court in pursuance of this section'.

The court will apply to all tests, or oppression and reliability, as formulated for evidence tendered by the prosecution but the standard applied to the co-defendant will be the balance of probabilities. The court may consider s. 126(1) **CJA 2003**, which provides an exclusionary discretion for hearsay statement, but it is unlikely it will be applied to prevent Christine producing evidence of her innocence.

The contrast between Joan's statement at trial and her earlier silence at interview raises the possibility of inviting the jury to consider s. 34 or s. 36 if the issue at interview was explaining the presence of drugs. More information is needed on the circumstances of the interview, particularly the nature of the legal advice and how much Joan was told of the case against her. In *R* v *Compton* [2002] EWCA Crim 2835 the court considered that it was sufficient for the police questioner to say that he was investigating drug trafficking, without being specific about the offence. Joan's explanation appears to go to the central issue, i.e. she is denying dealing in drugs. It is established that s. 34 may apply even if the jury in drawing an adverse inference would effectively determine guilt. Lord Woolf CJ in **Gowland-Wynn** [2002] 1 Cr App 569 stated that s. 34 applied when a 'defendant could be expected to comment about something which goes to the heart of his defence'. If other conditions apply then Joan's silence may be admissible.

The other issue to consider here is that at the interview room she said she was not a user of drugs. If the prosecution had used this it is arguable that a *Lucas* direction is required, since Jane appears to have told an out-of-court lie. In *R* v *AO* (2000) **Crim LR 617** the Court of Appeal held that 'where the same response was relied upon both as a lie and a failure to mention a fact relied on by the defence, then both directions should be given'. The judge should therefore give a *Lucas* direction as well as one on failure to mention a fact if the conditions apply. The lie by Joan must be admitted or proved beyond reasonable doubt and the jury told that the mere fact that the defendant lied is not in itself evidence of guilt since defendants may lie for innocent reasons. So only if the jury is sure that Joan did not lie for an innocent reason can the lie support the prosecution case.

Question 7

Hilda is charged with criminal damage. The prosecution case is that she painted slogans on the wall of a local factory farm which she considered was treating chickens cruelly. There had been a spate of such desecrations and police had set up watch in a neighbouring house and identified Hilda as the offender. Hilda suspects that the surveillance took place and wishes to cross-examine the prosecution witness about the quality of his observation because she contests the identification. The police have searched Hilda's lodgings with a search warrant and find pots of paint identical to the colours used on the wall slogans. The police wish to call Norman, Hilda's estranged husband, as a witness. He still lives in the same house as her and had made a statement to the police that Hilda came in very late on the night in question and her hands were covered with paint. He is called at the trial for the prosecution but refuses to give any evidence. There is medical evidence to the effect that Hilda is in any case unfit to stand trial because she suffers from a mental instability and the defence are considering whether to plead this. The defence have discovered that the police had secretly recorded a conversation between Hilda and her solicitor while Hilda was in police custody.
   Advise on evidence.

Commentary

A pot-pourri of issues, which means that you must have the law relating to them at your finger tips. Taking the issues in order:

- Can the police be compelled to disclose the identity of the surveillance? This turns on the question of public interest immunity and the protection of informers, including how far this stretches to surveillance sites.

- Is evidence arising from the search admissible? Consider whether the evidence is relevant.

- Is Norman a compellable witness? What is the status of estranged spouses? Consider s. 80 **PACE** and appropriate case-law.

- If Norman does not appear as a witness, may his evidence be presented in any other form, for example under the hearsay exceptions of the **Criminal Justice Act 2003**?

- What is the burden and standard of proof on the issue of Hilda's competence to testify?
- What view will the court take of the secret police recording? Will the prosecution go ahead?

Answer plan

- Identity of premises may be relevant to Hilda's defence
- Relevance of paint if supports other identification evidence—*R* v *Reading* (1966), CJA 2003, s. 101(1)(d) and s. 103(1)(a)
- Competence and compellability of Norman as witness
- Possible admissibility of Norman's evidence under **CJA 2003**
- Burden of proof on fitness to plead
- Possible stay of proceedings

Suggested answer

The secret recording by the police of the conversation between Hilda and her solicitor is likely to be taken very seriously by the court. In *R* v *Grant* [2005] 3 WLR 437 the court held that a prosecution should have been stayed for abuse of process since the police had by recording a conversation between the accused and their solicitors, interfered with the right to communicate in confidence, even though evidence was obtained as a result. (See also *Brennan* v *UK* (2001) 34 EHRR 507.) In the event the trial does go ahead. There are a number of issues arising from the evidence.

The police may wish to keep the identity of the house they are using secret, either because the people who allowed them to use it have been promised confidentiality or in order not to deter other possible assistance. However, the identity of the premises may be important to Hilda's defence so she can cross-examine the police witness on the quality of the identification evidence. The rule in *Marks* v *Beyfus* (1890) 25 QBD 494, allows the identity of informers to be protected as a matter of public policy. In *R* v *Rankine* [1986] QBD 861 this rule was held to apply also to the identity of persons who have allowed their property to be used as an observation post. However, if the owners do not wish to maintain secrecy, there would be no objection to identifying the premises. In any case, the prosecution must lay down a basis for the anonymity if it is required. In *R* v *Johnson* [1988] 1 WLR 1377, the Court of Appeal said it was necessary for the prosecution to satisfy the court that there was a particular need for the observation post and for anonymity before suppression would be accepted. In the event the identity in that case was not revealed. In *R* v *Brown*, *R* v *Daley* (1987) 87 Cr App Rep 52, the Court of Appeal held that the extension of the exclusionary rule to surveillance sites was intended to protect the owner or occupier, not the post *simpliciter*. Here details of an unmarked police car ought to have been revealed. It is necessary then to see whether on the facts the address is relevant information and to establish the attitude of the occupier. In view of these authorities it may be possible for Hilda to have discovery of the identity of the premises. If the prosecution wishes to refuse disclosure then depending on the sensitivity of the material it must follow the procedures set out in the **Criminal Procedure and Investigations Act 1996**. The House of Lords considered this in *R* v *H, R* v *C* **[2003] UKHL 3**. This is an area where the Strasbourg court has had considerable impact (see *Rowe and Davis* v *UK*). In some cases partial disclosure may be possible. One new procedure is that of appointing Special Counsel at application hearings to argue the case for the defendant. Special Counsel would not be permitted to disclose information to the defendant.

It is arguable that the evidence of the paint is relevant if it goes to support other identification evidence, as it does here. In *R* v *Reading* **[1966] 1 WLR 836** the court held that if otherwise innocent-seeming articles, in that case walkie-talkie radios and imitation police uniforms, could be used for criminal purposes it is not necessary that any particular occasion on which they were used be identified. It thus appears sufficient that there is identification evidence linking Hilda to the offence to make the submission of the paint as real evidence relevant in the case. The evidence may be admitted under **CJA 2003** s. 103(1)(a) and s. 101(1)(d).

It is assumed that Norman is a competent witness. Under the **Police and Criminal Evidence Act 1984 (PACE)**, s. 80(5), former spouses are treated as any other witnesses. However, that only applies if the marriage has been ended by divorce or if it was voidable and has been annulled. The common law position remains that a marriage is treated as subsisting even if there has been a judicial separation, as the court held in *Moss* v *Moss* **[1963] 2 QBD 799**. Thus Norman is a competent witness for the prosecution by virtue of s. 53 of the **Youth Justice and Criminal Evidence Act 1999**. He is not, however, compellable, since the offence in question does not fall within the categories of s. 80(3) **PACE**; that is, an offence that involves a violent or sexual attack on the spouse or a person under 16 years.

If he persists in refusing to testify the prosecution may need to consider whether the evidence can be adduced in any other way. His statement to the police is clearly hearsay in that the purpose of adducing it is to suggest it is true. It is arguably endorsed by him and therefore would fulfill the requirement of firsthand hearsay in s. 116 **Criminal Justice Act 2003**. However, there is difficulty in adducing it since on the facts there does not appear to be any reason for not calling him as a witness. The lack of one of the acceptable reasons listed in s. 116(2) is likely to be fatal to admissibility. Can the statement be adduced under s. 117, which admits statements received and created in the course of trade, business or profession? The Court of Appeal held in *R* v *McGillivray* **(1992) 97 Cr App R 232** that the predecessor to s. 114, s. 23 was the appropriate section for police statements, so s. 117 is unlikely to be held to be available here. In any case, since the document was prepared for criminal proceedings, the same problem arises of giving a reason for non-appearance of the witness. It is unlikely that the additional reason that the witness could not reasonably be expected to remember the matters dealt with will apply. In fact however, the prosecution will find it impossible to evade the protection a statute affords to witnesses by using a statutory exception to the rule against hearsay. Even if the requirements of the statute were fulfilled, the court's discretion would surely militate against admissibility under s. 126. One final point on this is that the prosecution cannot use Hilda's failure to call Norman as the occasion of an adverse comment, by virtue of s. 80(A) **PACE**, nor should a judge invite a jury to draw adverse inferences from her failure to testify.

With regard to the possible plea of unfitness to plead, if the prosecution disagree with the contention raised by the defence, then the defence has the legal burden of proof to the civil standard, as held by the Court of Criminal Appeal in *R* v *Podola* [1960] 1 QB 325.

Selected bibliography

Allen, C., *Practical Guide to Evidence*, 4th edn (Routledge-Cavendish, 2008).

Ashworth, A., 'Criminal Proceedings After the Human Rights Act' (2001) Crim LR 855.

Ashworth, A., *Human Rights, Serious Crime and Criminal Procedure* (Sweet & Maxwell, 2002).

Ashworth, A., 'Criminal Justice Act 2003(2) Criminal Justice Reform: Principles, Human Rights and Public Protection' (2004) Crim LR 516.

Choo, A.L.-T., *Evidence* (OUP, 2006).

Cross & Tapper on Evidence, 11th edn (Lexis Nexis, 2007).

Dennis, I. H., *The Law of Evidence*, 3rd edn (Sweet & Maxwell, 2007).

Doak, J. and McGourlay, C., *Criminal Evidence in Context*, 2nd edn (Law Matters, 2008).

Durston, G., *Evidence Texts and Materials* (OUP, 2008).

Emson, R., *Evidence*, 4th edn (Palgrave Macmillan, 2008).

Kadri, S., *The Trial: A History from Socrates to OJ Simpson* (Harper Collins, 2005).

Keane, A., *The Modern Law of Evidence*, 7th edn (OUP, 2008).

Langbein, J., *The Origins of the Adversary Criminal Trial* (OUP, 2005).

McEwan, J., *Evidence and the Adversarial Process*, 2nd edn (OUP, 1998).

Munday, R., *Evidence. Butterworths Core Text Series*, 4th edn (Butterworths, 2007).

Murphy, P., *Evidence*, 10th edn (OUP, 2008).

Roberts, P. and Zuckerman, A., *Criminal Evidence* (OUP, 2004).

Sharpe, S., *Judicial Discretion and Criminal Investigation* (Sweet & Maxwell, 1997).

Taylor, R., Wasik, M., and Leng, R., *Blackstone's Guide to the Criminal Justice Act 2003* (OUP, 2004).

Zuckerman, A., *The Principles of Criminal Evidence* (Clarendon, 1989).

Index